Facets and Practices of State-Building

Legal Aspects of International Organization

Volume 49

Facets and Practices of State-Building

Edited by
Julia Raue and Patrick Sutter

MARTINUS
NIJHOFF
PUBLISHERS

LEIDEN • BOSTON
2009

Cover illustration: Abandoned helmets, Freiburg im Breisgau, Germany 1945.
Copyright Werner Bischof, Magnum Photos.

This book is printed on acid-free paper.

Library of Congress Cataloging-in-Publication Data

Raue, Julia.
Facets and practices of state-building / by Julia Raue and Patrick Sutter.
p. cm. — (Legal aspects of international organization ISSN 0924-4883 ; v. 49)
Includes index.
ISBN 978-90-04-17403-0 (hardback : alk. paper) 1. Nation-building. 2. State, The.
I. Sutter, Patrick, lic. iur. II. Title.
JZ6300.R38 2009
327.1—dc22

2008052502

ISSN 0924-4883
ISBN 978 90 04 17403 0

PRINTED IN THE NETHERLANDS

Contents

ISSUES

PROCESSES

Preface

The idea of this book was born in 2004 when – through efforts in Afghanistan, Iraq, Kosovo and Bosnia-Herzegovina – it became increasingly apparent that state-building is a multifaceted and challenging operation in need for more consistent analysis. Our aim is to contribute to a better understanding of the complexity of state-building.

Drawing on a mix of international academic and field expert work, this book presents and analyses contemporary state-building efforts. It offers studies on the theoretical and practical foundations and causes of state-building, identifies the role and responsibilities of key actors and points to vital issues which merit specific attention in state-building undertakings. The book attempts to offer lessons for the future of state-building relevant to both practitioners and the academic community.

We would like to warmly thank all the contributors for presenting their expert views with great professionalism and dedication. We are grateful for their patience and persistence.

Special thanks go to Brill for accepting our manuscript, in particular Peter Buschman and Ingeborg van der Laan for the excellent cooperation. Kai Spiekermann deserves heartfelt thanks for spending endless hours in supporting us during the last weeks of finishing the manuscript.

Finally, we wish to express our gratitude to Claudia Vogt and Sacha Wunsch-Vincent for their love, support and encouragement given to us during the preparation of this book.

December 2008 Julia Raue & Patrick Sutter

Foundations

State-Building or The Dilemma of Intervention: An Introduction

Patrick Sutter

Recent developments in international law and international politics have highlighted the importance of state-building. When states collapse, divide, or parts of states secede, new states need to be built. The challenges arising from this task are analysed in this book. In this introduction we not only develop the framework in which the international community acts when involved in the process of state-building (with Iraq serving as an example), but begin with a description of what we call "the dilemma of intervention", followed by a definition of the notion of "state-building" as it is used throughout the book.

I. *The era of interventions*

With the end of the relatively stable[1] Cold War era came the era of interventions. Looking back at the last fifteen years, one can identify a variety of reasons for these interventions:

(a) Humanitarianism;
(b) The right to self-defence;
(c) Realpolitik.

(a) *Humanitarianism*

It may be surprising, at first sight, that many of the recent interventions (which often lead to wars) are connected with the successful establishment and development of international humanitarian law and of international human rights law. Putting obligations on states that are supposed to be more than "just" morally

---

[1] On the legally undefined notion of 'stability' from the standpoint of International Relations see Jürgen Gross, *Friedlose Zukunft? Gewalt, Instabilität und Machtverteilung im internationalen System*, 18 Vierteljahresschrift für Sicherheit und Frieden 164 (2000).

binding implies the will to intervene with diplomatic or even – as an *ultima ratio* – military forces whenever these obligations are not complied with. The situation is, therefore, paradox: The triumphal march of the humanitarian idea, as symbolized in the protection of the civilian population and in the prohibition of certain weapons (e.g. weapons of mass destruction [WMD]),[2] implies the readiness to engage in a war as a final means. From *ius in bello* and human rights law derives a *ius ad bellum*. This paradox is brought about by a situation in which there is no ethically sublime position of indecision, because any decision (including the decision not to act) brings severely negative consequences with it. Even absolute pacifism can be ethically reprehensible.[3] Speaking of this "dilemma of intervention", one has to acknowledge different perceptions of it among the main actors: Whereas (continental) Europe generally tends to undervalue the consequences of non-intervention, the optimistic view of the United States very often leads to an underestimation of the consequences of intervening. Put differently: When Europeans still cling to diplomacy, the United States already think of the next – military – step.[4]

(b) *The right to self-defence*

The second main reason brought up as a justification for recent interventions is the right to self-defence as guaranteed by article 51 of the UN-Charter.[5] On the one hand, it is not necessary to discuss the inherent mistakes in the argument for "anticipated self-defence" or "pre-emptive/preventive warfare" from the perspective of international law here.[6] Instead we notice the *fact* that interventions

---

[2] On humanitarianism behind the ABC weapons control regime see Daniel Thürer & Malcolm MacLaren, *Might the Future of the ABC Weapons Control Regime lie in a Return to Humanitarianism?*, Swiss Review of International and European Law 339 (2003). Despite this humanitarianism behind the prohibition of WMD, it is still fair to say that "humanitarian rationale for invading Iraq was generally not believed or accepted" (Ryan Goodman, *Humanitarian Intervention and Pretexts for War*, 100 American Journal of International Law 107, 133 [2006]), since the American public's support of the Iraq war was based solely on the consideration of the WMD-argument as a matter of national security and not of humanitarianism (*ibid.*, 133–134).

[3] On these thoughts see Patrick Sutter, *Das Treuhandsystem der Vereinten Nationen als Mittel zum Peacebuilding?*, 24 Sicherheit + Frieden 26, 27 (2006); Beat Schweizer, *Moral dilemmas for humanitarianism in the era of "humanitarian" military interventions*, 86 International Review of the Red Cross 547 (2004).

[4] On the intervention *capacity* see Michael O'Hanlon & Peter W. Singer, *The Humanitarian Transformation: Expanding Global Intervention Capacity*, 46 Survival 77 ss (2004).

[5] Whether the UN-Charter only codified international customary law and whether there remains a non-codified part needs not be considered, here (see among others Stanimir Alexandrov, Self-defense against the Use of Force in International Law 93 ss [1996]).

[6] See among numerous others Carsten Stahn, *International Law at a Crossroad? The Impact of September 11*, 62 Heidelberg Law Journal 183, 211 (2002); Michael Bothe, *Terrorism and*

are led under this banner. On the other hand, there is no denying that recent developments in the structure of conflicts are a big challenge to the system of collective security, which needs to install an early warning and (diplomatic and military) intervention mechanisms or improve existing mechanisms.[7]

(c) *Realpolitik*

Last but not least, states are justifying unilateral or multilateral interventions (with or without UNSC authorization) as *Realpolitik*, especially with reference to the fear of spill-over effects caused by internal turbulences (such as political instability and refugee crisis on their own territories). These justifications are often closely related to the aforementioned arguments from humanitarianism or the right to self-defence.

II. *Legitimacy and legality of military and other interventions*[8]

In today's system of collective security, the duty and the right to intervene applies undisputedly only for military interventions authorized by the United Nations Security Council (UNSC). Mohammed Ayoob recently wrote: "If this is not the case, as the two most recent cases of Kosovo and Iraq demonstrate, then we immediately run into severe problems of legitimacy and credibility of the UN system. This is why attempts to dump post-conflict situations requiring reconstruction in the lap of the UN following unilateral or multilateral interventions not sanctioned by the SC should be strongly resisted. The SC and the UN's collective security mechanism should not be allowed to become tools in the hands of intervening powers who have done so without UNSC authorization, as happened in Kosovo and in Iraq."[9]

Ayoob apparently considers the recent interventions in Kosovo and Iraq illegal since they were not authorized by the UNSC. Apart from the discussion about the so-called "unreasonable veto" in the UNSC, which, according to some

the Legality of Pre-emptive Force, 14 EUROPEAN JOURNAL OF INTERNATIONAL LAW 227; Robert Kolb, *Self-Defence and Preventive War at the Beginning of the Millenium*, 59 ZEITSCHRIFT FÜR ÖFFENTLICHES RECHT 111 (2004); Dirk Hasler, *Das Recht der staatlichen Selbstverteidigung: von der zulässigen Ausnahme zur rechtswidrigen Regel?*, 24 SICHERHEIT + FRIEDEN 33 (2006); and the classical OTTO KIMMINICH, VÖLKERRECHT IM ATOMZEITALTER 303 ss (1970).

7 Christophe Eick, *"Präemption", "Prävention" und die Weiterentwicklung des Völkerrechts*, ZEITSCHRIFT FÜR RECHTSPOLITIK 200 (2004); Bothe, *supra* note 6, 236.

8 On legality and legitimacy of *military* interventions see JANE STROMSETH, DAVID WIPPMAN & ROSA BROOKS, CAN MIGHT MAKE RIGHTS? BUILDING THE RULE OF LAW AFTER MILITARY INTERVENTIONS 18 ss (2006).

9 Mohammed Ayoob, *Post-Conflict Reconstruction*, 1 (2005), *at* <http://www.un-globalsecurity.org/pdf/Ayoob_paper_postconflict.pdf>. See also A/Res/60/1, para. 77.

commentators, might legitimize the willing nations to act instead of the blockaded UN,[10] Ayoob's statement is certainly correct in the legal context of collective actions to defend an attacked state or humanitarian norms (such as grave breaches of human rights and the illegal possession or development of WMD). That said, it should, however, not be concealed that one of the leading objections to the legalization of *unilateral* humanitarian interventions – "the overriding concern that states would use the pretext of humanitarian interventions to wage wars for ulterior motives"[11] – has recently been convincingly challenged by Ryan Goodman, especially by considering the relationship between international and domestic political process and, thus, concluding "that encouraging aggressive minded states to justify force as an exercise of humanitarian intervention can facilitate conditions for peace."[12]

Despite of all these discussions, the UN Charter remains the agreed international framework. Its acceptance is demonstrated by the fact that states using force seek to justify their actions within that framework – revealing disagreements about what the Charter permits or prohibits.[13]

Concerning united action, we can generally state with Charles W. Kegley: "In short, a consensus of purpose is the best basis for united action, and no such consensus presently exists."[14] As history shows, it has never been more than a

---

[10] The proponents of the "unreasonable veto"-approach should in any case not confuse the UNSC's capability for consensus with the fact that its members generally represent their own national (sometimes regional) interests: "The argument which is often heard against recourse to the Security Council as a source of legitimization is that it is all too often blockaded. There is, indeed, a certain balance of power in the Council, a system of checks and balances, designed with some degree of political wisdom by the drafters of the Charter. As a consequence, a majority led by one of the permanent members of the Council does not necessarily have its way. This is a leverage which all permanent members of the Council have used to their advantage as they thought appropriate. But this is not what can appropriately be called a blockade. Negotiations leading to a reasonable result are not impossible, as they were during the times of the 'automatic' veto which characterized the era of the Cold War. In this new situation, recourse to a Security Council mandate is the only acceptable solution, both as a matter of law and policy [...]" (Bothe, *supra* note 6, 240). The deliberative potential of interactions in the Security Council is measured out by Ian Johnstone, *Security Council Deliberations: The Power of the Better Argument*, 14 European Journal of International Law 437 (2003), although I am very critical of the underlying "preconditions for effective discourse" as identified by Jürgen Habermas (see Patrick Sutter, Wissenschaft und Ethik in der Rechtssetzung 104–109 [2006]).

[11] Goodman, *supra* note 2, 107.

[12] Goodman, *supra* note 2, 116.

[13] Stromseth, Wippman & Brooks, *supra* note 8, 54.

[14] Charles W. Kegley, *International Peacemaking and Peacekeeping: The Morality of Multilateral Measures*, 10 Ethics & International Affairs 25, 39 (1996).

temporary consensus, anyway.[15] Therefore, legitimacy of such "internationalist" undertakings may vary over time.[16]

Politics and diplomacy consist of various institutions and ways to intervene in states where deemed necessary, *without* any kind of external military involvement.[17] Influence may be exerted by mechanisms of regulation that come with international (financial) aid or by preconditions for a membership to an international organisation (such as the World Trade Organisation, the International Monetary Fund, the European Union or the Council of Europe) and by controlling compliance with these norms after the accession.[18] These preconditions and norms often concern standards of "good governance". As David Chandler shows in his chapter, Great Powers and external institutions nowadays implement long-term strategies in order to enhance the non-Western states' capabilities of good governance. Whereas international law – under the aspect of sovereignty – is satisfied as long as this aid (with all its consequences) is granted with the permission of the affected state, Chandler makes clear to what extent these states lose their policy-making authority to the Great Powers' and external institutions' "responsibility to protect".

III. *The notion of state-building*

As the recent cases of Kosovo, Afghanistan and Iraq have been and still are demonstrating, it is not generally a problem to achieve the immediate goals of military intervention itself – due to the superior military capacities of the intervening powers. This is actually just the point in time when the real troubles begin: The struggle for a sustainable consolidation of peace, for a reconciliation of the

---

15 Nathaniel Berman, *Intervention in a 'Divided World': Axes of Legitimacy*, 17 European Journal of International Law 743, 746 (2006).

16 Berman, *supra* note 15.

17 This aspect goes beyond the question of the effects of human rights treaties in general. On the latter see Erik Claes & Arne Vandaele, *L'effet direct des traités internationaux*, Revue belge de droit international 411 (2001/2); Oona A. Hathaway, *Do Human Rights Treaties Make a Difference?*, 111 The Yale Law Journal 1935 (2002); Ryan Goodman & Derek Jinks, *Measuring the Effects of Human Rights Treaties*, 14 European Journal of International Law 171 (2003).

18 The Council of Europe, for example, follows a quite successful strategy of state-building by controlling compliance with human rights norms (see Julia Raue, *Die EMRK als Prüfstein für den Europaratsbeitritt*, *in* 30 Jahre EMRK-Beitritt der Schweiz: Erfahrungen und Perspektiven 269 [Patrick Sutter & Ulrich Zelger ed., 2003]; Pamela A. Jordan, *Does Membership Have Its Privileges?: Entrance into the Council of Europe and Compliance with Human Rights Norms*, 25 Human Rights Quarterly 660 [2003]). But, as Julia Raue shows in her chapter in this volume, the Council's influence covers other aspects of constitutional law, as well.

different opposed (or even long-time warring) parties and for the (re-)building of the missing or weak institutions of a state.[19]

All of these tasks are subsumed under the notion of *state-building* or *nation-building*. Francis Fukuyama points out that Europeans tend to be more aware of the distinction between *state* and *nation*, since in the national experience of the United States "cultural and historical identity was heavily shaped by political institutions like constitutionalism and democracy."[20] So, when speaking of state-building instead of nation-building, one acknowledges "that nation-building in the sense of the creation of a community bound together by shared history and culture is well beyond the ability of any outside power to achieve. [...]; only states can be deliberately constructed. If a nation arises from this, it is more a matter of luck than design."[21]

But state-building cannot only be seen as a resulting problem of *military* interventions; there are various other forms of interventions *without* any military involvement, as mentioned in Section 2 above. This second, maybe less spectacular but in practice quantitatively far more relevant facet of state-building is especially influential when it aims at stabilizing (potentially or already) unstable countries on the verge or in the midst of internal (armed or non-armed) conflicts (some of them considered so-called *failed states*),[22] in order to prevent the further weakening of their institutions or to rebuild and strengthen them.[23] In her chapter, Ann C. Mason provides an in-depth description of the reasons for Colombia's weakness as an example.

Whereas, in case of military interventions, state-building is by definition taking place in *post-conflict* situations, the second facet also deals with *pre-conflict state-building*. All these types of intervention can be placed along a continuum from more to less interventionist.

---

[19] Francis Fukuyama, State-Building: Governance and World Order in the Twenty-First Century 135–136 (2004).

[20] Fukuyama, *supra* note 19, 134. See also Simon Chesterman in note 15 of his chapter.

[21] Fukuyama, *supra* note 19, 134. On this, see also Kai Spiekermann in his chapter.

[22] *Failed and Collapsed States in the International System* (2003), *at* <http://www.globalpolicy.org/nations/sovereign/failed/2003/12failedcollapsedstates.pdf>; Daniel Thürer, *The "failed state" and international law*, 81 International Review of the Red Cross 731 (1999). Critical of this notion or paradigm of "failed states" is, as many others, Ralph Wilde, *Representing International Territorial Administration: A Critique of Some Approaches*, 15 European Journal of International Law 71, 89 (2004).

[23] Henning Melber, Edward Newman & Roland Rich, *Die andere Art der Intervention: Zur Rolle der Vereinten Nationen in Demokratisierungsprozessen*, 51 Vereinte Nationen 161 (2003); Rainer Tetzlaff, *Staatszerfall in der Dritten Welt – neue Kompetenzen für die UNO?*, *in* Praxishandbuch UNO: Die Vereinten Nationen im Lichte globaler Herausforderungen 83, 98 (Sabine von Schorlemer ed., 2003). See also the articles of the *Symposium: State Reconstruction after Civil Conflict*, 95 American Journal of International Law 1–119 (2001).

IV. *How much international influence in the process of state-building? The example of Iraq*

Since the most drastic consequences of interventions are generally showing in the aftermath of a military intervention, we introduce the reader to the general legal framework for international influence. The more specific legal aspects will be dealt with in later chapters.

As to international law, every people of an *existing* or *developing* state has a claim to self-determination. In the days of decolonization after World War II, the term "people of a developing state", on the one hand, meant the native people in the colonies.[24] And on the other hand, a typical example of a "people of an existing state" claiming self-determination is a people under occupation.[25] Therefore, despite Iraq's occupation by the Coalition, the Iraqi people were in every moment a people of an existing state in that sense and thus entitled to the right to self-determination by international law. This was shown in SC-Res. 1483 (2003) which emphasized "the right of the Iraqi people freely to determine their own political future" and demanded "that the day when Iraqis govern themselves must come quickly". This, of course, only pertains to the question of when to end occupation; during the occupation, the freedom of action of the occupying power(s) is limited only by international humanitarian law (e.g. articles 47 ss of the fourth Geneva Convention of 1949). Charles H. B. Garraway describes these limitations and rights in his chapter.

According to the United Nations "Friendly Relations Declaration" of October 24, 1970 (Res. 2625/XXV), the peoples of existing or developing states can exercise their right to self-determination in four different ways:

(a) by establishing a sovereign and independent state;
(b) by associating freely with an independent state;
(c) by integrating freely with an independent state; or
(d) by emerging into any other political status freely determined by the people.[26]

[24] For details see Patrick Sutter, *Nation building: Stabilität durch Selbst- oder durch Fremdbestimmung?*, *in* SELBSTBESTIMMUNG UND RECHT: FESTGABE FÜR RAINER J. SCHWEIZER ZUM 60. GEBURTSTAG 205, 208–215 (Patrick Sutter ed., 2003).

[25] See Felix Ermacora, *Autonomie als innere Selbstbestimmung*, 38 ARCHIV FÜR VÖLKERRECHT 285, 290 (2000).

[26] See Christoph Gusy, *Selbstbestimmung im Wandel: Von der Selbstbestimmung durch den Staat zur Selbstbestimmung im Staat*, 30 ARCHIV FÜR VÖLKERRECHT 385, 399–401 (1992); Ermacora, *supra* note 25, 288 and 290–291.

As long as the peoples under occupation have not agreed to the annexation of a territory, they are still entitled to the right to self-determination.[27] This right can be exercised through a referendum.[28] However, if circumstances do not allow a referendum to be carried out in a way that could reliably reflect the free will of the people, representatives traditionally recognized as legitimate, i.e. representatives of ethnic, religious and other constituent communities are entitled to take over this task.[29] In that sense, SC-Res. 1483 (2003) "*support[ed]* the formation, by the people of Iraq with the help of the Authority and working with the Special Representative, of an Iraqi interim administration as a transitional administration run by Iraqis, until an internationally recognized, representative government is established by the people of Iraq and assumes the responsibilities of the Authority."

In the case of the lately discussed options of rejuvenating the system of UN-Trusteeship for the purposes of state-building,[30] the fourth option was examined, which covers any status not falling under any of the preceding three options. It says that any political status based on a free decision by the affected people stands essentially unopposed by international law and must, therefore, be respected by the international community.

---

[27] Gusy, *supra* note 26, 401–402. In the case of Iraq, a citizens group reportedly collected some 1.7 mio signatures in support for the United Nations to organize a referendum on whether the conditional attachment of the Mosul Vilayet to Iraq in 1926 shall be made permanent or reversed (at <http://www.solami.com/petition.htm>).

[28] On this *procedural* dimension of the law of self-determination see Catriona Drew, *The East Timor Story: International Law on Trial*, 12 European Journal of International Law 651, 658 (2001).

[29] On the aspect of representation in Afghanistan (calling it the "most fundamental of political questions" that "pervades every aspects of the process of re-establishing political authority in Afghanistan") see Alexander Their & Jarat Chopra, *Considerations for Political and Institutional Reconstruction in Afghanistan*, The Journal of Humanitarian Assistance 12 (2002) *at* <http://www.jha.ac/articles.htm>. On the troubles of defining such legitimate representatives in Iraq see Isam al Khafaji, *A Few Days After: State and Society in a post-Saddam Iraq*, *in* Iraq at the Crossroads: State and Society in the Shadow of Regime Change 77 (Toby Dodge & Steven Simon ed., 2003). As Ray Salvatore Jennings, *Military Peacebuilding: Stability Operations and the Strengthening of Peace in War-Torn Societies*, The Journal of Humanitarian Assistance 9 (2003) *at* <http://www.jha.ac/articles/a119.htm>, points out such leaders can play a very dangerous role by preying on latent animosities and, thus, manufacturing fear for their own ends.

[30] In favour of making use of the system of UN-Trusteeship as a means for state-building (in certain situations) Sutter, *supra* note 3, and William Bain, *Trusteeship: A Response to Failed States*, Paper Presented at the Conference on Failed States and Global Governance, April 10–14, 2001. Opposed to such use Andreas Zimmermann & Carsten Stahn, *Yugoslav Territory, United Nations Trusteeship or Sovereign State? Reflection on the Current and Future Legal Status of Kosovo*, 70 Nordic Journal of International Law 423, 429 (2001).

Nevertheless, for all four options international law's peremptory norms (*ius cogens*) *limit* the freedom of choice. Such limitations to the exercise of the right to self-determination become relevant in circumstances jeopardizing the protection of elementary human rights and of international humanitarian law, respect for the prohibition of force and/or the maintenance of international peace. From these limitations derive rights and obligations for the occupation powers in particular and the international community in general: These agents are at the same time entitled and obliged to commit themselves to the protection of the aforementioned peremptory norms.[31] Actions designed to fulfil these obligations are justified restrictions of the right to self-determination as long as they are limited to what is necessary (*proportionality*).

In case of danger to international peace and security, due to the risk of a conflict in an occupied state to spill over into one or more neighbouring states, the exercise of the right to self-determination must, in principle, await the emergence of conditions excluding said danger. However, and particularly if the occupation itself is the reason for the inner-state conflict, the very exercise of the right to self-determination need not fuel but may in fact contribute significantly to the resolution of said conflict. Therefore, one criterion is whether the withdrawal of the troops and the ending of the occupation would lead to peace or to civil war – in any case, such a prediction needs a sufficient level of plausibility.[32]

Moreover, rights and obligations are not restricted to ensuring security and peace by military and police only. The occupied people can and must be informed of the various constitutional options to secure peace and security after the era of occupation – a right and obligation which is compatible with the right to self-determination and which is a *key issue* of state-building. For better understanding, and as it touches on the principle of non-interference, it is advisable for the international community to fully analyse and draw on the experiences made in earlier cases of state-building.[33]

But the law of self-determination also confers certain substantive entitlements on a people that restrict any international influence: the right to exist demographically and territorially as a people, the right to territorial integrity, the right

[31] As Sylvain Vité, *Re-establishing the Rule of Law under Transitional Administration*, *in* Security Governance in Post-Conflict Peacebuilding 187, 190 (Alan Bryden & Heiner Hänggi ed., 2005) rightly points out: "Respect for IHL and human rights is fundamental for strengthening the legitimacy of such interventions."

[32] On this in detail see Sutter, *supra* note 24, 215–220. On the particular situation in Iraq after Spain's decision (in 2004) to withdraw its troops see Patrick Sutter, *Völkerrecht und Truppenrückzug aus dem Irak: Die Rechte und Pflichten einer Besetzungsmacht*, Neue Zürcher Zeitung 9 (March 31, 2004).

[33] On an integrative concept of comparative law see Sutter, *supra* note 24, 226–238, and Palermo & Lollini in their chapter.

to permanent sovereignty over natural resources, the right to cultural integrity and development and the right to economic and social development.[34]

We therefore come to the *conclusion* that state-building is permitted in the light of the right to self-determination as long as the offered solutions (a) ensure the protection of and compliance with the peremptory norms of international law, and (b) are subject to a free decision either by the people themselves in a referendum or by the traditionally legitimized representatives of their ethnic, religious and other constituent communities.

V. *The concept and content of this book*

Any (ethically and legally acceptable) intervention presupposes that the agents have adequate insights into the effects it may cause. Since the deficit of knowledge in the field of state-building has become more and more obvious with the experiences made in Afghanistan, Iraq and elsewhere, serious commentators rightly ask whether the people in countries like these would not be better off today without the international interventions.[35] Considering the responsibility the agents take, one cannot hold back the impression that many of these interventions have been undertaken almost negligently. Thus, knowledge about state-building is a prerequisite for intervention.

With the legal complexity corresponds a demand for thorough investigations on the factors making possible legal solutions successful in practice: Decision-makers should know about the causes of situations which may make interventions necessary, about the various options on the scale of intensity as described above, about the various actors and the experiences they have made so far. Legal and political scholars are, therefore, employed to come up with legally admissible creative frameworks, in which these questions are answered, and to develop strategies for engagement and disengagement.[36]

The emerging list of literature that has already done so is not only too large to cite here; some of these authors are also engaged in this book in their field of research, trying to define the deficits of the experiences made so far and to draw the consequences for future undertakings. The following chapters present

---

[34] Drew, *supra* note 28, 663.

[35] Among many others Fukuyama, *supra* note 19, 134–141.

[36] Jarat Chopra, *UN Civil Governance-in-Trust*, *in* The United Nations and Civil Wars 69, 86–87 (Thomas G. Weiss ed., 1995); Richard Caplan, A New Trusteeship? The International Administration of War-torn Territories 11 (2002). Critical of the voices within academic literature that are trying to obscure or downgrade the importance of the far-reaching normative and practical questions of international territorial administration by unmasking their discursive strategies is Wilde, *supra* note 22.

the *causes* for the growing need for knowledge on state-building and the difficult circumstances in which state-building takes place, the major *actors* on the political stage and their track records, and present *key elements* of successful state-building. The book results in the insight that, due to the complexity, constitution-building processes should no longer be undertaken based on the classical notion of constituent power exercised by a more or less representative political body in a delimited time. Constitutions should rather be "built" (by the plurality of actors over a relatively long period of time) than "made"; and this process should include a comparative interpretation of the experiences made in other parts of the world rather than transplant solutions.

Great Power Responsibility and "Failed States": Strengthening Sovereignty?

David Chandler

State-building – the development of international practices addressing cases of state 'failure' or at shoring up 'failing states' – is increasingly becoming the dominant framework for the Great Power regulation of and intervention within non-Western states. This chapter seeks to examine the development, content and consequences of the statebuilding discourse and the treatment of Great Power responsibility within it. Locating state-building as a response to the consequences of the 1990s decade of humanitarian intervention, it engages with changing theoretical approaches to state sovereignty, which redefine sovereignty as state capacity rather than as political independence. This has the effect of recasting intervention as strengthening sovereignty rather than undermining it. Today this intervention often no longer appears as external Great Power coercion but as an internal matter of administrative assistance for 'good governance' or 'institutional capacity-building'.

I. *Introduction*

In the dominant discourses surrounding state-building practices, the issue of the 'Failed State' is commonly held to be the most pressing problem facing global security. According to Francis Fukuyama, "state-building is one of the most important issues for the world community" and today has "risen to the top of the global agenda".[1] Robert I. Rotberg argues that state-building has "become one of the critical all-consuming strategic and moral imperatives of our terrorized time".[2] As the 2002 US National Security Strategy states: "America is

---

[1] F. Fukuyama, State-Building: Governance and World Order in the Twenty-First Century ix–xi (2004).

[2] R. I. Rotberg, *The Failure and Collapse of Nation-States: Breakdown, Prevention and Repair, in* When States Fail: Causes and Consequences 42 (R. I. Rotberg ed., 2004).

now threatened less by conquering states than we are by failing ones."[3] It seems that no international policy or strategy document can be complete without the focus on state-building as a key objective: in August 2004 the US government established a state-building department, the Office of the Coordinator for Reconstruction and Stabilization;[4] in February 2005 the UK Government's Strategy Unit report *Investing in Prevention – An International Strategy to Manage Risks of Instability and Improve Crisis Response* viewed state-building as a key part of its 'partnerships for stability' agenda;[5] in March 2005, at the High Level Meeting of the OECD Donor Assistance Committee in Paris, the Ministers of Development of OECD countries agreed to a set of 'Principles for Good International Engagement in Fragile States' with a 'focus on state-building as the central objective';[6] the same month the Commission for Africa report, welcomed the fact that more than a quarter of bilateral aid to Africa is already channelled directly into state capacity-building;[7] in September 2005 the UN world summit agreed on the establishment of a proposed Peace-Building Commission to coordinate international activity in this area.[8]

The focus on state capacities and institutions seems to herald a shift away from the 1990s when new, more interventionist, norms were heralded which challenged the fundamental rights of state sovereignty – those of self-government and non-intervention. These rights took their clearest institutional form in the UN Charter framework of international law which emphasised the rights of peoples to self-government (Article 1.2), the sovereign equality of member states (Article 2.1), and the principle of non-intervention – outlawing the threat or use of force (Article 2.4).[9] Throughout the Cold War, successive judgements of the International Court of Justice upheld these rights to self-government and

3 *The National Security Strategy of the United States of America*, Section 1 (2002), *at* <http://www.whitehouse.gov/nsc/nssall.html>.

4 The website of the Office of the Coordinator for Reconstruction and Stabilization is available *at* <http://www.state.gov/documents/organization/43429.pdf>.

5 UK Prime Minister's Strategy Unit Report, *Investing in Prevention – An International Strategy to Manage Risks of Instability and Improve Crisis Response* (Feb. 2005), *at* <http://www.strategy.gov.uk/downloads/work_areas/countries_at_risk/report/index.htm>.

6 OECD *Principles for Good International Engagement in Fragile States*, OECD document DCD(2005)11/REV2, 8, *at* <http://www.oecd.org/dataoecd/4/25/35238282.pdf>.

7 Commission for Africa, *Our Common Interest*, 136 (March 11, 2005), *at* <http://www.commissionforafrica.org/english/report/introduction.html>.

8 2005 World Summit Outcome, United Nations General Assembly, A/60/L.1 (Sept. 15, 2005), § 97–105, *at* <http://daccessdds.un.org/doc/UNDOC/LTD/N05/511/30/PDF/N0551130.pdf?OpenElement>.

9 The Charter of the United Nations (1945), *at* http://www.un.org/aboutun/charter/.

denied the existence of any legitimate grounds for external intervention, even on the basis of 'humanitarian' or 'human rights' justifications.[10]

After the end of the Cold War, the focus appeared to shift to an emphasis on the rights of individuals, often posed counter to the rights of states. States were no longer seen to be the primary security referent and state sovereignty was not considered to be an absolute barrier to external intervention. Following extended intervention in Iraq, to protect the Kurds and Marsh Arabs after the 1991 Gulf War, and external military intervention for humanitarian purposes in Somalia (in 1992–3) and Bosnia (1993–5) the high point of this new focus on individuals rather than states was the NATO-led international intervention over Kosovo in 1999.

Today, the state is once more at the centre of security concerns. It now appears that states, particularly those that have been marginalized by the world economy or weakened by conflict, can no longer be ignored or isolated. In the aftermath of 9/11 – where the failure of the Afghan state to control its borders and the activities of its citizens was held to have opened the way for Al Qaeda's operations – the state is no longer viewed from a mainly negative perspective. Non-Western states now appear less obviously as objects of opprobrium and are more likely to be fêted by international institutions and leading Western states, offering programmes of poverty reduction, capacity-building, democratisation, and good governance.

This chapter questions the visions of Great Power responsibility and of the non-Western state which are at the centre of international policy-making. The following section puts the state-building discussion in the context of current problems in conceptualising the role of states and in response to the 1990s decade of humanitarian intervention. Further sections then lay out specific problems which highlight the corrosive nature of current policy practices in this area, noting how the redefinition of sovereignty, central to the statebuilding framework, facilitates the erosion of ties linking power and accountability, enabling Great Power interveners to evade political responsibility an to distance themselves from the policies they promote.

II. *From the 'Right to Intervene' to State-Building*

The discussion of state-building – of international mechanisms to capacity-build weak states – seems, at face value, to herald a return to traditional frameworks of international relations. This chapter suggests, that this focus on a familiar

[10] D. Chandler, From Kosovo to Kabul: Human Rights and International Intervention 157–66 (2002).

political form should not obscure, what is, in effect, a radical transformation of the mechanisms of international regulation. Everyone seems to be agreed that states are not what they used to be. As Fukuyama notes, "for well over a generation, the trend in world politics has been to weaken stateness", this trend has been particularly marked since the end of the Cold War.[11] It is only in the context of current uncertainties over the role and purpose of the state that we can understand the novel processes at the heart of state-building policy and practice.

It would seem that non-Western states are losing their capacities rather than gaining them. Several commentators, have highlighted that the result of 1990s humanitarian and human rights interventions has been the 'sucking out' of state capacity as core state functions have been taken over by UN agencies, international institutions and international NGOs, undermining the legitimacy and authority of non-Western state[12] For many commentators, this is clearly a positive shift.[13] Across the board of social theory, from historical sociology to postmodern international relations, states have been increasingly cast as problems rather than solutions. Charles Tilly's work is regularly drawn on to argue that states are merely government-run 'protection rackets' based on the repression and exploitation of their citizens in the interest of criminal or self-interested elites.[14] Postmodernists draw on the work of Foucault to argue that Clausewitz's famous dictum should be inverted to reveal the illegitimacy of the liberal democratic state and understand "politics as the continuation of war by other means".[15] David Campbell, Mary Kaldor and others argue that it was the state-orientated perspective of the international community that encouraged many post-Cold War conflicts, such as the Bosnian war.[16]

There is little doubt that international policy intervention in the 1980s and 1990s tended to bypass or reduce the non-Western state's administrative and

---

11 Fukuyama, *supra* note 1, 161.

12 For example Fukuyama, *supra* note 1, 139; M. Ignatieff, Empire Lite: Nation-Building in Bosnia, Kosovo and Afghanistan (2003); European Stability Initiative, *The Helsinki Moment: European Member State Building in the Balkans*, 10 (Feb. 1, 2005), *at* <http://www.esiweb.org/pdf/esi_document_id_65.pdf>.

13 Re-imagining Political Community: Studies in Cosmopolitan Democracy (D. Archibugi, D. Held & M. Kohler eds., 1998); A. Linklater, The Transformation of Political Community (1998); Governance Without Government: Order and Change in World Politics (J. N. Rosenau & E. Czempiel eds., 1992).

14 C. Tilly, *War Making and State Making as Organized Crime*, *in* Bringing the State Back In (P. B. Evans, D. Rueschemeyer & T. Skocpol eds., 1985).

15 M. Foucault, Society must be Defended: Lectures at the Collège de France 1975–76 (2003).

16 D. Campbell, National Deconstruction: Violence, Identity and Justice in Bosnia (1998); M. Kaldor, New and Old Wars: Organized Violence in a Global Era (1998).

political institutional capacity. However, the key element of these interventions was their overtly external and coercive nature. The relations of authority were transparent; nowhere more so than in the prolonged discussion of the 'right of humanitarian intervention' and in the practices of aid conditionality where international financial institutions specified detailed policies which the recipient countries had to accept. It was clear that, in these cases, non-Western governments, particularly those in Africa, were more accountable to international donors than to their own people.[17]

Bearing this context in mind, this chapter suggests that the new focus on the non- Western state has less to do with the desire for strong non-Western states, or a new found confidence in non-Western governing elites, than a desire on the behalf of Western states to avoid direct accountability for policy interventions, which have thrown up as many problems as they have answered. The key difference, with the overtly 'interventionist' approach of the 1990s is that the emphasis is now on the non-Western state rather than those states and institutions doing the intervening. The transition away from justifying and holding intervening powers to account was presaged by the International Commission on Intervention and State Sovereignty (ICISS) *Responsibility to Protect* report, published in December 2001, and formulated prior to 9/11.

In this widely cited report, the Commission proposed a shift in language away from the 'human-centred' framework of a 'right to intervention' and towards a 'state-centred' framework of the 'responsibility to protect'. Whereas the 'right of intervention' put the emphasis on the international interveners to justify and legitimise their actions, the 'responsibility to protect' sought to avoid this 'attention on the claims, rights and prerogatives of the potentially intervening states'.[18] The 'responsibility to protect' seeks to off-load responsibility onto the non-Western state at the same time as these states increasingly lose their policy-making authority.

The ICISS report successfully set out to "shift the terms of the debate" and has facilitated the evasion of any clarification of the competing rights of state sovereignty and of those of intervening powers, by arguing that state rights of sovereignty can coexist with external intervention and state-building. The report spells out that, in its view, "sovereignty then means accountability to two separate constituencies: internally, to one's own population; and internationally, to the community of responsible states".[19] As the Commission co-chairs note,

---

[17] Highlighted *in* Commission for Africa, *supra* note 7, 92.

[18] International Commission on Intervention and State Sovereignty (ICISS), Responsibility to Protect 16 (2001).

[19] ICISS, *supra* note 18, 11 (2001).

this shift changes "the essence of sovereignty, from control to responsibility".[20] The major implications which this shift would have for accountability (a power which is accountable to another, external, body clearly lacks sovereign authority – the capacity for self-government) have been consistently played down by the report's authors and academic commentators. Robert Keohane, for example, disingenuously argues that the ICISS report is not at all 'devaluing' sovereignty, merely that it is 'reinterpreting' it, to bring the concept more into line with the modern world.[21]

Rather than the 1990s debate, where international intervention was posed in terms of a clash of competing rights – the 'right of intervention' against the 'right of state sovereignty' – today the language is one of 'shared responsibilities' and 'new partnerships'. Where the non-Western state was the subject of overtly coercive external intervention by Great Powers it is now more likely to be the focus of supportive, empowering, and capacity-building practices and new modalities of surveillance. The product of this change has been the enthronement of the state-building discourse as the framework for discussing Western regulation of and intervention in non-Western states.

III. *States without Sovereignty*

Sovereignty in international relations signifies political and legal autonomy; constitutional independence. It is a legal concept which is unconditional and indivisible. As Robert Jackson summarises:

> [It is] legal in that a sovereign state is not subordinate to another sovereign but is necessarily equal to it by international law [...]. Absolute [unconditional] in that sovereignty is either present or absent. When a country is sovereign it is independent categorically: there is no intermediate condition. Unitary [indivisible] in that a sovereign state is a supreme authority within its jurisdiction.[22]

Prior to decolonisation in the last century, the sovereign state form was only one of several kinds of international status. Under European colonialism territorial entities took the form of 'colonies', 'protectorates', 'mandates', 'trust territories', or 'dominions'.[23] What these various forms had in common was

[20] G. Evans & M. Sahnoun, *The Responsibility to Protect*, 81 (6) Foreign Affairs 101 (2002).

[21] R. Keohane, *Political Authority after Intervention: Gradations in Sovereignty*, *in* Humanitarian Intervention: Ethical, Legal and Political Dilemmas 276 (J. L. Holzgrefe & R. O. Keohane eds., 2003).

[22] R. Jackson, Quasi-states: Sovereignty, International Relations and the Third World 32 (1990).

[23] Ibid., 33.

formal legal subordination to a foreign power; they were a denial of sovereignty. There is nothing inevitable or natural about the sovereign state form or about its universalisation in the twentieth century, in the wake of World Wars One and Two.[24]

Few people engaged in the field would argue that international state-building in post-conflict situations is a framework for the creation or support of traditional sovereign entities. This can be seen clearly in practice in the cases of international engagement in Bosnia, Afghanistan, the handing over of 'sovereignty' in Iraq, and moves to make Kosovo an independent state in 2008, and more broadly in the UN and G8 proposals for state capacity-building in Africa. The sovereign state forms are held up but sovereignty is being redefined (or 'unbundled' in Stephen Krasner's phraseology),[25] emphasising the importance of the legal shell of the state form while abandoning its political content of self-government and autonomy.

This is done in three ways. Firstly, by redefining sovereignty as a variable 'capacity' rather than an indivisible right; legitimising a new hierarchy of variable sovereignty and undermining the UN Charter principle of sovereign equality. Secondly, by redefining sovereignty as a duty or responsibility rather than a freedom; legitimising external mechanisms of regulation, held to enhance 'sovereignty' despite undermining the traditional right of self-government or autonomy. Thirdly, by exaggerating the formal importance of international legal sovereignty; this formal shell then facilitates the repackaging of external domination as 'partnership' or 'country ownership' and the voluntary contract of formally equal partners.

1. *Sovereignty as capacity?*

The most important challenge to traditional conceptions of sovereignty has been the conflation of the formal political and legal right to self-government (an absolute quality) with the question of state capacity (a variable quantity), usually formulated in terms of 'good governance'. The conception of sovereignty as a capacity, rather than as a formal legal right to self-government and international legal equality, creates a structure of a 'continuum' of sovereignty or a hierarchy of sovereignty where some states are considered to be more sovereign than others. This approach was famously developed by Robert Jackson, with his conception of 'quasi-states'.[26] For Jackson, the sovereignty granted to post-colonial states was artificial. Not because they were often still under the influence of their former

---

[24] M. Wight, Power Politics, 23 (H. Bull & C. Holbraad ed., 1978); H. Morgenthau, Truth and Power: Essays of a Decade 1960–1970, 258–61 (1970).

[25] S. Krasner, Sovereignty: Organized Hypocrisy (1999).

[26] Jackson, *supra* note 22.

colonial rulers, but because many of these states did not have the capacity to regulate and control their societies to the same extent as states in the West. For Jackson, these states possessed *de jure* sovereignty, formal international legal rights, but lacked *de facto* sovereignty, the capacity to govern domestically.

This idea of the 'unbundling' of sovereignty into its different attributes was popularised by Stephen Krasner in his 1999 book *Sovereignty: Organized Hypocrisy*. In his more recent work, he has focused on sovereignty as a 'bundle' of three separate attributes: 'domestic sovereignty', the capacity of domestic governance structures; 'Westphalian/Vattelian sovereignty', i.e., self-government or political autonomy; and international legal sovereignty, formal juridical independence.[27] Krasner uses the problem of weak capacity to argue that self-government should not be a barrier to international intervention. Whereas in the 1990s intervention would have been posed as a conflict between human rights (or the right of intervention) and the right of state sovereignty (self-government and autonomy), in Krasner's terminology there is no conflict with sovereignty because human rights would be protected if governments possessed adequate governing capacity ('domestic sovereignty'):

> Honoring Westphalian/Vattelian sovereignty [...] makes it impossible to secure decent and effective domestic sovereignty [...] To secure decent domestic governance in failed, failing, and occupied states, new institutional forms are needed that compromise Westphalian/Vattellian sovereignty for an indefinite period.[28]

The discovery that the equality of sovereignty hides the inequality of state capacities was not a new one. The same problem, although to a lesser extent, is present in domestic politics, where equality at the ballot box or under the law in liberal democracies does not necessarily ameliorate social and economic inequalities between individuals. In the domestic context, of course, relatively few people would argue that these inequalities should mean that formal political and legal equalities should be abandoned. In the international sphere, the existence of vast inequalities of power was one of the reasons that state sovereignty, held to be unconditional and indivisible, was the founding principle of international society. It was only on this basis, of formally upholding the equality and autonomy of states and the sovereign rights of non-intervention, that post-colonial societies could be guaranteed the rights to self-government. UN General Assembly declarations during the Cold War regularly asserted that differences in state capacity could never be grounds for undermining the rights of state sovereignty.

---

27 S. Krasner, *Sharing Sovereignty: New Institutions for Collapsing and Failing States*, 29 (2) International Security 85, 87–88 (2004).

28 Ibid., 89.

The affirmation that differences in capacity were no justification for the unequal treatment of sovereign equals was confirmed most notably in the UN General Assembly Declaration on the Granting of Independence to Colonial Countries and Peoples of 14 December 1960 (Resolution 1514 (XV)) which proclaimed that: "all peoples have the right to self-determination; by virtue of that right they freely determine their political status and freely pursue their economic, social and cultural development" and that "inadequacy of political, economic, social or educational preparedness should never serve as a pretext for delaying independence".[29]

By associating sovereignty with a sliding scale of 'capacities', rather than political and legal rights of equality, not only is a new international hierarchy legitimised but intervention can be framed as supporting 'sovereignty' at the same time as it is undermining the rights of self-government. This inversion of the concept of 'sovereignty' is formulated in the clearest terms in the UK Overseas Development Institute (ODI) working paper report 'Closing the Sovereignty Gap'. In this report, by Ashraf Ghani, Clare Lockhart and Michael Carnahan, sovereignty is understood in functional rather than political or legal terms:

> The consensus now emerging from global economic, military and political institutions signals that this gap between *de jure* sovereignty and *de facto* sovereignty is the key obstacle to ensuring global security and prosperity. The challenge is to harness the international system behind the goal of enhancing the sovereignty of states – that is, enhancing the capacity of these states to perform the functions that define them as states. Long-term partnerships must be created to prepare and then implement strategies to close this sovereignty gap.[30]

Here sovereignty is no longer conceived of as a right to self-government. Sovereignty is merely a capacity which can be 'enhanced' or, presumably, 'weakened'. The conflation of external intervention for the purposes of 'capacity-building' with enhancing state sovereignty and independence is central to the state-building discourse. In Africa, where state capacity is held to be a fundamental concern for external powers engaged in supporting a multitude of empowering projects, headlined by the UN's Millennium Development goals, these governance interventions have gone furthest.[31]

If sovereignty is defined as the capacity of non-Western states for 'good governance' there would seem to be little wrong in Great Powers and external

---

[29] *At* <http://www.unhchr.ch/html/menu3/b/c_coloni.htm>.

[30] A. Ghani, C. Lockhart & M. Carnahan, *Closing the Sovereignty Gap: an Approach to State-Building* 4 (Sept. 2005) *at* <http://www.odi.org.uk/publications/working_papers/wp253.pdf>.

[31] See for example Tony Blair's Commission for Africa report (*supra* note 7, Chapter 4) and the Sachs report (UN Millennium Project, *Investing in Development: A Practical Plan to Achieve the Millennium Development Goals* [2005], *at* <http://www.unmillenniumproject.org/reports/index_overview.htm>)

institutions implementing strategies for long-term engagement in these societies in order to enhance their 'sovereignty'. In fact, governments which resisted this external assistance could, in the Orwellian language of international state-builders, be accused of undermining their own sovereignty. The key to the success of this conceptual conflation is not in its legitimisation of external intervention (already accepted in the 1990s) but in its portrayal of external regulation as somehow empowering or strengthening non-Western states. Here is the virtuous circle for intervening powers, one that was not possible in the post-conflict interventions of the 1990s: the more intervention there is the more the target state is held to be responsible and accountable for the consequences of these practices.

2. *Sovereignty as responsibility?*

The second shift articulated by the advocates of state-building as empowerment is the assertion that non-Western states have the 'responsibilities' of sovereignty rather than the rights of sovereignty. What these 'responsibilities' consist of is not held to be a decision made solely by the citizens of a state or their representatives, but in 'partnership' with external bodies. Rather than being a barrier to external interference, sovereignty becomes a medium through which non-Western states and societies become integrated into networks of external regulation. International regulatory mechanisms of intervention are legitimised, firstly through the role of international institutions in deciding the content of the 'responsibilities' of sovereignty, and, secondly, through holding states to external account for 'failings' in the exercise of sovereignty (now discussed in the language of responsibility/capacity).

Sovereignty as 'responsibility' enables a new consensual or 'partnership' approach to state-building. Non-Western states are in a poor position to resist new international mechanisms of regulation which come replete with carrots of international aid, trade privileges, debt forgiveness, or integration into international organisations, in return for external support for governance reforms and institutional capacity-building. Statebuilding or 'sovereignty-building' involves non-Western states being firmly embedded in international institutional frameworks, over whose decision-making processes they have little influence. For the UK's Overseas Development Institute, the focus on strengthening sovereignty entails a much more interventionist role by external institutions:

> We define a sovereignty or state-building strategy as [...] the alignment of the internal and external stakeholders [...]. In order to design and implement statebuilding strategies, the operation of the current international system must be reorientated towards a model where partnership and co-production of sovereignty becomes the aim of both national leaders and international partners.[32]

[32] Ghani, Lockhart & Carnahan, *supra* note 30, 13.

This 'co-production of sovereignty' follows the strategies adopted by the European Union towards Balkan states from 2000 onwards where international partnerships, enmeshing applicant states in a network of international institutional processes, were coordinated through the Stability Pact, the Stabilisation and Association Process, the Community Assistance for Reconstruction, Development and Stabilisation programme, and the 'European Partnership' process. Since 2000, the concept of state-building through international partnerships to enhance governance capacities has increasingly replaced external pressures.

Where the incentive of European membership is not available a wide range of other governance partnerships have been established around acceptance that the core problem of non-Western states is that of state capacity and that the solution lies with the shared 'responsibilities' of both the non-Western state and international institutions. The general rule of thumb appears to be that the greater the inequalities at play in the relationship between non-Western states on the one hand and Great Powers and international institutions on the other hand the more grandiose the language of partnership. As would be expected, it is in relation to Africa that the rhetoric and reality are most out of step. Here the language is of 'African leadership' and an entirely 'new kind of partnership' not based on inequality and hierarchy but 'mutual respect and solidarity'.[33] The UN Millennium Development Goals (MDG) project, following and extending the 'country ownership' approach of the interventionist Poverty Reduction Strategies, requires that states engage in far reaching governance reform and open up every area of domestic policy-making to international scrutiny and involvement. The 'responsibilities' or 'leadership' or 'ownership' lie with the domestic state but their partners (or joint 'stakeholders', in the language of the ODI authors) decide the policies:

> The host country should lead and own the effort to design the MDG strategy, drawing in civil society organisations; bilateral donors; the UN specialized agencies, programs, and funds; and the international financial institutions, including the IMF, the World Bank, and the appropriate regional development bank. The contributions of the UN specialized agencies, programs and funds should be coordinated through the UN Country Team, and the UN Country Team should work closely with the international financial institutions.[34]

Policy 'coherence' is the new buzzword for external capacity-building; this coherence is gained from closely tying international aid to new institutional frameworks of regulation and monitoring. In effect, this transforms external assistance from being a subject of international relations, between states, to one of domestic politics, of management and administration. This radical transformation in the relationship between non-Western states and international institutions

[33] Commission for Africa, *supra* note 7, 17.
[34] UN Millennium Project, *supra* note 31, 53.

is highlighted forcefully by the Commission for Africa report which stresses that it is: "not simply recommending throwing money at the problems" but a "fundamental change in the way in which aid works".[35]

Once international financial institutions have a more direct role in the *internal* governance mechanisms of non-Western states, aid is much less likely to be based on overt external regulation in the form of *external* conditionality. Graham Harrison usefully highlights the 'post-conditionality' regimes of international financial institutions in states like Tanzania and Uganda, where the influence of external donors is better conceived not as a 'strong external force' but as 'part of the state itself', through direct involvement in policy-making committees.[36] The undermining of sovereign autonomy and the enmeshing of subject states in international institutional frameworks fundamentally blurs the lines of accountability and control and the relationships of power behind these mechanisms. The relationship between Western institutions and non-Western states is a highly coercive one which forces these states to cede their sovereign powers to external institutions; the fiction of 'partnership' then relies heavily on an exaggeration of the importance of international legal sovereignty.

3. *International legal sovereignty?*

Today, despite the new interventionist consensus and the international attention given to 'failing' states and the lack of governance capacities in 'zones of instability', there is surprisingly little support for the return of international protectorates and direct external administrations. Only a small number of commentators argue that states should, in fact, be 'allowed to fail' and more capable neighbours allowed to directly govern these territories,[37] or that the UN Security Council should establish new international trusteeships.[38]

Intervening Great Powers and international institutions seem to have a particularly strong desire to preserve the formal trappings of sovereignty. The contradictory desire to intervene but also to avoid responsibility is most sharply posed in questions of military intervention, such as post 9/11 'regime change' in Afghanistan and Iraq. Few acts are as fundamentally undermining of sovereignty as the external removal of a state's government. Yet, no sooner have intervening

---

[35] Commission for Africa, *supra* note 7, 94.

[36] G. Harrison, *Post-Conditionality Politics and Administrative Reform: Reflections on the Cases of Uganda and Tanzania*, 32 Development and Change 669 (2001); see also G. Harrison, The World Bank and Africa: The Construction of Governance States (2004).

[37] For example, J. Herbst, *Let Them Fail: State Failure in Theory and Practice: Implications for Policy*, *in* When States Fail: Causes and Consequences 302–18 (R. I. Rotberg ed., 2004).

[38] G. B. Helman & S. R. Ratner, *Saving Failed States*, 89 Foreign Policy 3 (1993); P. Sutter, *Das Treuhandsystem der Vereinten Nationen als Mittel zum Peacebuilding?*, 24 Sicherheit + Frieden 26 (2006).

actors destroyed sovereignty than they are talking up its fundamental importance and pledging to restore authority to local actors at the soonest possible moment. State-building is the process of negotiating these contradictory drives towards intervention and away from responsibility for outcomes.

Leading US policy advisors and international think tanks are increasingly singing from the same hymn sheet, suggesting that international regulation should no longer be seen in the old ways. Today's policy context means that the old restrictions on international intrusion no longer exist. In the absence of Cold War rivalries between competing Great Powers, external intervention no longer needs to be overtly recognised in the undermining of sovereignty and open return to trusteeships and protectorates. In fact, the maintenance of formal sovereignty is at the heart of new approaches to 'neotrusteeship',[39] 'pooled sovereignty',[40] or 'shared sovereignty'.[41] In the words of Krasner:

> Shared sovereignty would involve the engagement of external actors in some of the domestic authority structures of the target state for an indefinite period of time. Such arrangements would be legitimated by agreements signed by recognized national authorities. National actors would use their international legal sovereignty to enter into agreements that would compromise their Westphalian/Vattellian sovereignty [self-government/autonomy] with the goal of improving domestic sovereignty [governing capacity]. One core element of sovereignty – voluntary agreements – would be preserved, while another core element – the principle of autonomy – would be violated.[42]

The key difference between new forms of external regulation – 'neo-trusteeship' or, even more user-friendly, 'shared sovereignty' – and traditional notions of a trust or protectorate is that, today, the subordinated territory will formally be a contracting legal equal. International legal sovereignty is maintained while political autonomy – self-government is given up. The Bosnian peace agreement at Dayton in 1995 is the classic example of the voluntary surrender of sovereignty; the 'neo trusteeship' was legitimised not through war and intervention or through international legal agreement (the UN Security Council's blessing was bestowed retrospectively) but through the signature of the Bosnian parties.[43]

---

[39] J. D. Fearon & D. D. Laitin, *Neotrusteeship and the Problem of Weak States*, 28 (4) International Security 5 (2004).

[40] R. Keohane, *Ironies of Sovereignty: The European Union and the United States*, 40 Journal of Common Market Studies 743 (2002).

[41] Krasner, *supra* note 27.

[42] Ibid., 108.

[43] D. Chandler, *From Dayton to Europe*, 12 International Peacekeeping 336 (2005).

Law and reality no longer coincide when considering the location of sovereign power and authority.[44] Kosovo, for example, is, at the time of writing, formally part of the state of Serbia-Montenegro, but again the lack of fit between the formal location of sovereignty and external mechanisms of regulation makes discussions of final status hard to resolve as decision-making authority lies neither with the elected Kosovo government in Pristina nor the Serbian government in Belgrade. Afghanistan and Iraq have the juridical status of independent states despite their dependence on the political and security role of the US. The artificial nature of these regimes is highlighted by the fact that their governments' writs seldom extend outside the protected security zones of the capitals. The restrictions on the Iraqi interim government's authority has meant that the formal transfer of Iraqi sovereignty from the US-led Coalition Provisional Authority to an Iraqi government in June 2004 did not reflect any change in the real relations of authority.[45]

Here we have states without sovereignty. States exist on paper, in terms of juridical status, for example, as members of the United Nations, with national flags, and maybe their own currencies, but not as independent political subjects capable of self-government. As Robert Keohane argues:

> We somehow have to reconceptualize the state as a political unit that can maintain internal order while being able to engage in international cooperation, without claiming the exclusive rights... traditionally associated with sovereignty [...]. The same institutional arrangements may help both to reconstruct troubled countries that are in danger of becoming 'failed states', and to constrain the autonomy of those states.[46]

He suggests that state-building can establish the 'institutional arrangements' which are capable of taking responsibility for maintaining order ('domestic sovereignty') but without giving rise to rights of self-government ('Westphalian sovereignty'). He recommends an exit strategy for Kosovo, for example, where there is a shift from existing trusteeship status, which could be called 'nominal sovereignty', to 'limited sovereignty' with external powers able to override domestic authorities, to a final stage of 'integrated sovereignty' where the state is locked into international institutions able to override domestic authorities.[47] This would resolve the problem of Kosovo's independence as it would never achieve independence beyond the purely formal trappings of statehood: "West-

---

[44] See A. Yannis, *The Concept of Suspended Sovereignty in International Law and its Implications in International Politics*, 13 European Journal of International Law 1049 (2002).

[45] See, for example, N. Klein, *Baghdad Year Zero, in* No War: America's Real Business in Iraq 7–41 (Klein et al. eds., 2005).

[46] Keohane, *supra* note 21, 277.

[47] Ibid., 296–7.

phalian sovereignty [...] is simply bypassed in the movement from limited to integrated sovereignty".[48]

His proposals are strikingly similar to those later advocated by the International Commission on the Balkans. The commission's April 2005 report, *The Balkans in Europe's Future*, talks about Kosovo's 'independence without full sovereignty', to be followed by 'guided sovereignty' with 'reserve powers' for the EU and a final stage of 'full and shared sovereignty'.[49] Here state-building is held to be able to build a new type of state; one which has 'sovereignty' but is still in essentially the same position as it was when it was formally a protectorate. The difference being that formal accountability has been shifted back to the non-Western state.

James Fearon and David Laitin suggest a similar approach arguing that a return to traditional forms of sovereignty is not the solution, but instead that the transfer of power in cases of post-conflict intervention and regime change should be "not to full sovereignty but rather as a state embedded in and monitored by international institutions".[50] Krasner argues the point even more openly in his support for the concept of 'shared' sovereignty, which similarly uses 'sovereignty' as a means for enabling external Great Power regulation. Here, international legal sovereignty allows post-conflict states to enter into 'partnerships' which informally violate their sovereign rights:

> For policy purposes, it would be best to refer to shared sovereignty as "partnerships". This would more easily let policymakers engage in organized hypocrisy, that is, saying one thing and doing another. Shared sovereignty or partnerships would allow political leaders to embrace sovereignty, because these arrangements would be legitimated by the target state's international legal sovereignty, even though they violate the core principle of Westphalian/Vattellian sovereignty: autonomy [...]. Shared sovereignty or partnerships would make no claim to being an explicit alternative to conventional sovereignty. It would allow actors to obfuscate the fact that their behaviour would be inconsistent with their principles.[51]

IV. *Conclusion*

It is this 'obfuscation' of the maintenance of international legal sovereignty that enables Great Powers and international institutions to present themselves as facilitating partners in a shared project rather than as coercive external powers.

---

48 Ibid., 297.

49 International Commission on the Balkans, *The Balkans in Europe's Future*, 18–23 (2005), *at* <http://www.balkan-commission.org/activities/Report.pdf>.

50 Fearon & Laitin, *supra* note 39, 42.

51 Krasner, *supra* note 27, 108.

Robert Cooper, focusing particularly on the enlargement policies of the European Union, describes this as a new conflict-free 'postmodern' or 'voluntary' form of imperialism.[52] Mark Leonard argues that unlike the old imperialism based on conflict and overt subordination, the EU is completely transforming states from the inside, rather than ruling them from above, for example: "Europe is changing all of Polish society, from its economic policies and property laws to its treatment of minorities and what gets served on the nation's tables."[53]

The more 'sovereignty' is voluntarily shared between target states and Great Powers or international institutions, coercive external conditionality is exchanged for internal forms of 'enhanced surveillance' through the reporting mechanisms generated by the good governance requisites of openness and transparency enforced by international institutions.[54] Policy-advisers can no doubt see the gains to be made in enabling Great Powers to talk about sovereignty and accountability in non-Western states, while avoiding policy responsibility and political accountability for their actions and policy prescriptions.

---

[52] R. Cooper, The Breaking of Nations: Order and Chaos in the Twenty-first Century (2003).

[53] M. Leonard, Why Europe Will Run the 21st Century 6 (2005).

[54] Commission for Africa, *supra* note 7, 376.

The Interplay between Security and Legitimacy: Security Sector Reform and State-Building

Fairlie Chappuis & Heiner Hänggi

I. *Introduction*

The predicament of failing and collapsed states has become a key concern among the security challenges of the post-Cold War era. The events of 9/11 and the aftermath of the interventions in Afghanistan and Iraq, added urgency to these concerns and triggered evermore complex externally assisted (or imposed) peacebuilding and state-building operations. The international community has prescribed a remedy for the pathology of failed statehood based on ending conflict, establishing security and (re)building institutions to allow the liberal democratic state to emerge and deliver security, representation and welfare.[1] The range of activities implied by this agenda is broad and complex, and security sector reform (SSR) is taking its place as a keystone among them. The growing prominence of SSR on the international agenda is due at least in part to the lessons of recent experiences which have brought home the importance of security to successful peacebuilding and state-building. Where fragile state capacity is threatened by an ineffective or partisan security sector, reform of these institutions can create a platform for political processes that will restore legitimacy to the nascent state and a sense of security to its people. This mutually reinforcing relationship between security and legitimacy lies at the heart of the SSR concept and has made it an essential part of the peacebuilding and state-building agendas.

The concept of peacebuilding has suffered from a certain amount of conceptual stretching and has been expanded to include a broad range of activities. Definitions range from minimalist concepts of safeguarding an absence of violent conflict (peacekeeping) to maximalist formulations dealing with 'root causes' of

---

[1] See Jennifer Milliken & Keith Krause, *State Failure, State Collapse, and State Reconstruction: Concepts, Lessons and Strategies*, 33 Development and Change 753 (2002), and Rolf Schwarz, *Post-Conflict Peacebuilding: The Challenges of Security, Welfare and Representation*, 36 Security Dialogue 429 (2005).

conflict and implying the provision of social goods such as equality, well-being and justice.[2] Nevertheless the central idea remains that of consolidating peace and within this wider agenda, the institutionalisation of peace through the instrument of the state is frequently the key component of international attempts to deal with failing and collapsed states. State-building, interpreted as the attempt to create the institutional capacity necessary to sustain a minimally functional liberal, democratic state, has been the focus of recent international efforts to bring sustainable peace to conflict-affected states.[3] SSR can be considered as a form of institution building aimed at restoring the state's capacity to provide for its own security and that of its people in an efficient and effective way and within a framework of legitimate, ideally democratic governance.[4] What makes SSR distinct from traditional means of re-establishing security in post-conflict societies is the connection it embodies between the provision of security and another key function of the state, legitimate, representative rule. By subjecting the use of force to norms of democratic governance SSR helps to restore the legitimacy of fledgling state capacity by putting the needs and input of citizens at the centre of the state security agenda. SSR thus reinforces the state's capacity not only to provide security, but to provide security by legitimate means.

Conceived first of all in terms of post-conflict environments where fragile or collapsed states are the subject of state-building efforts, this chapter will first consider to what extent state-building is deemed feasible before turning to discuss the intimate relationship between security and representation as core state functions. This will be followed by a discussion of the rather recent and still contested SSR concept and how it links the provision of security to the legitimacy of the state, which is a particularly challenging task in post-conflict settings. Having laid the conceptual foundations of SSR in the state-building context, we will finally consider the implications of the SSR concept in practice across a number of recent instances of state-building, namely Afghanistan, Kosovo, Sierra Leone and Timor Leste. To the extent that SSR is a way of building institutions, this chapter will contend that it is a key element in a functional approach to state-building where security and legitimacy become mutually reinforcing.

---

[2] Charles T. Call, *Building States to Build Peace*, *in* BUILDING STATES TO BUILD PEACE 4–7 (Charles T. Call & Vanessa Wyeth eds., 2008).

[3] Ibid., also see FROM WAR TO DEMOCRACY: DILEMMAS OF PEACEBUILDING (A. K. Jarstaad & T. D. Sisk eds., 2008).

[4] See Heiner Hänggi, *Security Sector Reform (SSR)*, *in* POST-CONFLICT PEACEBUILDING: A LEXICON (Vincent Chetail ed., 2009).

II. *Different Perspectives on State-building*

State-building most simply understood refers to the creation or buttressing of institutions of government.[5] The intervention of external actors in the affairs of states in order to reshape their politics is as old as the idea of states themselves, yet the era of peacebuilding and state-building beginning after the Cold War has redefined the goal of international intervention. In general terms the aim is to supply the stability and capacity necessary to empower a weakened or collapsed state to fulfil its core competencies. Yet attempts by the international community to meet this appealingly simple goal have yielded mediocre results at best.[6] The search for greater effectiveness has resulted in a number of innovations in thinking about how best to restore state capacity in view of stable and durable peace. Indeed this profusion of approaches has spawned a confusion in terminology; juxtaposed by some, the terms state-building and nation building are used interchangeably by others. While terms may vary, a clear analytical distinction can be made between more expansive, maximalist and more minimalist, conservative definitions. These different perspectives on state-building fall broadly into three categories based on the scale of social transformation implied in undertaking to (re)build a state. Drawing on Schneckener's typology which defines strategies of peacebuilding according to the elements of peace they prioritise,[7] we can distinguish three distinct perspectives on the nature of state-building in post-conflict environments.

The first and most expansive approach to state-building is based on a maximalist definition of what external actors ought to aim for in their efforts to re-establish peace and stability. In an influential study of American experiences of nation-building, Dobbins et al. provide an example of what this could include: "the use of military force in the aftermath of a conflict to underpin rapid and fundamental societal transformation" and including "comprehensive efforts that

---

5 Fukuyama, for example, defines state-building as "the creation of new governmental institutions and the strengthening of existing ones". Francis Fukuyama, State-building: Governance and World Order in the 21st Century ix (2004).

6 Determining the success or failure of peacebuilding and state-building efforts remains a subject of wide debate: see for example, Michael Doyle & Nicholas Sambanis, *International Peacekeeping: A Theoretical and Quantitative Analysis*, 94 American Political Science Review 779 (2000); also Virginia Page Fortna, *Does Peacekeeping Keep Peace? International Intervention and the Duration of Peace After Civil War*, 48 International Studies Quarterly 269 (2004).

7 Ulrich Schneckener, *Addressing Fragile Statehood: Dilemmas and Strategies of International State-building*, *in* Strategies for Peace: Contributions of International Organisations, States and Non-State Actors 193 (Volker Rittberger & Martina Fischer eds., 2008). Schneckener's typology in fact includes four strategies for peacebuilding however, for simplicity's sake we have restricted ourselves to the three categories which are most immediately relevant from the state-building perspective.

aimed to engineer major social, political, and economic reconstruction".[8] This maximalist perspective on state-building is ambitious in so far as it aspires to affect deep-seated social change as a means to democratisation and stabilisation. Chesterman, Ignatief and Thakur reflect a similar position in underlining the fact that state-building necessarily requires building or rebuilding the faith of a population in the very idea of a state.[9] While this point in itself is not controversial, controversy does arise over the utility of efforts to rebuild states in the absence of such social transformation. Chesterman et al. maintain that the idea of a generic mode of institution building that could be applied in post-conflict settings without regard for the deeper transformation of "hearts and minds" is "wrongheaded".[10] In Schneckener's terminology this approach would be equivalent to the *Liberalisation-First* strategy which, inspired by democratic peace theory and neo-Wilsonisn liberalism, is based on the idea that a politically and economically liberal society is the foundation of lasting peace.[11] This perspective sees social change on a large scale as necessary and asserts that such transformation can be affected through external intervention. This approach is typified by the view that a community of shared values and identity can be created through the targeted reconstruction of state capacity and goes by the name of nation-building within American discourse.[12] Fukayama suggests that this specifically American use of the term "nation-building" reflects the particular historical experience of emerging nationhood and the concurrent establishment of the institutions of state.[13] Eschewing the complex social and cultural dynamics inherent in the notion of nationhood and nation building, European usage of the term state-building has tended towards a skinnier definition focussed on the technicalities of institution-building.[14]

Reflecting a certain scepticism in the face of what is considered to be ambitious "social engineering",[15] this approach suggests that while external actors

---

[8] James Dobbins, John G. McGinn, Keith Crane, Seth G. Jones, Rollie Lal, Andrew Rathmell, Rachel Swanger & Anga Timilsina, America's Role in Nation-Building: From Germany to Iraq xiii (2003).

[9] Simon Chesterman, Michael Ignatieff & Ramesh Thakur, Making States Work: From State Failure to State-Building 8 (2004).

[10] Chesterman et al., *supra* note 9, 8.

[11] Ulrich Schneckener, International Statebuilding: Dilemmas, Strategies and Challenges for German Foreign Policy 16–17 (October 2007).

[12] Francis Fukuyama, *Nation-Building and the Failure of Institutional Memory, in* Nation-Building: Beyond Afghanistan and Iraq 3 (Francis Fukuyama ed., 2006).

[13] Fukuyama, *supra* note 5, 99.

[14] Ibid.

[15] Schwarz, *supra* note 1, 438. See also, Keith Krause & Oliver Jütersonke, *Peace, Security and Development in Post-Conflict Environments*, 36 Security Dialogue 451 (2005); Roland Paris, At War's End: Building Peace After Civil Conflict 4–6 (2004).

can transplant established methods of institution-building and bureaucratic state capacity, these efforts will at best become vectors of organic social change if the right conditions obtain. Equivalent to Schneckener's *Institutionalization-First* strategy which emphasises habits of government, this approach is rooted in institutionalist theories of international relations.[16] Looking to the history of the emergence of the modern state in Europe, this perspective reflects that the long historical process of evolution from medieval order to liberal democracy, via war, feudalism and industrial revolution cannot be circumvented or replicated by the efforts of external actors in post-conflict environments.[17] Although Europe's long historical process may have made states and nations synonymous, Fukayama contends that while states can be built, nations must evolve.[18] Instead of building nations, state-building in this guise aims lower: Call and Cousins thus define the goal of state-building in post-conflict peacebuilding contexts as establishing a "minimal threshold of nationally recognized, sufficiently effective and broadly legitimate institutions" such that a minimally functional state might endure once external support is withdrawn.[19] This approach is firmly rooted in a functional vision that defines the state according to the public functions it performs through its institutions. State-building from this perspective is not intended as an end in itself but as a means to democratisation and political consensus in so far as the institutions established can become conduits for non-violent political contestation.[20] The "institutionalisation before liberalisation" approach to peacebuilding developed by Paris taps directly into this logic by contending that the nascent state needs to be protected from the stresses of competitive political processes and market liberalisation by a framework of effective governmental capacity.[21] Developing state capacity through effective institutions thus makes state-building the cornerstone of a wider post-conflict peacebuilding agenda.

Optimism about how much can be achieved through such inorganic governance mechanisms is the point of difference that distinguishes the second perspective on state-building from the third. Standing in stark contrast to the view that state-building must imply deep social transformation to succeed, is the perspective that such change may be necessary but cannot be affected by external actors. On this view the most that external actors can hope to achieve is a minimal guarantee of security that may allow political contestation to unfold in a non-violent way, hence why Schneckener describes this as the *Security-First*

---

[16] Schneckener, *supra* note 11, 207–208.

[17] See Milliken & Krause, *supra* note 1.

[18] Fukuyama, *supra* note 12, 3.

[19] Charles T. Call & Elizabeth M. Cousins, *Ending Wars and Building Peace: International Response to War-Torn Societies*, 9 International Studies Perspectives 9 (2008).

[20] Ibid.

[21] Paris, *supra* note 15, 205–207.

approach.[22] Etzioni has also used this terminology to explain that basic security is a pre-requisite for democratisation, which may or may not develop according to Western models.[23] Taking an essentially (neo-)realist approach to the assessment of security, this perspective is embodied in the practice of peacekeeping that aspires to create a physically safe space for the dangerous game of politics among local power brokers.[24] Institution-building can only be achieved by local actors by virtue of the fact that only they can give appropriate forms of political organisation the significance that qualifies them as institutions. Ottaway characterises this approach by pointing out that external actors can put organisational mechanisms in place but that these mechanisms will not become institutions in a meaningful governance sense unless they become "significant and established" in the minds of local populations, something which can only occur through an internally led process of politics and power brokerage.[25] According to this third perspective, institution building in the sense that the institutionalisation-first perspective might imply, is an almost marginal activity that succeeds because of and never in spite of local political processes. Ultimately this view is based on the idea that the state itself is constituted by internal political dynamics of negotiation, conflict and compromise and institutions are meaningful only in so far as they embody these political processes. Proponents of this view question the efficacy of state-building operations in so far as they are premised on the notion that changes in institutional mechanisms can shape the evolution of political processes when in fact something closer to the opposite would be a truer reflection of reality.[26]

While all accounts acknowledge that durable peace in the aftermath of violence requires fundamental social transformation, they differ in terms of the extent to which institution-building as state-building can plausibly affect such change. The security-first view of state-building disputes the efficacy of governance mechanisms in containing political processes and thereby directly questions the contention inherent in other state-building approaches that political disputes can be channelled into non-violent resolution mechanisms. On the liberalisation-first view, state-building means social transformation while an institutionalisation-

---

[22] Schneckener, *supra* note 11, 206–207.

[23] See Amitai Etzioni, Security First: For a Muscular, Moral Foreign Policy ix (2007).

[24] Ibid. It should be noted that Schneckener describes SSR as the key activity of a security-first approach to peacebuilding but that this assessment is based on a narrower definition of SSR than is employed here. Taking the broader view of SSR and the security concept it reflects (see below), SSR is more likely to be part of the institutionalisation-first approach.

[25] Marina Ottaway, *Rebuilding State Institutions in Collapsed States*, 33 Development and Change 1004 (2002).

[26] David Chandler, *Back to the future? The limits of neo-Wilsonian ideal of exporting democracy*, 32 Review of International Studies 4759 (2006).

first perspective suggests that state-building can create a solid institutional foundation acting as a conduit for social transformation. In contradistinction, the security-first view sees state-building as a process of fundamentally political negotiation between internal actors which institution building can at best facilitate if a favourable balance of power prevails.

III. *Bridging Security and Legitimacy in State-building*

The definitional fuzziness surrounding the concept of state-building is a reflection of the breadth of challenges subsumed under this task. While the restoration of state capacity is certainly integral to each approach, debates about the nature of that capacity drive directly to the heart of the question of stateness. The issue at stake is the very nature of what is being (re)built; to what end is institutional capacity to be built?

Milliken and Krause argue that the search for an idealised definition of statehood reifies the idea of a state to the point that its nature as an ongoing political process is obscured. Regarding the state as an institutional arrangement to be technocratically constructed ignores the historical forces that have always been instrumental in its development. The example of how historical forces shaped the emergence of Europe's modern states in a dynamic social process of successive war inspired Charles Tilly's influential formulation "states make war and wars make states".[27] In so far as such accounts of state formation explain a long historical process, modern state-building constitutes, as Ottaway puts it, a conscious "short-cut to the Weberian state", that is to the legitimate monopoly on the use of force.[28] Disagreements over approaches to state-building reflect the extent to which such a short-cut is deemed feasible rather than disagreement over whether such a short-cut is desirable.

During the 20th century, juridical, de jure statehood came to be defined as "effective government".[29] This account of statehood which establishes war and instability as pathologies deviating from a supposed norm triggered an optimistic third-wave of democratisation that aspired to 'fix' these weak states with relative ease.[30] The impression that statehood could be cured by almost 'surgical' intervention on the part of the international community created unrealistic

[27] Charles Tilly, *War-Making and State-Making as Organised Crime*, *in* Bringing the State Back In 169 (P. Evans, D. Reuschmeyer & T. Skocpol eds., 1985).

[28] Ottaway, *supra* note 25, 1004.

[29] Milliken & Krause, *supra* note 1, 763–765.

[30] Ibid.

expectations in the diagnosis of "failing states".[31] Since no differentiation was to be made between state *failure* and state *collapse*, the various processes that lead to each are obscured. Arguing for a distinction between state decay, political crisis and civil war, the idea of a "failing state" can be refined to allow for state *collapse* (the institutional disintegration of the state apparatus) and state *failure* (the functional incapacity of an existing apparatus).[32] According to this schema, cases of actual state collapse have been rare in recent years while sloppy definitions have given the impression of an increasing trend towards collapse when in fact state failure is more often at issue.[33]

The broadening of the concept of security that has occurred over recent years under the rubric of human security for example[34] or multidimensional security as conceived by Buzan,[35] takes the issue of state failure from a different angle. Where states fail to guarantee the well-being of their citizens, their legitimacy is called into question turning the assertion that 'states make war, and wars make states' on its head. From this point of view war-making can also unmake states when instruments of state violence are co-opted by narrow interest groups (through kleptocratic, rentier or predator states), when the state's legitimate monopoly on the use of force is eroded (through the internationalisation, privatisation or criminalisation of security), or when security comes at the cost of welfare or representation.[36] These tensions in the modern vision of sovereignty show why concern with the security sector and its reform – or reconstruction – has become key to practical agendas of state-building.

SSR is based on the idea that there are at least two intimately connected answers to the question of what function states should perform; the first is that states must provide security, and the second is that they must do so legitimately. These are certainly not innovative responses to the question of statehood for although definitions of what functions the state should embody vary as widely as definitions of how to build states themselves, the provision of security is a key element in almost every understanding of what constitutes a legitimate state. Reflective of a long tradition first articulated by Hobbes and later Weber, the state's control of the use of force in order to protect its citizens from arbitrary victimisation is the primary guarantee of the state's legitimacy.

---

[31] Ibid.

[32] Schwarz, *supra* note 1, 430.

[33] Milliken & Krause, *supra* note 1, 764.

[34] See Keith Krause, Towards a Practical Human Security Agenda (2007).

[35] Barry Buzan, People, States and Fear (1983).

[36] See Schwarz, *supra* note 1.

Legitimacy itself remains a contested concept.[37] In so far as the nature of the legitimacy of the state remains tied to its representation function, it is firmly embedded in an international discourse of liberal democratic governance. This brings a distinctly normative angle to the SSR agenda which further distinguishes SSR from technical military or security focussed assistance. Establishing the legitimacy of nascent state institutions has become a key element of the state-building agenda and an increasingly important aspect of statehood itself through the promulgation of such concepts as the responsibility to protect. This recent innovation in the concept of sovereignty places limits on the state by defining its remit to extend only so far as is in the interest of its population. Making this connection between human security and state legitimacy fundamentally alters the nature of the state as the lynchpin of the international system. Thus modern experiences of state-building have been clearly focused not merely on building states that can guarantee security but rather on building states that can guarantee security legitimately in the eyes of their population and the international community. In practice this has meant that the international community has endeavoured to establish liberal democracies where the state's ability to supply security cannot be separated from its legitimacy.[38] Ensuring that repression cannot become part of the state function is thus as much a part of the modern state-building agenda as the goal of creating capacity to govern, and SSR is a key means to accomplish both.

Articulating the relationship between security, legitimacy and stateness shows why SSR as an exercise in institution building is so integral to the state-building agenda. According to Milliken and Krause, the three core functions of the state are the provision of "security, representation and welfare".[39] However these functions are only analytically separate thus the ability to monopolise the use of force is only equivalent to the provision of security when coercion is governed by the rule of law. A transition from war to peace then entails what Rubin describes as "the transformation of the organisational control of the use of force".[40] This is why the essential element of an SSR agenda calls for channelling the use of force through mechanisms of democratic governance that vouch for the

---

[37] See for example, on input and output legitimacy, F. W. Scharpf, *Economic integration, democracy and the welfare state*, 4 Journal of European Public Policy 18 (1997); on legitimacy in state-building contexts, Katia Papagianni, *Participation and State Legitimacy, in* Building States to Build Peace (Charles T. Call & Vanessa Wyeth eds., 2008).

[38] Roland Paris, *International peacebuilding and the 'mission civilisatrice'*, 28 Review of International Studies 637 (2002).

[39] Milliken & Krause, *supra* note 1, 756. See also Krause & Jütersonke, *supra* note 15; Schwarz, *supra* note 1; Barnett R. Rubin, *The Politics of Security in Postconflict Statebuilding, in* Building States to Build Peace 25 (Charles T. Call & Vanessa Wyeth eds., 2008).

[40] Rubin, *supra* note 39, 31.

legitimacy of the state. In so doing, legitimacy and security should grow together in a way that also enhances the welfare provision function of the state and its general capacity to govern.

Many have questioned the plausibility of the idea that this positive feedback between security and legitimacy can succeed in engendering democracy where stability is so inorganic. The fact that restoring the core state functions of security, representation and welfare may entail inherent contradictions for a state-building agenda is mirrored in the larger context of peacebuilding where the goals of negative and positive peace may entail contradictory approaches. This is attributed to the fact that the conditions for a stable peace are not necessarily the conditions of a stable democratic transition, although the two are not always mutually exclusive.[41] The fact that contemporary efforts by the international community at state-building increasingly involve an explicit agenda of democratisation only increases the need for robust reform of the security sector. Where democratisation is incompatible with stability, a democratically controlled, minimally efficient security sector can become essential in preventing a destabilising slide back into conflict that has sometimes been the result of a return to competitive politics.[42]

The lessons of bitter recent experience have taught the international community that establishing a secure environment for individuals and groups is an integral part of establishing a stable and prosperous peace – negative or positive – and has thus become an increasingly prescient concern in state-building enterprises as the theory and practice of building peace and development have evolved. Where once the security-development nexus was taken to imply that states which suffered from a lack of development were prone to conflict, understandings of the linkages between security and development have now evolved to demonstrate that security is a precondition for development as much as it is the result.[43] In post-conflict situations this has meant questioning how to establish security and justice where rampant insecurity is so often perpetuated or worsens after both sides have formally laid down their arms.[44] This problem also illustrates why SSR has come to the fore as a key concern on the state-building agenda, a fact which is symptomatic of a larger international consensus on the importance of

---

[41] See Jarstaad & Sisk, *supra* note 3.

[42] Virginia Page Fortna, *Peacekeeping and democratization*, *in* From War to Democracy: Dilemmas of Peacebuilding 47 (A. K. Jarstaad & T. D. Sisk eds., 2008).

[43] Deepa Narayan, with Raj Patel, Kai Schafft, Anne Rademacher, Sarah Koch-Schulte, *Listening to the Voices of the Poor*, *in* Voices of the Poor: Can Anyone Hear Us?, Vol. III (Poverty Group, PREM World Bank ed., Dec. 1999).

[44] Charles T. Call, *What We Know and Don't Know About Post-Conflict Justice and Security Sector Reform*, *in* Constructing Justice and Security After War 4 (Charles T. Call ed., 2007).

the rule of law to almost every other state-building and foreign policy goal from human rights to fighting terrorism.[45]

While the provision of security has always been a fundamental goal of the analysis of civil-military relations and defence diplomacy that predate SSR discourses, SSR is different in so far as it links the effective provision of security to the crucial state attribute of legitimacy. By promoting norms of governance rooted in human rights and development agendas, SSR aims to secure both state and human security. Where the interrelationships between security and development are taken seriously, human security can also be seen as a means of promoting national security. Rubin states that "the success of SSR requires growing the legitimacy of the state" but this neglects the fact that the success of SSR can be what the legitimacy of the state depends on because the demilitarisation of politics makes non-militarized political processes meaningful and important.[46] This angle is emphasised even further in the case of post-conflict settings where the state has sometimes been an instrument of terror and oppression in the past. This observation reveals why transitional justice and justice reform are key components of SSR if understood in its broad sense and in a post-conflict environment (see below).

In sum, SSR can be crucial, especially in post-conflict contexts, when an efficient and accountable security sector proves the relevance of the state to a disillusioned or hostile population and proves its own relevance at the same time: successful SSR thus links the provision of security to the legitimacy of the state. Stability based on security can become the basis for development which in turn helps to restore the welfare function of the state and also contributes to state legitimacy. Increasing state welfare and development also make a minimally functional and democratically controlled security sector necessary in order to protect against plunder of or by the state. Of course the fact that a functional and democratically controlled security sector cannot be easily co-opted by entrenched interests for narrow economic or political purposes is also what makes SSR itself a fundamentally political activity focussed on the reordering of power relations. Looking more closely at the concept of SSR gives a better understanding of how SSR links security to legitimacy.

IV. *The Concept of Security Sector Reform*

Security sector reform is a relatively new concept. The term SSR first came to prominence in the late 1990s through the speeches of the UK Secretary of State for International Development Clare Short and policy statements by the newly

45 Ibid.

46 Rubin, *supra* note 35, 39.

created Department for International Development (DfID). However the need for comprehensive reform of the security sector had been recognised earlier and as an idea, SSR grew out of three particular trends typical of the post-Cold War reordering of international affairs.

The first trend reflected the expansion of development agendas to include previously circumscribed issues, such as levels of military expenditure vis-à-vis development challenges, the application of good governance paradigms of public sector management to the security sector, and the recognition of development as a precondition for security. In this context SSR provided the conceptual justification for development actors to substantively engage with security agendas for the first time. Thus following the lead established by DfID, bilateral and multilateral donors began to incorporate SSR activities into their development programmes. A second important trend that influenced the emergence of SSR was the new emphasis given to democracy promotion in the aftermath of the ideological deadlock that ended with the Cold War. In the framework of their "new defence diplomacy",[47] Western governments worked bilaterally and multilaterally to encourage democratic civil-military relations among Central and Eastern European transition states. Through actors such as the European Union (EU) and the Council of Europe, non-military security elements took on growing importance and the focus expanded to include border guards, police and justice institutions. Similar patterns of emphasis on the democratic governance of the security sector became key elements in the political transitions of countries in Latin America, the Asia-Pacific and Africa. Thus throughout the 1990s multilateral security actors and states engaged in a broad range activities that constituted SSR in all but name. Finally, and most importantly for the subject of this chapter, the new engagement of the international community with the task of stabilising failing or collapsed states has seen the broad scope of the SSR concept provide a coherent framework for understanding the short- and long-term challenges of security governance in conflict-affected states. As the number of UN peace operations and externally assisted reconstruction efforts has mounted, SSR has become an increasingly important conceptual tool in understanding the interrelationships between the challenges of disarmament, demobilisation and reintegration (DDR), the control of small arms and light weapons (SALW), mine action, transitional justice and the rule of law in post-conflict settings.[48] As a result the concept has gained ever more momentum among actors involved in such diverse fields as development assistance, democracy promotion, conflict

[47] On "old" and "new defence diplomacy" see ANDREW COTTEY & ANTHONY FORSTER, RESHAPING DEFENCE DIPLOMACY. NEW ROLES FOR MILITARY COOPERATION AND ASSISTANCE (2004).

[48] See SECURITY GOVERNANCE IN POST-CONFLICT PEACEBUILDING (Alan Bryden & Heiner Hänggi eds., 2005).

prevention and post-conflict peacebuilding. The trend is exemplified most recently by the attention devoted to the development of explicit SSR policies as a key instrument of peacebuilding and state-building approaches by the EU, the OECD and UN.[49]

Despite its growing ubiquity in international relations discourse and practice, SSR remains a contested concept, particularly regarding understandings of the scope of the security sector, with different actors embracing broader and narrower interpretations. The narrow notion reflects traditional state-centric understandings of security, focusing on those public sector institutions responsible for the provision of internal and external security, as well as on the civilian bodies relevant for their management, oversight and control. An expanded understanding that still falls within the state-centric notion of the security sector would include justice institutions in recognition of the linkages and the complementary relationships between security and justice. This view, however, is not necessarily shared by the entire SSR community: on the one hand, there is concern that the justice sector might become "securitised" by its incorporation in the SSR concept, whereas others fear a lack of clarity and focus if the security sector is not confined to core security actors. Broader understandings of SSR emphasise that more often than not security and justice services are delivered by non-state actors ranging from customary justice providers to armed groups and private military and security companies, and that civil society organisations have an important role to play owing to their potential for monitoring government policy and practice on security (and justice) issues. The broadest notion of SSR demands the inclusion of all those with a stake in security and therefore extends to the inclusion of non-state actors such as civil society organisations, customary and traditional justice systems and all kinds of armed groups.[50] The shift from an exclusive focus

---

[49] See for example, Council of the European Union, *EU Concept for ESDP support to Security Sector Reform (SSR)* (Document No. Council doc. 12566/4/05, Brussels, 2006); European Commission, *A Concept for European Community Support for Security Sector Reform* (Document No. COM (2006)253 Final, Brussels, May 24, 2006); OECD DAC, *Security System Reform and Governance – DAC Guidelines* (Paris: OECD, 2005); OECD DAC, *OECD DAC Handbook on Security System Reform* (Paris: OECD, 2007); United Nations General Assembly/Security Council, *Securing peace and development: the role of the United Nations in supporting security sector reform* (Report of the Secretary-General, Document No. A/62/659–S/2008/39, Jan. 23, 2008).

[50] The widely used OECD DAC guidelines on SSR define the security sector – or the security system as it is referred to by the DAC – as including all those institutions, groups, organisations and individuals both state and non-state, that have a stake in security and justice provision. These include: (i) Core security actors: armed forces; police service; gendarmeries; paramilitary forces; presidential guards; intelligence and security services (both military and civilian); coast guards; border guards; customs authorities; and reserve or local security units (civil defence forces, national guards, militias); (ii) Management and oversight bodies: the executive, national security advisory bodies, legislative and legislative select committees; ministries of defence,

on government (narrow understanding) to governance (broad understanding) is particularly relevant in post-conflict situations where security and justice have in important respects been both privatised and internationalised, suggesting that SSR entails far more than simply the reconstruction of the state security forces and relevant oversight institutions.

Nevertheless, from a state-building perspective, the recognition of non-state actors as a component part of the security sector may be seen as problematic, because this could undermine the state's institutional capacity to provide security, representation and welfare, which the state-building project aims to reconstruct. This is less a problem for the involvement of civil society organisations which have the potential to play a key enabling role in strengthening legitimate, representative rule. The situation is quite different with regard to armed non-state actors who – more often than not – constitute part of the problem rather than part of the solution in the state-building project. This view is strongly held by governments of fragile states facing armed resistance.[51] Against this backdrop, armed non-state actors can be granted a role in SSR only to the extent that they support the re-establishment of the state's legitimate monopoly on the use of force, which means that these non-statutory security forces must eventually be either disarmed and demobilised or integrated into statutory security forces.

The point of departure for SSR is a dysfunctional security sector, i.e. a security sector which does not provide security to the state and its people in an efficient and effective way or, even worse, which is itself a cause of insecurity and violent conflict. Moreover, in line with the normative dimension of the SSR concept, and in view of the fact that authoritarian states may also have efficient and effective security sectors (though primarily for the purpose of regime security), a security sector must be considered dysfunctional if it is deficient in terms of civilian control and democratic accountability. Thus, SSR is meant to turn a dysfunctional security sector into a functional one, with security and justice

---

internal affairs, foreign affairs; customary and traditional authorities; financial management bodies (finance ministries, budget officers, financial audit and planning units); and civil society organisations; (iii) Justice and rule of law: judiciary and justice ministries; prisons; criminal investigation and prosecution services; human rights commissions and ombudsmen; customary and traditional justice systems; (iv) Non-statutory security forces: liberation armies, guerrilla armies, private security companies, political party militias. See OECD-DAC, *Security System Reform and Governance – DAC Guidelines* (Paris: OECD 2005), *available at* <http://www.oecd.org/document/33/0,3343,en_2649_34567_33800289_1_1_1_1,00.html>.

[51] To illustrate the sensitive nature of this issue, the UN Secretary-General's report on SSR, while subsuming 'civil society groups' under management and oversight bodies, cautiously refers to 'customary or informal authorities and private security services' as being 'other non-State actors that could be considered part of the security sector'. Consequently, armed groups such as guerrilla forces, warlord armies and non-statutory paramilitary forces are not viewed as component parts of the security sector. See UN GA-SC, A/62/659–S/2008/39, *supra* note 49, para. 14.

institutions performing their statutory functions – to deliver security to the state and its people – efficiently and effectively. It is crucial but not sufficient that the security forces perform their statutory functions efficiently and effectively; they must also conform to principles of good governance, democratic norms, the rule of law and human rights. Consequently, reforms aimed solely at modernising and professionalising the security forces and thereby increasing their capacity without ensuring their democratic accountability are not consistent with the SSR concept.[52] Such activities would instead tend to come under the heading of technical assistance in the framework of "old defence diplomacy", which was aimed at strengthening the capacity of the armed and security forces of allied states irrespective of governance considerations. This double objective – effective and efficient provision of state and human security within a framework of legitimate, ideally democratic governance – constitutes the largely uncontested core of the SSR concept and is also reflected in the authoritative definitions offered by the relevant policy documents of multilateral and bilateral donors.[53] This accounts for the cross-cutting role of SSR, bridging security and legitimacy in state-building.

As such SSR aims to enable the state to supply security but within the normative bounds of a democratic governance framework, thus including cross-cutting issues such as human rights, humanitarian law, gender and child protection. With this goal in mind, dimensions of SSR focus simultaneously on increasing the efficacy of the security sector while strengthening its civilian management and democratic oversight. SSR activities focussed on efficacy tend to revolve around institutional reform and the integration of non-state actors into the governance framework while measures aimed at improving governance centre on ministerial, legislative, parliamentary and judicial reform and policy development as well as capacity building among civil society actors. These efforts in turn need to be oriented toward long-term needs for stability and development whilst also catering to short term agendas. SSR is thus typified by a holistic approach that ties

[52] This distinction reflects the misperception of SSR that would account for Schneckener's categorisation of SSR as a key element in the security-first approach to state-building (see *supra* note 24). When the good governance aspect of SSR is given appropriate importance, SSR falls more naturally into an institutionalisation-first approach.

[53] SSR means – according to the OECD DAC definition – 'transforming the security system, which includes all the actors, their roles, responsibilities and actions – working together to manage and operate the system in a manner that is consistent with democratic norms and sound principles of good governance and thus contributing to a well-functioning security framework': OECD DAC, 2005. According to the Secretary-General's report, SSR 'describes a process of assessment, review and implementation as well as monitoring and evaluation led by national authorities that has as its goal the enhancement of effective and accountable security for the State and its peoples without discrimination and with full respect for human rights and the rule of law'. See UN GA-SC, A/62/659–S/2008/39, *supra* note 49, para. 17.

piece-meal reform efforts across government branches together into a coherent framework of democratic governance that includes non-state actors. This does not however indicate that SSR has become an unworkably broad concept but rather that an imperative for reform in one area must take account of overall efforts and ideally coordinate with those efforts.

Although state-building and SSR occur in diverse contexts, they are particularly relevant in post-conflict settings. The post-conflict setting is typified by the complexity of challenges it poses and also the particular opportunities it presents. On the one hand, there is often considerable public demand for change in these countries, including the "right-sizing" and reform of the security sector, and the willingness of the international community to actively support security sector reforms. On the other hand, SSR seems to be particularly difficult where insecurity is endemic, state institutions are weak or absent, political situations are fragile and socio-economic conditions precarious. Such settings are more often than not characterised by the strong presence of armed non-state actors, such as rebel groups and warlords, whose political ambitions and economic stakes will have to be taken into account. Thus in such contexts SSR is an extremely political exercise that, as mentioned above, implies engaging with fragmented patterns of power and governance including non-state armed forces as well as wider civil and uncivil society. Ultimately SSR may act as a power sharing arrangement among interested parties. That security provision in post-conflict contexts tends to be both internationalised and privatised also means that SSR can be instrumental in restoring an important function of Weberian state sovereignty.

Despite these distinct patterns, SSR in post-conflict settings follows the same two key principles as SSR in non-conflict environments, namely (re-)establishing security within a framework of legitimate, ideally democratic governance. What makes post-conflict SSR different, however, is the fact that it has to tackle a third objective: addressing the specific legacies of conflict through such SSR-related activities as DDR, mine action, rule of law, transitional justice and SALW control for example. As noted by the UN Security Council in July 2005, in the context of post-conflict environments, SSR "is inextricably linked with the promotion of rule of law, transitional justice, DDR, and the protection of civilians, among others".[54] Indeed these activities can prove determinant in the eventual success or failure of SSR in post-conflict contexts and will inevitably define the parameters of an SSR strategy.[55]

While post-conflict SSR is in most cases an externally driven exercise, a collision between local needs and externally-generated reform agendas will inevitably

---

[54] United Nations Security Council, "Statement by the President of the Security Council," Document No. S/PRST/2005/30 (July 12, 2005), para. 10.

[55] See Bryden & Hänggi, *supra* note 48.

lead to failure. Ensuring that SSR involves local commitment and reflects local needs from the outset while balancing the involvement of a broad coalition of state and non-state actors against the risk of spoilers is an inherent tension within the SSR agenda, and one that is of particular relevance to state-building. The importance of local ownership is only underscored by the fact that international intervention is the rule of post-conflict peacebuilding rather than the exception, and often for a considerably longer period of time than initially expected. This tends to be contrasted with a shortage of local capacity and, thus, by a lack of local ownership in state-building and reconstruction efforts, including SSR.[56]

The upshot of this discussion in terms of the role of SSR is to show that different approaches to state-building will fit differently with various versions of the SSR concept. Hence a liberalisation-first approach to state-building will emphasize the governance angle of the broad concept of SSR. An institutionalisation-first approach will aim for a minimal threshold of institutional efficiency so as to privilege accountability and exclude the threat of violence from politics. Finally a security-first approach would imply securing a certain margin of action for political actors without much regard to the governance elements of security sector management and therefore is hardly compatible with even the most narrow understanding of SSR.

V. *Security Sector Reform in Practice*

While SSR activities have been a staple of state-building for a long time and many peace operations with mandates related to state-building have included activities constituting SSR in all but name, there are nonetheless relatively few examples of explicit attempts at SSR in post-conflict state-building contexts. The first explicit acknowledgement by the Security Council of the need to engage in SSR came in 2002 in the context of operations in Sierra Leone. Since then more and more peace operations have been tasked with conducting SSR activities, increasingly at the request of recipient states and carried out in close collaboration with other multilateral and bilateral actors.[57] Looking at several recent examples of state-building serves to illustrate a number of the points raised in the preceding analysis of the role of SSR and state-building. While many cases present themselves as explanatory and useful in relation to this question, we have chosen to focus on the examples of Timor Leste, Kosovo, Afghanistan and Sierra Leone because of the illustrative points each makes about the role of SSR

---

[56] See Local Ownership and Security Sector Reform (Tim Donais ed., 2008).

[57] See Security Sector Reform and UN Integrated Missions (Heiner Hänggi & Vincenza Scherrer eds., 2008); UN GA-SC, A/62/659–S/2008/39, *supra* note 49.

in state-building. We will briefly compare these cases in terms of the nature of SSR activities each implied and the key lessons that can be drawn from each.

1. *Timor Leste: Legitimacy without security*

The case of Timor Leste demonstrates the need to build minimally effective and democratically controlled security institutions at the risk of seeing progress in every other area of the state-building agenda put in jeopardy. In Timor Leste, the conditions for state-building were almost uniquely favourable, a fact which bolstered the impression that this was one of the most successful state-building enterprises ever conducted by the UN. External forces in the guise of the Australian-led International Force for East Timor (INTERFET) credibly guaranteed security both internal and external, ensuring a relatively benign environment in which to put the pieces of the new state together. The United Nations Transitional Administration in East Timor (UNTAET) and the United Nations Mission of Support in East Timor (UNMISET) were endowed with permissive mandates stipulating the establishment of effective and democratic public institutions, a mandate which ostensibly extended to include development of the security sector.[58] Nevertheless the withdrawal of Indonesian forces after decades of occupation created a formidable challenge making necessary the construction of a new security sector in the context of a total collapse in territorial administration.[59] While the question of Timor Leste's armed forces was initially postponed, police reform became the focus of SSR activities. Ultimately short-comings in planning and capacity resulted in a politicized and poorly vetted police force that presented a threat to the human security of the people of Timor Leste as a result of growing abuse in the face of impunity and a general impression among the population that the police were not to be trusted.[60] Perhaps because of the relatively benign security environment, the question of how to deal with the defunct rebel forces which had fought the Indonesian occupation was delayed in an atmosphere of political indecision stemming from initial confusion over the legal implications of engaging armed non-state actors.[61] When action was taken, it came in the form of a deeply flawed DDR process that politicised recruitment of the new armed forces leading disgruntled veterans to form groups which became a source of insecurity.[62] This chain of events highlights the interdependent nature

58 Edward Rees, *Security Sector Reform (SSR) and Peace Operations: "Improvisation and Confusion" from the Field* 16–17 (United Nations Department of Peacekeeping Operations, March 2006).

59 International Crisis Group, *Timor-Leste: Security Sector Reform* (2008).

60 Ludovic Hood, *Security sector reform in East Timor, 1999–2004*, 13 International Peacekeeping 60 (2006).

61 Ibid., 61.

62 International Crisis Group, *supra* note 59, 19–20.

of SSR and DDR activities in post-conflict situations and the importance of acknowledging these linkages in state-building agendas.

Furthermore, the need for effective institutions to manage the security sector was neglected creating a policy vacuum around the security sector, which nurtured confusion over the appropriate division of labour between the police and the armed forces. This confusion was exacerbated when politicians called on the army to restore domestic order that had been entrusted to an under-prepared and under-resourced police force. The result of this blurring of appropriate roles was fierce competition between the police and the army eventually leading to armed clashes in 2006 that threatened to jeopardise the substantive progress made since the transition from occupation.[63] The failure to make SSR a cornerstone of the state-building effort put the nascent state's security at risk and nearly brought the international community's show-case example of state-building to the brink of state collapse.

Indeed the dangers of not building security institutions as illustrated in Timor Leste show how the legitimacy of the new state can be undone by a lack of security. The precarious state of security in Timor Leste, despite one of the largest and most intense efforts by the international community to build an effective state, bears sad testament to the necessity of ensuring minimal institutional efficacy in the management of the security sector. In terms of the role of SSR in state-building, the case of Timor Leste also shows that while SSR activities may be an explicit part of the state-building agenda, a failure to coordinate such activities within such an agenda can too easily result in a botched attempt at institution-building. In other words, although SSR was a goal of the state-building agenda in Timor Leste, it did not fit well within the larger state-building approach.

2. *Kosovo: Security without legitimacy*

A similar lesson about the need to ensure that SSR fits cohesively with larger state-building efforts can be drawn from the experience of Kosovo. Progress on SSR was slow in the first years of the mission in Kosovo even though the security situation was stabilised as the remnants of the Serb security forces were ousted from the territory. Institutional and bureaucratic miss-fit between multiple actors stemmed from fact that the SSR mandate was implicit rather than precise and explicit.[64] Mandates distributed across the Organisation for Security and Cooperation in Europe (OSCE), the United Nations Mission in Kosovo (UNMIK),

---

63 Ibid., 2–3.

64 Eric Scheye, *UNMIK and the Significance of Effective Programme Management: The Case of Kosovo*, *in* Security Sector Reform and UN Integrated Missions 176–177 (Heiner Hänggi & Vincenza Scherrer eds., 2008).

and the Kosovo Force (KFOR) led by the North Atlantic Treaty Organization (NATO) arguably contributed to confusion and a complicated chain of command. The negative effects of this state of affairs included a lack of clarity over the future role of the Kosovo Liberation Army, a fact which again highlights the cardinal importance of DDR to successful SSR efforts. Furthermore, delays in the development of effective justice and security institutions, particularly in the area of police reform, created opportunities for organised crime and allowed residual ethnic violence to become an increasing threat to internal security within Kosovo.[65] Ultimately a growing sense of police impunity in the face of ethnic violence contributed to the outbreak of riots in March 2004 which posed a major setback for security and SSR in Kosovo.[66]

The case of Kosovo is unique in terms of the role of SSR in state-building in so far as it turns the standard formula of SSR as a means of state-building on its head by effectively excluding the "state" from the "building". In Kosovo, SSR helped establish norms of democratic governance by paving the way for the Provisional Institutions of Government to assume control of the territory but without the synonymous goal of reinforcing state legitimacy per se. Indeed during the nine years that Kosovo's final status remained an open question, the international community invested unprecedented sums in creating the democratic institutional parameters of an undefined future. Working in collaboration with the OSCE and NATO, the goals of the UNMIK mission implied an expansive SSR effort in so far as establishing efficient and democratically controlled security and justice institutions was deemed integral to the larger task of building "provisional democratic self-governing institutions".[67] Yet these institutions were nevertheless provisional and the "state-hood" that was under construction was resolutely de facto as opposed to the de jure or juridical sovereignty that is usually the subject of state-building efforts. The fact that Kosovo's security sector was relatively successful in ensuring minimal levels of security without the juridical status of de jure sovereignty shows that SSR generates de facto legitimacy and security from the institutions it builds.[68]

The case of Kosovo also presents an interesting counter-point to the example of Timor Leste, in so far as it is also an example of how the failure to ensure

---

[65] Colette Rausch, *From Elation to Disappointment: Justice and Security Reform in Kosovo*, *in* Constructing Justice and Security After War 271 (Charles T. Call ed., 2007).

[66] A. Heinemann-Grüder & I. Grebenschikov, *Security governance by internationals: The case of Kosovo*, 13 International Peacekeeping 43 (2006).

[67] United Nations Security Council Resolution 1244, Document No. S/RES/1244 (June 10, 1999).

[68] This highlights the fact that SSR is a practical agenda rooted in results on the ground rather than the theoretical or normative constructs that give it analytical scope.

the legitimacy of state-building efforts can jeopardise security. Although after the 2004 and 2006 crises relative security and stability was restored and public confidence in the new security services is now relatively high, this was accomplished under external auspices. This fact had negative repercussions on the general level of confidence in the supposedly self-sustaining institutions which were supposed to have been built by the international task force. The foundations of democratic governance had been laid in the form of the Constitutional Framework for Provisional Self-Government issued in 2001 but while the Framework was a blue-print for democratic institution building, it also vested ultimate authority irrevocably in the hands of UNMIK and the Special Representative of the Secretary General. Responsibility for the security sector including justice remained with the external authorities longer than for any other institutional oversight capacity. This control over the institution building process came at the expense of genuine Kosovar autonomy with concomitant adverse effects for local ownership. The international community was accused of dealing in a high-handed manner with the tasks of administration.[69] The case of Kosovo tested the limits of principle in building a democracy non-democratically and thus shows how institutions can supply security at the cost of legitimacy if sufficient efforts are not made to assure local ownership and to create wide-spread consensus over the shape and form of the security sector.

3. *Afghanistan: Security versus legitimacy*

SSR in Afghanistan provides a different example of the relationship between legitimacy and security highlighting the fact that these concerns are not always mutually reinforcing. Military reform, under US control, was perhaps the most successful element of the international SSR programme;[70] however, efficiency was apparently achieved at the price of governance in what has become a classic example of a contradiction between domestic interests and external agendas. US interest in SSR was largely driven by the overriding policy imperative of the war on terror and the need to establish an effective counter-terrorism force in a key strategic region.[71] However this policy imperative was not always in harmony with the goal of creating an effective Afghan military.

The 2002 Bonn Agreement became the blueprint for Afghanistan's state-building and issues of DDR and SSR were afforded a certain importance, yet the exigencies of political compromise and the realities of insecurity on the ground nevertheless created tensions with the holistic and comprehensive vision of SSR

[69] Heinemann-Grüder & Grebenschikov, *supra* note 54, 66.

[70] Mark Sedra, *Security sector reform in Afghanistan: The slide towards expediency*, 13 International Peacekeeping 97 (2006).

[71] Rubin, *supra* note 30, 40.

that donors had envisaged.[72] A lack of coordination among stakeholders hindered efforts to rehabilitate Afghanistan's crumbling judicial system.[73] Police reform took the oft-cited critique to heart that SSR should focus on long-term needs at the cost of short-term gains in law and order.[74] The result was a general decline in human security as an atmosphere of impunity set in.

Furthermore, the conditions of SSR and state-building in Afghanistan in general cannot be separated from the continuing conditions of conflict, insurgency and insecurity. The exigencies of state-building "under-fire" led to a focus on operational capacity-building to the neglect of long-term training and the sustainability of reforms.[75] Hence SSR in Afghanistan demonstrated a close fit with the larger state-building agenda in some terms (e.g. police reform, DDR and judicial reform) but less so in others (military reform). This contradiction in agendas led to a contradiction between human security and state security as the ability of the state to protect itself increased with the efficiency of the army but human security deteriorated in great part due to unsuccessful police reform. This contradiction helped short-circuit the link between security and legitimacy, in this case drawing them into contradiction.

Afghanistan is also an example of how local ownership can be a double-edged sword. The inclusiveness of the Bonn Agreement, which co-opted warlords and factional leaders into the political process, has been praised for giving these potential spoilers a stake in the future order of political affairs.[76] Yet the same local ownership made it possible for interested actors to entrench their influence early on in the transitional administration with highly detrimental effects for the effectiveness of the SSR process.[77] Thus the ministry of defence for example became a politicised instrument of factional politics actively working against the agenda of donors at different stages.[78] In response, donors shifted their tactics to increase the effectiveness and reach of their reform agendas, however this strategic response required the sacrifice of the holistic approach to SSR that had been the hallmark of early policy formulations. Efficiency, to the extent that it has been

[72] This process is what prompted Sedra to describe SSR in Afghanistan as a 'slide towards expediency': see *supra* note 70.

[73] Sedra, *supra* note 70, 100.

[74] Ibid., 97–98.

[75] Jake Sherman, *Afghanistan: Nationally Led Statebuilding, in* Building States to Build Peace 303 (Charles T. Call & Vanessa Wyeth eds., 2008).

[76] Papagianni, *supra* note 37, 62.

[77] Antonio Giustozzi, *Local Ownership and Security Sector Reform in Afghanistan, in* Local Ownership and Security Sector Reform (Tim Donais ed., forthcoming 2008); Sherman, *supra* note 75, 304.

[78] See Giustozzi *supra* note 77; Sherman, *supra* note 75.

achieved, has come at the cost of democratic governance principles and local ownership demonstrating how security and legitimacy can stand in opposition when human security is not the focus of the normative agenda.

4. *Sierra Leone: Security through legitimacy*

Sierra Leone's long and tragic history of conflict provides the final perspective on how SSR can influence state-building. In comparison to Timor Leste, Kosovo and Afghanistan, the process of SSR in Sierra Leone is much older having begun ostensibly in 1996 under President Kabbah.[79] Yet attempts at SSR ended in abject failure when in 1997 the downsizing of the armed forces prompted a faction within the military to stage a coup d'état against the democratically elected government.[80] To the extent that SSR was at all possible at the time, it was not effective in countering the volatile security situation and indeed the failure to strengthen Sierra Leone's armed forces was part of the reason why the country slid back into instability and conflict. When British assistance was offered through the International Military Assistance Training Team (IMATT) it was in the knowledge that a stronger national army could have likely resisted the advances of the rebels who in 1999 had threatened to take Freetown and overthrow the democratically elected government but for the last minute arrival of British forces. In this sense Sierra Leone provides an object lesson in the importance of ensuring that a state can credibly defend its national territorial integrity. The same example also shows that a framework of democratic governance is important in removing the threat of the use of force against elected officials and that absent that guarantee, weak governments may have no wish to see the security sector strengthened.

Sierra Leone is also an example of how a post-conflict situation can generate a demand for reform. The country's long history of conflict made the need to reform the security sector clear and the principle of democratic control over the armed forces as a cornerstone of stability and economic development was duly inscribed on government policy; first through the 1999 Lomé Accords, in 2000 as part of the Interim Poverty Reduction Strategy Paper, and later as a cornerstone of the 2005 Poverty Reduction Strategy Paper.[81] Embedding SSR in the national poverty reduction strategy was part of the recognition that security

[79] Osman Gbla, *Security Sector Reform in Sierra Leone*, in Challenges to Security Sector Reform in the Horn of Africa 13 (L. Le Roux & Y. Kidane eds., 2007).

[80] Peter Albrecht, The Sierra Leonean State in 2005: Revisiting the Root Causes of the Conflict 4–5 (Sept. 2005).

[81] Osman Gbla, *Security sector reform under international tutelage in Sierra Leone*, 13 International Peacekeeping 83 (2006).

is the bedrock of development in a country struggling to restore itself after more than a decade of vicious conflict. This approach is symptomatic of a development-focussed approach to SSR which might not have been possible in more volatile circumstances. This approach also aptly shows to what extent the state functions of security and legitimacy are intertwined with the provision of welfare.

Under the protection of a security guarantee from the UK, the first steps towards stability and reform were ad hoc and poorly coordinated within an institutional governance structure rife with corruption.[82] Given the recent history of military interference in political life, the possibility of replacing Sierra Leone's armed forces with a more robust police force was briefly considered before being laid aside in view of the precarious regional security situation.[83] Thus reform of the armed forces began under the tutelage of IMATT and over a period of years has achieved increased efficiency despite continuing deficits in governance and oversight.[84] While the process of institution building has been slow and not always comprehensive, it has been considered relatively successful and is perhaps the best example of why long time horizons and locally driven reform agendas are the hallmarks of success in SSR, no matter how modest. Nevertheless the situation is far from perfect, with the on-going presence of external actors drawing questions about sustainability and the fact that the growing number of Sierra Leoneans in decision-making positions seem to operate as if "remotely controlled by foreigners".[85] This state of affairs demonstrates that a slow-going approach while offering certain advantages vis-à-vis the short time horizons of other reform programmes nonetheless carries with it its own pitfalls. The process in Sierra Leone ultimately demonstrates that attention to efficiency in security provision within a framework of consultative democratic governance can augment the legitimacy of a state recovering from conflict and that of the state-building project that goes with it.

VI. *Conclusion*

The schematic overview of these diverse recent experiences in state-building show that the relationship between the state functions of legitimacy and security are neither linear nor static. Security can reinforce legitimacy by empowering the state to prove its relevance to the daily lives of people, while insecurity or

---

[82] See International Crisis Group, *Sierra Leone: The State of Security and Governance* (2003).

[83] Gbla, *supra* note 19, 79.

[84] Gbla, *supra* note 81, 89–90.

[85] Al-Hassan Kondeh, *Sierra Leone*, *in* Challenges of Security Sector Governance in West Africa 298 (A. Bryden, B. N'Diaye & F. Olonisakin eds., 2008).

security that is focussed elsewhere than the interests of citizens, can undermine the relevance of the state itself. Conditions in Timor Leste demonstrate that the legitimacy of a new-born state cannot guarantee its internal security, just as Kosovo shows that security can be undone more easily where legitimacy lacks. It is nearly trite to observe that both security and legitimacy are necessary to new and newly empowered states, yet Afghanistan shows that not just any security will do. This insight is underlined by the case of Sierra Leone, where a broad notion of security based on the intimate relationship between security and development helped guarantee that state legitimacy and security concerns were mutually reinforcing rather than contradictory.

The complexities of the relationship return to the importance of context in approaching SSR but also underline the difficult question of assessing success both in terms of state-building and SSR. While addressing the 'root causes' of instability will always be a worthy goal, it provides an impossible standard against which to judge the achievements of state-building and reform. Similarly a minimalist definition focussed on shallow indicators such as an absence of violence or the holding of elections is equally unsatisfying in guiding progress towards a stable and productive society. Mixed approaches based on various indicators of governance and security over time, have supplied mixed results in determining which approaches to state-building are the most promising. Hartzell et al. define successful peace on the basis of a 5 year measurement dated from a negotiated settlement reasoning that institutions and their effects will change over time, just as the factors driving conflict will likely attenuate over time.[86] This logic is appealing from an institutionalisation-first state-building perspective, rooted as it is in the assertion that while institutions do matter to a lasting peace, they cannot make all the difference.

A liberalisation-first approach to state-building implies embracing SSR in its broadest aspiration with a strong emphasis on the transformative potential of the democratic governance aspects of the agenda. While this may have positive repercussions in terms of the broad-based consensus that can be built across a range of state and non-state actors, it also sets very high expectations about what institutional reform can achieve. From this point of view institutions are the embodiment of a new political order and can be determinant in political outcomes allowing external actors to shape both security and legitimacy through the instrument of state reform or reconstruction. The goal of this agenda would be to strengthen institutional capacity as a form of social change and according to a normative agenda of democratic governance: the legitimacy of the state so constructed should constitute a guarantee of greater security. Such an

[86] Caroline Hartzell, Matthew Hoddie & Donald Rothchild, *Stabilizing the Peace After Civil War: An Investigation of Some Key Variables*, 55 International Organization 187 (2001).

approach however tends to overestimate the efficacy of institutional reform in driving normative transformations. In this regard, the liberalisation-first approach establishes a standard of success that is all but unreachable in the short- to mid-term if indeed it is attainable at all. Ultimately, SSR within a liberalisation-first approach to state-building runs the risk of establishing legitimacy at the cost of security.

In contra-distinction a security-first approach emphasises the conditions of security in order to create space for political processes to unfold without the threat of violence. Based on the assumption that institutions cannot affect political outcomes, SSR in any meaningful sense is anathema from this point of view. Technical military assistance, or bilateral aid aimed at improving the operational efficiency and effectiveness of security forces is more obviously relevant to guaranteeing the minimal physical security that this approach implies. However, without embracing the wider governance aspects of the SSR agenda, a security-first approach risks becoming a security-only approach as legitimacy through accountability is excluded from the equation. This approach clearly provides security at the cost of legitimacy. At best, security may result in legitimacy if the prevailing political context permits.

Compared to a liberalisation-first approach, a more modest approach based on an institutionalisation-first strategy is less ambitious and therefore more achievable. By lowering expectations of the socially transformative role of democratic governance, space is created for organic political processes to give institutions their own meaning. This does not mean that institution-building is ineffectual, as a security-first approach would posit, but rather that SSR can define the parameters of political contestation by excluding the use of violence from politics. This also creates scope for governance solutions that are not necessarily modelled on Western, liberal democratic models of statehood and are therefore more responsive to the exigencies of context. External actors can contribute to the strengthening of institutional capacity according to this approach and still pursue a normative agenda based on the legitimacy of democratic governance but within limits of influence that are more clearly demarcated. A broad-based consensus among security sector stakeholders will still be necessary to the success of SSR, but the emphasis is more likely to fall on government institutions. Approaching SSR in this way offers an opportunity to make security and legitimacy mutually reinforcing under the right circumstances and with judicious attention to context. Where security and legitimacy become mutually reinforcing the question of social transformation is left for societies themselves to answer through organic political processes.

Thus the contention of this analysis remains that an inclusive institutionalisation-first approach to state-building can empower a new or recovering state to supply a minimal level of security legitimately, and that SSR is a key means towards this end.

Causes

State-Building and the Transformation of Warfare

Monika Heupel

I. *Introduction*

The concept of state-building refers to the (re-)building of public institutions that enable weak, failing or failed states to (re-)gain the capacities to perform the core functions of modern states. The literature on state failure and state-building converges towards the view that a state is expected to perform three core functions: First, a state is to assure security both internally towards its citizens and externally towards other states and their citizens. Second, a state is supposed to provide basic welfare services to its citizens. Third, a state must be perceived as representative and legitimate by its citizens.[1] Thus, in a nutshell, empowering a state to assure internal and external security, provide basic welfare services to its citizens, and establish institutions that advance its legitimacy constitutes state-building.[2]

State-building is crucial in the wake of domestic armed conflict or war. Even if all relevant parties have signed a peace treaty and vowed to terminate warfare, a state emerging from armed conflict or war often does not have the monopoly

---

[1] See for example Jennifer Milliken & Keith Krause, *State Failure, State Collapse and State Reconstruction: Concepts, Lessons and Strategies, in* State Failure, Collapse and Reconstruction 1 (Jennifer Milliken ed., 2003), who name security, welfare and representation as the three core functions of the modern state. See also Sebastian von Einsiedel, *Policy responses to state failure, in* Making States Work: State Failure and the Crisis of Governance 13 (Simon Chesterman, Michael Ignatieff & Ramesh Thakur eds., 2005). For literature on state failure see for example Robert H. Jackson, Quasi-states: sovereignty, international relations and the Third World (1990). See also Daniel C. Esty et al., *State Failure Task Force Report: Phase II Findings*, July 31, 1998, *at* <http://globalpolicy.gmu.edu/pitf/SFTF%20Phase%20II%20Report.pdf> (last access 22 May 2008).

[2] For the concept of state-building see for example Simon Chesterman, You, the People: The United Nations, Transitional Administration, and State-Building (2004). See also Ulrich Schneckener, *International Statebuilding. Dilemmas, Strategies and Challenges for German Foreign Policy* (2007), *at* <http://www.swp-berlin.org/en/common/get_document.php?asset_id=4428> (last access 22 May 2008).

on the use of force. In addition, in the immediate aftermath of domestic armed conflict or war a state usually does not have the capacities and resources to develop and implement sustainable economic and social policies. Moreover, in the course of protracted violent conflict democratic institutions tend to erode and the legitimacy of the state tends to be undermined. Post-conflict state-building as a specific form of state-building therefore aims at restoring the governmental monopoly on force, strengthening the capacities of the state to provide urgently needed basic welfare services and reconstituting the legitimacy of governmental institutions. Therefore the rebuilding of public institutions that enable a war-torn state to (re-)gain capacities to perform its three core functions is regarded as the key to effective post-conflict peacebuilding.[3]

With the end of the Cold War, state-building as a means to stabilize peace processes in countries emerging from armed conflict or war has become more important for two reasons. First, the demand for state-building has increased. In the late 1980s and early 1990s several so-called proxy wars ended once the superpowers lost interest in supporting allied guerrilla groups in the developing world. Second, the United Nations expanded their scope and are more frequently engaged in state-building. Accordingly, the United Nations were increasingly able to authorize and dispatch missions in post-conflict settings that – like those in Bosnia-Herzegovina and East Timor – were given encompassing and intrusive mandates for institution building, supposed to lay the foundations for stable peace.[4]

At the same time, though, the contemporary transformation of warfare poses fundamental challenges to state-building and makes institution building in the wake of domestic armed conflict or war difficult. With the end of the Cold War so-called "new wars" have gained in importance. These "new wars" are characterized by the involvement of numerous private, internally fragmented actors, increased significance of economic motives, spread of brutal violence against the civilian population, and proliferation of criminal activities such as natural resources trafficking as a means to fund warfare.[5] Each of the features of

---

[3] For an elaboration of (re-)building state institutions in the wake of armed conflict or war see Marina Ottaway, *Rebuilding State Institutions in Collapsed States*, *in* State Failure, Collapse and Reconstruction 245 (Jennifer Milliken ed., 2003). See also Robert Rotberg, *The Failure and Collapse of Nation-States: Breakdown, Prevention, and Repair*, *in* When States Fail: Causes and Consequences 1 (Robert Rotberg ed., 2004). See also Roland Paris, At War's End: Building Peace After Civil Conflict (2004).

[4] For the evolution of United Nations peace missions see Volker Rittberger & Bernhard Zangl, International Organization: Polity, Politics and Policies 123–144 (2006).

[5] For the features of the "new wars" see Monika Heupel & Bernhard Zangl, *Von "alten" und "neuen" Kriegen – Zum Gestaltwandel kriegerischer Gewalt*, 45 Politische Vierteljahresschrift 346 (2004).

the "new wars" constitutes a particular challenge to state-building in the aftermath of intra-state armed conflict or war. All these features – the privatization of actors, the economization of motives, the brutalization of strategies and the criminalization of war economies –, render post-conflict state-building more demanding and require specific strategies to meet the new challenges.

The purpose of this chapter is to highlight how the emergence and proliferation of the phenomena associated with the "new wars" pose a challenge to state-building in the aftermath of intra-state armed conflict or war. To this end, the chapter will unfold as follows. It will start by briefly outlining the concept of post-conflict state-building (II.). In a second step, it will show how the transformation of warfare poses a challenge to state-building in the wake of domestic violent conflict (III.). Finally, the conclusion will summarize the main arguments (IV.).

II. *The Concept of Post-Conflict State-Building*

In the aftermath of internal armed conflict or war states normally want the capacities and resources to fulfil the three core functions assigned to them, that is to provide security, basic welfare services, and representation. Public institutions, which warrant security internally and externally, make basic welfare services available, and facilitate legitimate governance, are vital requirements for effective peacebuilding in the wake of violent conflict. By enabling states to meet their three core functions, post-conflict state-building aims to prevent the recurrence of violent conflict and to create the foundations for stable peace.[6]

To guarantee security – both internally towards its citizens and externally towards other states and their citizens – a state needs the monopoly on the use of force. In the aftermath of domestic armed conflict or war, however, states typically lack the monopoly on force. Rebel groups, even if they have agreed to the termination of warfare and to the disarming and demobilizing of their combat units, generally still have armed forces at their disposal. Hence, disarming and demobilizing irregular armed forces is considered to be one pivotal element of post-conflict state-building. Usually the disarmament and demobilization of irregular armed forces is embedded in a broader reform of the security sector. Such a reform normally includes the integration of members of all relevant conflict parties into the security forces, the establishment of civil control over

[6] For literature on post-conflict state-building see Ottaway, *supra* note 3, Rotberg, *supra* note 3, and Paris, *supra* note 3. For the concept of state-building in general see Chesterman, *supra* note 2, and Schneckener, *supra* note 2.

the army and the police, as well as the restriction of the army's brief to national defence against external threats.[7]

Furthermore, in the wake of armed conflict or war states frequently lack the capacities and resources to provide basic welfare services to their citizens. This may have highly detrimental implications for the stabilization of fragile peace processes, as individuals and societal groups are more likely to accept a peace process if it improves their socioeconomic well-being. Accordingly, the less the population in general and former members of rebel groups in particular are satisfied with the peace dividend, the less probable is their acceptance of and participation in post-conflict state-building. Strengthening the capacities of states to develop and implement social, educational and health policies, build infrastructure, and stimulate sustainable economic growth is thus a further core element of the (re-)construction of states emerging from violent conflict.[8]

Finally, in the course of domestic armed conflict or war democratic and constitutional values tend to be undermined and the legitimacy of the state frequently erodes. State-building in the aftermath of violent conflict aims therefore not only to enable the state to provide security and basic welfare services, but also to restore its legitimacy in the eyes of its citizens. According to this, the development of a constitution in which democratic norms and the rule of law are inscribed is regarded as a central component of post-conflict state-building. Furthermore, the establishment of an independent judicial system, as well as the organization of free and fair elections, contributes to the legitimacy of the state. This may comprise power-sharing agreements to guarantee the integration of all relevant actors into the political process. Eventually, establishing public institutions such as tribunals and truth commissions that can facilitate reconciliation and coming to terms with the past may help to revive the legitimacy of a state in the aftermath of violent conflict.[9]

---

[7] See for example Elizabeth M. Cousens, *Introduction, in* Peacebuilding as Politics: Cultivating Peace in Fragile Societies 1 (Elizabeth M. Cousens & Chetan Kumar eds., 2001). See also Nicole Ball, *The Challenge of Rebuilding War-Torn Societies, in* Turbulent Peace – The Challenges of Managing International Conflict 719 (Chester A. Crocker, Fen Osler Hampson & Pamela Aall eds. 2001). See also Kees Kingma, *Demobilisation and Reintegration of Ex-combatants in Post-war and Transition Countries: Trends and Challenges of External Support* (2001), *at* <http://www.bicc.de/publications/other/gtz_studien/demob/demobilisation.pdf> (last access 22 May 2008).

[8] See for example Christian Drews, Post-Conflict Peace-Building (2000). See also Kingma, *supra* note 7, and Hugh Miall, Oliver Ramsbotham & Tom Woodhouse, Contemporary Conflict Resolution: The prevention, management and transformation of deadly conflict (1999).

[9] See for example Samuel H. Barnes, *The Contribution of Democracy to Rebuilding Postconflict Societies*, 95 The American Journal of International Law 86 (2001). See also Roy Licklider, *Obstacles to Peace Settlements, in* Turbulent Peace – The Challenges of Managing

III. *State-Building and the Transformation of Warfare*

After the end of the Cold War, so-called "new wars" have emerged and spread, posing specific challenges for state-building in the wake of domestic armed conflict or war. These "new wars", which differ both from inter-state wars and from the classical civil wars of the Cold War period, did not displace other forms of violent conflict, but have gained increased significance since the early 1990s. The "new wars" can be distinguished from the classical intra-state wars of the Cold War period with regard to four dimensions: the actors involved in the conflict, the motives they pursue, the strategies they apply, and the war economy through which they supply themselves.[10] With respect to every dimension, the "new wars" pose special demands to post-conflict state-building and render the (re-)building of public institutions more difficult. This section outlines the transformation of warfare in terms of the actor-, motive-, strategy- and war-economy-dimension and depicts implications for effective state-building in the aftermath of domestic armed conflict and war.

1. *The privatization of actors and its implications for state-building*

The classical intra-state wars of the Cold War period were characterized by a limited number of conflict parties. Normally, the state was confronted by only one or few guerrilla groups. These guerrilla groups were usually organized along vertical command structures and therefore displayed a considerable degree of internal coherence. The individual units of the guerrilla groups generally acted fairly independently from each other, but were controlled by their leadership and followed a common strategy. Governments entangled in domestic armed conflict or war mainly relied on regular combat units to respond to the guerrilla operations. In addition, governments deployed paramilitary forces, but these acted widely under their control.[11]

The "new wars", in contrast, feature a privatization of actors. This does not mean that private actors increasingly interfere with the state's monopoly of warfare, as this applies to all domestic wars, both the classical civil wars of the Cold War period and the "new wars" alike. Rather, the privatization of actors

---

INTERNATIONAL CONFLICT 697 (Chester A. Crocker, Fen Osler Hampson & Pamela Aall eds. 2001) and PRISCILLA HAYNER, UNSPEAKABLE TRUTHS: FACING THE CHALLENGE OF TRUTH COMMISSIONS (2002).

[10] For the notion of the "new wars" see MARY KALDOR, NEW AND OLD WARS – ORGANIZED VIOLENCE IN A GLOBAL ERA (2006) and HERFRIED MÜNKLER, THE NEW WARS (2004). For the dimensions to distinguish "new wars" from the classical intrastate wars of the Cold War period see Heupel & Zangl, *supra* note 5.

[11] See Kaldor, *supra* note 10. For the strategic and tactical guidelines of classical guerilla warfare see MAO TSE-TUNG, ON GUERILLA WARFARE (1961).

refers, firstly, to the involvement of more and novel private actors that operate largely independently from each other. The most prominent private actor of the "new wars" is the figure of the warlord who aims at fulfilling the tasks of a military leader, a politician, and an entrepreneur at the same time. In addition, private security companies have more frequently become involved in intra-state wars like for example in Uganda and Angola, where governments hired foreign mercenaries to fight against rebel groups. Also, in the course of many violent conflicts, such as in Bosnia-Herzegovina, self-defence units have been formed to protect local communities against assaults of marauding troops and militias. Secondly, the privatization of actors refers to the internal fragmentation of the parties involved in the conflict. Thus, in the "new wars" the traditionally hierarchical structures of conflict parties erode, and individual units and combatants tend to act more autonomously from their leadership.[12]

The privatization of actors has negative implications for state-building in the aftermath of domestic armed conflict or war. This assessment rests upon two assumptions. Firstly, the stabilization of a peace process is more difficult the higher the number of parties involved in the conflict. This is because a peace process can only be stabilized if it is accepted by all relevant parties and therefore all relevant parties have to be integrated in the post-conflict peacebuilding process. The higher the number of parties involved in the conflict, the more complicated is the integration of all relevant parties in the peace process as is illustrated by the conflict in Darfur. Besides, a high number of conflict parties also raises the likelihood that more than one so-called spoiler – an actor aiming at violently undermining the peace process – has to be accommodated. This entails dilemmas, as measures to weaken one spoiler potentially strengthen another spoiler. In Afghanistan, for example, the U.S.-led coalition supported local warlords in order to win allies in their campaign against the Taliban and al-Qaeda. This might have impaired the Taliban and al-Qaeda, but at the same time empowered local warlords, who subvert the authority of the central government and undermine state-building.[13]

---

[12] See Münkler, *supra* note 10. See also Paul B. Rich, *The Emergence and Significance of Warlordism in International Politics, in* Warlords in International Relations 1 (Paul B. Rich ed., 1999). See also Sven Chojnacki, *Wandel der Kriegsformen: Die Dimensionen neuer, privatisierter Kriege* (2002), *at* <http://www.wz-berlin.de/~svencho/pdf/Bad-Boll-2002–1.pdf> (last access 31 May 2005).

[13] See Michael W. Doyle & Nicholas Sambanis, *International Peacebuilding: A Theoretical and Quantitative Analysis*, 94 American Political Science Review 779 (2000). See also Heiko Nitzschke, *Transforming War Economies: Challenges for Peacemaking and Peacebuilding, Report of the 725th Wilton Park Conference, in association with the International Peace Academy* (2003), *at* <http://www.ipacademy.org/pdfs/TRANSFORMING_WAR_ECONOMIES.pdf> (last access 22 May 2008). See also Stephen John Stedman, *Spoiler Problems in Peace Processes*, 22 International Security 5 (1997).

Secondly, some scholars point out that the internal fragmentation of conflict parties exacerbates the difficulty of state-building and the stabilization of peace processes in the wake of domestic armed conflict or war. A peace treaty can only be implemented if the elites of the involved parties have the ability to enforce the obligations they agreed to when signing a peace treaty. The more decentralized the organizational structure of a conflict party, the more difficult it is for its leadership to enforce arranged stipulations against the resistance of individual commanders or units. In addition, the more the leadership anticipates opposition of individual commanders or units in the first place, the less likely is its active engagement in implementing peacebuilding measures.[14] However, this argument hinges on the premise that the leadership of a rebel group is generally more inclined to partake in peace implementation and state-building than individual commanders and units. In some cases though, such as the Cambodian peace process, the leadership defies peace implementation and state-building, while individual commanders and units display more willingness to participate in post-conflict peacebuilding and separate from the leadership. Under these circumstances, a decentralized organizational structure of rebel groups can promote peacebuilding.[15]

2. *The economization of motives and its implications for state-building*

In the classical civil wars of the Cold War period rebel groups fought primarily for ideological motives – as in the anti-regime wars – or for identity-based motives – as in the decolonization and secession wars. In the anti-regime war in Guatemala, for instance, the social-revolutionary Guatemalan National Revolutionary Unity (URNG) took up arms against the conservative government in order to change the prevalent form of government. In decolonization wars, such as that of the Algerian National Liberation Front (FLN) against France, rebel groups challenged colonial powers to found independent states. And in secession wars, such as between Eritrea and Ethiopia, rebel groups strove for autonomy rights or the establishment of an independent state based on an ethnically, religiously or culturally defined identity. Certainly, economic goals did play a role in the

[14] See Michael W. Doyle, *War Making and Peace Making: The United Nations' Post-Cold War Record*, *in* TURBULENT PEACE – THE CHALLENGES OF MANAGING INTERNATIONAL CONFLICT 529 (Chester A. Crocker, Fen Osler Hampson & Pamela Aall eds. 2001). See also Gilles Carbonnier, *Undoing War Economies: A Prerequisite For Peace?*, 22 REFUGEE SURVEY QUARTERLY: REPORTS, DOCUMENTATION, LITERATURE SURVEY 165 (2003).

[15] For this argument see also Philippe Le Billon, *Risiko Ressourcenreichtum: Ursachen und Wirkung der „Neuen Kriege"*, *in* MEDICO REPORT 24: UNGEHEUER IST NUR DAS NORMALE: ZUR ÖKONOMIE DER „NEUEN" KRIEGE 28, 45 (2002).

domestic wars of the Cold War period as well, but they have not been the main motivating forces.[16]

In the "new wars", ideological and identity-based motives are increasingly mixed and intertwined with economic motives.[17] Often economic motives play only a minor role in the outbreak and early stages of violent conflicts, but gain in importance as soon as the parties involved in the conflict open up sources of income in the course of warfare. However, the emergence and proliferation of economic motives does not imply that rebel groups do not aspire to assume national power any more. Rather, rebel groups like, for example, Charles Taylor's National Patriotic Front of Liberia (NPLF) still aim to assume political power, as this provides better conditions to generate profits. Ideological and identity-based war motives do not disappear but are to an increasing degree applied merely as rhetoric means to mobilize followers for an ultimately economically motivated conflict. In Sierra Leone, for example, the Revolutionary United Front (RUF) rebel movement justified its struggle with ideological motives, although in the course of the war the control of the country's lucrative diamond deposits had become more and more the actual objective of its fighting.[18]

The increase of economic motives renders state-building in the wake of armed conflict or war more difficult. This is because conflict parties that are predominantly motivated by ideological or identity-based reasons are normally interested in ending a war, whereas actors that are predominantly motivated by economic reasons are usually interested in the continuation of warfare. According to this, rebel groups that fight for a specific form of government, autonomy rights, or a state of their own are commonly ready to end an armed conflict or a war if the conditions of peace widely coincide with their objectives. In contrast, rebel groups that primarily wage war in order to enrich themselves have fewer incentives to abandon warfare, since their trafficking of natural resources or looting of the population usually depends on the perpetuation of warfare. Being involved in the implementation of a peace treaty and post-conflict state-building means to share income from the resource sector with the government or with government-licensed companies. For rebel groups which are primarily motivated by economic reasons, abandoning warfare and taking part in state-building is

---

[16] See Chojnacki, *supra* note 12.

[17] Not all proponents of the "new wars"-thesis share the assumption of the increased significance of economic motives. Kaldor, *supra* note 10, for instance, rather presumes that actors in the "new wars", even though political and economic goals increasingly mix with each other, are primarily motivated by identity-based and ideological goals.

[18] See Nitzschke, *supra* note 13. See also Neil Cooper, *State Collapse as Business: The Role of Conflict Trade and the Emerging Control Agenda*, 33 Development and Change 935 (2002). See also Paul Collier, *Doing Well out of War: An Economic Perspective, in* Greed & grievance: economic agendas in civil wars 91 (Mats Berdal & David M. Malone eds., 2000).

therefore attractive only if the peace dividend promises higher profits than the perpetuation of warfare.[19]

Some scholars contend that wars primarily fought for economic motives are easier to end than wars fought primarily for ideological or identity-based motives. They maintain that actors who pursue ideological or identity-based motives fight for indivisible values and are therefore only rarely ready to change their attitudes. In contrast, conflicts which are fought for economic motives are interest-led conflicts over divisible goods guided by rational cost-benefit calculations. Hence, it is argued, actors pursuing predominantly economic motives can be influenced by reducing the profits which can be gained during warfare, thereby lowering the incentives for the continuation of warfare.[20] However, these considerations presuppose that profits obtained in the course of an armed conflict or war can actually be reduced by external intervention. In doing so, the difficulties of preventing conflict parties from supplying themselves via war economies based on illicit economic activities are underestimated. If, however, efforts at reducing incentives for the continuation of warfare fail, actors seeking divisible goods are unlikely to partake in peace implementation and state-building.[21]

3. *The brutalization of strategies and its implications for state-building*

During the classical civil wars of the Cold War period, guerrilla groups did not only try to avoid direct confrontation with the government forces, but also widely refrained from deliberately resorting to violence against civilians. Support from the population was considered to be a necessary condition of successful guerrilla warfare, as the guerrilla fighters were supposed to move among the local population "like a fish in the water". Rather, the strategy applied by the guerrilla groups of the classical intrastate wars was to wear down the state and its armed forces through attacks on infrastructure facilities and public institutions. Nevertheless, violence against civilians has undoubtedly been a widespread feature of the intra-state wars of the Cold War period. Frequently, government-sponsored paramilitary forces intentionally applied brutal force against civilians in the framework of so-called counter-insurgency measures in order to deter local support for guerrilla units. In El Salvador, for instance, government-sponsored

---

[19] See Karen Ballentine, *Beyond Greed and Grievance: Reconsidering the Economic Dynamics of Armed Conflict, in* The Political Economy of Armed Conflict: Beyond Greed & Grievance 259 (Karen Ballentine & Jake Sherman eds., 2003). See also Stephen John Stedman, *International Implementation of Peace Agreements in Civil Wars: Findings from a Study of Sixteen Cases, in* Turbulent Peace – The Challenges of Managing International Conflict 737 (Chester A. Crocker, Fen Osler Hampson & Pamela Aall eds. 2001).

[20] See Leiv Lunde, Economic Driving Forces of Violent Conflict and War (2001) (quoted from Ballentine, *supra* note 23, 273–274). See also Licklider, *supra* note 9.

[21] For a similar criticism see Ballentine, *supra* note 23, 274–275.

death squads systematically used brutal force against civilians to deprive the guerrilla from local assistance.[22]

In the "new wars", however, the civilian population falls victim to consciously applied violence to an increasing degree. In the "new wars" the use of deliberate brutal violence against civilians is no longer largely restricted to government-sponsored paramilitary forces, but has increasingly become a strategy applied by rebel groups also. Accordingly, since the end of the Cold War, the number of refugees and internally displaced persons has risen and the ratio of military to civilian casualties has further shifted towards civilian casualties. Violent acts against the civilian population sometimes lose every restraint and break previously respected taboos, as the systematic mutilations during the war in Sierra Leone display. In doing so, brutal violence against the civilian population is neither irrational nor a side effect of warfare, but rather a deliberate strategy, which aims at expelling civilians from certain areas. In Bosnia-Herzegovina, for example, irregular Serbian combat units tried to gain control over particular areas by purposely using brutal force against the Muslim population. Thus, the massacre against Muslim men in Srebrenica and the mass rape of Muslim women was no collateral damage of warfare but part of a rational strategy.[23]

The rise in deliberate brutal violence against civilians has negative implications for post-conflict state-building. This claim rests on several assumptions: Firstly, states whose population has notably suffered from brutal violence in the course of armed conflict or war are likely to lack the necessary capacities for sustainable development in post-conflict situations and thus need support to provide basic welfare services to their citizens. Secondly, war crimes and massive human rights violations targeted at the civilian population tend to engender mistrust and mutual rejection between different population groups, which renders reconciliation between population groups more demanding. And finally, after violent conflicts that were marked by numerous civilian casualties and a large number of refugees and internally displaced persons, the parties involved in the conflict are likely to confront each other with distrust. Correspondingly, they tend to doubt the other parties' willingness to abide by the terms of a peace treaty and actively engage in state-building. Hence, (re-)building public institutions in a state emerging from armed conflict or war that featured widespread brutal violence against the civilian population faces particular obstacles. To overcome these obstacles, state-building requires encompassing and deep forms of external

---

[22] See Kaldor, *supra* note 10. See also Peter Waldmann, *Bürgerkrieg – Annäherung an einen schwer fassbaren Begriff*, 25 Leviathan 480 (1997).

[23] See Mary Kaldor, *New Types of Conflict*, *in* Gewalt und Konflikt in einer globalisierten Welt: Festschrift für Ulrich Albrecht 24–25 (Ruth Stanley ed., 2001). See also Brian S. Turner, *The Globalization of Human Rights: Violence, New Wars and Failed States*, 37 Korea Observer 23 (2006), and Chojnacki, *supra* note 12.

intervention to attenuate the security dilemma of post-conflict settings and enforce state-building against feasible resistance.[24]

4. *The criminalization of war economies and its implications for state-building*

During the Cold War guerrilla groups were typically supplied by the local population and by external sponsors. The local population, for whose concerns the guerrilla claimed to fight, supported the guerrilla more or less voluntarily. Besides the assistance from the population in the territory they controlled, rebel groups were normally backed by allied great or superpowers. According to Cold War logic, rebel movements could act on the assumption that they would be supported either by the United States or by the Soviet Union, contingent on their purported or actual ideological orientation. Both superpowers tried to prevent countries in the developing world from falling to the sphere of influence of the other side and therefore cooperated with local conflict parties, be it governments or rebel groups. In Guatemala, for instance, the United States provided assistance to the government, while the Soviet Union backed the leftist rebel movement. In Nicaragua, in contrast, the government was supplied by the Soviet Union, whereas the Contras were helped by the United States.[25]

The ebbing of superpower assistance with the end of the Cold War has triggered a criminalization of the way warfare is funded, for parties involved in conflict increasingly relied on compensating the loss of superpower aid with other – mostly criminal – channels of supply. On the one hand, rebel groups turn to supply themselves within the conflict zone by criminal activities. In Sierra Leone, for instance, warlords urged their fighters to loot the belongings of civilians to save pay and food for their militias. On the other hand, rebel groups try to cooperate with transnationally organized criminal networks to balance the loss of superpower assistance. More and more, rebel groups begin acquiring legal or illegal natural resources in the territories they control and sell them on the legal or illegal global market with the help of transnational criminal networks. The proceeds are used for the import of weapons, ammunition and other goods needed for the maintenance of armed forces. Again, criminal networks play an important role in these transactions. In the Democratic Republic of Congo,

---

24 See Doyle & Sambanis, *supra* note 13. See also Betty Bigombe, Paul Collier & Nicholas Sambanis, *Policies for Building Post-conflict Peace*, 9 JOURNAL OF AFRICAN ECONOMIES 323 (2000). See also Albrecht Schnabel, *Post-Conflict Peacebuilding and Second-Generation Preventive Action*, 9 INTERNATIONAL PEACEKEEPING 7 (2002).

25 See Philipp Genschel & Klaus Schlichte, *Wenn Kriege chronisch werden: Der Bürgerkrieg*, 25 LEVIATHAN 501 (1997). See also Rudolf Hamann, *Einleitung: Die Sicherheit des Westens*, *in* DIE ‚SÜDDIMENSION' DES OST-WEST-KONFLIKTES: DAS ENGAGEMENT DER SUPERMÄCHTE IN KRISEN UND KRIEGEN DER DRITTEN WELT 7 (Rudolf Hamann ed., 1986).

for example, numerous militias relied on illegal trade in coltan, gold, copper, diamonds, coffee and other goods. And in Myanmar, various rebel groups that controlled the north of the country funded military operations by trafficking drugs and timber.[26]

The transformation of the way parties to a conflict maintain their combat forces and finance warfare constitutes a major challenge to effective post-conflict state-building. Conflict parties unable to maintain and equip their combatants after the termination of an armed conflict or war usually lack the capacities to seriously undermine state-building in the wake of violent conflict. Correspondingly, rebel groups, which used to obtain assistance from superpowers during the Cold War, but did not succeed in opening up alternative sources of income in the late 1980s and early 1990s, were normally unable to continue warfare and derail post-conflict state-building. In Mozambique, for instance, one reason for the relative success in stabilizing the peace process in the 1990s has been the failure of the Mozambican National Resistance (RENAMO) rebel movement to compensate the deprivation of external support after the end of the Cold War and its inability to hamper peacebuilding decisively.[27]

In contrast, state-building in the wake of violent conflict is far more challenging if the parties involved have access to valuable resources that they can sell on the global market. Unlike conflict parties that draw on external assistance from allied states to finance warfare, conflict parties supplying themselves via trafficking in natural resources are normally able to maintain their revenue streams after the end of an armed conflict or war. Thus, unless commodity sanctions, certificate of origin regimes, or other instruments aiming to obstruct illicit trade in natural resources are implemented, conflict parties relying on natural resources-based war economies are likely to have continued revenues to maintain armed forces at their disposal. Consequently, even without support from allied governments, these conflict parties have capacities to undermine post-conflict state-building as soon as it does not proceed in line with their interests.[28] The incapacity to dry up the criminalized war economies of the "new wars" and transform them into sustainable peace-time economies has seriously undermined post-conflict state-

---

[26] See Economies des Guerres Civiles (François Jean & Jean-Christophe Rufin eds., 1996). See also Neil Cooper, *Conflict Goods: The Challenges for Peacekeeping and Conflict Prevention*, 8 International Peacekeeping 21 (2001). See also Michael Ross, *What Do We Know About Natural Resources and Civil War?*, 41 Journal of Peace Research 337 (2004).

[27] See Fen Osler Hampson, Nurturing Peace: Why Peace Settlements Succeed or Fail 214–216 (1996).

[28] See Mats Berdal & David M. Malone, *Introduction*, *in* Greed & grievance: economic agendas in civil wars 1 (Mats Berdal & David M. Malone eds., 2000). See also Ross, *supra* note 30, and James D. Fearon, *Why Do Some Civil Wars Last So Much Longer Than Others?*, 41 Journal of Peace Research 275 (2004).

building and fuelled repeated outbreak of warfare in the past. In Cambodia, for instance, post-conflict state-building failed as long as the Khmer Rouge were able to invest revenues from the illicit trade in timber and gems in the armament and maintenance of their fighters. In Angola, the peace process could only be stabilized after efforts to cut off the diamond trade of the Union for the Total Independence of Angola (UNITA) rebel group had become increasingly effective. And in Afghanistan, state-building is still weakened by the Taliban and various warlords gaining profits from trading in opium and heroine.[29]

IV. *Conclusion*

In the aftermath of domestic violent conflict – of a classical civil war of the Cold War period and a "new war" of the post-Cold War period alike – a state normally fails to perform the core functions a modern state is supposed to live up to: In a post-conflict setting, a state does not have the monopoly on force at its disposal and therefore can hardly provide security. Likewise, a post-conflict state lacks the capacities and resources to provide basic welfare services to its citizens. Moreover, in the course of an armed conflict or war, the legitimacy of public institutions usually erodes seriously.

States emerging from classical civil wars and states emerging from "new wars" are both in need of state-building to stabilize post-conflict peace processes and lay the groundwork for stable peace. However, the features of the "new wars" pose particular challenges to state-building. The rise in the number of private conflict parties and the internal fragmentation of the parties involved in conflicts render the integration of all relevant parties into a state-building process and the enforcement of agreed-upon state-building measures more demanding. The proliferation of economic motives undermines the disposition of parties to assent to terminating warfare and take part in state-building. The spread of brutal violence targeted intentionally at the civilian population degrades both the competencies and the willingness of post-conflict societies to engage in state-building. Finally and most importantly, access to precious tradable natural resources in the wake of violent conflict enables spoilers to oppose state-building by force if it runs counter to their interests.

Therefore, effective state building must account for the specific challenges posed by the actual transformation of warfare. To ensure the participation of all relevant parties in a state-building process, the integration of the members of the major conflict parties into political and military institutions through

---

[29] See Monika Heupel, *Shadow-Trade War Economies and their Challenge to Peacebuilding*, 9 Journal of International Relations and Development 140 (2006).

power-sharing arrangements could prove fundamental. The prevalence of economic motives suggests putting special emphasis on boosting the capacities of post-conflict states to provide basic welfare services and assure socio-economic well-being of the population in general and former combatants in particular. The destabilizing legacies of massive human rights violations necessitate more substantive forms of external intervention to help overcome mistrust and ensure the participation of all relevant actors in state-building. Ultimately, given the spread of financing warfare through natural resources trafficking, state-building in the aftermath of armed conflict or war must include strengthening public institutions which can prevent spoilers from generating income from illegal resources transactions.

Does contemporary state-building take the challenges posed by the emergence and spread of the features of the "new wars" into consideration? In recent years state-building in general has gained increased attention. In the wake of the terrorist attacks from September 11, 2001, the United States and the European Union have increasingly acknowledged that terrorist groups and criminal networks benefit from weak, failing or failed states. They have therefore attributed greater significance to state-building in their respective Security Strategies from 2002 and 2003.[30] Moreover, in late 2005 the United Nations General Assembly and Security Council established a Peacebuilding Commission, which is to support state-building and other operations in countries emerging from armed conflict or war.[31] Nevertheless, whether this increased focus on state-building takes the specific challenges posed by the transformation of warfare into account is ambiguous. On the one hand, the United Nations, the European Union and other actors involved in state-building have already developed some strategies and capacities to meet the challenges posed by the emergence of the "new wars" when engaging in post-conflict state-building. In the Democratic Republic of Congo, for instance, the United Nations has pushed for the formation of a very broad transitional government to integrate representatives of the numerous parties to the conflict into a common government.[32] Another example is the framework

[30] U.S. National Security Strategy (Sept. 2002), *at* <http://www.whitehouse.gov/nsc/nssall.html> (last access 22 May 2008); European Security Strategy (A Secure Europe in a Better World) (Dec. 12, 2003), *at* <http://ue.eu.int/uedocs/cmsUpload/78367.pdf> (last access 22 May 2008).

[31] For the Peacebuilding Commission see Gerhard Thallinger, *The UN Peacebuilding Commission and Transitional Justice*, 8 GERMAN LAW JOURNAL 681 (2007). See also NYU Center on International Cooperation (CIC) and International Peace Institute (IPI), *Taking Stock, Looking Forward: A Strategic Review of the Peacebuilding Commission* (April 2008), *at* <http://www.cic.nyu.edu/peacebuilding/docs/takingstocklookingforward.pdf> (last access 22 May 2008).

[32] International Crisis Group, *Pulling back from the Brink in the Congo*, (July 7, 2004), *at* <http://www.crisisgroup.org/library/documents/africa/central_africa/041217_back_to_the_brink_in_the_congo.pdf> (last access 22 May 2008).

of the Kimberley Process, where both the United Nations and the European Union backed the establishment of a certificate of origin regime for the trade in rough diamonds.[33] On the other hand, these achievements notwithstanding, practitioners involved in (re-)building public institutions after violent conflict still feel the need for a comprehensive strategy. Such a strategy should systematically integrate responses to the specifics of the "new wars" into the approach to post-conflict state-building. The Peacebuilding Commission, which is supposed to help overcome coordination and coherence problems among the various institutions involved, could be the framework for the development of such an encompassing strategy. However, whether it will gain sufficient political and financial support from the community of states is yet to be seen.

[33] The Website of the Kimberley Process is accessible at http://www.kimberleyprocess.com/ (last access 22 May 2008).

Citizenship Scarcity and State Weakness: Learning from the Colombian Experience

*Ann C. Mason**

A robust civil society is one of the hallmarks of strong states. Previous political science approaches that viewed the state as dichotomous from society has generally given way to a conceptualization of the state as incorporating both components. Measurements of stateness that focus exclusively on the coercive powers and institutional capacity of the government proved to be incomplete: a cohesive and activated civil society that participates in the political process, societal practices and beliefs that legitimate state institutions, a unifying sense of national identity that inspires public responsibility and loyalty are undoubtedly also crucial determinants of overall state strength and performance.

Citizenship, whether understood in legal terms as nationality, as a status associated with a bundle of relational rights and obligations, as civic praxis, or as identity derived from belonging to a particular political community, is closely related to civil society and society's bond with the state.

Current citizenship debates are primarily concerned with how citizenship is responding to social changes within the world's advanced democracies. The principal theoretical traditions all address domestic challenges to the state-society relationship and the best way for nation-states to adapt to changing global conditions. These deliberations seem to have largely eclipsed the issue of citizenship in developing countries or in state-building contexts, however. Even when evolving notions of citizenship take into account conditions in the global periphery, the primary concern is how these circumstances, such as massive migration, affect citizenship rules and practices in developed, strong states. Will Kymlicka and Wayne Norman note that advanced democracies can "become difficult to

* The author would like to thank Lothar Brock, Hans-Henrik Holm and Michael Stohl for their observations and recommendations on a previous draft of this article presented at the 5th Failed States Conference in Santa Barbara, California, September 9–11, 2002. Special thanks also to Catalina Arreaza, Roxana Alejandra Trujillo and Carolina Santacruz for their very helpful research assistance.

govern, even unstable" without strong citizenship qualities.[1] If so, examining the role citizenship plays in new or developing countries, given their vulnerability to ingovernability and instability, is of particular urgency.

To the extent that vigorous citizenship rules and practices are associated with strong states, it seems intuitive that these same attributes would be feebler in weak and failing states. Still, given the tremendous variation among states, as well as the multiple theories of citizenship, it is not clear what dimension or type of citizenship is associated with state weakness. Many states may have insubstantial notions of citizenship as a result of incomplete nation-building projects. Some weaker states may be wracked by divided and competing loyalties common in ethnically plural societies. States may be incapable or unwilling to fulfill basic obligations to their citizens, undermining society's loyalty, sense of we-ness, and patriotism that characterize a strong citizenry. In extreme cases of violent internal conflict or security emergencies, the citizen-state bond may be ruptured almost entirely. Still others are challenged by having a transnational population that has been permanently dispersed by war or other internal calamity, making the construction of a unifying citizenship project problematic.

What does citizenship look like in relatively weak states, and weak democracies in particular? Is the idea of the citizenry and the relation between state and society the same in weak states, only less developed, or are there operative fundamentally different definitions of what it means to be a citizen? Are weaker notions of citizenship necessarily one of the markers of weak states? And thus, what is the importance of citizenship to state building?

This paper explores these issues through a reflection on citizenship in Colombia. First, the principal strains of citizenship theory and current debates will be reviewed. The chapter then continues with an analysis of contemporary citizenship in Colombia through the lens of each theoretical tradition, identifying deficiencies in the quality of its citizenship project as an element to consider in evaluating Colombian stateness. Drawing on Colombia's experience, the paper concludes with some observations on the links between citizenship, state strength and state building.

I. *Citizenship Classification and Theory*

The conceptual disarray surrounding the concept of citizenship is familiar territory. Judith Shklar sums it up this way: "There is no notion more central in politics than citizenship, [yet] none more variable in history, or contested in

[1] Will Kymlicka & Wayne Norman, *Return of the Citizen: A Survey of Recent Work on Citizenship Theory*, *in* THEORIZING CITIZENSHIP 284 (Ronald Beiner ed., 1995).

theory."[2] We are all citizens of somewhere, but we do not share the same rights and obligations as citizens. The citizen emerged from democratic philosophy and practices, and yet citizenship bonds in non-democratic states may be as strong, or stronger, than in modern democracies. An individual can be a citizen of more than one country at the same time, with contradictory obligations to those political communities. Many comply with the formal political and civic duties of being a citizen, but feel a stronger attachment and loyalty to another type of community. In short, what does it mean to be a citizen?

In broad strokes, citizenship can be understood in four distinct, yet overlapping, ways.[3] In its least problematic form it is a legal category related to formal membership in a nation-state. Conflated with what is popularly understood as nationality, this definition of citizenship identifies the political community to which an individual belongs. This attribution was historically assigned by virtue of being born in a particular territorial designation, *jus soli*, or as the result of a parent's nationality, *jus sanguinis*. Just as territorial boundaries sharply demarcate state sovereignty, so nationality laws establish strict criteria for distinguishing between citizens and aliens. Indeed, the "politics of citizenship" in receptor states in the North define strict naturalization laws that determine inclusion in and exclusion from the state.[4] This legal definition of citizenship reflects a world order that privileges the state as the primary political unit, denying, in most cases, the possibility of citizenship status deriving from non-state criteria, such as ethnicity or religion, or from sub-national or transnational communities.

The citizenship-as-identity perspective distinguishes formal membership in a state from an individual's sense of association, belonging, and loyalty to a particular community.[5] A collective consciousness traditionally rooted in culturally homogenous ethnonational communities has steadily evolved into a modern national identity based on association with a state organization. Still, for many individuals a civic national identity associated with the modern nation-state exists alongside the persistence of identities deeply rooted in prepolitical cultural associations. Regardless of the origin, citizenship-as-identity becomes a common denominator that supersedes competing sub-national identifications, embodies

---

[2] Judith Shklar, American Citizenship: The Quest for Inclusion 1 (1991).

[3] There is no one organizing scheme for citizenship. Kymlicka & Norman, *supra* note 1, distinguish among three approaches: citizenship-as-rights, citizenship-as-activity, and citizenship-as-identity, each of which is widely represented in the literature on citizenship. For my purposes I include a fourth category of citizenship as legal status as suggested by Linda Bosniak, *Denationalizing Citizenship, in* Citizenship Today: Global Perspectives and Practices 237 (T. Alexander Aleinikoff & Douglas Klusmeyer eds., 2001).

[4] Rogers Brubaker, *Immigration, Citizenship, and the Nation-State in France and Germany, in* The Citizenship Debates 138 (Gershon Shafir ed., 1998).

[5] Kymlicka & Norman, *supra* note 1, 301.

collective allegiance to the political community, and fosters patriotism to the nation-state, its myths and its symbols.[6]

A third interpretation of citizenship is as a status derived from the possession of a set of rights and obligations with relation to the state. This rights-based notion of citizenship has its origins in the emergence of the modern nation-state and the social contract. The French Revolution marks a turning point in the development of citizenship models, where for the first time the conception of citizenship came to be synonymous with the rights of citizens against the absolutism of the monarch, the arbitrariness of state power, and the legal and political privileges of aristocratic society.[7] Implicit in this idea of citizenship derived from legal rights was the equality of these protections as well as equal participation in the democratic process. Thus, freedom *from* the state meant an equal right *to* the state as well. Citizen-as-status involves a fundamental set of rights in exchange for the obligation to comply with the directives that emerge from the democratic process.[8]

Lastly, citizenship is conceived in terms of praxis. The earliest notion of the citizen, and what remains for many the ideal[9] or the myth[10] of citizenship, is the Aristotelian view of public service. That is, citizenship refers to the active participation in political and civic life. One is a citizen by virtue of vigorous involvement in the polity and commitment to the exercise of those rights and duties.[11] Within this framework of "high citizenship" the "citizen transcends the limits of his private interest" through participation in public life and deliberation with fellow citizens.[12] In both classical and modern communitarian and civic republican variations on this citizenship-as-activity theme, the emphasis is on the

[6] See for details David Miller, Citizenship and National Identity (2000).

[7] Stephen Castles & Alastair Davidson, Citizenship and Migration: Globalization and the Politics of Belonging (2000).

[8] Jürgen Habermas, *Citizenship and National Identity: Some Reflections on the Future of Europe*, 12 Praxis International 4 (1992).

[9] See for details J. G. A. Pocock, *The Ideal of Citizenship since Classical Times, in* The Citizenship Debates (Gershon Shafir ed., 1998).

[10] Michael Ignatieff, *The Myth of Citizenship, in* Theorizing Citizenship 53 (Ronald Beiner ed., 1995).

[11] Habermas, *supra* note 8, 3; Ronald Beiner, *Why Citizenship Constitutes a Theoretical Problem in the Last Decade of the Twentieth Century, in* Theorizing Citizenship 19 (Ronald Beiner ed., 1995).

[12] Richard Flatham, *Citizenship and Authority: A Chastened View of Citizenship, in* Theorizing Citizenship 105 (Ronald Beiner ed., 1995), distinguishes between "high citizenship", or robust civic involvement associated with the republican tradition, and "low citizenship", which refers to liberalism's more restricted conception of rights and entitlements. The quote is from Ignatieff, *supra* note 10, 53.

collective practices of membership in the life of the polity with the stated goal of bettering the common good and fostering public-mindedness and civility.

These traditions for classifying citizenship form the arena within which contemporary theoretical debates take place. Certain philosophical positions regarding citizenship neatly coincide with these categories, while others traverse them in a rather complex web. The following sections will provide a thumbnail sketch of the principal theories and controversies regarding citizenship of concern to political theorists and practitioners alike, as an introduction to the analysis of the institution of citizenship in Colombia, and of the relationship between citizenship and state-building.

1. *Liberalism*

Citizenship viewed through the lens of liberal theory is largely about safeguarding personal liberty. Liberalism's emphasis on the freedom to pursue private values conceives of the citizen not in public, civic terms, but rather as an autonomous individual who is to be protected from government interference. The prerogative of the citizen is to enjoy his inalienable rights and pursue his own welfare in the private sphere free from public imposition, in exchange for minimal political obligations and civic responsibilities such as voting, paying taxes and complying with the law. "The role of politics in this approach remains negative" according to Gershon Shafir, where the function of public institutions is to protect private self-interest, enhance private privileges, and guarantee equal treatment under the law.[13] The freedom valued in the liberal citizenship paradigm is essentially passive: freedom from excesses of the state, the right to accumulate property, religious freedom and freedom of expression.[14] A contractual liberal view is that the state provides a public good in the form of institutional mechanisms that protect liberty and order valued by the citizen, in return for compliance. Charles Taylor concludes that liberalism offers an individualist model of citizenship, in which public institutions "have an entirely instrumental significance" and "no value is put on participation in rule for its own sake".[15] Shafir is even blunter: "citizenship, in the liberal view, is an accessory, not a value in itself.[16]

[13] Gershon Shafir, *Introduction: The Evolving Tradition of Citizenship, in* The Citizenship Debates 10 (Gershon Shafir ed., 1998).

[14] Ignatieff, *supra* note 10, 53.

[15] Charles Taylor, *The Liberal-Communitarian Debate, in* Liberalism and the Moral Life 178 (N. Rosenblum ed., 1989).

[16] Shafir, *supra* note 13, 10.

2. *Republicanism*

Republican citizenship is the most readily distinguished from the liberal model, with the opposing visions of each tradition remaining one of the central debates that concern citizenship theorists.[17] If the liberal theory of citizenship gives pride of place to citizen rights and the private sphere, the republican perspective stresses citizen duties and the public sphere. Civic republicanism, largely inspired by Rousseau, invokes images of the involved, active citizen with a strong sense of civic duty. The Republican test of citizenship is "performance of the duties" required of the citizen related to involvement in public issues, and more exactly, assuming public office. In *Politics*, Aristotle presents the ideal citizen as one who both rules and is ruled, depicting this enmeshment of the public and private spheres and the idea that the complete citizen also takes part in governing. For Will Kymlicka and Wayne Norman, in modern contexts, this amounts to "an extreme form of participatory democracy [with] emphasis on the intrinsic value of political participation for the participants themselves".[18] There is only one kind of citizen, the "active citizen", whose identity and sense of worth are derived from civic participation within the political community, which for Adrian Oldfield "is not only the most inclusive, but also the highest, form of living-together that most individuals can aspire to".[19]

3. *Communitarianism and Civil Society*

Few would dispute that the civic republican conception of citizenship is out of step with attitudes and practices in modern democracies. The liberal critique would be that individuals are more often than not indifferent to an alienating political process in which they participate only minimally, preferring to direct their energies toward private economic interests.[20] Civil society theorists, however, point to a different deficiency of the republican ideal. While sharing a belief in the importance of community involvement, they are skeptical about the republican single-minded insistence that "politics is our highest calling".[21] Citizen virtue is not cultivated through political participation, and human fulfillment

[17] The debate is nicely encapsulated in Amy Gutmann, *Communitarian Critics of Liberalism*, 14 Philosophy and Public Affairs 308 (1985) and Robert B. Thigpen & Lyle A. Downing, *Liberalism and the Communitarian Critique*, 31 American Journal of Political Science 637 (1987).

[18] Kymlicka & Norman, *supra* note 1, 293.

[19] Adrian Oldfield, *Citizenship and Community: Civic Republicanism and the Modern World, in* The Citizenship Debates 79 (Gershon Shafir ed., 1998).

[20] Ignatieff, *supra* note 10, 55.

[21] Michael Walzer, *The Civil Society Argument, in* Theorizing Citizenship 155 (Ronald Beiner ed., 1995).

is not found in political life, but rather through membership in the voluntary associations that make up plural societies. "Because we are by nature social, before we are political or economic, beings", we realize our status as citizens by associating with others in organizations that represent society: neighborhood associations, churches, schools, ethnic leagues, sports clubs, social movements, support groups, or other single interest associations.[22] Involvement in political organizations or party chapters may be one among a wide range of citizen activities.[23] Just as society is understood as being complex and plural, so should citizens have the "associational freedom" to choose their causes.[24] Citizenship requires active involvement in civil society, for it is *here* that citizens learn the tolerance, responsibility, self-restraint, civility, and public-spiritedness necessary to a vigorous community, values considered increasingly absent from liberal societies.[25]

4. *Social Democracy*

T.H. Marshall's influential, postwar reformulation of citizenship rights gave birth to the idea of the social citizen, and opened up a new debate on the relationship between state and individual.[26] Against the backdrop of class struggles in postwar Britain and the establishment of the welfare state, Marshall made the case that formal political equality alongside the persistence of economic and social inequities was a fundamental contradiction.

Basing his theory of citizenship on the social-welfare conditions in Great Britain from the 18th to the 20th century, Marshall identified three dimensions of citizenship privileges that had emerged in historical progression: civil, political and socioeconomic. Civil rights provided legal protection from the state and guaranteed basic provisions, such as freedom of speech and the right to trial. Civil liberty guarantees were followed in 19th century Britain by advances in political citizenship through the development of electoral rights and the formation of political parties which provided access to the democratic process. The third leg of citizenship was established in the twentieth century with the expansion of social rights that guaranteed basic standards of economic and social well-being

[22] Ibid., 162.

[23] Enrique Peruzzotti, *Towards a New Politics: Citizenship and Rights in Contemporary Argentina*, 6 Citizenship Studies 77 (2002), considers the possibility of citizen activities, associations and social movements as also having a highly political content and being the source of a renovated Latin American democracy.

[24] Walzer, *supra* note 21, 163.

[25] Ibid., and William Galston, Liberal Purposes: Goods, Virtues, and Duties in the Liberal State (1991).

[26] See for details T. H. Marshall, Class, Citizenship and Social Development: Essays by T. H. Marshall (1965).

through access to employment or claims to social security provisions. For Marshall, these social rights finally permitted the working class genuine participation in society as citizens. This shift toward a liberal socialist theory of citizenship reflected the view that equality of political rights was impossible in the face of inequality in social, economic and cultural conditions.[27] That is, citizenship went beyond civil and political rights to encompass a third generation of rights in the form of socioeconomic claims.

5. *Nationalism*

More than any other citizenship framework, the nationalist perspective goes to the heart of what it means for an individual to feel a sense of attachment and belonging to a collectivity, which confers a powerful, unifying identity on its members. One version of national citizenship is decidedly "nationalistic". Roger Scruton, bucking current multicultural trends, argues that citizenship derives from belonging to a group whose identity is unambiguously sociocultural.[28] One dominant national idea born of social and cultural commonalities inspires loyalty and allegiance to the country. Nationalism based on shared history, culture and language creates a sense of belonging that is the essence of citizenship. A nationalist spirit is not necessarily ethnic, but it *is* prepolitical. Thus the national consciousness that inspires a citizen to commit what Rogers Brubaker calls "sacred acts", such as dying for one's country, is rooted in the shared sanctification of and loyalty to a unifying vision that is the core of national citizenship.[29]

Modern political nationalism, on the other hand, amounts to a "denationalized" citizenship model, in that the nation is not considered a requirement to form a political community and inspire patriotism. Jürgen Habermas argues that the gradual formation of an identity linked to the sovereign state paralleled the change in the meaning of "nation" in post-French Revolution Europe "from designating a cultural entity to something that was supposed to play a constitutive role in defining the political identity of the citizen within a democratic polity".[30] Thus, the modern national identity emerges not from an ethnocultural community, but rather from a "nation of citizens".[31] Linking a citizenship identity with a political collectivity is, in fact, frequently in contrast to competing identities related to region, ethnicity, or religion. While articulated national identities may evoke historical myths based on common cultural origins, what

[27] Castles & Davidson, *supra* note 7, 105.

[28] Roger Scruton, *In Defense of Nation, in* The Philosopher on Dover Beach 299 (Scruton ed., 1990).

[29] Brubaker, *supra* note 4, 132.

[30] Habermas, *supra* note 8, 3.

[31] Ibid.

distinguishes a secular citizenship identity is its basis in a "political culture and not [...] an ethical-cultural norm of life as a whole".[32]

6. *Multiculturalism and Differentiated Citizenship*

As a response to the growing cultural pluralism of many nation-states, the differentiated model proposes that citizenship rights and protections be bestowed on the multiple cultural, religious, national, or even social groups found in diverse societies. Largely motivated by the relentless waves of immigration that continue to transform the demographic landscape of the global north, this view considers the best way to unify a heterogeneous citizenry is by accommodating different nationalities within an inclusive society. This can be achieved by adding "cultural citizenship rights to the congeries of civil, political and social citizenship rights".[33] A group-based model of citizenship rights that affirms and formalizes its plural character and acknowledges immigrant groups' persistent feelings of loyalty toward their nation of origin, is the basis of social unity in multinational states.[34] "If there is a viable way to promote a sense of solidarity in a multinational state", argues Kymlicka, "it will involve accommodating, rather than subordinating, national identities".[35]

In a more radical rejection of the "myth" of universal citizenship, Iris Marion Young suggests that group rights be assigned not only on the basis of ethno-cultural heritage, but also to any disadvantaged or oppressed group that has a coherent identity.[36] The "politics of difference" principle seeks equal protection under the law for groups such as women, gays and lesbians, blue collar workers, senior citizens, and the disabled. According to Young, the particularities of such groups establish near insurmountable barriers to full access to equal rights, impeding the liberal citizenship ideal.

7. *Postnationalism and Cosmopolitanism*

The newcomer to the citizenship debate, postnationalism argues that notions of citizenship linked to the sovereign state have lost meaning in a globalized world, where individuals are no longer categorized according to state territories. For Yasemin Soysal, "a new and more universal concept of citizenship has

---

32 Ibid., 17.

33 Shafir, *supra* note 13, 19.

34 Will Kymlicka, *Multicultural Citizenship, in* The Citizenship Debates 179 (Gershon Shafir ed., 1998); John Rawls, A Theory of Justice (1979) and Political Liberalism (1993).

35 Kymlicka, *supra* note 34, 182.

36 See Iris M. Young, Justice and the Politics of Difference (1990), and *Polity and Group Difference: A Critique of the Ideal of Universal Citizenship, in* Theorizing Citizenship 175 (Ronald Beiner ed., 1995).

unfolded in the post-war era, one whose organizing and legitimating principles are based on universal personhood rather than national belonging".[37] Using the trend toward transnational citizenship as established in the European Union as the best example of the disjuncture between national citizenship and universal rights and laws, Soysal proposes a model of "post-national belonging" in which citizenship is linked to global governance schemes.[38]

Cosmopolitan citizenship is also based on the ongoing reconfiguration of states, but places the emphasis on universal moral commitments and entitlements.[39] More modest than postnational citizenship, "cosmopolitan citizenship [...] argues that member states and non-state actors within post-Westphalian structures have additional obligations to ensure just treatment for the rest of humanity".[40] Migration theorists contribute to the discussion with their notion of translocal or transnational identities forming migrant communities that create dense networks of social, economic and political relations spanning the spaces between the country of origin and country of residence.[41] These perspectives suggest the formation of postnational identities and the need to reconceptualize citizenship's exclusive link to the territorial state.

II. *Citizenship in Colombia*

Many of today's citizenship tensions in Colombia have been recurring themes throughout its history. Like many newly liberated colonies in South America, Colombia had a fairly narrow conception of democracy and citizenship upon gaining its independence from Spain in 1819. Direct, democratic participation was limited to free, literate males, and by the middle of the century property requirements were added to the education restriction such that the right to

---

[37] Yasemin Soysal, Limits to Citizenship: Migrants and Postnational Membership in Europe 1 (1994). See also K. Hutchings, *Political theory and cosmopolitan citizenship, in* Cosmopolitan Citizenship (K. Hutchings & R. Dannreuther eds., 1999).

[38] Soysal, *supra* note 37; See also Michael Muetzelfeldt & Gary Smith, *Civil Society and Global Governance: The Possibilities for Global Citizenship*, 6 Citizenship Studies 55 (2002).

[39] See Arjun Appadurai, *Sovereignty Without Territoriality: Notes for a Postnational Geography, in* The Geography of Identity 40–58 (Patricia Yaeger ed., 1996), and Andrew Linklater, The Transformation of Political Community: Ethical Foundations of the Post-Westphalian Era (1998).

[40] Linklater, *supra* note 39, 206.

[41] On translocal identities, see Peter Mandaville, *Territory and Translocality: Discrepant Idioms of Political Identity*, 28 Millennium: Journal of International Studies 653 (1999). For transnational migration and citizenship, see Rainer Baubock, Transnational Citizenship: Membership and Rights in International Migration (1994).

vote became little more than an aristocratic privilege.[42] A new constitution in 1863 aimed to reconquer democracy through a liberal reform project that involved separation of church and state, limits on executive powers, freedom of religious expression, and freedom of speech.[43] Interest in freeing the state from the Church's conservative influence also resulted in radical reforms aimed at providing universal, free, and secular education for the purpose of "constructing citizens [...] to serve the Republic".[44] Colombia's flirtation with liberalism was short-lived however. A reactionary backlash undid the modest reforms, replacing them with a return to centralism, greater presidential authority, limits on voting rights, and the reestablishment of the Catholic Church in the seats of power.

A bitter civil war that lasted 1,000 days from 1899 to 1902 was the backlash against the conservative state-church regime. The political pendulum did swing back toward liberalism again in the 1930's, when civil liberties related to voluntary associations and the right of labor unions to organize were granted, along with full male suffrage. But this progress was outweighed by increasingly conflictive social relations between Bogotá's ruling elite and the working and agrarian class in the rest of the country. The government's incapacity to unify the regionally and socially fragmented nation through a modern democratic project, the state's mechanisms of exclusion and repression, and the economic downturn that had begun in the 1920's, inaugurated a period of violence that, some would argue, continues today.[45]

The assassination of Jorge Elicier Gaitan in 1946, a liberal presidential hopeful who represented Colombia's urban masses and rural poor, sparked a vicious period of violence between Liberal and Conservative factions. A power sharing agreement, in which in an interesting twist on modern democracy the two leading parties agreed to alternate the presidency and to share all elective and appointive positions, finally put an end to a decade of brutal violence and economic hardship during which 300,000 lives were claimed. The bipartisan National Front regime reduced sectarianism, although it also contributed to the institutional exclusion of third parties from political power, did little to address underlying social discontent, and was unable to neutralize the many peasant vigilante groups that had proliferated during the period known as *la Violencia*.

The persistence of entrenched economic, social, and land disparities during the 1960's and 1970's were seized on by leftist revolutionary movements that

---

[42] Alvaro Tirado, El Estado y la Política en el Siglo XIX 19–20 (2000).

[43] Pierre-Luc Abramson, Las Utopías Sociales en América Latina en el Siglo XIX (1999).

[44] Jaime Jaramillo, *El proceso de la educación en la República (1830–1886), in* Nueva Historia de Colombia, Toma 2, 228 (Camilo Calderon & Jaime Jaramillo eds., 1989).

[45] William Ramírez, *Violencia, Guerra Civil, Contrato Social, in* Colombia: Cambio de Siglo 25 (William Ramírez et al. eds., 2000).

had a series of grievances against the rules of the political game that favored landowners, the economic elite, and the political oligarchy. The very weakness of political institutions led to "new political violence in the form of class struggles [...] to defend rural property rights threatened by official violence".[46] The most important insurgent movement in Colombia today, the Fuerzas Armadas Revolucionarias de Colombia (FARC), slowly consolidated its base of support among disenfranchised, landless peasants, and by the mid 1980's had become an independent, well-established guerrilla organization with its own political agenda and military doctrine. Narcotraffickers and paramilitary forces also created large militias to protect their private interests and imposed crude forms of social order in remote areas of the country with little or no state presence.

Colombia limped its way through the 1980's and 1990's, plagued by a political model that did not work, widespread insecurity, violence, and human rights abuses, the growth of armed subversive and para-institutional groups, corruption and crime related to the drug industry, poverty, and inequality. The adoption of a new constitution in 1991 was intended to offer lasting solutions to these problems by establishing an effective democratic state based on the principles of inclusion and representation, and through the granting of extensive human, socioeconomic, and civil protections. The following section looks at current state-society relations and at how well Colombia's citizenship model lives up to the various definitions reviewed above.

1. *Poor Protection of Citizen Rights*

Formally, the current Colombian constitution is one of the most progressive and "liberal" in Latin America.[47] It establishes an impressive political, civil and human rights package, offers legal mechanisms for citizens to seek redress from the state, creates an independent constitutional court, establishes political privileges for historically under-represented minorities, and limits the power of the military. These institutional protections and guarantees, taken in conjunction with nearly unbroken civilian rule, result in Colombia being hailed as one of the oldest and most robust democracies in South America.

The reality of Colombia's democracy, however, is somewhat different. Colombia unarguably meets the basic democratic test by holding regular competitive multiparty elections. Citizen access to the political process actually improved with the 1991 constitution, which strengthened both participation and opposition. Indeed, that Colombia has managed to maintain its unbroken record of

---

[46] Ibid., 47.

[47] John Dugas, *La Constitución Política de 1991, in* La Constitución de 1991: Un Pacto Político Viable? 28 (John Dugas ed., 1993).

elections in the face of pervasive threats to its institutionalism can be considered evidence of the robustness of its democracy.

Nevertheless, Colombia has been less successful at fulfilling democracy's liberal expectations related to citizenship claims in the form of respect for the rule of law, separation of powers, and guarantees of basic civil freedoms. Weak controls on executive power, an uneven record on observance of the rule of law, and restrictions on individual liberties have variously earned Colombia the labels of semi-democracy, besieged democracy and illiberal democracy.[48] In this regard Colombia's claim to be a liberal democracy is unconvincing, as it does not systematically provide institutionalized and accessible procedures for protecting the liberties of individual citizens.[49] Paradoxically, the tendency toward formal democratization in Colombia, "which includes the elimination of prior restrictions and the broadening of the space for political participation and competition" has paralleled "a tendency toward [the] deterioration of the indicators of 'civility', or respect and protection of basic rights and liberties".[50]

At the same time, the presence of illegal organizations has seriously compromised the freedoms that lie at the core of a liberal citizenship model. The activities of subversive groups, paramilitaries, and narcotrafficking organizations, which in different ways all compete directly with state power and authority, have perpetuated Colombia's ongoing internal conflict and branded the country one of the most violent and insecure in the world. In spite of significant improvements in Colombia's internal situation during the current administration of President Alvaro Uribe beginning in 2002, the levels of violence and human rights abuses that characterized Colombian society for decades and that became especially virulent in the 1990's, continue to be linked to this deterioration in rights protections for its citizens.

No other country formally at peace registers the level of violence found in Colombia. Criminal and social violence intertwine with conflict dynamics to form a complex humanitarian situation. Although the overall human rights panorama has improved due to the Uribe Administration's Democratic Security Policy and

---

[48] For a full discussion of the various ways of classifying and qualifying democracy in Colombia, see Ana María Bejarano & Eduardo Pizarro, *From Restricted to Besieged: The Changing Nature of the Limits to Democracy in Colombia, in* ADVANCES AND SETBACKS IN THE THIRD WAVE OF DEMOCRATIZATION IN LATIN AMERICA (Frances Hagopian & Scott Mainwaring eds., 2004). See also Scott Mainwaring, Daniel Brinks & Anibal Pérez-Liñán, *Classifying Political Regimes in Latin America, 1945–1999*, 36 STUDIES IN COMPARATIVE INTERNATIONAL DEVELOPMENT 37 (2001); David Collier & Steven Levitsky, *Democracy with Adjectives: Conceptual Innovation in Comparative Research*, 49 WORLD POLITICS 430 (1997).

[49] Guillermo O'Donnell, *Horizontal Accountablility in New Democracies*, 9 JOURNAL OF DEMOCRACY 112 (1998).

[50] Bejarano & Pizarro, *supra* note 48, 241.

the government's efforts to demobilize the paramilitaries, many regions remain engulfed in violence, with civilians bearing the brunt of the conflict. In 2006 there were 17,479 violent deaths in Colombia, representing a homicide rate of 37 per 100,000 individuals.[51] A significant decrease from the all time high murder rate of 79 in 1991, this national figure does not depict the bleak panorama in areas of intense conflict where the number of violent deaths is even higher.[52] Citizens in conflict zones are also the victims of land mines, direct attacks on villages, land seizures, forced conscription, and displacement.[53] Children are particularly hard hit by Colombia's conflict: 11,000 combatants, or 1 in 4, are believed to be under age 18.[54] Colombia also has the dubious distinction of having the highest kidnapping rate in the world, with 687 kidnappings officially reported in 2006.[55] Nevertheless, due to the higher number of abductions in previous years, it is estimated that a far greater number of citizens are currently being held for ransom, some having been held for as many as ten years.[56] Between 1997 and 2007, more than 200 kidnapped Colombians died in captivity. In

---

[51] Policia Nacional de Colombia, *Crime Report 2006, at* <http://www.policia.gov.co/pls/portal/docs/page/observatorio_del_delito/home/crimereport2006.pdf > (visited September 24, 2008). Colombia's homicide rate is estimated to be 10 times the global average, and higher than the Latin America average. In the 1990's, only El Salvador's homicide rate exceeded Colombia's. See Steven Levitt & Mauricio Rubio, Understanding Crime in Colombia and What Can Be Done About It 3–4 (Aug. 20, 2000).

[52] The homicide rate in some departments reached as high as 61 due to the presence of insurgent groups and narcotraffickers, according to Fundacion Seguridad y Democracia, *Perspectivas de Seguridad 2006: Balance de Seguridad 2005, Análisis Trimestral Octubre-Deciembre de 2005*, 11 Coyuntura de Seguridad 43 (2006).

[53] Colombia is the country with the second highest number of internally displaced persons after Sudan. According to the NGO Consultoria para los Derechos Humanos y el Desplazamiento (Codhes), in the 22 year period from 1985 to 2007, over 4 million Colombians experienced displacement, or 8.7% of the population. See Codhes press release, Feb. 5, 2008 *at* <http://www.pda-alemania.org/descargas/descar_esp/prensa_codhes.pdf> (visited Sept. 24, 2008); Internal Placement Monitoring Center, *Newly Displaced People in Colombia Yearly, at* <http://www.internal-displacement.org/idmc/website/countries.nsf/httpEnvelopes> (visited May 2, 2006). Estimates place current IDP's between 2 and 3 million individuals. See Codhes, *El Desplazamiento Forzado, Crisis Nacional, at* <http://www.codhes.org/index.php?option=com_content&task=view&id=227&Itemid=1> (visited May 15, 2006).

[54] Human Rights Watch, *Colombia in Human Rights Watch World Report 2006, at* <http://www.hrw.org/wr2k6/americas/index.html> (visited May 8, 2006).

[55] Figures are according to the Policia Nacional de Colombia, *supra* note 51.

[56] The highest number of kidnappings was registered in 2002, when close to 3,000 citizens were abducted, according to the Policia Nacional de Colombia, *supra* note 51. On the number of detained citizens, see United Nations, Comision de Derechos Humanos, *Informe de la Alta Comisionada de las Naciones Unidas para los Derechos Humanos sobre la situación de los derechos humanos en Colombia, at* <http://www.hchr.org.co/documentoseinformed/informed/altocomisionado/Informe2007_esp.pdf> (visited Sept. 24, 2008).

2006 there were 37 confirmed massacres, in which 193 people were killed, and 687 citizens were forcibly "disappeared" in the same period.

Certain sectors of society, including human rights activists, journalists, teachers, labor leaders and academics are among the most frequent victims of "political" violence in the form of assassinations and disappearances. Colombia has the highest homicide rate against the press in the hemisphere, with 40 journalists murdered since 1991 and 30 others forced into exile by the threat of violence.[57] Human rights activists also are particular targets, with 73 murdered between 1996 and 2002.[58] According to Freedom House, Colombia is also the most dangerous place in the world for organized labor, with approximately 2,500 labor leaders and activists assassinated in the last decade.[59]

This chilling scenario points to the state's failure to fulfill perhaps its most elementary obligation to its citizens – the provision of internal order and security. Vast areas of the country have only a marginal government or police presence as drug producers, *guerrilla* forces, and paramilitaries violently vie for control of strategic coca growing regions and transhipment corridors, and target civilian populations and their land. Many decommissioned paramilitary units devolve into criminal gangs dedicated to drug producing and trafficking, while the FARC, although very hard hit during 2007 and 2008, continues its attacks on the public force and civilians. In some areas these illegal actors exercise de facto control of territory, markets, and political structures. The incapacity of the state to adequately provide security is aggravated by a weak system of justice. Not only do many areas in conflict operate according to extra-legal criminal codes and rudimentary systems of justice and conflict resolution, but an estimated impunity rate of well over 50% points to the difficulties to adequately respond to soaring levels of criminality and politically-motivated violence.[60]

A liberal analysis would conclude that the Colombian state exhibits a manifest failure to comply with its part of the social contract of providing the basic public

---

[57] The situation for journalists in Colombia is particularly dramatic. According to the Interamerican Commission for Human Rights, as reported in Amnesty International, *Colombia: Informar, hacer campaña y servir a la ciudadanía sin temor: los derechos humanos de periodistas, candidatos electorales y funcionarios electos, at* <http://www.amnesty.org/library/Index/ESLAMR230012006>, between 1998 and 2005, 31 journalists were assassinated by the FARC, paramilitaries and the state security forces. During 2005 alone, 9 journalists were threatened and some were forced to flee the country, one was kidnapped, and there were 4 attacks on media buildings and offices. See Fundación para la Libertad de Prensa, *Diagnóstico de la Libertad de Prensa en Colombia, at* <http://www.flip.org.co/informes/especiales/comunidado> (visited May 9, 2006).

[58] United Nations, Comision de Derechos Humanos, *supra* note 56, 34.

[59] Freedom House, *Freedom in the World: Colombia: Country Report, at* <http://www.freedomhouse.org/template.cfm> (visited May 15, 2006).

[60] See Elvira María Restrepo & Mariana Martinez, Impunidad penal: mitos y realidades (2004).

goods of liberty, order, and justice. In spite of extensive individual protections provided for in the constitution, state institutions have been unable to ensure these rights and protections uniformly across all regions and socioeconomic levels.[61] This dismal picture is made worse by the fact that many of the violations of civil and human rights committed during the internal conflict in Colombia involved the state apparatus. Military modernization and reforms have led to significant improvements in this regard, yet there continues to be credible evidence of ongoing extra-judicial executions, arbitrary detentions, and involvement in criminal activity by security forces acting independently.[62]

Another crucial dimension of the liberal notion of basic civil rights is that these protections be equal for all citizens. Here again, the Colombian citizenship model falls short. Government institutions are permeated by corruption and bias, and the protections that do exist are not provided equally. The persistence of clientelist practices by the state, in the words of Francisco Gutiérrez, convert "rights into favors", or citizens into clients.[63] With poor mechanisms of accountability and vertical legitimacy, corruption is rampant in nearly all branches and levels of government.[64] For Michael Mann, the patron-client networks and corruption that characterize Colombian democracy rupture the state-society bond and pose a major obstacle to genuine citizenship.[65]

Given this scenario, it is no surprise that many Colombians routinely search for ways to avoid compliance with their obligations to the state, and even toward society in general. At the same time, the suspicion that class privileges, corruption, and clientelist practices are such that those who are able shirk their obligations, creates a payoff structure that encourages cheating or non-compliance. This lack of civic-mindedness can be observed in many facets of Colombian public life, from tax evasion to avoidance of mandatory military duty.[66] With the rules of

---

[61] Freedom House ranked civil liberties in Colombia a 2 in 1972, on a scale of 1 (the best) to 7 (the worst). By 1990 it had fallen to 4, and today is at 3. In combination with the ranking of 3 in the area of political rights, Freedom House classifies Colombia as partly free for the period ending November 2005. See <http://freedomhouse.org/uploads/pdf/Charts2006.pdf>.

[62] United Nations, Comision de Derechos Humanos, *supra* note 56.

[63] Francisco Gutiérrez, La Ciudad Representada: Política y Conflicto en Bogotá 33 (1998).

[64] According to the Transparency International, Colombia was ranked 4.0 on a scale from zero (highly corrupt) to ten (highly clean), placing it 56th out of 159 countries on the ranking. See Transparency International, *Corruption Perceptions Index 2005, at* <http://www.transparency.org/policy_research/surveys_indices/cpi/2005>.

[65] Michael Mann, *La Crisis del Estado-Nación en América Latina, in* La Crisis Política Colombiana (Ann Mason & Luis Javier Orjuela eds., 2002).

[66] It is estimated that 35% of Colombian taxpayers evade fully paying their tax obligation. See Gustavo Hernández et al., Exenciones tributarias: costo fiscal y análisis de incidencia (2000).

military conscription favoring the privileged classes, perhaps the most elementary feature of the social contract – universal rights and suffrage in exchange for universal military service – does not exist in Colombia.

2. *Violence and Communitarianism*

There is an ongoing debate in Colombia regarding the effects of the conflict on civil society, and what this may mean for Colombian citizenship. The conventional position is that the persistent levels of violence since the late 1940's have in effect hindered the consolidation of a national citizenship project. Under conditions of sustained, collective, organized violence against both state institutions and society, the state inevitably constrains civil freedoms, while citizen participation is curtailed. Drawing on democratic theorists' emphasis on the indispensability of civil rights to the democratic process, Carlo Nasi considers that the violence in Colombia has kept the state from fulfilling the liberal and collective guarantees which protect opposition and dissent.[67] Without such citizen rights and the rule of law to competently resolve societal conflicts, democracy has floundered, civil society has splintered, and "citizenship" has been incapacitated.[68] Others go further, arguing that political violence permeates all aspects of the sociocultural experience, reproducing subjective identities based on the day to day experience of multiple forms of violence.[69]

On the other hand, some point to the strengthening of civil society as one of the unintended or counterintuitive consequences of the armed conflict.[70] The state's inability to put an end to the internal conflict, to protect society from violence, and to provide sustained solutions to critical socioeconomic problems has, according to this view, resulted in a more activated and engaged citizenry. Citizens have looked to alternative means of expressing collective interests and resolving conflicts. The explosion in the number of cooperatives, NGO's, civic organizations, private foundations and new social movements in the last decade is evidence of how citizenship in Colombia is increasingly expressed through

---

[67] Carlo Nasi, *Violencia política, democratización, y acuerdos de paz: algunas lecciones de América Latina*, 8 REVISTA DE ESTUDIOS SOCIALES 93 (2001).

[68] Daniel Pecaut, *Crisis y Construccion de lo Publico, in* Violencia y Política en Colombia: Elementos de Reflexión (Daniel Pecaut ed., 2003).

[69] Myriam Jimeno, *Cuerpo Personal y Cuerpo Política: Violencia, Cultura y Ciudadanía Neoliberal*, 63 UNIVERSITAS HUMANÍSTICA 15 (2007); and Sonia Liliana Vivas, *La Experiencia de Violencia en Colombia: Apuntes para Pensar la Formación Ciudadana*, 63 UNIVERSITAS HUMANISTICA 269 (2007).

[70] ANGELIKA RETTBERG, BUSCAR LA PAZ EN MEDIO DEL CONFLICTO 11 (2006). This debate parallels another controversy in Colombian political science, over whether the internal conflict is a force for state creation in the long run in the Tillian tradition, or a structure that has ritualized violence and fragmentation as a "normal" part of Colombian political and social life.

civil society as an antidote to a fractured political community and constraints on civil freedoms. These voluntary associations offer private spaces for civil association and for seeking collective solutions to the country's problems. One of the most striking examples of direct civic involvement are the peace rallies and antikidnapping marches that have taken place in Colombia in 2008 to protest against both the FARC and paramilitaries with massive citizen participation across the country.[71]

Communitarianism in Colombia can also take very different forms, however. The construction of "alternative social contracts" and "alternative political orders" has been a recurring theme in Colombian history.[72] The leftist insurgency, although a principal sponsor of current violence, was also in part born out of a closed, exclusionary political system and the state's practice of systematic violence against it. These armed actors originated in response to local and regional civil society needs, provided a rudimentary form of order and authority, and are now "negotiating", albeit violently, an alternative social contract with the Colombian state.[73] Like their leftist counterparts, Colombia's paramilitary movements also claim, with some legitimacy, to represent civil society in certain parts of the country.

The Colombian experience with communitarianism is perhaps symbolic of one of the weaknesses of the civil society theory of citizenship – what is the "community" and what is that community's notion of the common good that can replace the civic republican vision? Colombian civil society is at once unified against violence and insecurity, but fractured and subsumed by that very violence. Colombians are increasingly active in "civil" associations, but many of these, such as the paramilitaries or urban vigilante groups, are a substitute for political order, hardly a "social" complement to public life where civic virtues are inculcated. No one would disagree that effective citizenship in Colombia must involve a growing sense of community and civil involvement, but the results of this model will continue to be highly varied so long as profound disagreement persists within Colombian society regarding the broader collective good.

---

71 A massive transglobal demonstration, with over 1 million demonstrators in Bogotá alone, against the FARC, its practice of kidnapping, and other violent actors such as the paramilitaries took place in 2007, see <http://www.eltiempo.com/archivo/documento/CMS-3945957#> (visited Sept. 24, 2008), for further information see <http://www.semana.com/noticias-on-line/colombia-cansada-violencia/109991.aspx> (visited Sept. 24, 2008).

72 Ramírez, *supra* note 45, 61; María Teresa Uribe, *Las soberanías en disputa, conflicto de identidades o de derechos, in* Museo, Memoria y Nación 458 (Gonzalo Sánchez & María Emma Wills eds., 2000).

73 Ramírez, *supra* note 45, 61–62.

3. *A Paucity of Participation*

Citizen participation in public life in most modern democracies does not resemble Republican civic idealism. Colombia is no exception. Traditionally, Colombia was an elite dominated political system in which institutional arrangements granted the two main parties a preponderant role in politics, and partisan clientelism distorted participation. Such political centralization, in conjunction with rigid social hierarchies, shaped an exclusionary political culture incompatible with the liberal aspects of representative democracy and "the exercise of meaningful democratic citizenship for non-elite citizens".[74]

The rules of representation opened significantly with the 1991 constitutional redesign, however. Increased access to the political system was achieved through the facilitation of new political parties and movements, the number of which have increased dramatically since 1991, and through new provisions for minority representation.[75] For the first time, Colombia's democratic process was free from restrictions on political participation and competition.

In spite of these formal advances, the ongoing theme of violence in Colombia has continued to act as a powerful constraint on civic participation, measured in terms of voting practices and running for public office. On the one hand, in the most recent legislative elections in March 2006, the abstention rate was close to 60%.[76] Intimidation and direct threats of violence are the most immediate form of limiting the citizens' right to vote freely, and indeed in provinces with a strong guerrilla influence, abstention tends to be higher than the national average.[77] At the same time, both the guerrilla and paramilitaries constrain free participation in the areas they dominate by manipulating the voter process through threats

[74] Sonia Alvarez, Evelina Dagnino & Arturo Escobar, *Introduction: The Cultural and the Political in Latin American Social Movements*, *in* CULTURES OF POLITICS, POLITICS OF CULTURES 12 (Sonia Alvarea, Evelina Dagnino & Arturo Escobar eds., 1998).

[75] Bejarano & Pizarro, *supra* note 48, 236.

[76] *La abstención: el fantasma de siempre*, EL COLOMBIANO, *at* <http://www.elcolombiano.terra.com.co/BancoConocimiento> (visited May 9, 2006). See also *La abstención, protagonista de las elecciones colombianas*, EL MUNDO, *at* <http://www.elmundo.es/internacional/eleccionescolombia98/eleccionescolombia98.html> (visited Sept. 24, 2008). As a point of comparison, abstention in the 2000 parliamentary elections in the United States was 48.5%, according to the International Institute for Democracy and Electoral Assistance (IDEA), *at* <http://www.idea.int>, while the average rate of abstention in "partly free" democracies between 1945 and 1997 averaged 41%. See <http://freedomhouse.org>.

[77] In the 2002 presidential elections, the national rate of abstention was 58%, compared to 65% in Putumayo and 73% in the case of Caqueta, departments with high levels of violence and a strong guerrilla presence, according to Miguel Garcia, *Sobre balas y votos: violencia política y participación electoral en Colombia, 1990–1994, in* ENTRE LA PERSISTENCIA Y EL CAMBIO. RECONFIGURACIÓN DEL ESCENARIO PARTIDISTA Y ELECTORAL EN COLOMBIA (Diana Hoyos ed., 2007).

of violence, fraud and bribery.[78] Armed actors have also penetrated the political process by controlling political forces and candidates for public office in their areas of influence.[79]

The high levels of violence to which politicians, candidates, judges, and even civil servants are exposed also have a chilling effect on the involvement of Colombian civil society in political life. Political assassinations are a particularly virulent tool of the armed actors, with mayors, congressional representatives, local assemblymen, and candidates for public office the most frequent targets. 2005 experienced a sharp increase in political violence in anticipation of the 2006 legislative and presidential elections: 25 local assemblymen were assassinated, 200 had their lives threatened, and 325 were banished from their towns by credible threats of violence.[80] In 2006, there were 153 politically related murders throughout the country, including one sitting and four former mayors.[81] 47 individuals from both the national and local levels are currently being held by the FARC as political kidnapping victims.[82] That 11 assemblymen from the city of Cali, kidnapped by the FARC in 2002, were assassinated *en masse* after five years in captivity attests to the high stakes for political participation in Colombia.

As Bejarano and Pizarro conclude, "violence distorts democracy's participatory and competitive dimensions, both before and after elections".[83] Violence and threats discourage citizens from voting, armed actors restrict alternative parties and manipulate candidates and votes, and violence against politicians and public figures stifles direct participation in public life. The state's inability to provide security for its citizens has curtailed civic participation in all aspects of Colombia's democracy.

---

[78] It is estimated that voting in nearly 50% of the country's municipalities in the March 2006 elections was tampered with by guerrilla or paramilitary groups, according to Diego Perez, *Eleciones al Congreso: Reinvencion de la democracia o consolidacion del poder de las elites?, at* <http://www.dhcolombia.info/article.phps?id_article=285> (visited May 9, 2006).

[79] Since the parapolitics scandal first exploded in 2006, 45 regional and nationally elected congressional representatives from 16 regions have been prosecuted for direct collusion with local paramilitaries, and 18 are currently in prison.

[80] United Nations, Comision de Derechos Humanos, *supra* note 56.

[81] Among the victims was the sister of ex-President and ex-head of the OAS Cesar Gaviria, murdered by the FARC in a botched kidnapping attempt in April 2006. See, *Cae otro implicado en el asesinato de hermana de César Gaviria*, La Opinión, *at* <http://www.laopinion.com/latinoamerica/?rkey=00060508191513175321> (visited Sept. 24, 2008).

[82] Following the extraordinary July 2008 rescue of ex-presidential candidate Ingrid Betancourt, three U.S. Military contractors, and 11 members of the public force, there are still approximately 47 police and public office holders being held in captivity by the FARC, see <http://www.ejercito.mil.co/?idcategoria=204730> (visited Sept. 24, 2008).

[83] Bejarano & Pizarro, *supra* note 48, 242.

4. *Social Inequality*

Marshall's social democratic critique, although widely criticized and generally considered to have been superseded by more current theorizing, nevertheless seems relevant to an understanding of citizenship dynamics in Colombia.[84] Not unlike what Marshall observed in postwar Great Britain, the Colombian citizenship problematic is closely bound up with the persistence of poverty, inequality, and a lack of meaningful opportunities experienced by the majority of Colombian citizens. The radicalness of the 1991 Constitution lay in part with the adoption of extensive economic, social, cultural, and human rights, with the stated goal, echoing Marshall, of establishing the minimum conditions necessary for achieving full and equal access to civil and political rights.[85] Indeed, public spending in Colombia has increased during the last decade, with important gains made in the areas of education and health coverage.

But again, the contrast between formal guarantees and reality is instructive. High levels of inequality that characterize Colombian society, even fifteen years after adoption of the new constitution, undermine the possibility of true parity of socioeconomic rights. With a Gini Coefficient of 0,535 in 2005, Colombia's concentration of income is one of the highest in Latin America, the second highest in the region after Brazil.[86] The concentration of wealth in Colombia has also become more acute, with the wealthiest 10% earning 78.4 times what the poorest 10% earn, an increase of 25% in less than ten years.[87] In 2005, 49.2% of all Colombians lived below the poverty line, with 14.7% of the entire population indigent.[88] The national unemployment rate in 2007 was 12%, with 31% of the employed estimated to work in the informal economy.[89] Given that there is no government safety net for those who lose their source of income,

---

[84] For a review of the standard objections to Marshall's theory of citizenship, see Bryan S. Turner, *Outline of a Theory of Citizenship*, 24 Sociology 189 (1990).

[85] Libardo Sarmiento, *Balance Social de la Constitución de 1991: Desconocimiento, derechos y explotación de necesidades*, 4 Revista Foro 27 (2001).

[86] United Nations Development Programme, *Human Development Report for 2001*, <http://www.undp.org/hdr2001/>. Camilo Herrera & John Valles, *Estudios de consume Radar, la concentración del consumo en Colombia, at* <http://www.eumed.net/cursecon/ecolat/co/08/hmv.htm> (visited Sept. 24, 2008).

[87] Colombian Government's National Planning Department (DNP), Santiago Montenegro Trujillo, *Estimaciones pobreza e indigencia en Colombia 2005* 8 (2006), *at* <http://www.presidencia.gov.co/sne/2006/enero/18/presentaci%F3ncifraspobreza2005.pdf>, (visited Sept. 24, 2008) and the United Nations Development Programme (UNDP), *Informe de Desarrollo Humano para Colombia* (2000).

[88] DNP, *supra* note 87, 8; World Bank, *Colombia at a Glance, at* <http://devdata.worldbank.org/AAG/col_aag> (visited May 9, 2006).

[89] Organizacion Internacional de Trabajo, *Panorama Laboral 2007: America Latina y el Caribe, at* <http://www.oit.org.pe/WDMS/bib/publ/panorama/panorama07.pdf> (visited Sept. 24, 2008).

unemployment in Colombia can be catastrophic, often affecting an extended group of people who may all depend on one employable family member. According to the World Bank, 15% of Colombian children between the ages of 12 and 14 are estimated to be working.[90] A third of all Colombians had no access to health care in 2005.[91] For many, entrenched poverty, unemployment, and lack of social mobility strain what is an already precarious level of existence, with restricted access to health care, education and basic services.

Marshall's fundamental insight that the full exercise of citizenship is unattainable when there is socioeconomic exclusion seems appropriate to the Colombian case. The individual Colombians who make up the statistics presented above are certainly less likely to access the set of civil and political rights that privileged Colombians enjoy. The impossibility of receiving the rights and protections as stipulated by the state, in turn create enormous barriers to meet citizenship's obligations. Colombia's social and economic exclusion and the state's failure to respond to the needs of a vast segment of its population have seriously eroded confidence in public institutions and democracy. This has fueled disillusionment, resentment and rising social discontent, leading many to simply disengage from political and civic processes in which they have no stake, and making others vulnerable to crime and urban vigilante groups. This socioeconomic panorama also resonates with the guerrilla's revolutionary platform, and is a persuasive recruitment tool with the rural disenfranchised. Either way, that the state does not hold up its end of the social contract has, as in many other countries in Latin America and the Andean region in particular, led to disillusionment with democracy and a deterioration in relations between state and society, thwarting Colombia's citizenship project.[92]

5. *Multiple Nationalisms*

Like many national identities, Colombia's is not easy to nail down. Catholicism and the ideologies of the liberal-conservative party system are credited with having articulated an "imagined" Colombian nation (or rather nations) at different moments in the historical consciousness, and yet both are obsolete to an

---

On informal labor statistic, see CARMEN ELISA FLOREZ, THE FUNCTION OF THE URBAN INFORMAL SECTOR IN EMPLOYMENT: EVIDENCE FROM COLOMBIA 1984–2000 (April 2002).

90 World Bank, *supra* note 88. Global March, *Colombia Child Labour, at* <http://www.globalmarch.org/resourcecentre/world/colombia.pdf> (visited May 10, 2006). OIT – Oficina Regional para América Latina y el Caribe, *Panorama Laboral 2005: América Latina y el Caribe (Avance primer semestre), at* <http://www.oit.org.pe/portal/documentos/avance_panorama_laboral_2005.pdf> (visited May 5, 2006).

91 World Bank, *supra* note 88.

92 Paul Drake & Eric Hershberg, *Crises in the Andes, in* STATE AND SOCIETY IN CONFLICT: COMPARATIVE PERSPECTIVES ON ANDEAN CRISES (Paul Drake & Eric Hershberg eds., 2006).

understanding of modern Colombian national identity.[93] Is Colombian citizenship rooted in a sense of belonging to a community of Colombians? If so, what is that unifying idea that bonds citizen to nation? Or in the words of Ronald Beiner, what is it that prompts a Colombian "to feel that [he] belongs to *this* political community rather than to *that* political community"?[94] At the risk of doing disservice to an enormous literature on this topic, it is perhaps fair to say that there is probably no single notion of Colombian nationalism, but rather multiple, overlapping, and competing identities. What is more, these identities are in an ongoing process of change and becoming.

Important differences related to territory, class and ethnicity have been a constant in Colombian history and in the difficulties of constructing a single, unifying national project.[95] In this regard Colombia exhibits a striking absence of a nationalism rooted in a shared ethnocultural heritage. Entrenched regional attachments and identities stand out as one of the primary challenges to a single national identity.[96] At the same time, the inequalities in the country have created a nation so socially stratified, that a university educated *Bogotano* most likely identifies more with a professional from any other major Latin American city or even developed north than she does with the poorest of the poor in Colombia. Other significant fault-lines in Colombian society include the urban-rural divide, and the white European versus the Andean indigenous and the Afrodescendant communities.

With the 1991 Constitution, Colombia formally acknowledged its cultural diversity for the first time. Indigenous groups that had long been organized at the regional level were now granted collective rights and were articulated as political actors on the national stage with guaranteed representation. At the same time, social movements of women, youth, and religious practitioners have gained a

---

93 On religion and identity, see María Emma Wills, *De la nación católica a la nación multicultural: rupturas y desafíos, in* Museo, Memoria y Nación 385 (Gonzalo Sánchez & María Emma Wills eds., 2000). On how the party system shaped nacional identities, see Gonzalo Sánchez, Guerra y Política en la Sociedad Colombiana (1990) and Carlos Mario Perea, Porque la Sangre es Espíritu: Imaginario y Discurso Político en las Elites Capitalinas (1942–1949) (1996). The pioneering work on imagined communities is Benedict Anderson, Imagined Communities: Reflections on the Origin and Spread of Nationalism (1983).

94 Beiner, *supra* note 11, 19.

95 See David Bushnell, Colombia. Una nación a pesar de sí misma (1999); Marco Palacios, Entre la Legitimidad y la Violencia: Colombia 1875–1994 (1995); Fernan Gonzalez, Poderes Enfrentados: Iglesia y Estado en Colombia (1997).

96 A telling anecdote: A student of mine from Medellin, Colombia's second city and capital of one of the most prosperous and modern of the country's departments, referred to her coming to Bogotá to attend university as "moving to Colombia". On the regional loyalty issue, Robert Putnam, Making Democracy Work: Civic Traditions in Modern Italy (1993), may be a model for reconciling national citizenship with a strong sense of local identity in Colombia.

new prominence in Colombian society, giving weight to Colombia's pluralism. Still, Colombia's commitment to diversity has not been put to the test by massive waves of immigration by different ethnocultural groups, but rather has had to adjust to the multiculturalism that has always existed, but never been recognized, within its national territory. There is no mass clamoring for collective rights by specific identity groups, and Young's differentiated citizenship seems rather limited in the Colombian context.

Neither does Habermas's idea of a nationalism related to political community appear to be much in evidence in the case of Colombia. As has been stressed throughout this essay, perhaps the greatest "failure" of Colombia lies in its historical incapacity to consolidate a national democratic project on the principles of representation, participation, and universal rights. Neither the ideologies of the Liberal and Conservative parties, nor the bipartisan compromise during the National Front period, were able to unite the country. Politics seems to have done more to divide the polity than it has to unify it. This is no where more evident than in the 40 year plus internal conflict, in which alternative political arrangements directly and violently compete with that of the state.

That said, Colombians exhibit great national pride, if not exactly patriotism, and articulate a sense of being Colombian. In contrast to the bond of a single political model or a shared ethnocultural heritage, there are multiple attributes of the Colombian experience that can be associated with the palpable feeling of we-ness that diffuses society. Some suggest that violence and war have emerged as the common denominator of the Colombian experience, providing the core of a modern collective consciousness and sense of nation.[97] Historian Jorge Orlando Melo argues that the Colombian national identity is essentially a discourse constructed and reconstructed by shared language, symbols, myths, stereotypes, and collective images present from the time of infancy and reproduced through the mass media.[98] Thus, ordinary cultural practices related to food, music, and dance become the shared idiom of the nation. Related to this interpretation of identity as the "everyday", others point to popular cultural representations that have extraordinary unifying powers within Colombia. For Germán Ferro, Catholic iconography such as the Christ Child has become a symbol of the nation, of urban solidarity, and a cultural rallying point.[99] Likewise, the popular rituals of beauty contests and football also tend to produce a potent collective reaction in the national consciousness that spans ideology, region, ethnicity,

---

[97] Maria Teresa Uribe, Nación, ciudadano y soberano (2001).

[98] Jorge Orlando Melo, *Etnia, región y nación: el fluctuante discurso de la identidad*, *in* Memorias del V Congreso de Antropología en Colombia 27 (ICFES ed., 1989).

[99] Germán Ferro, *El Divino Niño, ícono de una nación*, *in* Belleza, fútbol y religiosidad popular 9 (Ingrid Bolívar, Germán Ferro & Andrés Dávila eds., 2001).

class and gender.[100] Finally, Colombian nationalism also exhibits a dimension of "topophilia" or "geopiety", which Daniel Deudney defines as "identity and loyalty based on experience of and feeling of connectedness to a particular place or area".[101] The rhetoric of modern Colombian nationalism is indeed highly naturalistic, and Colombians express a near reverence for the national geography and specific landscapes.

6. *The Global Colombian*

Regarding post-territorial models of citizenship, there is incipient evidence to suggest that Colombians are beginning to construct new forms of social, economic and cultural connectedness that go beyond the nation-state. The most tangible indication of this tendency is found in current migration patterns. The internal conflict, insecurity and lack of economic opportunities are factors which have made Colombia one of the chief emigrant countries in Latin America. As of 2005, 4 million Colombians, or an estimated 10% of the population, were residing outside national territory, while the Colombian government reports that between 1996 and 2004, 1.8 million citizens permanently left the country.[102] In 2005 alone, 123,000 Colombians relocated to other countries.[103] What is different about this current wave of Colombian migration, however, is that many of the activities and attitudes of Colombians living abroad imply the existence of a transnational field of action formed by a complex web of relations that link them to their home society. Contrary to previous migration patterns in which Colombians made a discrete move out of one country and into a new life in another, today's migrants maintain deep political, cultural, and socioeconomic ties with Colombia. Colombian migrants in the United States and Spain display consistent and complex commercial, financial, cultural and even criminal practices linking both national domains.[104] Legislation in Colombia and the United States that permits dual citizenship weakens the exclusivity of the state citizen bond,

---

[100] Ingrid Bolivar, *Estetizar la política: lo nacional de la belleza y la geografía del turismo, 1947–1970*, and Andrés Dávila, *La nación baja uniforme: la selección Colombia*, both *in* BELLEZA, FÚTBOL Y RELIGIOSIDAD POPULAR (Ingrid Bolívar, Germán Ferro & Andrés Dávila eds., 2001).

[101] David Deudney, Ground Identity: Nature, Place, and Space in Nationalism, *in* THE RETURN OF CULTURE AND IDENTITY IN IR THEORY 131 (Yosef Lapid & Friedrich Kratochwil eds., 1996).

[102] Centro de Estudios Migratorios Latinamericanos-Banco Interamericano de Desarrollo, *Colombia: Flujos Migratorios y Remesas de Trabajadores, at* <http://www.cemla-remasas.org/PDF/seminariomx/0510MX-ES-PPT-Colombia.pdf> (visited May 6, 2006).

[103] World Bank, *Movement of People, in* WORLD DEVELOPMENT INDICATORS 2006, *at* <http://www/devdata.worldbank.org/wdi2006/contents/Section6.htm> (visited May 9, 2006).

[104] Luis Eduardo Guarnizo & Luz Marina Díaz, *Transnational migration: a view from Colombia*, 22 ETHNIC AND RACIAL STUDIES 397 (1999).

and contributes to the formation of multiple associations, rights, nationalisms and even identities.

At the same time, new authority relations related to global governance projects also are affecting the citizen-state relationship in Colombia, along the lines of a post-national conception of citizenship. New global spheres of authority, involving overlapping internal and external jurisdictions, a proliferation of new global actors, and changing authority criteria, all point to the formation of more direct associations between Colombian citizens and global citizenship schemes. This dynamic is particularly apparent in the case of global processes and norms related to human rights and the internal conflict. The loosening of territorial parameters has legitimated nonstate actors within the domestic sphere and helped create new legitimacy sentiments toward global institutions, such as NGO's and the International Criminal Court in the Hague.[105] Although a postnational scheme is far from replacing a national model in Colombia, new rules and institutions related to the global human rights regime in particular have established authority relations with nonterritorial communities, altering the sense of citizenship based exclusively on the national domain.

III. *Citizenship, State Strength and State Building*

In weakened states, countries with security emergencies, or cases of outright collapse, citizen engagement is not a high priority item. National governments in crisis are concerned with maintaining control, avoiding coups, and staving off intervention. The international community, for its part, may be more interested in imposing order and shoring up domestic capabilities and institutions. Even in reconstruction projects with a longer time horizon and a broader political program, the goal is externally imposed self-governance.

Triage approaches to state strengthening or building, whether domestic or international, share the immediate objective of buttressing the instrumental aspects of institutions. After all, institutions must be effective at performing specific functions related to the collective good: territorial control, public order, government administration and basic services, and mechanisms of justice. A critical component of state building, however, is the legitimation of the state and its institutions by civil society and the subordination of allegiances to competing claims to political authority. Modern stateness requires both problem-solving capacity *and* legitimacy. Creating and maintaining legitimate, accountable state

---

[105] Ann Mason, *Constructing Authority Alternatives on the Periphery: Vignettes from Colombia*, 26 International Political Science Review 37 (2005).

institutions, in turn, can only be achieved with broad-based societal involvement and pressure.[106]

The aptitude for governance, the provision of public goods, and the ability to mediate social conflicts according to the rule of law are all inextricably linked with the degree and quality of public authority.[107] Contrary to the attitudes exhibited by some world leaders, it is society that legitimates state authority and power. Where society disputes the underlying rules of social order on which the state claims authority, where the state's provision of public goods such as justice, security, property rights, and economic development is inadequate, or where there are competing claims to authority, citizens may withhold consent, protest against the government, or violently contest state power. Attempts to govern based solely on coercion and unsanctioned power will eventually collapse under the weight and cost of the regime's violence, threats and repression. Indeed, the total breakdown of authority in failed states provides dramatic evidence for the importance of legitimacy rooted in society's validation of the state's right to rule, to overall state strength and internal order.[108] Although elusive and difficult to measure, the state-society relationship is one of the most critical determinants of any state building project.

While constructing a social base of public power is a long, daunting task for any weak state, it poses a particular difficulty for state-building efforts from the outside. When authority effectively resides in another sovereign entity or the United Nations, the state-society bond in effect has been broken. "If states are constructed as administrative centres, directed from Brussels or Washington", says David Chandler, "there is little possibility that they will be able to strengthen their relationship with their societies. This is particularly problematic in situations where states have a weak social basis or their societies are particularly divided or fragmented".[109] Francis Fukuyma goes even further, arguing that state-building efforts have, paradoxically, made public institutions even weaker, undermining the national projects capable of uniting societal forces with state elites.[110]

A durable state must be built in partnership with society. This is true for reconstruction projects, as well for weak states such as Colombia whose state-building project is still in process. Nevertheless, many weak states are characterized by a fractured social contract between state and society, widespread citizen

---

106 David Chandler, *The Problems of 'Nation-Building': Imposing Bureaucratic Rule from Above*, 17 Cambridge Review of International Affairs 577 (2004).

107 Mason, *supra* note 105, 50.

108 David Beetham, The Legitimation of Power 28 (1991).

109 David Chandler, *How 'State-Building' Weakens States*, Spiked Essays (Oct. 24, 2005), *at* <http://www.spiked-online.com/Articles/0000000CADDB.htm>.

110 Francis Fukuyama, State-Building: Governance and World Order in the Twenty-First Century 5 (2004).

alienation from the political system, high levels of insecurity, and competing or ambivalent national identities, all of which tend to have a corrosive effect on effective citizenship.

The starting point for citizenship projects in weak states and the developing world more generally is the state's granting and protection of civil and political rights. In contrast with the advanced, industrialized north, where basic needs and liberties are largely guaranteed, weaker states have done a relatively poor job at protecting rights. Even where rights are formally provided for, incomplete separation of powers, excessive autonomy and politicization of security forces, and a spotty adherence to the rule of law are such that many weaker states in practice do not systematically uphold basic freedoms.

According to Michael Doyle, the democratic qualities that most induce peace are related to constitutionalism and liberalism.[111] Not surprisingly, unchecked power and poor protections of the bundle of freedoms associated with constitutional liberalism are highly correlated with internal instability and violence in weak state contexts. Procedural democracy is not in and of itself enough to strengthen states or build capacity. Democracies must also establish and provide for the effective protection of society's civil rights and liberties. Although liberal citizenship theory is widely criticized for its instrumentalism, institutional mechanisms to guarantee protections are the cornerstone of any citizenship project in the global south. Government failure to fulfill that responsibility results in deteriorating state-society relations, citizen opposition, and instability. To the extent that constructing a social base of public power is critical to the state-building task, liberalism's instrumental individualism is precisely what is needed in developing contexts.

The quality of the state-society bond in peripheral states also depends on institutionalized channels of participation in political life. For many states, and a particular challenge in reconstruction efforts, this will mean guaranteeing access to participation in multi-party, competitive elections. For others with already institutionalized mechanisms, pervasive violence or internal conflicts often impede citizen involvement in multiple aspects of public life, including voting, serving in police forces, running for elected office, or turning out for political rallies. Again, the Colombian case is instructive: formal rules offering participation and free competition are a necessary but insufficient condition to achieve society's participation in political life. Yet without such engagement, the society's stake in the state is tenuous.

Citizenship practices in weaker states also diverge from those in developed democracies with regard to society's involvement in the non-political aspects of communal life, such as NGO's and voluntary associations. In weak and state-building contexts, it is virtually impossible to separate out private interests from

[111] Michael Doyle, Ways of War and Peace: Realism, Liberalism, and Socialism 253 (1997).

political agendas. Almost all non-public organizations in which private citizens participate have mandates that are in essence, political. Within the developing world, they typically spring from the need to supplement, or replace, the state in particular issue areas such as health, education, security, or justice, where the government has failed to provide public goods. In contrast to contemporary forms of civic engagement in the United States,[112] which are increasingly oriented toward private, particularistic and apolitical agendas, communitarian involvement and activism on the periphery is more political than not.

The social model of citizenship has been largely discredited in the developed north for leading to a sense of entitlement and a clientelist attitude regarding what the state can offer.[113] Valid in countries that offer sufficient economic opportunities to achieve an acceptable standard of living, this critique is off the mark in the developing world where large portions of the population have a precarious level of existence. Political and civil rights are relatively meaningless in societies marked by persistent poverty, inequality, lack of employment, restricted access to education and health care, and little hope of upward mobility. The ruptured state-society relationships found throughout the Third World are closely bound up with poor economic performance and failed development strategies, even in nominally competitive democracies. In many weak states, expectations that prosperity would result from democratization and neoliberal reforms have been dashed, resulting in widespread disillusionment and rising social discontent, and thwarting constructive citizenship projects. Marshall's social democratic theory of citizenship seems highly relevant to understand the importance of socioeconomic development to the state-society bond in peripheral and new states.

A vibrant civil society and civic engagement are indispensable dimensions of state strength. The quality of governance and the performance of institutions in state-building and developing contexts are powerfully influenced by norms, practices and networks of civil engagement. The state-society relation must be such that the citizenry has a clear stake in public life and institutions. Although much concern is expressed over the passive reliance of society on government in new democracies without much experience in self-government, Colombia's experience tells us that the greater risk is that citizens will seek alternative, extra-institutional channels of participation, which inevitably lead to social fragmentation and atomization. A collective sociopolitical framework of government and society within which there is a social base of state authority, citizens with incentives and opportunities for diverse forms of participation, and public institutions that are accountable to the polity are all prerequisites for a constructive citizenship project and the creation of sustainable states in the developing world.

---

112 Robert Putnam, *Bowling Alone: America's Declining Social Capital*, 6 Journal of Democracy 65 (1995).

113 Turner, *supra* note 84, 211.

Actors

State-Building and the United Nations: A Critical Overview

*Simon Chesterman**

Is it possible to establish the conditions for legitimate and sustainable national governance through a period of benevolent foreign autocracy under UN auspices? This contradiction between ends and means has plagued recent efforts to govern post-conflict territories in the Balkans, East Timor, Afghanistan, and Iraq. Such state-building operations combine an unusual mix of idealism and realism: the idealist project that a people can be saved from themselves through education, economic incentives, and the space to develop mature political institutions; the realist basis for that project in what is ultimately military occupation.

In early 1995, chastened by the failed operation in Somalia, the failing operation in Bosnia and Herzegovina, and inaction in the face of genocide in Rwanda, UN Secretary-General Boutros Boutros-Ghali issued a conservative supplement to his more optimistic 1992 *Agenda for Peace*. The *Supplement* noted that a new breed of intra-state conflicts presented the United Nations with challenges not encountered since the Congo operation of the early 1960s. A feature of these conflicts was the collapse of state institutions, especially the police and judiciary, meaning that international intervention had to extend beyond military and humanitarian tasks to include the "promotion of national reconciliation and the re-establishment of effective government." Nevertheless, he expressed caution against the United Nations assuming responsibility for law and order, or attempting to impose state institutions on unwilling combatants.[1] General Sir Michael

---

* Many thanks to David M. Malone, Neclâ Tschirgi, Sebastian von Einsiedel, Dino Kritsiotis, Kimberly Marten, and Ramesh Thakur for their comments on an earlier version of this text. The views expressed are those of the author alone. This text reproduces ideas discussed at greater length in Simon Chesterman, You, The People: The United Nations, Transitional Administration, and State-Building (2004), and Making States Work: State Failure and the Crisis of Governance (Simon Chesterman, Michael Ignatieff, & Ramesh Thakur eds., 2005).

[1] Supplement to An Agenda for Peace: Position Paper of the Secretary-General on the Occasion of the Fiftieth Anniversary of the United Nations, UN Doc. A/50/60–S/1995/1, paras. 13–14 (1995), *at* <ttp://www.un.org/Docs/SG/agsupp.html>

Rose, then commander of the UN Protection Force in Bosnia (UNPROFOR), termed this form of mission creep crossing "the Mogadishu line."[2]

Despite such cautious words, by the end of 1995 the United Nations had assumed responsibility for policing in Bosnia under the Dayton Peace Agreement. The following January, a mission was established with temporary civil governance functions over the last Serb-held region of Croatia in Eastern Slavonia. In June 1999, the Security Council authorized an "interim" administration in Kosovo to govern part of what remained technically Serbian territory for an indefinite period; four months later a transitional administration was created with effective sovereignty over East Timor until independence. These expanding mandates continued a trend that began with the operations in Namibia in 1989 and Cambodia in 1993, where the United Nations exercised varying degrees of civilian authority in addition to supervising elections.

Efforts to construct or reconstruct institutions of the state are hardly new: nation-building coincided with the dismantling of colonial structures and efforts to support weak governance have long been a feature of UN post-conflict reconstruction. What was novel about the missions undertaken in Kosovo and East Timor was the amount of executive authority assumed by the United Nations itself, placing it in the position of an occupying power. Though this power was, presumably, understood to be exercised in a benevolent fashion, problems associated with foreign rule repeated themselves with some predictable results in the cases examined here.

The present chapter surveys the brief history of UN transitional administration, before elaborating on three contradictions that have emerged in the conduct of such operations. The emphasis is on operations in which the United Nations has exercised some form of executive control – most prominently in East Timor, where it exercised effectively sovereign powers for over two years. This is the subject matter of section one. More recent operations in Afghanistan and Iraq have shifted the terms of this debate: the state-building agenda in such operations has been determined less by the needs of the post-conflict society than by the strategic interests of the United States. Section two therefore turns to the relationship between state-building and the war on terror.

I. *The contradictions of transitional administration*

Though colonialism is now condemned as an international crime, international humanitarian law – specifically the 1907 Hague Regulations and the Fourth

---

[2] Michael Rose, *The Bosnia Experience, in* PAST IMPERFECT, FUTURE UNCERTAIN: THE UNITED NATIONS AT FIFTY 139 (Ramesh Thakur ed., 1998).

Geneva Convention of 1949 – provides the legal basis for an occupying power to exercise temporary authority over territory that comes under its control. The occupying power is entitled to ensure the security of its forces, but is also required to "take all the measures in his power to restore, and ensure, as far as possible, public order and safety, while respecting, unless absolutely prevented, the laws in force in the country." In addition to other positive obligations, such as ensuring public health and sanitation, as well as the provision of food and medical supplies, the occupying power is prohibited from changing local laws except as necessary for its own security and is limited in its capacity to change state institutions. As the purpose of transitional administration is precisely to change the laws and institutions, further legal authority is therefore required. In most of the cases examined here, that authority has tended to come from the UN Security Council. Here, as with much of the Council's work, practice has led theory, with some members of the Council and the wider UN community apparently allergic to the development of doctrine.

These UN missions, sometimes referred to as complex peace operations, bear a curious heritage. In the heady days of the early 1990s, traditional or "first generation" peacekeeping, which was non-threatening and impartial, governed by the principles of consent and minimum force, was swiftly succeeded by two further generations. Second generation or "multidimensional" peacekeeping was used to describe post-Cold War operations in Cambodia, El Salvador, Mozambique, and Angola, but, retrospectively, might also have included the Congo operation in 1960–1964. Third generation peacekeeping, sometimes called "peace enforcement," operating with a Chapter VII mandate from the Security Council, began with the Somalia operation. The genealogy was curious – the third generation appearing a mere six months after the second – but the terminology also misleadingly suggested a linear development in peacekeeping doctrine. Evolution is a more appropriate metaphor than selective breeding, with essentially unpredictable events demanding new forms of missions.[3]

If military doctrine developed through natural selection, civil administration was a random mutation. The fact that such operations continue to be managed by the UN Department of Peacekeeping Operations is suggestive of the ad hoc approach that has characterized transitional administration, an historical accident perpetuated by the reluctance to embrace temporary governance of post-conflict territory as an appropriate and necessary task for the United Nations. This was evident in the Brahimi Report on UN Peace Operations, which noted the

---

[3] For a six generation model, see Ramesh Thakur & Albrecht Schnabel, *Cascading Generations of Peacekeeping: Across the Mogadishu Line to Kosovo and Timor, in* United Nations Peacekeeping Operations: Ad Hoc Missions, Permanent Engagement 3 (Ramesh Thakur & Albrecht Schnabel eds., 2001).

likely demand for such operations as well as the "evident ambivalence" within governments and the UN Secretariat itself concerning the development of an institutional capacity to undertake them. Because of this ambivalence it was impossible to achieve any consensus on recommendations, so the Department of Peacekeeping Operations continues to play the dominant supporting role.[4]

These doctrinal and operational concerns are valid, but have frequently overshadowed the more basic political problems confronting transitional administration. This section discusses three sets of contradictions in the very idea of creating a legitimate and sustainable state through a period of benevolent autocracy: the means are inconsistent with the ends, they are frequently inadequate for those ends, and in many situations the means are inappropriate for the ends.

1. *The means are inconsistent with the ends*

UNMIK in Kosovo and the High Representative in Bosnia and Herzegovina have governed through military occupation. In East Timor, the United Nations completed the task of decolonization. The fact that these powers have been exercised benevolently does not deprive them of their imposed character. More important than the benevolence of intention is the acceptance of the subject population that power is being exercised for ends that are both clear and achievable. The post-war experiences of Germany and Japan suggest that it is not impossible to create democracies through military occupation, but those operations were very different from more recent instances of transitional administration, with the possible exception of Iraq. Decolonization may be a more fitting model, but there are valid concerns about embracing such language only half a century after one-third of the world's population lived under colonial rule. Whatever euphemism is used, however, it is both inaccurate and counter-productive to assert that transitional administration depends upon the consent or "ownership" of local populations. It is inaccurate because if genuine local control were possible then a transitional administration would not be necessary. It is counter-

[4] *Cf.* Strengthening of the United Nations: An Agenda for Further Change, UN Doc. A/57/150, para. 126 (2002): "To strengthen further the Secretariat's work in international peace and security, there is a need to bring a sharper definition to the existing lead department policy, which sets out the relationship between the Department of Political Affairs and the Department of Peacekeeping Operations. The Department of Political Affairs will increase its focus in the fields of preventive diplomacy, conflict prevention and peacemaking. The Department will also intensify its engagement in policy formulation across the full spectrum of the Secretariat's tasks in the domain of international peace and security. It will continue to be the lead department for political and peace-building offices in the field. The Department of Peacekeeping Operations will be the lead department for the planning and management of all peace and security operations in the field, including those in which the majority of personnel are civilians."

productive because insincere claims of local ownership lead to frustration and suspicion on the part of local actors.

Clarity is central to the effective management of post-conflict reconstruction. Instead of institutional transformations, such as rejuvenating the Trusteeship Council or creating a new body to administer territories under the auspices of the United Nations, a modest but important area of reform would be to require clarity in three key areas: as to the strategic objectives; as to the relationship between international and local actors and how this will change over time; and as to the commitment required of international actors in order to achieve objectives that warrant the temporary assumption of autocratic powers under a benevolent international administration. Structured discussion within the UN Security Council would be one way to achieve this, in the form of transitional administration committees, modelled on the sanctions committees that now routinely monitor the implementation, effects, and humanitarian impact of economic sanctions.

In a case like East Timor, the strategic objective – independence – was both clear and uncontroversial. Frustration with the slow pace of reconstruction or the inefficiencies of the UN presence could generally be tempered by reference to the uncontested aim of independence and a timetable within which this was to be achieved. In Kosovo, failure to articulate a position on its final status inhibited the development of a mature political elite and deterred foreign investment. The ambiguity derived from a compromise that was brokered between the United States and Russia at the end of the NATO campaign against the Federal Republic of Yugoslavia in 1999, formalized in Security Council resolution 1244 (1999). Nevertheless, it is the United Nations itself that was blamed for frustrating the aspirations of Kosovars for self-determination.

Obfuscation of the political objective leads to ambiguity in the mandate. In a speech at the tenth anniversary of the Department of Peacekeeping Operations in 2002, Jacques Paul Klein, former Special Representative of the Secretary-General for the UN Transitional Administration for Eastern Slavonia (UNTAES), contrasted his own mandate with that governing international efforts to bring peace to Bosnia. The UN Protection Force (UNPROFOR) was governed by no less than 70 Security Council resolutions and dozens of Presidential statements. Political negotiating authority was divided between the United Nations, the European Union, and the Contact Group. The Dayton Peace Agreement had 150 pages, 11 Annexes, 40 pages of Peace Implementation Council declarations, 92 post-accession criteria for membership of the Council of Europe, and a host of further agreements – most of which were never fulfilled.

> In contrast, the mandate of UNTAES contained just thirteen sentences that could be distilled into six quantifiable objectives. [...] My point here is twofold: if you start out and don't know where you want to go, you will probably end up somewhere else. And secondly, the mandate is the floor (but not the ceiling) for everything the

> Mission does. If the mandate is vague for whatever reason – including the inability of Security Council members to agree on a political end state – dysfunction will plague the lifespan of the Mission.[5]

This echoed sentiments in the Brahimi Report applicable to peace operations generally.[6]

Niche mandate implementation by a proliferation of post-conflict actors further complicates the transition. More than five years after the Dayton Peace Agreement, a "recalibration" exercise required the various international agencies present in Bosnia to perform an institutional audit to determine what, exactly, each of them did.[7] Subsidiary bodies and specialized agencies of the United Nations should in principle place their material and human resources at the direct disposal of the transitional administration: all activities should be oriented towards an agreed political goal, which should normally be legitimate and sustainable government. Ideally, the unity of civilian authority should embrace command of the military also. In reality, the reluctance of the United States and other industrialized countries to put their troops under UN command makes this highly improbable. Coordination thus becomes more important, to avoid some of the difficulties encountered in civil-military relations in Afghanistan.

Clarity in the relationship between international and local actors raises the question of ownership. This term is often used disingenuously – either to mask the assertion of potentially dictatorial powers by international actors or to carry a psychological rather than political meaning in the area of reconstruction. Ownership in this context is usually not intended to mean control and often does not even imply a direct input into political questions. This is not to suggest that local control is a substitute for international administration. As the operation in Afghanistan demonstrates, a light footprint makes the success of an operation more than usually dependent on the political dynamic of local actors. Since the malevolence or collapse of that political dynamic is precisely the reason that power is arrogated to an international presence, the light footprint is unsustainable as a model for general application. How much power should be transferred and for how long depends upon the political transition that is required; this in turn is a function of the root causes of the conflict, the local

---

[5] Jacques Paul Klein, "What Does It Take to Make UN Peacekeeping Operations Succeed? Reflections from the Field" (paper presented at the 10th Anniversary of the Department of Peacekeeping Operations, New York, Oct. 29, 2002).

[6] Report of the Panel on United Nations Peace Operations (Brahimi Report), UN Doc. A/55/305–S/2000/809, para. 56 (2000), *at* <http://www.un.org/peace/reports/peace_operations/>.

[7] International Crisis Group, *Bosnia: Reshaping the International Machinery*, 13 (ICG Balkans Report No 121, Nov. 29, 2001), *at* <http://www.crisisgroup.org>.

capacity for change, and the degree of international commitment available to assist in bringing about that change.[8]

Local ownership, then, must be the end of a transitional administration, but it is not the means. Openness about the trustee-like relationship between international and local actors would help locals by ensuring transparency about the powers that they will exercise at various stages of the transition. But openness would also help the states that mandate and fund such operations by forcing acknowledgement of their true nature and the level of commitment that is required in order to effect the transition that is required.

Clarifying the commitment necessary to bring about fundamental change in a conflict-prone territory is, however, a double-edged sword. It would ensure that political will exists prior to authorizing a transitional administration, but perhaps at the expense of other operations that would not be authorized at all. The mission in Bosnia was always expected to last beyond its nominal 12 month deadline, but might not have been established if it had been envisaged that troops would remain on the ground for a full decade or more. Donors contemplating Afghanistan in November 2001 baulked at early estimates that called for a ten year, $25 billion commitment to the country. In the lead up to the war with Iraq, the Chief of Staff of the US Army was similarly pooh-poohed by the leadership of the Defense Department when he testified to the Senate that 200,000 soldiers would be required for post-war duties. Political considerations already limit the choice of missions, of course: not for lack of opportunity, no major transitional administration has been established in Africa, where the demands are probably greatest.

Resolving the inconsistency between the means and the ends of transitional administration requires a clear-eyed recognition of the role of power. The collapse of formal state structures does not necessarily create a power vacuum; political life does not simply cease. Rather, power comes to be exercised through informal political and legal structures, complicating efforts to construct political institutions and to instantiate the rule of law. Constructive engagement with power on this local level requires both an understanding of culture and history as well as respect for the political aspirations of the population. Clarity will help here also: either the international presence exercises quasi-sovereign powers on a temporary basis or it does not. This clarity must exist at the formal level, but leaves much room for nuance in implementation. Most obviously, assertion of executive authority should be on a diminishing basis, with power devolved as appropriate to local institutions. This is not, therefore, an argument for unilateralism

---

[8] Michael W. Doyle, *War-Making and Peace-Making: The United Nations' Post-Cold War Record, in* TURBULENT PEACE: THE CHALLENGES OF MANAGING INTERNATIONAL CONFLICT 529, 546 (Chester A. Crocker, Fen Osler Hampson, & Pamela Aall eds., 2001).

in the administration of post-conflict territories, but an argument for the transfer of power to be of more than symbolic value: once power is transferred to local hands, whether at the municipal or national level, local actors should be able to exercise that power meaningfully, constrained only by the rule of law. Unless and until genuine transfer is possible, consultation is appropriate but without the pretence that this is the same as control. In such situations, additional efforts should be made to cultivate civil society organizations such as local non-governmental organizations (NGOs), which can provide a legitimate focus for the political activities of the local population and lobby international actors. Where international actors do not exercise sovereign power – because of the size of the territory, the complexity of the conflict, or a simple lack of political will – this is not the same as exercising no power at all. Certain functions may be delegated to the international presence, as they were in Cambodia and Afghanistan, and international actors will continue to exercise considerable behind-the-scenes influence either because of ongoing responsibilities in a peace process or as a gatekeeper to international development assistance. In either case, the abiding need is for clarity as to who is in charge and, equally important, who is *going* to be in charge.

2. *The means are inadequate for the ends*

Speaking in Cincinnati, Ohio, on 7 October 2002, US President George W. Bush made one of his strongest early statements concerning the threat that Iraq posed to the United States. In the course of his speech, he also alluded to the aftermath of war, stating that the lives of Iraqi citizens would "improve dramatically if Saddam Hussein were no longer in power, just as the lives of Afghanistan's citizens improved after the Taliban."[9] Ten months after the Bonn Agreement, Afghanistan was hardly a success story – Bush's remarks could equally have been intended as an optimistic assessment of that troubled mission, or a pessimistic downplaying of expectations for what might follow the impending war with Iraq.

Iraq is, of course, distinct from the UN transitional administrations considered here, but the ephemeral nature of international interest in post-conflict operations is, unfortunately, a cliché. When the United States overthrew the Taliban regime in Afghanistan, Bush likened the commitment to rebuild the devastated country to the Marshall Plan. Just over twelve months later, in February 2003, the White House apparently forgot to include *any* money for reconstruction in the 2004 budget that it submitted to Congress. Legislators reallocated $300

[9] George W. Bush, *President Bush Outlines Iraqi Threat* (Cincinnati, Ohio, Oct. 7, 2002), *at* <http://www.whitehouse.gov>.

million in aid to cover the oversight.[10] Such oversights are disturbingly common: much of the aid that is pledged either arrives late or not at all. This demands a measure of artificiality in drafting budgets for reconstruction, which in turn leads to suspicion on the part of donors – sometimes further delaying the disbursement of funds. For example, $880 million was pledged at the Conference on Rehabilitation and Reconstruction of Cambodia in June 1992. By the time the new government was formed in September 1993, only $200 million had been disbursed, rising to only $460 million by the end of 1995. The problem is not simply one of volume: Bosnia has received more per capita assistance than Europe did under the Marshall Plan, but the incoherence of funding programmes, the lack of a regional approach, and the inadequacy of state and entity institutions have contributed to it remaining in financial crisis.[11]

Many of these problems would be reduced if donors replaced the system of voluntary funding for relief and reconstruction for transitional administrations with assessed contributions, which presently fund peacekeeping operations. The distinction between funds supporting a peacekeeping operation and those providing assistance to a government makes sense when there is some form of indigenous government, but is arbitrary in situations where the peacekeeping operation *is* the government. Given existing strains on the peacekeeping budget, however, such a change is unlikely. A more realistic proposal would be to pool voluntary contributions through a trust fund, ideally coordinated by local actors or a mixed body of local and international personnel, perhaps also drawing upon private sector expertise. Even more modest proposals along these lines have faced stiff resistance from the larger donors – in part due to concerns about accountability and additional red tape, in part due to fears that this would remove the discretion to direct funds to projects that are more popular at home than they are necessary abroad. At the very least, a monitoring mechanism to track aid flows would help to ensure that money that is promised at the highpoint of international attention to a crisis is in fact delivered and spent.

Parsimony of treasure is surpassed by the reluctance to expend blood in policing post-conflict territories. In the absence of security, however, meaningful political change in a post-conflict territory is next to impossible. Unless and until the United Nations develops a rapidly deployable civilian police capacity, either military tasks in a post-conflict environment will include basic law and

---

10 Paul Krugman, *The Martial Plan*, N.Y. Times, 21 February 2003; James G. Lakely, *Levin Criticizes Budget for Afghanistan; Says White House Isn't Devoting Enough to Rebuilding*, Washington Times, 26 February 2003. Aid was later increased further: David Rohde, *US Said to Plan Bigger Afghan Effort, Stepping Up Aid*, N.Y. Times, 25 August 2003.

11 See, for example, International Crisis Group, *Bosnia's Precarious Economy: Still Not Open for Business* (ICG Balkans Report No. 115, Aug. 7, 2001), *at* <http://www.crisisgroup.org>.

order functions or these functions will not be performed at all. The military – especially the US military – is understandably reluctant to embrace duties that are outside its field of expertise, but this is symptomatic of an anachronistic view of UN peace operations. The dichotomy between peacekeeping and enforcement actions was always artificial, but in the context of internal armed conflict where large numbers of civilians are at risk it becomes untenable. Moreover, as most transitional administrations have followed conflicts initiated under the auspices or in the name of the United Nations, inaction is not the same as non-interference – once military operations commence, external actors have already begun a process of political transformation on the ground. And, as the Independent Inquiry on Rwanda concluded, whether or not a peace operation has a mandate or the will to protect civilians, its very presence creates an expectation that it will do so.

A key argument in the Brahimi Report was that missions with uncertain mandates or inadequate resources should not be created at all:

> Although presenting and justifying planning estimates according to high operational standards might reduce the likelihood of an operation going forward, Member States must not be led to believe that they are doing something useful for countries in trouble when – by under-resourcing missions – they are more likely agreeing to a waste of human resources, time and money.[12]

Applied to transitional administration, this view finds some support in the report of the International Commission on Intervention and State Sovereignty, *The Responsibility to Protect*, which calls for the "responsibility to rebuild" to be seen as an integral part of any intervention. When an intervention is contemplated, a post-intervention strategy is both an operational necessity and an ethical imperative.[13] There is some evidence of this principle now achieving at least rhetorical acceptance – despite his aversion to "nation-building," Bush stressed before and during operations in Afghanistan and Iraq that the United States would help in reconstructing the territories in which it had intervened.

More than rhetoric is required. Success in state-building, in addition to clarity of purpose, requires time and money. A lengthy international presence will not ensure success, but an early departure guarantees failure. Similarly, an abundance of resources will not make up for the lack of a coherent strategy – but the fact that Kosovo has been the recipient of 25 times more money and 50 times more troops, on a per capita basis, compared with Afghanistan, goes

---

[12] Brahimi Report, *supra* note 6, para. 59.

[13] International Commission on Intervention and State Sovereignty, *The Responsibility to Protect*, paras. 2.32, 5.1–5.6 (2001), *at* <http://www.iciss.ca>.

some way towards explaining the modest achievements in developing democratic institutions and the economy.[14]

3. *The means are inappropriate for the ends*

The inappropriateness of available means for the desired ends presents the opposite problem to that of the inadequacy of resources. While the question of limited resources – money, personnel, and international attention – depresses the standards against which a post-conflict operation can be judged, artificially high international expectations may nevertheless be imposed in certain areas of governance. Particularly when the United Nations itself assumes a governing role, there is a temptation to demand the highest standards of democracy, human rights, the rule of law, and the provision of services.

Balancing these against the need for locally sustainable goals presents difficult problems. A computerized electoral registration system may be manifestly ill-suited to a county with a low level of literacy and intermittent electricity, but should an international NGO refrain from opening a world-class clinic if such levels of care are unsustainable? An abrupt drop from high levels of care once the crisis and international interest passes would be disruptive, but lowering standards early implies acceptance that people who might otherwise have been treated will suffer. This was the dilemma faced by the International Committee of the Red Cross, which transferred control of the Dili National Hospital to national authorities in East Timor almost a year before independence.

Although most acute in areas such as health, the issue arises in many aspects of transitional administration. In the best tradition of autocracies, the international missions in Bosnia and Kosovo subscribed to the vast majority of human rights treaties and then discovered *raisons d'Etat* that required these to be abrogated. Efforts to promote the rule of law tend to focus more on the prosecution of the highest profile crimes of the recent past than on developing institutions to manage criminal law in the near future. Humanitarian and development assistance is notorious for being driven more by supply than demand, with the result that those projects that are funded tend to represent the interests – and, frequently, the products and personnel – of donors rather than recipients. Finally, staging elections in conflict zones has become something of an art-form, though more than half a dozen elections in Bosnia have yet to produce a workable government.

Different issues arise in the area of human resources. Staffing such operations always takes place in an atmosphere of crisis, but personnel tend to be selected from a limited pool of applicants (most of them internal) whose skills may be

[14] See James Dobbins et al., America's Role in Nation-Building: From Germany to Iraq 160–66 (2003).

irrelevant to the tasks at hand. In East Timor, for example, it would have made sense to approach Portuguese-speaking governments to request that staff with experience in public administration be seconded to the UN mission. Instead, it was not even possible to require Portuguese (or Tetum or Bahasa Indonesia) as a language. Positions are often awarded for political reasons or simply to ensure that staff lists are full – once in place, there is no effective mechanism to assess an individual's suitability or to remove him or her quickly if this proves warranted. A separate problem is the assumption that international staff who do possess relevant skills are also able to train others in the same field. This is an entirely different skill, however, and simply pairing international and local staff tends to provide less on-the-job training than extended opportunities to stand around and watch – a problem exacerbated by the fact that English tends to be used as the working language. One element of the "light footprint" approach adopted in Afghanistan that is certainly of general application is the need to justify every post occupied by international staff rather than a local. Cultivating relations with diaspora communities may help address this problem, serving the dual function of recruiting culturally-aware staff and encouraging the return of skilled expatriates more generally.

The "can-do" attitude of many people within the UN system is one of the most positive qualities that staff bring to a mission. If the problem is getting a hundred tonnes of rice to ten thousand starving refugees, niceties of procedure are less important than getting the job done. When the problem is governing a territory, however, procedure is more important. In such circumstances, the "can-do" attitude may become a cavalier disregard for local sensibilities. Moreover, many staff in such situations are not used to criticism from the population that they are "helping," with some regarding it as a form of ingratitude. Where the United Nations assumes the role of government, it should expect and welcome criticism appropriate to that of the sort of political environment it hopes to foster. Security issues may require limits on this, but a central element in the development of local political capacity is encouraging discussion among local actors about what sort of country theirs is going to be. International staff sometimes bemoan the prospect of endless consultation getting in the way of their work, but in many ways that conversation is precisely the point of their presence in the territory.

II. *State-building and the war on terror*

The primary barrier to establishing transitional administration-type operations in areas such as Somalia, Western Sahara, and the Democratic Republic of the Congo has less to do with the difficulty of such operations than with the absence of political will to commit resources to undertake them. The "war on terror" has transformed this agenda, though triage is performed less according to need than to the strategic priorities of the dominant actors, most prominently the United States. Though the operations in Afghanistan and Iraq are not transitional administrations as understood in this chapter, they are suggestive of how the state-building agenda has changed.

In the course of the US-led intervention in Afghanistan in late 2001 – in particular, as the likelihood of capturing Osama bin Laden "dead or alive" diminished – a rhetorical shift became evident in the Bush administration's war aims. "Nation-building,"[15] something that Bush had previously derided as inappropriate for the US military, came back onto the US agenda. And, with increasing frequency, the Taliban regime and its mistreatment of the Afghan civilian population were presented as the real evil, rather than being ancillary to the man and the organization that attacked the United States on 11 September 2001. These developments highlighted the changing strategic and political environment within which state-building takes place. The proximate cause was the adoption of state-building as a tool in the "war on terror," but underlying this was an emerging view that the United States should be more ready to use its power in the world.

1. *Nation-building and the national interest*

During the 2000 US presidential campaign, candidate Bush was openly critical of the use of US military resources for nation-building purposes. He affirmed this position once in office, including statements in July 2001 stressing that the United States military "should be used to fight and win war."[16] Bush made similar comments in the weeks after the 11 September 2001 attacks, when he stated that "we're not into nation-building, we're focused on justice."[17] Days before the United States commenced military operations in Afghanistan, however, the President's spokesman marked a slight shift in position as it became apparent that international support for the impending conflict might depend on the broader consequences for the Afghan people: the United States had no intention of engaging in nation-building, but it would "help those who seek a

[15] The term "nation-building," sometimes used in this context, is a broad, vague, and often pejorative one. Although it continues to be used in this context, "nation-building" has a more specific meaning in the post-colonial context, in which new leaders attempted to rally a population within sometimes arbitrary territorial frontiers. The focus here is on the *state* (that is, the highest institutions of governance in a territory) rather than the *nation* (a people who share common customs, origins, history, and frequently language) as such.

[16] George W. Bush, *Remarks by the President in Roundtable Interview with Foreign Press* (Washington, DC, July 17, 2001), *at* <http://www.whitehouse.gov>.

[17] George W. Bush, *Remarks by President Bush and Prime Minister Koizumi of Japan in Photo Opportunity* (Washington, DC, Sept. 25, 2001), *at* <http://www.whitehouse.gov>.

peaceful, economically-developing Afghanistan that's free from terrorism."[18] This was elaborated by the President himself in a news conference after the military action had begun, including a more substantial role for the United Nations in rebuilding Afghanistan:

> I believe that the *United Nations* would – could provide the framework necessary to help meet those conditions. It would be a useful function for the United Nations to take over the so-called "nation-building" – I would call it the stabilization of a future government – after our military mission is complete. We'll participate; other countries will participate [...]. I've talked to many countries that are interested in making sure that the post-operations Afghanistan is one that is stable, and one that doesn't become yet again a haven for terrorist criminals.[19]

US war aims thus evolved from a retributive strike, to a defensive response, and finally to embrace the broader goals of ensuring the stability of post-conflict Afghanistan. As the war aims changed, so, with the benefit of hindsight, did the asserted motivation for US military operations in the first place. This appeared to be a carefully scripted shift, as shown in two important speeches by President Bush. Speaking to the United Nations in November 2001, he equated the Taliban regime with the terrorists who had attacked the United States: the regime and the terrorists were "virtually indistinguishable. Together they promote terror abroad and impose a reign of terror on the Afghan people. Women are executed in Kabal's [*sic*] soccer stadium. They can be beaten for wearing socks that are too thin. Men are jailed for missing prayer meetings. The United States, supported by many nations, is bringing justice to the terrorists in Afghanistan."[20] Then, in his 2002 State of the Union Address, Bush sought to expand this into a more general doctrine intimating that the US action stemmed from goals loftier than self-defence:

> We have no intention of imposing our culture. But America will always stand firm for the non-negotiable demands of human dignity: the rule of law; limits on the power of the state; respect for women; private property; free speech; equal justice; and religious tolerance. America will take the side of brave men and women who advocate these values around the world, including the Islamic world, because we have a greater objective than eliminating threats and containing resentment. We seek a just and peaceful world beyond the war on terror.[21]

---

[18] Ari Fleischer, *Press Briefing* (Washington, DC, Oct. 4, 2001), *at* <http://www.whitehouse.gov>.

[19] George W. Bush, *President Holds Prime Time News Conference* (Washington, DC, Oct. 11, 2001), *at* <http://www.whitehouse.gov>.

[20] George H. W. Bush, *Address to the United Nations General Assembly* (New York, United Nations, Sept. 21, 1992), *at* <http://bushlibrary.tamu.edu/research/papers/1992/92092100.html>.

[21] George W. Bush, *State of the Union Address* (Washington, DC, 29 January 2002), *at* <http://www.whitehouse.gov>.

One year after the 11 September 2001 attacks, nation-building was implicitly included in the National Security Strategy issued by the White House. Much of the document elaborated and justified the concept of pre-emptive intervention; together with the stated policy of dissuading potential adversaries from hoping to equal the power of the United States, it implicitly asserted a unique status for the United States as existing outside of international law as it applies to other states.[22] At the same time, however, the National Security Strategy noted that threats to the United States now came not from fleets and armies but from "catastrophic technologies in the hands of the embittered few." In such a world, failing states pose a greater menace to US interests than conquering ones.[23]

The transformed strategic environment presents both opportunities and dangers for state-building. Recognition that weak states can create threats that reach beyond their borders may increase the level of international interest in supporting those states, indirectly providing benefits to the populations. This argument has been made, for example, to encourage intervention for human protection purposes in Liberia by the United States and in the South Pacific by Australia, although in both cases the link with terrorism was tenuous.[24] The connection was also made in the National Security Strategy, which stressed that when violence erupts and states falter, the United States will "work with friends and partners to alleviate suffering and restore stability."[25] When interventions are justified by the national interest, however, this may lower the standards to which post-conflict reconstruction is held. The level of physical and economic security required in Afghanistan to prevent it becoming a terrorist haven, for example, is not the same as that required for the basic peace and prosperity of the general population. This was reflected in the methods used by the United States to pursue its objectives in Afghanistan: by minimizing the use of its own troops in favour of using Afghan proxies, more weapons were introduced into a country that was already heavily armed, empowering groups that fought on the side of the United States – whether or not they supported the embryonic regime of Hamid Karzai. Many Afghans saw these power relations as reinforced

---

22 The National Security Strategy of the United States of America (President of the United States, Washington, DC, Sept. 2002), *at* <http://www.whitehouse.gov/nsc/nss.html>. Cf. the draft Defense Planning Guidance leaked in 1992: *Excerpts from Pentagon's Plan: "Prevent the Re-Emergence of a New Rival,"* N.Y. Times, March 8, 1992. The 1992 document was drafted by Paul D. Wolfowitz, then Under-Secretary of Defense for Policy and later Deputy Secretary of Defense under President George W. Bush, for approval by Dick Cheney, Secretary of Defense in 1992 and later Vice-President. Criticism of its unilateralist message led to a substantial redrafting.

23 National Security Strategy, *supra* note 22, 1.

24 *See, e.g.*, Augustine Toure, *Liberia: Why Doing Too Little May Hurt US Long-term Interest*, New Democrat, July 16, 2003; Elsina Wainwright, *Our Failing Neighbour: Australia and the Future of Solomon Islands*, 14 (June 2003), *at* <http://www.aspi.org.au>.

25 National Security Strategy, *supra* note 22, 9.

by the Emergency Loya Jirga in June 2002, which appeared to show that the position of warlords and other local commanders would not be challenged by international actors.[26]

None of this, of course, is new. Coercive diplomacy, the use of force, and military occupation have long been used by powerful states to further their interests; claims that occupation serves noble motives have an equally long pedigree. What is relatively new is the rejection of colonization as an element of foreign policy from around the middle of the twentieth century. Modern sensibilities therefore prevent explicit reference to occupation or colonization as a model for transitional administration, a constraint that at times prevents the learning of valuable lessons from decolonization in particular. There is a danger, however, that strategic interests may now begin to erode this prohibition in favour of a greater preparedness not merely to intervene, but to occupy and transform other states along the models of Afghanistan and Iraq. Such a development would be undesirable in principle, as it forms part of a broader attack on international law that proposes to order the world not around norms and institutions but the benevolent goodwill of the United States.[27] And yet it would also be undesirable in practice, as it is far from clear that the United States is either willing or able to fulfil such a role.

2. *The indispensable nation*

In debates within the United Nations and elsewhere, much attention has been focused on the unwillingness of the United States to engage in state-building. But there is also some evidence that the United States is not well-suited to such activities. The importance of domestic politics in the exercise of US power means that it has an exceptionally short attention span – far shorter than is needed to complete the long and complicated task of rebuilding countries that have seen years or decades of war, economic ostracism, and oppression under brutal leaders. More importantly, when the United States has assumed state-building responsibilities in Afghanistan and Iraq, it was justified at home as an element of the war on terror. This was reflected in the strategies adopted in each case, with military priorities ranking well above political goals for either country.

The United States is not alone in suffering from foreign policy "attention deficit disorder," but its hegemonic position and global footprint increase the significance of this condition. The United States spends more on its defence budget than the next 15 countries combined, it is the only country with five military commands

---

[26] Chris Johnson et al., *Afghanistan's Political and Constitutional Development* (2003), *at* <http://www.odi.org.uk/hpg>.

[27] *See, e.g.*, Richard Perle, *Thank God for the Death of the UN*, Guardian, March 21, 2003.

spanning the entire planet, and it is unrivalled in its capacity to move troops and hardware. Reference to US imperialism, which increased exponentially with the invasions of Afghanistan and Iraq, was common during the years of the Vietnam War. What is different in its contemporary manifestation is that the discussion is often neither hostile nor apologetic – indeed, a common criticism of the perceived US empire is that it does not exercise its power sufficiently. Michael Ignatieff has termed this phenomenon "Empire Lite," though it bears similarities to the British policies of indirect rule.[28] Whereas indirect rule was developed in part out of weakness, however (notably the practical impossibility of administering Nigeria), US imperial ambivalence derives in equal part from its democratic traditions, its isolationist tendencies, and its adherence to anti-colonial norms that it helped to establish. The potential for a US imperium is also constrained by the changed nature of how power is exercised: US military power may be unrivalled, but its economic strength is not. Both economically and culturally, the United States has greater influence than any other state, but that influence depends upon a free flow of capital and ideas that would be undermined by extensive reliance upon military might.[29]

This may change. How the United States manages its de facto empire and the choices that it makes between unilateral and multilateral responses to problems that are increasingly global will determine much of twenty-first century history. Machiavelli advised his Prince that it was better to be feared than loved, but this was only because it was difficult to unite both qualities in one person.[30] It is perhaps a uniquely American notion that countries inferior in power to the United States should not resent their subordinate status – that, if it is nice enough, Washington might construct a benevolent empire in which all love it.[31] Afghanistan and Iraq may serve as proving grounds for this vision.

III. *Conclusion*

> Above all we must remember that the ways of Orientals are not our ways, nor their thoughts our thoughts. Often when we think them backward and stupid, they think us meddlesome and absurd. The loom of time moves slowly with them, and they

---

[28] Michael Ignatieff, Empire Lite: Nation Building in Bosnia, Kosovo, Afghanistan (2003). See also Niall Ferguson, Empire: The Rise and Demise of the British World Order and the Lessons for Global Power (2003).

[29] See generally Joseph S. Nye, The Paradox of American Power: Why the World's Only Superpower Can't Go It Alone (2002).

[30] Niccolò Machiavelli, The Prince and the Discourses ch. xvii ([1531] 1950).

[31] Stephen Peter Rosen, *An Empire, If You Can Keep It*, 71 The National Interest 51 (Spring 2003).

> care not for high pressure and the roaring of the wheels. Our system may be good for us; but it is neither equally, nor altogether good for them. Satan found it better to reign in hell than to serve in heaven; and the normal Asiatic would sooner be misgoverned by Asiatics than well governed by Europeans.
>
> George Nathaniel Curzon[32]

A measure of the speed with which the UN Interim Administration Mission in Kosovo was established is the name itself. UN operations typically operate under an acronym, but "UNIAMIK" was dismissed as too much of a mouthful. "UNIAK" sounded like a cross between "eunuch" and "maniac" – associations judged unlikely to help the mission. "UNMIK" was the final choice, having the benefits of being short, punchy, and clear. Only in English, however. Once the operation was on the ground, it was discovered that *anmik*, in the dialect of Albanian spoken in Kosovo, meant "enemy." No one within the United Nations was aware of the confusion until it was too late, at which point instructions went out to pronounce the acronym "oon-mik."

Just as generals are sometimes accused of planning to re-fight their last war, so the United Nations experiments in transitional administration have reflected only gradual learning. Senior UN officials now acknowledge that, to varying degrees, Kosovo got the operation that should have been planned for Bosnia four years earlier, and East Timor got that which should have been sent to Kosovo. Afghanistan's very different "light footprint" approach draws, in turn, upon the outlines of what Lakhdar Brahimi argued would have been appropriate for East Timor in 1999.

The United Nations may never again be called upon to repeat operations comparable to Kosovo and East Timor, where it exercised sovereign powers on a temporary basis. Even so, it is certain that the circumstances that demanded such interventions will recur. Lessons derived from past experiences of transitional administration will be applicable whenever the United Nations or other international actors engage in complex peace operations that include a policing function, civilian administration, development of the rule of law, establishment of a national economy, the staging of elections, or all of the above. Learning from such lessons has not, however, been one of the strengths of the United Nations.

The proposal to establish a Peacebuilding Commission within the UN system had initially raised the prospect of a change in this trend. However, the watering down of the analytical capacity of its proposed support office and the removal of any early warning function disappointed those who had hoped for the new body to have a meaningful impact on strategic issues. However its role may evolve in the years to come, a key question will be how the Commission includes the

---

32 George N. Curzon, Persia and the Persian Question 630 (1966).

voices of populations on the receiving end of benevolent autocracy. Curzon's observations from his 1889 trip to Persia on "the ways of Orientals," quoted above, were insightful but uncharacteristic. As Viceroy of India, he did not appoint a single Indian to his advisory council; when asked why, he replied, absurdly, that in the entire country there was not an Indian fit for the post. Modern trusteeships demand, above all, trust on the part of local actors. Earning and keeping that trust requires a level of understanding, sensitivity, and respect for local traditions and political aspirations that has often been lacking in transitional administration. How that trust is managed will, in large part, determine its legacy.

Transitional administration will remain an exceptional activity, performed on an ad hoc basis in a climate of institutional and political uncertainty. But in those rare situations in which the United Nations and other international actors are called upon to exercise state-like functions, they must not lose sight of their limited mandate to hold that sovereign power in trust for the population that will ultimately claim it.

The European Union as a State-Builder: Policies towards Serbia and Sri Lanka

*Marlies Glasius & Denisa Kostovicova**

I. *EU External Policies: "High" and "Low" Politics*

The founders of the original European Coal and Steel Community believed that if they promoted integration at the level of society through common infrastructure like steel and coal, through economic relations such as trade and finance, and through people-to-people links, the high politics of security and foreign policy would eventually follow. In keeping with this founding philosophy, the European Union's emphasis, and its greatest strides, have until recently always been in the area of "low politics". This is true for its external relations as well as its domestic policy. But the European Union has in recent years become more ambitious in terms of its global role in "high politics," in particular in relation to security and crisis management.

The failure of the European Union (EU) to act in an effective and co-ordinated way during the crises in the former Yugoslavia led to a revision in the provisions on Common Foreign and Security Policy (CFSP) in the Amsterdam Treaty, and the appointment of Javier Solana as High Representative or "face" of the EU's external policies. The EU has since set "headline goals" both for its military capabilities and civilian personnel that could be deployed in crisis situations outside the Union. In 2003 it deployed its first external missions, to Bosnia-Herzegovina, Former Yugoslav Republic of Macedonia and the Congo, and at the time of writing it was engaged in no less than sixteen military, civilian or mixed missions.[1] But because the member states wish to keep close control over their high politics, high and low politics are developed by different institutions,

---

* An earlier version of this article was published in 56 (1) SÜDOSTEUROPA 84–114 (2008).

[1] Human Security Study Group, *A European Way of Security: The Madrid Report of the Human Security Study Group Comprising a Proposal and Background Report* 3 (Nov. 8, 2007), *at* <http://www.lse.ac.uk/Depts/global/PDFs/Madrid%20Report%20Final%20for%20distribution.pdf>.

	High Politics	**Low Politics**
Institution:	Council/Member states	Commission
Priority:	Stability, good relations	Development
Instruments:	Negotiation, intervention	Aid and trade
Aimed at:	Governments	Societies

Countries and Regions:

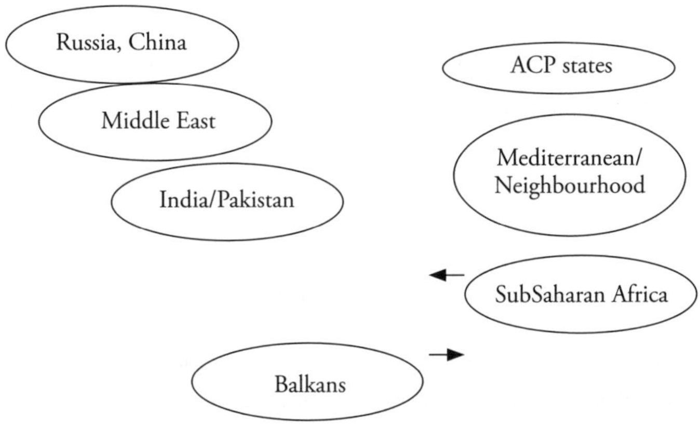

Figure 1 EU External Policies: High and Low.

with different logics, more or less in isolation from each other. Some regions are primarily subject to high politics, other primarily to low politics (see fig. 1).

EU foreign policy remains split between the Council and the Commission. Outside events, topics, and indeed entire regions get coded "security" or "development," and accordingly one or the other institution responds. Until now, security issues have been looked after by the inter-governmental Council, while development has been taken care of by the supra-national Commission. Both institutions are now heavily involved in what might be termed "state-strengthening," but each has different traditions, assumptions and instruments, and therefore different limitations. Moreover, where the two approaches do meet, policies are prone to becoming guided more by bureaucratic struggles between the Council and the Commission than by the needs of citizens of weak states or the aspirations of European citizens.

The failed European Constitution made several proposals to mitigate this competition, including having a single representative for foreign policy, and an amalgamated European external action service answerable to this figure. The Lisbon Treaty has largely reincorporated these proposals, albeit in more modest terms. However, even if the Treaty does achieve universal ratification, the legacy of separated and competing strands of foreign policy is not likely to be undone at a stroke.

Within the framework of state-building, we focus on "state-strengthening," i.e. developing policies designed to reinforce weak states, rather than rebuilding from scratch entirely failed states. State-strengthening captures a set of challenges the EU and other institutions encounter much more frequently than pure state failure, which tends to dominate the state-building literature. We focus on "ailing" states,[2] whose malfunction both in terms of provision of national cohesion and public goods stems from their weakness. This weakness is self-perpetuating and not necessarily heading for state failure.

Without rational, accountable and liberal institutions, the state is an empty shell and a protective shield at the disposal of the few. At the same time, it is an indispensable infrastructure for predatory political elites and their clients in the pursuit of partial interests. In fact, the state's complete failure would jeopardise their interests. These elites are "ruminants," as Wade describes them, borrowing from John Waterbury, since they graze the resource base while fertilising it at the other end. Hence, they are to be distinguished from "vampire"-type elites that extract so much from the state as to debilitate.[3] In sum, state weakness, that becomes a chief source of non-traditional security threats with local and global implications, is in their vested interest.

We compare two "ailing states," Serbia and Sri Lanka, which have been treated very differently by the EU, but which, we argue, have much in common in terms of structural weaknesses and hidden strengths, in order to illustrate the problems raised by the two separate approaches pursued by the EU.[4] On the basis of these case studies, we will argue that the EU could overcome the myopia of its security or development approaches by basing all its external state-building efforts on a coherent human security vision underpinned by a set of principles that would apply throughout European foreign policy.

II. *Commonalities between the "Ailing States" Serbia and Sri Lanka*

1. *Contested Polities*

The borders of both Serbia and Sri Lanka are contested. In both cases, some areas are effectively out of control of the central government, while their international status is dubious, and at least part of the citizenry feels they should be under government control.

---

2 We acknowledge Shiral Lakhtilala of the Berghof Foundation, Colombo, as our source for this appropriate term.

3 Robert Wade, Governing the Market: Economic Theory and the Role of Government in East Asian Industrialization 358 fn. 3 (2004).

4 In the case of Sri Lanka, we focus on the response to the tsunami as epitomising both the character of state weakness and the flaws in EU policy.

In 2000, Serbia emerged out of the wars of the previous decade and embraced the democratisation project as an "improvised state."[5] The violent implementation of the Serbian national project of uniting "all Serbs in one state", centred on Serb-populated areas in Croatia and Bosnia-Herzegovina as well as the forceful termination of Kosovo's autonomy, failed to produce the desired outcome. The territorial integrity of Croatia and Bosnia-Herzegovina was preserved, so was that of the then Federal Republic of Yugoslavia, subsequently Serbia and Montenegro. However, at the same time, the borders of Serbia and Montenegro were left open to the possibility of future revision. By early 2008, Serbia was confronted with a "double loss:" a loss of Montenegro after the disintegration of the state of Serbia and Montenegro, and a loss of Kosovo. Although fears of major destabilisation in the region after these two events turned out to be wrong, they have had a direct impact on Serbia's interaction with the EU.

After the regime-change in Belgrade, Serbia faced an independence movement from Montenegro, its sister republic, comprising the Federal Republic of Yugoslavia (FRY). The crisis between Serbia, which sought to preserve the federation, and Montenegro was resolved under the auspices of the EU in 2002. Based on the policy of preservation of the joint state, EU's Foreign Policy Chief Javier Solana brokered the creation of the union of Serbia and Montenegro, accordingly nicknamed "*Solania*". A belated adoption of the Constitutional Charter by the FRY parliament in early 2003 marked the beginning of the new state. Importantly, it removed the possibility of an immediate referendum on independence in Montenegro, which, it was believed, would trigger a referendum in Kosovo. The moratorium on a referendum on Montenegro's independence expired in 2006, coinciding with the beginning of the negotiations on the final status on Kosovo. By that time, the dysfunctional nature of the new state had emerged as yet another obstacle in the process of European integration of both Serbia and Montenegro. Consequently, it forced a change in the EU's original approach that favoured the union between the two states.[6] In the event, the role of the EU in brokering the terms of the independence referendum by setting the threshold for a "yes" vote at 55 percent and in appointing its representative to the Montenegrin Electoral Commission, which was critical for certifying the result, had an important legitimating impact on the entire process.[7] The current role of the EU in Kosovo is already subject to a legitimacy challenge.

---

[5] Cf. Slobodanka Ast, *Milan St. Protić: Meni niko ne treba da soli pamet!* [Milan St. Protić: I don't need preaching!], VREME No. 554, Aug. 16, 2001.

[6] Cf. Karsten Kris, *The Referendum in Montenegro: The EU's 'Postmodern Diplomacy'*, 12 EUROPEAN FOREIGN AFFAIRS REVIEW 67–88 (2007).

[7] Srdjan Darmanović, *Montenegro: A Miracle in the Balkans?*, 18 JOURNAL OF DEMOCRACY 152–159 (2007).

After the NATO intervention in 1999 ended the Serb minority rule and the ethnic violence in Kosovo, Kosovo became a UN protectorate. The original conflict over the ethnic claims to Kosovo remained unresolved. On the one hand, Serbs in Serbia and minority Serbs in Kosovo claimed Kosovo to be an integral part of Serbia. On the other hand, Kosovo's majority Albanians sought independence. The 1244 United Nations Security Council Resolution that introduced the UN administration stipulated that Kosovo's final status would be determined in negotiations, which began in February 2006. The final status talks took place in Vienna under UN auspices, chaired by former Finnish President, Martti Ahtisaari. The talks were focused on a discussion of non-status issues, given that the two sides entered the process with diametrically opposite views. The final status question overshadowed the talks and any constructive engagement by the parties remained elusive, prompting a change of strategy. The UN Special Envoy was given the task of drafting a solution. This move signalled the attempt to impose a solution with the backing of the international community. In March 2007, Ahtisaari submitted a document to the UN Secretary General, along with a report, that says that "the only viable option for Kosovo is independence, to be supervised for an initial period by the international community."[8] The document itself contains a detailed outline of the internal governance architecture of the future independent Kosovo, accompanied by an elaborate outline of international supervision with civilian and military presence.[9] The adoption of the package by the UN Security Council in spring 2007 was blocked by Russia's opposition to a non-negotiated and imposed solution, which led to another 120 days of negotiations under the auspices of the Contact Group. The futility of yet another round of talks led to the unilateral declaration of independence by Kosovo Albanians on 17 February 2008, though not without coordination with their partners in the international community, primarily the US, the United Kingdom, France and Germany. While the EU remained divided over the recognition of independence, Serbia and Russia opposed the move, requesting, in vain, its annulment by the UN Security Council.

In the post 2000 period, the prospects and the eventual independence of Kosovo and Montenegro enhanced the anxiety of the Serbian political elites. They elevated the concerns with Serbia's borders and territory into a priority issue competing with and even sidelining the post-Communist and post-conflict

[8] *Letter Dated 26 March 2007 from the Secretary-General Addressed to the President of the Security Council; Report of the Special Envoy of the Secretary General on Kosovo's Future Status*, United Nations S/2007/168, March 26, 2007, *at* <http://www.unosek.org/docref/report-english.pdf>.

[9] *Letter Dated 26 March 2007 from the Secretary-General Addressed to the President of the Security Council*; Addendum, *Comprehensive Proposal for the Kosovo Status Settlement*, United Nations S/2007/168/Add.1, March 26, 2007, *at* <http://www.unosek.org/docref/Comprehensive_proposal-english.pdf>; <http://www.unosek.org/unosek/index.html>.

reform agenda.[10] At the same time, Serbia's uncertain borders accentuated the need for the EU to act as a security provider in the region, while at the same time attempting to advance its enlargement agenda with various degrees of success.

After independence, Sri Lanka increasingly moved, in law and in fact, towards the model of a unitary, majoritarian state, favouring the Sinhala majority over Tamil speakers and condoning periodic massacres. This sparked armed rebellion of Tamil youngsters in the late 1970s, with the Liberation Tigers of Tamil Eelam (LTTE) emerging as the dominant group. It seeks an independent homeland, "Tamil Eelam" for ethnic Tamils, and has held territory designated as the core of a nascent Tamil Eelam since the mid-1980s. Periods of barren peace negotiations and open warfare have followed each other intermittently since. The last ceasefire agreement, dating from 2002, was officially abrogated by the government in early 2008, although severe and numerous breaches on both sides had long since made it a dead letter. The shortcomings of the 2002–2005 negotiations have been extensively documented elsewhere,[11] but one of the main weaknesses was the underlying assumption that the government could "deliver" universal support for the process on the part of the Sinhala majority, and the LTTE could similarly "deliver" the Northeast.

Instead, the last government relied on the minority support of the left-nationalist party JVP (*Janatha Vimukthi Peramuna* – People's Liberation Front), which was dead-set against the peace process, while the iron grip of the LTTE leadership over the Tamil people also came under challenge. In March 2004 a break-away faction was formed, led by commander Karuna, who claimed that LTTE privileged the needs of Northern over East Coast Tamils. LTTE has since tried to exterminate Karuna and his followers, while elements of the army and military intelligence exploited the Karuna split, which challenges the idea that the Tamils are a homogeneous group and the LTTE is their sole legitimate representative. This low-intensity but bitter three-way conflict is marked primarily by assassinations, bombings and disappearances. The military significance of the Karuna faction may have dwindled, with Karuna himself now being held in custody in the United Kingdom, but his group, the TMVP (*TamilEela Makkal Viduthalai Pulikal* – TamilEela People's Liberation Tigers), continues to compete for political power in the East. It has recently won local elections, marred by violence on all sides, in Batticaloa.[12]

---

[10] Slobodan Cuparić, *Gordo posrtanje* [Proud stumbling], NEZAVISNA SVETLOST, April 4, 2002, *at* <http://www.svetlost.co.yu>.

[11] Cf. JONATHAN GOODHAND & BART KLEM, AID, CONFLICT AND PEACE BUILDING IN SRI LANKA, 2000–2005 (2005), *at* <http://www.asiafoundation.org/publications/pdf/208>; LIZ PHILIPSON & YUVI THANGARAJAH, THE POLITICS OF THE NORTH-EAST (2005) *at* <http://www.asiafoundation.org/publications/pdf/212>.

[12] Randeep Ramesh, *Jailed Tamil Warlord Has Deadly Influence on Election in Batticaloa*, THE GUARDIAN, March 7, 2008.

Moreover, as the peace negotiations appeared to be bringing Tamil self-government a step closer to reality, there has been increasing conflict between Tamils and Muslims in Eastern Sri Lanka. Muslim youths have in recent years become increasingly radicalised, frustrated about being squeezed between the main parties in the conflict, and encouraged by the apparent example set by the LTTE experience, that the use of violence buys respect and a place at the negotiating table.[13] While Muslims live in geographically dispersed areas, a "Pondicherry model" of Muslim autonomy in a series of non-contiguous areas predominantly inhabited by Muslims has been floated.[14]

The contested nature of the territory has a double deleterious effect on the governability of both Serbia and Sri Lanka. First, it raises practical problems in every field of government, from the birth registry to transport policies to customs or crime prevention. Secondly, it means that every area of policy becomes poisoned with the "national question", and contingent upon hotly contested "final solutions."

2. *State Weakness*

In Serbia, like in its West Balkan neighbours, state weakness is a manifestation of a double legacy of Communism and conflict. The state in the Balkans is weak in a structural as well as a political sense: it cannot provide public goods and it lacks political, national and social cohesion. Weak state capacity is exacerbated by a predatory project of the elites set on extracting resources from the state itself. Consequently, a weak state becomes both a subject and an obstacle of political and democratic liberalisation, as it creates space for corruption and unofficial economy, hinders structural economic reform and development, and accounts for the inability to establish proper market institutions.[15]

In addition, the Balkans have seen an expansion of organised criminal networks, which had been cultivated during the conflict.[16] The end of the war precipitated global integration of these networks in a quest for new sources of income. In this context, the Balkans as a region assumed several roles. It established itself as a transit route, as a destination, but, also, due to impoverishment and insecurity, as a source of illicit commodities. Revenues generated by organised crime in cooperation with transnational networks, are used directly to undermine the state's political institutions and economy. A combination of informal practices

---

[13] Goodhand & Klem, *supra* note 11, 53; Interview with Mirak Raheem, Research Associate, Centre for Policy Alternatives, Colombo, Sept. 1, 2005.

[14] Goodhand & Klem, *supra* note 11, 54.

[15] Cf. Ivan Krastev, *Weak State as a Security Threat*, 44 (4) Südosteuropa Mitteilungen 102–116 (2004).

[16] Peter Andreas, *Criminalized Legacies of War: The Clandestine Political Economy of the Western Balkans*, 51 (3) Problems of Post-Communism 3–9 (2004).

and institutions, and of organised crime linked to the criminalised elements of the state, has undermined the democratisation project. The assassination of the Serbian Prime Minister Zoran Djindjić in 2003 by the criminal underground demonstrated how criminal elements had infiltrated the state security services. Criminal networks are also suspected of having been involved in war crimes.[17]

But this is not a scenario of a weak state necessarily edging into failure.[18] Rather, as Reno notes, in the post-Communist context, the existence of organised and informal structures depends on a state's ability to provide some public goods.[19] The perpetuation of state weakness becomes a self-interest to these structures, hence leading to a situation of sustained but unconsolidated democracy.[20] At the same time, a strong state also becomes a barrier to the predatory project of the elites. Hence, a perverse consensus operates between the elites and the underground on maintaining state weakness, without destroying the state altogether.

The daily manifestation of the state's omission to provide public goods since Milošević's fall, amidst a pervading sense of insecurity, has discredited the democratic process among the populace. Citizens have been left feeling helpless, or finding alternative recourses to fill the human security gap created by state corruption, criminalisation and inactivity. As the legitimacy of the elected as opposed to unelected institutions plummets, the opinion polls have recorded that 18 per cent of respondents trust the Serbian parliament and 22 per cent trust the government, while 63 per cent trust the Serbian Orthodox Church and 41 per cent trust the army.[21] In sum, according to the Centre for Free Elections and Democracy, citizens of Serbia have greater trust in social institutions or the so-called "people institutions," such as relatives, neighbours, priests, work colleagues, doctors, than the state institutions.[22]

While Sri Lanka is probably less penetrated by transnational criminal networks, the form that state weakness takes is remarkably similar to that in Serbia. As

---

[17] Miloš Vasić, Atentat na Zorana [Zoran's Assasination] 2005.

[18] Robert I. Rotberg, *The failure and collapse of nation-states: breakdown, prevention, and repair, in* When States Fail: Causes and Consequences 1 (Robert I. Rotberg ed., 2004).

[19] William Reno, *Shadow States and the Political Economy of Civil Wars, in* Greed and Grievance: Economic Agendas in Civil Wars 43, 55 (Mats Berdal & David M. Malone eds., 2000).

[20] Valerie Bunce, *Rethinking Recent Democratization: Lessons from Postcommunist Experience*, 55 World Politics 167 (2003).

[21] Centar za slobodne izbore i demokratiju (CeSID), *Socijalni i politički milje predsedničkih izbora. Istraživanje javnog mnenja Srbije, zima 2007/08. godine* [The Social and Political Milieu of the Presidential Elections. Public Opinion Poll in Serbia, Winter 2007/2008], 3 (2008), *at* <http://www.mediacenter.org.yu/upload/documents/izbori_2008/Izvestaj_CeSID_decembar_januar.pdf>.

[22] Ibid., 4 (Tabela 2: Ne/poverenje u društvene institucije jun 2007–decembar 2007 [Table 2: The lack of confidence in social institutions June 2007–December 2007]).

Frerks and Klem have put it, "the government may sometimes better not be seen as an agent necessarily acting for the common good, but rather as a structure through which individual agents operate for their own benefit."[23]

Governments are unstable, politics are personalised and subject to patronage, but a certain level of service provision is maintained, and the system is structurally weak, but by no means sliding into "state failure."

A combination of weak capacity, bureaucratic rigidity and rapacity was demonstrated in the central government's response to the tsunami. After having been virtually absent in the first week, the state response became extremely centralised. President Kumaratunga created various Colombo-based coordinating bodies, headed by personal confidants, sidelining even her own ministers. The most lasting of these bodies, the Task Force to Rebuild the Nation (TAFREN) has been singled out for particular criticism by all who dealt with it. It described itself as "facilitators, enablers, coordinators,"[24] but was treated with scorn by local NGO actors and foreign aid officials alike.[25] In an interview in September 2005, nine months after the tsunami, a TAFREN official acknowledged that they had been slow to establish a presence in the tsunami-affected regions, but expressed the hope that there would be such a presence in six to eight weeks.[26] As a result of centralisation, the district authorities, who had had a mixed but not wholly inadequate record in the immediate response, became paralysed.

A second effect of central government involvement was that aid became subject to patronage. The then Prime Minister, now the President, Mahinda Rajapakse, gave a particularly egregious example, concentrating his efforts on his own constituency, the Hambantota district. He stands accused of directing 83 million rupees (approximately € 665,000) of international donor money into the private "Helping Hambantota" fund.[27] Generally, national politicians focused on the South coast, because most of their constituency comes from the Sinhala majority in the South of the country.

In Sri Lanka as in Serbia, the weak and corrupt state has three effects on the citizenry: it fuels a generalised distrust of the state, it feeds into existing suspicions

---

[23] Georg Frerks & Bart Klem, Tsunami Response in Sri Lanka: Report on a Field Visit from 6–20 February 2005 (2005).

[24] Interview with Rachel Perera, NGO Coordinator, Task Force to Rebuild the Nation (TAFREN), Sept. 2, 2005.

[25] Interviews with Shiral Lakthilala, Senior Advisor, Berghof Foundation, Colombo, Aug. 29, 2005; Chammika Mallawaarachchi, Consortium of Humanitarian Agencies, Colombo, Aug. 29 2005; Merce de Torres LLosa, Development Cooperation Advisor, Delegation of the European Commission to Sri Lanka, Sept. 2, 2005.

[26] Interview Perera, *supra* note 24.

[27] *Police Probe PM Tsunami Fund*, BBC, Sept. 15, 2005, *at* <http://news.bbc.co.uk/1/hi/world/south_asia/4250190.stm>.

and envy between different communities, but also, perhaps more positively or at least ambiguously, it sparks local-level citizen initiatives to provide human security where the state is failing to do so.

3. *Lack of Social Cohesion*

As a consequence of ethnic nationalism and wars, the UN sanctions from 1992–1995, the translation of political loyalty into economic privilege during Milošević's rule, the disappearance of the middle class, and the reluctance by the state to confront the past after the wars, Serbia has emerged as a deeply fragmented society. The lines of division cut across the lines of welfare, ethnicity and ideology. The latter schism is reflected in a lack of consensus among the political elites and the population to work towards a liberal state.

Some 10 percent of the population in Serbia live below the poverty line. However, subjective perception of poverty is much more pronounced due to a dramatic decline of general welfare (in the 1990s the Gross Domestic Product [GDP] per capita dropped by some 50 percent) and high expectations of democratic change.[28]

At the same time, Serbia is the most ethnically diverse state in the Western Balkans, affected by occasional flare-ups of ethnic tensions. This, in turn, sustains an ethnic as opposed to civic dimension of Serbian identity. Even excluding Kosovo, it has significant ethnic minority populations of Hungarians and Slovaks in Vojvodina, Bosniaks in Sanjak, Albanians in Southern Serbia, Roma, etc.

Lastly, Serbia's democratisation has been overshadowed by a denial of its responsibility for war crimes on the territory of former Yugoslavia. This issue provides a key challenge for Serbia's European integration. On the one hand, Serbia's full cooperation with the International Criminal Tribunal for former Yugoslavia (ICTY) is one of the conditions for Serbia's advance in the process of European integration. On the other hand, the failure to face the nationalist past and break with it demonstrates an incompatibility between the state's tolerance for nationalism and its proclaimed Europeanisation.[29]

In Sri Lanka, the most obvious division, between Sinhala and Tamil, expressed in the military opposition between the army and the LTTE, obscures many more complicated divisions of religion, caste and region. Hill-country Tamils of recent

---

[28] Vlada [Republike Srbije], *Prvi izveštaj o implementaciji Strategije za smanjenje siromaštva u Srbiji* (2005), *at* <http://www.prsp.sr.gov.yu/download/Prvi%20izvestaj%20o%20implementaciji%20SSS.pdf>; Government of the Republic of Serbia, *First Progress Report on the Implementation of the Poverty Reduction Strategy in Serbia* (2005), *at* <http://www.prsp.sr.gov.yu/download/PRS%20Progress%20Report%20–%20English%20FINAL.pdf>.

[29] Denisa Kostovicova, *Civil Society and Post-Communist Democratization: Facing a Double Challenge in Post-Milošević Serbia*, 2 Journal of Civil Society 21–37 (2006).

Indian descent are looked down upon by the Tamils who have inhabited the island for millennia. East Coast Tamils resent Jaffna Tamils for dominating the LTTE when they have born the brunt of the conflict, and the high caste urban and rural elites, both Tamil and Sinhala, are believed to treat lower castes with disdain and indifference.

The response to the tsunami fed into all these long-standing grievances.[30] On the positive side, there have apparently not been any instances of severe deprivation: food, health care and transitional shelters were adequate for all, and while the latter leave a lot to be desired for long-term habitation, they are generally built to a better standard than is customary for IDP camps. The unsystematic response to the tsunami, and the lack of information available, has left almost every victim feeling that others have it better. At the macro-level, people in the North and East are convinced that victims in the South are better off because they received more government aid. In the South, the North and East are resented because they received the bulk of the international and Non Governmental Organisation (NGO) aid. These differential commitments might have become complementary, were it not for the fact that the international community has been severely hampered in implementing its plans for the North and East by the increased level of hostilities since early 2006.[31]

The complaints of different communities are not necessarily based on facts concerning the actual situation in other provinces. They feed into long-standing grievances concerning differential treatment of different ethnic groups. At the micro-level, too, there is a general perception that other communities, sometimes, but not necessarily of a different religious or ethnic affiliation, have received more, and are better off. The expression "golden tsunami" is often heard, always applying to what other people (for instance "the villages on that side of the bay")[32] have received.

Just as in Serbia, the civic dimension of what might constitute a Sri Lankan identity is overshadowed by ethnic identity, with the majority ethnicity attempting to conflate the two. Moreover, again similar to Serbia, citizenship is constructed as a claim to a share of the collective pie, of which too much is always grabbed by others, rather than a set of obligations and entitlements.

---

[30] For a more extensive discussion of the aftermath of the tsunami, see Marlies Glasius, *The EU Response to the Tsunami and the Need for a Human Security Approach*, 11 European Foreign Affairs Review 353–378 (2006).

[31] European Commission, *2007 Progress Report on the EC Post Tsunami Rehabilitation and Reconstruction Programme* 21–28 (Dec. 17, 2007), *at* <http://ec.europa.eu/world/tsunami/docs/2007_report_final.pdf>.

[32] Interview with women engaged in cash-for-work programme, Navaladi, Sept. 5, 2005.

4. *Local Civil Society Initiatives*

The citizens of Serbia and Sri Lanka are not always apathetic in the face of a malfunctioning state. They do organise in small groups to collectively provide basic security or basic services.

An illustrative example of the self-organisation of citizens is the effort to combat drug dealing and trafficking in Novi Sad, Serbia. For five years a mother has been fighting to save her son, a heavy drug user, by pleading with state institutions to crack down on dealers. Her futile attempts convinced her of the collusion between the state and criminal networks. According to her, every time the parents reported the dealers to the police, they would leave just before the police came, if it showed up at all: "All this assured me that we are completely helpless, left to our own devices."[33] Consequently, she founded the Citizens' Association for the Fight against Drugs, which now gathers about 2,000 people, mostly the parents of drug addicts. She explains why: "The strongest motive [for setting up an NGO] was that there were no adequate institutions to help our children, both in healthcare, in the police, including the politicians, in general, state organs who could offer us help and protection, and treatment for our children."[34]

This is not an isolated example of individual insecurity, prompting self-organisation of non-state actors in order to engage an otherwise unresponsive weak state. In fact, with a spread of political apathy among the population at large, combined with the lack of trust in the state institutions, it demonstrates a trend of the NGO sector emerging as the only vocal corrective to the failings of the weak state. However, due to the legacy of Communism and an aversion of post-Communist citizens to join voluntary organisations, as well as the tendency of the post-Communist state to view civil society as an opponent rather than a partner, civil society, like the state, is weak.[35] It also lacks a capacity to contribute to the strengthening of the state, and has limited impact on ameliorating state weakness.

In Sri Lanka, society's capacity for self-help in the absence of an adequate state response was demonstrated in the immediate aftermath of the tsunami. While, as described above, it took the Sri Lankan government a week to even set up a coordinating body, the initial emergency response to the tsunami was spontaneous, uncoordinated, but largely successful. As a Batticaloa-based commentator put it, "people were better off the day after than the victims of Katrina."[36] Frerks and Klem describe the situation as follows: "In the immediate

---

[33] Interview with a mother who launched the initiative, Novi Sad, May 5, 2004.

[34] Ibid.

[35] Kostovicova, *supra* note 29; Marje M. Howard, The Weakness of Civil Society in Post-Communist Europe (2003).

[36] Interview with T. Jayasingham, Senior Lecturer, Eastern University, Chenkalady, Sept. 5, 2005.

aftermath of the tsunami, rescue and life saving activities have been undertaken nearly instantaneously. Necessary medical aid was given within hours, dead bodies were buried and relief aid was mobilised within a day."[37] As a result, "the worst did not happen:" there were no major outbreaks of disease contributing to the death toll.

Moreover, the initial effort remarkably transcended ethnic and political boundaries, and caused unlikely partners to work together. One of the more striking features of the local response, particularly in the conflict environment in the Northeast, was the immediate setup of inclusive district coordinating committees within 24 to 48 hours, involving the district administration, the LTTE, the local NGOs, the international agencies and in Trincomalee also the army.[38]

The emergence of these structures may be less remarkable than they appear when it is taken into account that local civil servants in the Northeast are by and large Tamil (Trincomalee is an exception), and by and large loyal to or at least afraid of the LTTE. Nonetheless, the immediate cross-community response "had a positive emotional appeal, everyone was talking about pulling together and reconciliation [...] Immediately after the tsunami there was this upsurge for living in harmony."[39]

But these initiatives did not last. In the context of generalised distrust, described above, they were always fragile, but additionally they were crowded out and marginalised by the rigid state response and the overweening international response combined.

III. *Background to EU Relations with Serbia and Sri Lanka*

1. *The EU and Serbia: From "High" to "Low" Politics*

The fall of Slobodan Milošević after the fraudulent presidential elections and the subsequent victory of the united Serbian opposition in 2000 heralded the EU's qualitatively novel engagement with Serbia. Hitherto Serbia had been considered a "rogue state" in the region, and the EU's involvement with this country had primarily fallen under the remit of the Council, and the domain of high politics of security and foreign relations. Democratic change in Belgrade paved the way for the role of the Commission and engagement with Serbia within the framework of the European enlargement, specifically, the Stabilisation and Association process (SAp), designed for the Western Balkan aspirants to the EU membership. The EU's enlargement to the countries on the other side of

---

[37] Frerks & Klem, *supra* note 23.

[38] Interviews with Jayasingham; Jalamudin (LTTE), Head Project Implementation Centre, Mullaitivu, Sept. 8, 2005.

[39] Interview with S. I. Keethaponcalan, Senior Lecturer, University of Colombo, Aug. 30, 2005.

the Cold War divide in Europe was the extension of Europe-as-a-peace project model: ensuring peace and security via political and economic integration.[40] It offered a prospect of a European future to all countries and entities of the Western Balkans through a contractual relationship in the form of Stabilisation and Association Agreements (SAA) accompanied by a programme of assistance and asymmetric trade liberalisation.[41]

The objectives and conditionalities of the SAp were evolved from the model applied to the post-Communist countries in Central and Eastern Europe, but were tailored to meet the double challenge of post-conflict and post-Communist transition. As such, the SAp conditions were more demanding and more multifaceted than the conditions applied to Central and Eastern Europe, which were already stricter than those applied to earlier newcomers to the EU.[42] However, they were also shaped by an imperative to deal with the political, economic and security fallout of ethnic conflict in the Balkans. The EU has not been able to entirely relegate the involvement with Serbia from the Council to the Commission, nor has Serbia been able to make a clear-cut shift from being a "security" to becoming a "transition" issue. Therefore, the EU has continued to pursue simultaneously both security and enlargement approaches and policies towards Serbia. Instead of being mutually reinforcing, the two approaches have led to policy spill-overs and interference, ultimately slowing down rather than accelerating Serbia's European integration process. This is best illustrated by the approach to the final status of Kosovo.

The EU has insisted on the artificial separation of the issue of Kosovo's final status and Serbia's EU integration. The EU strategy was based on attempting to get Serbia locked into the process of EU integration, preferably with the SAA agreement, in order to make it difficult for Serbia to abandon the process after Kosovo's declaration of independence. This policy has failed. As the Kosovars' declaration became imminent, following the Serbian presidential elections in January 2008, the EU's last-ditch attempt was to offer Serbia a partial political agreement – yet another, though much more feeble form of tying Serbia into.[43] The EU signed the SAA with Serbia on 29 April 2008. Nonetheless,

---

[40] Karen E. Smith, *The Evolution and Application of EU Membership Conditionality, in* The Enlargement of the European Union 105, 107 (Marise Cremona ed., 2003).

[41] Fraser Cameron & Andreas Kintis, *Southeastern Europe and the European Union,* 1 Journal of South East European and Black Sea Studies 94 (2001).

[42] Karen E. Smith, *Western Actors and the Promotion of Democracy, in* Democratic Consolidation in Eastern Europe. Volume 2: International and Transnational Factors 31–57 (Jan Zielonka & Alex Pravda eds., 2001).

[43] The initial Serbian 'no' to the EU was paved by the resolution adopted by the Serbian parliament of Dec. 26, 2007. See *Rezolucija Narodne skupštine Republike Srbije o zaštiti suvereniteta, teritorijalnog integriteta i ustavnog poretka Republike Srbije* [Resolution of the National Parlia-

Serbia went on to obstruct the deployment of the EU's biggest ever rule of law mission, EULEX, in Kosovo's Serb-populated areas.[44] After months of delay, the mission became operational in the entire territory of Kosovo in December 2008. However, the price was a critical procedural and operational concession to Belgrade. The EULEX received a go-ahead from Serbia only after the United Nations authorised the deployment of the mission, effectively disassociating it from the concept of Kosovo's supervised independence. Also, according to the new arrangement, police, customs officers and judges in the Serb areas will remain under the umbrella of the United Nations mission in Kosovo. From Belgrade's perspective, the UN's involvement affirmed Serbia's territorial integrity. However, from Albanians' perspective, it rolled back Kosovo's sovereignty. The arrangement heralded ethnic division of labour in Kosovo, with the EU and the UN overseeing Albanian and Serbian areas respectively.

In sum, the EU's simultaneous involvement in the Balkans through its European Security and Defence Policy (ESDP) and Enlargement portfolios led to policy compromises in both areas. The EU signed the SAA without Serbia fully meeting the ICTY conditionality. At the same time, in order to pursue its ESDP involvement, the EU gave in to Serbia's requests regarding the deployment of the EULEX, practically reinstating the UN's rule in parts of Kosovo.

2. *The EU and Sri Lanka: A Stronger Commitment?*

Sri Lanka is a small middle-income country, far from Europe and without significant strategic resources. As such, it generally receives only limited attention from the international community. Europe's attention to the conflict in Sri Lanka has been very scant, particularly compared to its involvement with conflicts in, for instance, the Balkans or the Middle East. Since 2002, the European Union has been one of the four co-chairs in the peace negotiations between the Sri Lankan government and the LTTE, but this has been largely a passive role.

Sri Lanka has been much more the subject of development policy than of political foreign policy on the part of the EU, but even Europe's aid role was small. From 2002 to 2004, it disbursed 10–15 million euros to Sri Lanka per year. This limited interest in Sri Lanka was reflected in the number of staff dedicated to Sri Lanka in Brussels and on the ground. Until 2005, the EU's External Action Service had precisely one diplomat in Colombo, a *chargé d'affaires*, supported by half a dozen contract staff with no diplomatic status and another four staffers

ment of the Republic of Serbia on the Protection of Sovereignty, Territorial Integrity and Constitutional Order of the Republic of Serbia], *at* <http://www.parlament.sr.gov.yu/content/lat/akta/akta_detalji.asp?Id=465&t=Z>.

[44] This was in line with the rejection of the Ahtisaari plan. *Koštunica: Misija EU poništava SSP* [Kostunica: The EU mission annuls the SAA], B92, Jan. 27, 2008, at <www.b92.net>.

in the European Commission's Humanitarian Aid Office (ECHO). Generally, the diplomatic community in Colombo is very small, with just six of the EU members represented. This also had advantages: ties were close and informal, EU political matters were routinely jointly handled by the *chargé d'affaires* and the EU chairing ambassador, and the rivalry between Council and Commission in Brussels did not surface at the country level. Partly because of the small size of the delegation and partly because all aid is disbursed indirectly, through partners, the EU and Sri Lanka were virtually invisible to each other.

This suddenly changed when the tsunami of 26 December 2004 struck, affecting virtually the entire coastline. Unlike India and Thailand, Sri Lanka requested international assistance within hours of the disaster, and the EU was one of the first and most generous respondents to this call. In the first few days after the tsunami, the European Commission wired € 23 million to the Red Cross and various UN agencies. In the next few months, the EU disbursed a further € 100 million in relief funds, approximately 40% of which went to Sri Lanka. The Council was much slower to get into action. Immediately after the tsunami, the problem arose how to organise the relief effort in the LTTE-held coastal areas, which had been hard-hit. In the post-tsunami upsurge of inter-communal solidarity, this problem was soon constructed as an opportunity for an initiative to set up a joint tsunami response mechanism including both the government and the LTTE, which, it was hoped, would build trust and spark wider peace negotiations. Arguably, an immediate political response to the tsunami from the EU, rather than just a humanitarian response, pushing immediately and hard for a joint relief mechanism, might have capitalised upon the early sentiments of cross-communal solidarity in Sri Lanka. The EU did in fact signal its support for the joint mechanism during a visit by External Affairs Commissioner Ferrero-Waldner in early March, but by this time, the central government and the LTTE had both responded in their own way, and accusations were flying back and forth.

The transition from relief to reconstruction was slow on the part of the EU as well as other donors and receiving governments. The European Commission presented its detailed plans for reconstruction in late May 2005, five months after the tsunami.[45] For Sri Lanka, it proposed a total package of € 95 million, divided into € 40 million towards rebuilding the main road from the South to the East and € 55 million towards livelihoods and community support in the North and East, the bulk of which was to be channelled through the joint mechanism

[45] European Commission External Relations Directorate General, *Tsunami Indicative Programme: Indonesia, Sri Lanka, Maldives (2005–2006)*, C (2005)1490, May 23, 2005, *at* <http://ec.europa.eu/world/tsunami/docs/tip_05–06_c1490.pdf>.

described above. When the joint mechanism ultimately collapsed after a legal challenge, the EU was left scrambling to hastily disburse its 2005 allocation for the Northeast to multilateral agencies (it was too late to consider a call for proposals from NGOs), and to seek alternatives for the rest of the programme. Since then, the funding to the South has been successfully disbursed, but most projects in the East and Northeast, the areas now doubly hit by tsunami and subsequent flare-up of the conflict, have been suspended indefinitely.[46]

The EU also monitored the 2005 presidential elections, an unprecedented fourth electoral mission in five years (a measure of the instability of the Sri Lankan political system as well as the EU's commitment). The EU's representation in Colombo has been upgraded from a lone *chargé d'affaires* with contract staff to a full delegation led by an ambassador and supported by six diplomatic staff, although none devoted specifically to political affairs. This should considerably increase the EU's capacity to implement any policies at all. The question is whether, given that Sri Lanka is still a small middle-income country without significant resources, this expansion, and the increased attention it signals, will be sustained.

After the tsunami, the EU also briefly took a more active interest in the conflict in Sri Lanka. The Council has taken a harder and more consistent line on the LTTE, first warning that the EU was "actively considering the formal listing of the LTTE as a terrorist organisation",[47] then proceeding to list the organisation in the face of continued attacks.[48] However, since then, its only visible policy in response to the escalating violence has been to issue a statement urging the LTTE and the Karuna faction to stop using child soldiers.[49]

---

[46] Ibid., 23–33.

[47] *European Union Declaration Condemning Terrorism in Sri Lanka*, Sept. 26, 2005, *at* <http://www.eu2005.gov.uk/servlet/Front?pagename=OpenMarket/Xcelerate/ShowPage&c=Page&cid=1115146994806&a=KArticle&aid=1127731929213&date=2005–09–26>.

[48] Council of the European Union, *Declaration by the Presidency on Behalf of the European Union Concerning Listing of the LTTE a Terrorist Organisation*, Brussels, May 31, 2006, 9962/06 (Presse 163), P 078/06, *at* <www.consilium.europa.eu/ueDocs/cms_Data/docs/pressData/en/cfsp/89790.pdf>.

[49] Council of the European Union, *Declaration by the Presidency on Behalf of the European Union on the Situation of Children Affected by Armed Conflict in Sri Lanka*, Brussels, Dec. 1, 2006, 16076/06 (Presse 347), P 141, *at* <http://www.consilium.europa.eu/ueDocs/cms_Data/docs/hr/news88.pdf>.

IV. *Shortcomings in EU Policies*

1. *Crude Use of Conditionalities*

Until recently, Serbia had been treated exclusively as a security problem by the EU, while Sri Lanka was exclusively treated with a development paradigm, with the civil war considered at most as a minor nuisance. In recent years, the EU has begun to apply more economic instruments to Serbia as a part of the SAp, and to concern itself with the conflict in Sri Lanka.

However, in both cases, the (belated) recognition that security and economic development are connected has been translated into a simplistic use of political and financial conditionality. In the Balkans, the objective and the conditionalities defined by the SAp have come under criticism for their ambiguous impact on furthering stabilisation. The impact of the SAp on shaping the reforms in the region has not been as comprehensive and effective as it was hoped. EU officials admit that the results of the EU strategy towards the Balkans have fallen behind the expectations.[50]

One reason is that the SAA remains only a stepping-stone to candidacy, and its implementation "a prerequisite for any further assessment by the EU of the country's prospects of accession."[51] Consequently, scholars argued that being exogenous to the enlargement has limited the impact of the SAp on the domestic political agenda.[52]

At the same time, the enhanced conditionality that encompasses a range of political, economic, social and security issues, has favoured states that have made greatest progress in reform. This, in turn, has created a new line of division in the region between the Balkan candidates and "potential candidates." From the start of the process, the European integration of the Western Balkans has been characterised by the "stability dilemma:" those countries that suffer from the greatest stability deficits qualify least for the EU's initiatives.[53] No policy follow-up was designed to fill in the vacuum created by the success of the individual

---

[50] Stefan Lehne, *Has the 'Hour of Europe' come at last? The EU's Strategy for the Balkans, in* The Western Balkans: Moving on 111 (Judy Batt ed., Oct. 2004), *at* <http://www.iss.europa.eu/uploads/media/cp070.pdf>.

[51] European Commission, *From Regional Approach to the Stabilisation & Association Process, at* <http://ec.europa.eu/enlargement/enlargement_process/accession_process/how_does_a_country_join_the_eu/sap/history_en.htm>.

[52] Dimitrios Triantaphyllou, *The Balkans between Stabilisation and Membership, in* Partners and Neighbours: A CSFP for a Wider Europe 60, 69 (Judy Batt et al. eds., Sept. 2003), *at* <http://www.iss.europa.eu/uploads/media/cp064e.pdf>.

[53] Andreas Wittkowski, *South-Eastern Europe and the European Union – Promoting Stability through Integration?*, 3 South-East Europe Review for Labour and Social Affairs 79, 85 (2000).

aspirants.[54] It is precisely this vacuum that is the strength of the transnational spoilers of the Europeanisation.

In Sri Lanka, as elsewhere, there are strong connections between security and development, or between freedom from fear and freedom from want aspects. It was a combination of exclusion from political and administrative positions and threats to physical safety by the Sinhala majority that drove certain Tamils to take up arms, sparking the present-day conflict. Moreover, the conflict does of course block both infrastructural development and especially private investment, although not in the whole country but almost exclusively in the conflict zone. According to one analysis, the unequally distributed benefits of neoliberal policies, fuelling disgruntlement of the poor in both communities, was one of the major reasons for the failure of the peace process that began in 2002.[55] At present, it is the poorest, least educated segments of the population that form a recruiting ground for the army, the LTTE, the Karuna's TMVP and the Marxist-nationalist JVP alike. On the one hand, these organisations may offer the only form of livelihood. On the other, their ideology of blame appeals precisely to those who feel most marginalised.

The connections between development policy and the peace process have not been as straightforward as donors previously hoped. Neither of the parties in the conflict has been easily influenced by aid "carrots," in fact the general perception has been that they have been rather better at manipulating donors than the other way around.[56] Nor has the ceasefire agreement had an immediate and significant effect on economic prosperity in the conflict area.

Security does not automatically lead to economic development, or vice versa. This would suggest that policies on security and development must be worked out in conjunction with each other, yet each for its own sake, without easy assumptions being made about an instrumental connection.

2. *Policies Ignore Regional and Global Context*

Foreign policy, even the foreign policy of a supra-national entity like the EU, still has a tendency to focus attention on areas that are defined in terms of statehood. Because of this, regional and transnational, as well as sub-national sources of state weakness, or potential strength, tend not to be taken into account.

In the case of Sri Lanka, there are three aspects to this. The first is the proximity of the regional power India. India has a fraught history with the conflict

---

[54] Dimitris Papadimitriou, *The European Union's Strategy in the Post-Communist Balkans*, 1 (3) Journal of Southeast European and Black Sea Studies 69–94 (2001).

[55] Goodhand & Klem, *supra* note 11, 29–30.

[56] Interviews with S.I. Keethaponcalan; Anthea Mulakala, Conflict Advisor, DFID, Colombo, Sept. 2, 2005.

in Sri Lanka, including a very unfortunate attempt at intervention in the 1980s, but its relations with both the government and the LTTE have in recent years become more normalised.[57] It has a rather more fortunate record with respect to the neglected issue of the rights of the hill-country Tamils of more recent origin.[58] Its preferences regarding resolution of the conflict, tending towards accommodation of minority rights rather than self-government for the Northeast, may well run parallel to those of the EU.

The second dimension is sub-national, but partly connected to India's proximity, and of an economic nature: Sri Lanka may well be reaping some benefit from India's spectacular recent growth, but such benefit may be felt exclusively in the South West of the country. Development policies should take account of, and try to counteract, the likelihood of growing economic inequality between different parts of Sri Lanka.

The final dimension is the role of the Tamil diaspora, which has been part of the problem in the military conflict, but could also be part of the solution. It is well-known that the LTTE is partly, perhaps even largely funded by diaspora communities, although no one really knows the extent and fluctuation of this funding. Little attempt has been made by the EU to have a dialogue with and within these communities, many of which are in Europe, about the peace process. The open letter by the European Commissioner Ferrero-Waldner addressed to the diasporas, justifying the Council's decision to list the LTTE as a terrorist organisation, could be seen as a step in that direction.[59] It was a one-way communication, and although it defended the Council decision, the move might also be interpreted as encroaching on the Council's turf. A joint statement, defending the decision but simultaneously inviting diaspora groups from both communities to contribute suggestions regarding Sri Lanka's future, would have been a real break-through. The diaspora has also been making spontaneous contributions to development, particularly of the Northeast and particularly after the tsunami. These efforts too could have been harnessed, and connected to the peace process at a time when it might still have been saved.

In the Balkans, the key question has been not of whether there are regional initiatives, but of what nature and, therefore, effectiveness they are. One of the main challenges that the EU still experiences in the region is "to identify correctly regional actors involved, their political agendas and likely strategies."[60]

---

[57] Goodhand & Klem, *supra* note 11, 65–66.

[58] Interview with Sunil Bastian, Deputy Director, International Centre for Ethnic Studies, Colombo, Sept. 9, 2005.

[59] *Open Letter from Commissioner Benita Ferrero-Waldner* [on EU Declaration to Combat Terrorism, July 17, 2006], *at* <http://ec.europa.eu/external_relations/sri_lanka/intro/open_letter_commissioner_june_2006.pdf>.

[60] Vesna Bojicic-Dzelilovic & Denisa Kostovicova, *Introduction, in* Austrian Presidency of the

In order to prepare the Western Balkans for accession to the European Union, the Stabilisation and Association Process has also been premised on a regional dimension. Ultimately, the regional cooperation became another explicit condition for the progress of the Western Balkans towards the EU integration.[61] The Balkan aspirants must show commitment to improving relations with neighbours and enhancing political and economic cooperation. At the same time, the EU retained an individual approach to the states in the Balkans awarding the leaders in transition with a candidate status.

Although nearly ten years of the EU's involvement in the region and its insistence on regionalism has undoubtedly advanced greater regional cooperation among the Balkan states, the policy has not been without contradictions.

Delević has pointed out different if not conflicting agendas regarding the regional cooperation: "The Western Balkan countries' aim is to further the prospects of their promised European Union membership, while the EU stresses the intrinsic benefits of cooperation, and more recently has become more ambiguous about the timetable of integration. Therefore it would be a mistake to take the existing consensus on regional cooperation for granted."[62]

With its focus on the state level cooperation, the EU's insistence on regionalisation has not substantially affected the effectiveness of transnational criminal and other informal and illicit networks that are "multi-ethnic, cross-border and integrated in Europe."[63] These have thrived on the weakness of the states in the region, despite the latter's official championing of the EU's regional approach. In fact, shady non-state transnationalisation of the region that has taken place in parallel with the official regional cooperation among the states continues to pose a threat to state strengthening and to de-ethnification of local politics.[64] Ultimately, these networks threaten the Europeanisation of the Balkans.

3. *Failure to Strengthen State and Civil Society Simultaneously*

In Serbia, the EU's focus has been overwhelmingly on trying to strengthen state institutions. In its declarations, the EU considers consolidation of civil society

---

EU: Regional Approaches to the Balkans 17, 19 (Denisa Kostovicova & Vesna Bojicic-Dzelilovic eds., 2006).

[61] Cf. Judy Batt, *Introduction: The Stabilisation/Integration Dilemma, in* The Western Balkans: Moving on 7–20 (Judy Batt ed., Oct. 2004), *at* <http://www.iss.europa.eu/uploads/media/cp070.pdf>.

[62] Milica Delević, *Regional Cooperation in the Western Balkans*, 99 (July 2007), *at* <http://www.iss.europa.eu/uploads/media/cp104_01.pdf>.

[63] Dejan Anastasijević, *Comment*, Study Group on Europe's Security Capabilities meeting, Brussels, Belgium, March 17, 2004.

[64] See Denisa Kostovicova & Vesna Bojicic-Dzelilovic (eds.), Transnationalism in the Balkans (2008).

fundamental to achieving a more accountable and accessible government. But the EU's assistance directed at civil society both in the SAp and in the Stability Pact framework indicates that non-state-centred investment has been considered neither strategic nor integral to a comprehensive state-building effort in contrast to a narrowly conceptualised state-building as institution-building. In addition, it has been almost entirely divorced from the security efforts, security being defined in terms of human security.[65] This is partly due to donors' preference for funding economic reconstruction projects, which produce concrete accountable results in the short or medium term, in contrast to "cumbersome," long-lasting projects with unquantifiable soft results in the field of democratisation.[66] The donors' reluctance is reinforced by the EU's ambivalence in making a conceptual shift in treating a non-state sector as a strategic actor in state-building. Even less on the radar is the transnational cooperation of the civil society in the Balkans, which could be a response to thriving illegal transnational links.

In Sri Lanka, the opposite has to some extent happened, in particular in response to the tsunami. In its frustration with the corrupt and bureaucratic central state, the international community has largely channelled its relief effort through NGOs, bilateral and UN agencies. But this has not benefited the local civil society efforts, which were responsible for the successful immediate relief operations. On the contrary, local groups have found themselves marginalised and losing staff to the much better-paying international organisations. Similarly, the local administration found itself disempowered. This is where the EU could have made a very practical contribution to state-building, boosting the capacity and self-confidence of local authorities in humanitarian crises by providing them with, for instance, vehicles, phones and computers as well as training. In addition, at the civil society level, the EU could play a role in funding, legitimising and raising the profile of consultations and negotiations between groups beyond the armed parties.

Thus, in the Balkans and particularly in Serbia, the focus has been on the state, while in Sri Lanka, in line with prevailing development orthodoxy until recently, civil society (in practice in the form of international NGOs) has been the panacea for development. A holistic approach to state-building in both countries would require a simultaneous focus on strengthening civil society and state capacity.

---

65 York University Centre for International and Security Studies (ed.) *The Security Sector Reform in South Eastern Europe: An Inventory of Initiatives, at* <http://ssr.yciss.yorku.ca>.

66 Wim van Meurs, *The Balkans and New European Responsibilities. Strategy Paper Presented to the Special Meeting of "The Club of Three and the Balkans"* (June 29–30, 2000), *at* <http://www.cap.uni-muenchen.de/download/2000/balkan1.PDF>; cf. Nenad Pandurevic, *Security Aspects of the Stability Pact for South Eastern Europe*, 32 Security Dialogue 311–324 (2001).

4. *Flawed Human Rights Policy*

In Sri Lanka the international community, including the EU, is still in the "Dayton-phase" of over-focusing on mediation between the armed parties at the expense of the ordinary people on the ground. None of the armed parties in question is a champion of human rights. It might still be possible for them to find agreement around financial and territorial power-sharing arrangements, without either party being inclined to look into the other's human rights record except for rhetorical value. Therefore, it must be a third party such as the EU which champions human rights, even if this appears to complicate negotiations in the short run. At present, the manner in which human rights violations are brought up with each party tends to be through a routine exchange, and does not make much of an impression. The International Independent Group of Eminent Persons (IIGEP), invited by the President to shadow his own Commission of Inquiry into recent human rights violations, and enthusiastically supported by the EU, has just quit in protest at having its suggestions to increase the independence and effectiveness of the Commission ignored.[67]

In Serbia emphasis on justice as pursued by the EU has rendered contradictory results on the ground. As mentioned above, the cooperation with the ICTY is the "condition of all conditions" for Serbia's path to the EU. Insofar as the cooperation is primarily interpreted in terms of extradition of war criminals it has done little to promote the cause of transitional justice in Serbia. The issue of transitional justice became a merely technical issue of extraditions, rather than reckoning with war crimes that would open up a possibility of regional reconciliation.

This is best illustrated by a spate of surrenders by Serbian war crimes suspects after the EU and the US stepped up pressure on Serbia.[68] The government headed by Prime Minister Vojislav Koštunica hailed a surrender by a former army general and a suspected war criminal as a "patriotic act."[69] Even though it glorified war criminals, the government was rewarded by the EU with a Feasibility Study, which is the first step towards the Stabilisation and Association Agreement. At the same time, vocal civil society groups that advocate recognition of Serbian responsibility for war crimes in former Yugoslavia, increasingly

---

[67] International Independent Group of Eminent Persons, *Public Statement: The Presidential Commission's Public Inquiry Process So Far Falls Short Of International Norms and Standards*, (March 5, 2008), *at* <http://www.ahrchk.net/statements/mainfile.php/2008statements/1408/>.

[68] International Crisis Group, *Serbia: Spinning its Wheels* (May 23, 2005), *at* <http://www.crisisgroup.org/library/documents/europe/balkans/b039_serbia___spinning_its_wheels.pdf>.

[69] D. Djevori & Lj. Staletović, *General ispunio patriotski čin* [The general carries out a patriotic act], Glas javnosti, Feb. 4, 2005, *at* <http://arhiva.glas-javnosti.co.yu/arhiva/2005/02/04/srpski/P05020301.shtml>.

at risk for their work both from the state and the non-state illiberal groups, have been excluded from the EU's justice policy. Neither is transitional justice specifically earmarked as one of the areas to be funded within the scope of EU's civil society programmes.

Human rights violations are one of the most contested issues both in Sri Lanka and Serbia. They are closely related to the conflict since they constitute part of the root causes for state weakness in both cases, and also affect national cohesion as one of the dimensions of state weakness. Insofar as the EU recognised the importance of human rights issues in Serbia, its state centred approach proved to have limited effectiveness. It resulted in the extradition of some, but notably not the most wanted fugitives. Radovan Karadžić has only very recently been transferred to The Hague, whilst Bosnian Serb war time commander Ratko Mladić remains at large. The exclusion from this policy, as well as a lukewarm support to civil society advocating confrontation with one's nation criminal past, allowed the culture of denial of Serbian war crimes in Serbia to be entrenched further.[70]

V. *Conclusion*

This comparative study of Sri Lanka and Serbia analysed through the lens of the EU's policy approach to "ailing states" has not argued that both countries should be treated equally in the EU's external portfolio in terms of commitment, attention and resources. The EU's privileging of the Western Balkans is consistent with the region being considered the EU's "near abroad." Or, as the EU's Enlargement Commissioner Olli Rehn summed up the EU's approach: either the EU will export stability to the Western Balkans through enlargement, or it will import instability.[71] Despite the EU's increased involvement in the aftermath of the tsunami, Sri Lanka is bound to remain one out of a number of competing areas on its state-building policy's receiving end. Our comparative approach was aimed at challenging the *nature* of the EU's attention.

We have shown that the outcomes of state-strengthening interpreted almost exclusively in a reductionist manner as institution-building, such as in the case of Serbia, or a narrow focus on development and humanitarian assistance, as in the case of Sri Lanka, are bound to be limited. Rather, state-building ought to be designed as a long-term and holistic project. It should involve both security and economy, civil society and state institutions, as well as a domestic and

---

70 Kostovicova, *supra* note 29.

71 Olli Rehn, *The Future of EU Enlargement: Consolidation, Conditionality and Communication*, Public Lecture, London School of Economics and Political Science (Jan. 20, 2006), transcript *at* <http://lse.ac.uk/collections/LSEPublicLecturesAndEvents/pdf/20060120-OlliRehn.pdf>.

regional perspective. In the context of "ailing states" prioritising specific policy areas over others creates voids. These are readily exploited by both domestic and transnational constituencies for the pursuit of their partial interests, one of the top ones being maintaining the state weakness.

Further, more policies on the part of the EU do not necessarily imply better results on the ground. Some scholars have argued that the EU's twin approach to the Western Balkans, embodied by a set of Enlargement and ESDP mechanisms, demonstrates the EU's growing strength in projecting stability into the region.[72] We, however, challenge this view. The parallel involvement of the Council and the Commission, without prior coordination and streamlining of the EU policy, has actually introduced another level of separation of the EU's policy instruments. This has not only chipped the legitimacy of the EU as an effective actor on the ground, as the locals observe and try to make sense of the EU's bureaucratic struggles. It has also had an unintended consequence of actually slowing the advance towards Europe. This is best illustrated by Serbia and Montenegro's inability to agree to economic harmonisation as stipulated in the Belgrade Agreement – itself an ESDP product. The deadlock nearly halted their advance in the SAp process.

In Sri Lanka, the increased focus on security is to be welcomed. The EU may have more credibility as an honest broker with both warring parties as well as with civil society actors than the US with its anti-terrorist agenda. However, it must guard against making the mistakes of the Balkans, where Council and Commission involvement have typically been in competition with each other.

The interrelated nature of challenges faced by the EU as a state-builder and the multiplication of the EU's policy instruments makes a strong case for a rethink of a best-suited strategy. We argue that this strategy should be defined at two levels: institutional and policy. Institutionally, the EU needs to do away with a distinction between "high" and "low" politics best achieved by closer coordination and inter-institutional learning between the Council and the Commission. Policy-wise, the intra-EU institutional streamlining should be guided by the application of a comprehensive human security vision. In our conclusion, we take inspiration from the "human security principles" developed by the Study Group on Europe's Security Capabilities.[73]

---

[72] See Milada A. Vachudova, *Strategies for democratization and European integration of the Balkans*, *in* The Enlargement of the European Union 141, 141 (Marise Cremona ed., 2003); Islam Yusufi, *Europeanizing the Western Balkans through Military and Police Missions: the Cases of Concordia and Proxima in Macedonia*, 2 (1) European Balkan Observer 8–12 (2004), *at* <http://www.wiiw.ac.at/balkan/files/EBO%203.pdf>.

[73] Study Group on Europe's Security Capabilities, *A Human Security Doctrine for Europe: The Barcelona Report of the Study Group on Europe's Security Capabilities. Presented to EU High Representative for Common Foreign and Security Policy Javier Solana* (Sept. 15, 2004), *at* <http://lse.ac.uk/Depts/global/Publications/HumanSecurityDoctrine.pdf>. We elaborate on five of the

1. *Primacy of Human Rights*

The primacy of human rights, encompassing economic and social rights as well as political and civil rights, is what distinguishes the human security approach from traditional state-based approaches. This principle has profound implications both for security policy and for development. In security terms, this implies serious attention must be paid to the *means* of the external involvement, not just the legitimacy of its *ends*. In development terms, the primacy of human rights has implications for conditionality. Ways have to be found to help the individual even where a country has poor governance or fails to meet various forms of conditionality. Different voices within a country should be consulted on the use of conditionality, and means have to be found to assist communities that bypass local authorities.

2. *Legitimate Political Authority*

The end goal of a human security strategy has to be the establishment of legitimate political authority capable of upholding human security. Again this applies both to issues of physical security, where the rule of law and a well-functioning system of justice are essential, and to material security, where issues of legitimate employment and the provision of infrastructure and public services require state policies. Legitimate political authority does not necessarily need to refer to a state, it could also refer to local government or regional or international political arrangements. Multilevel but always public monopolies of authority could emerge from such a policy that can compensate for each other's weaknesses.

3. *Bottom-up Approach*

Notions of "partnership," "local ownership" and "participation" are already key concepts in development policy. These concepts should also apply to security policies. Decisions about the kind of security policies to be adopted, whether or not to intervene and how, must take account of the most basic needs identified by the people who are affected by violence and insecurity. This is not just a moral issue, it is also a matter of effectiveness. People who live in the affected area are the best source of intelligence. Thus communication, consultation, and dialogues are essential tools for both development and security.

Study Group's seven principles as particularly relevant to its state-building role in Serbia and Sri Lanka. The other two, multilateralism and appropriate use of force, relate more to the use of military power in failed states.

4. *Regional Focus*

State-weakness is not sustained only through (in)activity of local actors. Rather, in a global setting, their impact in maintaining the "ailing state" depends on their full integration into a transnational diaspora and criminal networks. Most situations of severe insecurity are located in regional clusters. The tendency to focus attention on areas that are bounded by national borders, even the contested ones, has often meant that relatively simple ways of tackling the sources of insecurity have been bypassed. By the same token, a regional focus is important in restoring and/or fostering economic and trade co-operation. The breakdown of transport and trade links, associated with war, is often a primary reason for falls in production and employment that contribute to poverty and insecurity.

5. *Use of Legal Instruments*

For both development and security, the establishment or restoration of a rule of law is of critical importance. Whether we are talking about dealing with political violence or a criminalised economy, legal instruments that respect the dignity of the individual need to be available. Where there has been a breakdown of law and order, and in authoritarian states, where domestic law lacks legitimacy, legal frameworks need to be established which command widespread assent. Investment is also needed in civilian capabilities for law-enforcement, i.e. police, court officials, prosecutors and judges. Citizens in these situations need to regain the protection of the law, and to help transform it if the old laws were unjust or repressive.

In their focus, these five principles match the complexity of non-traditional security challenges spawned by "ailing" states. They coherently join up the low and the high end of external policies. Insofar as the EU has pursued or experimented with their individual aspects, albeit in a piecemeal fashion, both institutionally and policy-wise, it is well-positioned to adopt these principles in a comprehensive manner as a guide to broadening its policy vision and fine-tuning its institutional mechanisms. The alternative is letting the spoilers get away with their narrow vision focused on weak states, with major repercussions for the credibility of the EU as a human security actor, and for the security of Europe itself.

Constitution-Building in Eastern Europe: Achievements of and challenges to the Council of Europe

*Julia Raue**

Since the end of the Cold War, more than 20 countries from Eastern Europe have knocked on the door of the Council of Europe. All of them emerged from the former Soviet Union or had previously been under its sphere of influence. As such, all of them were confronted with the challenge to reform their constitutional systems in order to pursue their path to democracy.

The Council of Europe, which – until 1989 – could certainly be regarded as the "Council of Western Europe",[1] put itself in an entirely new role and decided to act as a "trainer" of these Eastern European states.[2] Opinions about this new approach varied widely. It implied to grant these countries membership of the Council even before they were able to bring their legal systems and practices in compliance with the Council's three fundamental standards, namely the principle of the rule of law, democracy, and respect for human rights and fundamental freedoms.

In the early 1990s, accessions of states from Eastern Europe were mostly greeted with appreciation since these countries had already made significant progress in reforming their constitutional systems. However, as of 1995 a new series of Eastern European countries applied for membership, whose constitutional structures

* This text draws on ideas discussed at greater length in JULIA RAUE, DER EUROPARAT ALS VERFASSUNGSGESTALTER SEINER NEUEN MITLGIEDSSTAATEN: VOM BEOBACHTER ZUM REFORMER IN OSTEUROPA? (2005). The views expressed are those of the author alone.

[1] In 1989, 23 states were members of the Council of Europe: Austria, Belgium, Cyprus, Denmark, Finland, France, Germany, Greece, Iceland, Ireland, Italy, Liechtenstein, Luxembourg, Malta, the Netherlands, Norway, Portugal, San Marino, Spain, Sweden, Switzerland, Turkey and the United Kingdom.

[2] Diana Pinto, *Assisting central and eastern Europe's transformation, in* THE CHALLENGES OF A GREATER EUROPE: THE COUNCIL OF EUROPE AND DEMOCRATIC SECURITY 49–51 (Council of Europe ed., 1996).

were far from being compliant with the Council's three fundamental standards. These admission requests were increasingly considered with hesitation.

In that moment, two schools of thought emerged. One favoured a quick enlargement process, arguing that an early admission to the Council would create a "school of democratisation."[3] The second opinion expressed doubts, preferring a more cautious, step-by-step approach in order to prevent the watering down of the Council's standards. Finally, the Council of Europe decided to opt for a quick enlargement process, which rapidly led to a truly pan-European Organisation.

The objective of this article is to present and analyse the Council of Europe's constitutional assistance to its new Eastern European member states. This assessment should help the Council to tackle the remaining major challenges resulting from its rapid enlargement process.

The article has four parts. In the first part, the Council's strategy for granting membership to the Eastern European states is explained. In the second part, the new mechanisms and bodies which were set up in the 1990s to prepare the organisation for its new tasks are introduced and briefly evaluated. The third part presents country-specific examples which illustrate both achievements and challenges of the Council's work in the period of national constitutional restructuring. A thorough study of these achievements and challenges will lead to findings on whether the Council's work has had meaningful impact on country-specific constitutional developments. Based on this analysis, the concluding part of the paper will outline a series of reform proposals for the Council of Europe.

I. *The Council's "commitments for membership" strategy*

What was the *modus operandi* applied by the Council of Europe in order to ensure that it could exercise its new function as a "trainer", while avoiding its standards to be watered down by the enormous undertaking of enlargement?

Prior to the actual accession and as an initial and "educative" step, the Eastern European states were granted special guest status to the Council's Parliamentary Assembly. This measure was adopted to let their parliamentary representatives get acquainted with the democratic rules applied at the European level.

Furthermore, with a view to future membership, the legal systems of each of the applicant states were examined in detail by experts of the organisation. Shortcomings in the areas of the Council's three fundamental standards were listed by the Council's Parliamentary Assembly and brought to the attention of

[3] Heinrich Klebes, *Le Caucase et la Grande Europe* 12, *at* <http://www.upmf-grenoble.fr/espace-europe/conf_pub/Klebes_coul.pdf>.

the aspirant members as well as the Council's executive body, the Committee of Ministers.

Following positive opinions issued by the Parliamentary Assembly,[4] the Eastern European countries were gradually offered membership of the Council on the condition that they undertake commitments in the area of the listed shortcomings.[5] Since the "democratic label" that came along with the Council's membership was in fact an acknowledgment by the international community,[6] the candidate states were more than willing to sign up to the suggested commitments.[7]

The character of these commitments varied widely. For instance, all applicant states had to commit themselves to abolish the death penalty by a certain timeline and, in the meanwhile, to establish a moratorium on executions. Also, all candidate states had to sign the European Convention on Human Rights and Fundamental Freedoms at the moment of accession and ratify it together with selected additional protocols by a certain date. Some states were urged to commit themselves to drawing up new constitutions compatible with the Council's fundamental principles.[8] In many cases, states committed themselves to adopt legislation providing for the protection of minorities. At times, the commitments entered into were quite detailed and often referred to amendments to a series of legislation, including the criminal and criminal procedural law, the prison administration systems, and the law on elections and political parties. In some cases, the Parliamentary Assembly even requested legal reforms that would, in specific cases, grant individuals access to the constitutional court.[9]

---

4 See for example, Parliamentary Assembly, Opinion 193 (1996), Russia's application for membership of the Council of Europe.

5 The Parliamentary Assembly played a very demanding role in this respect, making its positive opinion on whether to grant membership to the aspirant state depending on the state's willingness to enter into the suggested commitments.

6 See Hanna Machinska, *The Significance of Co-operation between the Council of Europe and the European Union for Countries preparing for Membership in the European Union*, *in* LAW IN GREATER EUROPE – TOWARDS A COMMON LEGAL AREA 294, 299 (Haller, Krüger & Petzold eds., 2000).

7 On the question whether these commitments are legally binding, see Vladimir Djeric, *Admission to Membership of the Council of Europe and Legal Significance of the Commitments Entered into by New Member States*, 60 HEIDELBERG JOURNAL OF INTERNATIONAL LAW 605 (2000), and JULIA RAUE, DER EUROPARAT ALS VERFASSUNGSGESTALTER SEINER NEUEN MITGLIEDSSTAATEN: VOM BEOBACHTER ZUM REFORMER IN OSTEUROPA? 57–84 (2005).

8 See for example, Parliamentary Assembly, Opinion 190 (1995), Ukraine's application for membership of the Council of Europe, paras. 6 and 11 v.

9 See Parliamentary Assembly, Opinion 221 (2000), Armenia's application for membership of the Council of Europe, para. 14 ii, and Opinion 222 (2000), Azerbaijan's application for membership of the Council of Europe, para. 15 ii.

On the basis of this "commitments for membership" strategy, 21 states from Eastern Europe joined the Council in a period of 12 years.[10]

II. *The Council's internal institutional adjustments in the era of constitution-building in Eastern Europe: Constitutional Engineering and Monitoring*

Starting in the early 1990s, the Council of Europe was confronted with the question of how to ensure that the newly admitted member states would initiate and implement reform processes that would eventually lead to the full compliance of the members' constitutional and legal systems and practices with the Council's fundamental principles. On the one hand a body offering advisory services to the new member states was essential. On the other hand, an instrument to ensure "post-accession-control" was needed for a meaningful impact of the Council's work on the constitutional developments in the Eastern European states.[11]

1. *The Venice Commission as a tool for emergency constitutional engineering*

Originally intended to serve as an academic platform of constitutional expertise, the purpose of the European Commission for Democracy through Law (Venice Commission) rapidly changed with the fall of the Berlin Wall. Established in 1990, the Venice Commission quickly evolved to a "tool for emergency constitutional engineering" in the early and mid 1990s. New member states of the Council, some even prior to their actual admission to the organisation, requested assistance from the Venice Commission when drafting new constitutions.[12]

The Commission is composed of experts appointed by its member states who are independent and impartial, acting in their personal capacity. Most experts are respected academics in fields such as public international and constitutional

[10] From 1990 to 2004, the following countries from Eastern Europe joined the Council of Europe: Hungary (1990), Poland (1991), Czechoslovakia (1991) [since 1993 Check Republic, and Slovak Republic], Bulgaria (1992), Lithuania (1993), Estonia (1993), Romania (1993), Slovenia (1993), Latvia (1995), Albania (1995), Former Yugoslav Republic of Macedonia (1995), Moldova (1995), Ukraine (1995), Croatia (1996), Russian Federation (1996), Georgia (1999), Armenia (2001), Azerbaijan (2001), Bosnia and Herzegovina (2002), Serbia and Montenegro (2003) (since 2006 Republic of Serbia through continued membership).

[11] Heinrich Klebes & Despina Chatzivassiliou, *Problèmes d'ordre constitutionnel dans le processus d'adhésion d'États de l'Europe centrale et orientale au Conseil de l'Europe*, 8 Revue universelle des droits de l'homme 269, 284 (1996).

[12] Garrone called this "dépannage constitutionnel", see Pierre Garrone, *La Commission de Venise à la veille de son dixième anniversaire*, 66 Rivista di studi politici internazionali 527, 529 (1999).

law, political scientists, active or retired judges of national high courts, and former diplomats. The Commission's work focuses *inter alia* on constitutional, legislative and administrative principles which serve the efficiency of democratic institutions and their strengthening.[13]

When providing constitutional assistance, the Commission appoints a working group, which is primarily drawn from its own members. Whenever possible the working group visits the country concerned, in order to meet with the different political actors involved. In general, the Commission provides assistance in the drafting of a constitutional text, prepares an opinion on whether the text meets the standards of the Council of Europe, or on how to improve the text on the basis of the European experience. Draft reports and opinions prepared by the respective working group are submitted to the Commission and voted upon during its plenary sessions.

In the case of Albania, for example, the Venice Commission assisted the country throughout the constitutional drafting process, from the outset of the country's democratisation process in 1991 until the eventual adoption of the new constitution in 1998. In the course of action, the Commission had a close and continuing dialogue with the authorities and issued various opinions on parts of the transitional constitution as well as on several draft constitutions.[14] Similarly, with regards to Ukraine, the Commission's experts prepared opinions on legal texts that were adopted to govern the transitional phase until the enactment of a new constitution. Subsequently, the Commission commented on draft constitutions and, eventually, also on the adopted constitution itself.[15]

2. *Establishment of monitoring procedures*

Following the first wave of accessions, which lasted until 1992, the problem of monitoring became apparent: to ensure that the new member states honour the commitments[16] they had entered into at the time of their accession, control structures were needed. Thus, monitoring procedures were gradually installed within the Parliamentary Assembly, the Committee of Ministers[17] and the Congress of Local and Regional Authorities.

---

[13] Article 1 (2) Revised Statute of the Venice Commission, see: Committee of Ministers, Resolution (2002) 3.

[14] For an overview of the co-operation of the Venice Commission with Albania see <http://www.venice.coe.int/site/main/Coop_ALB_E.asp>.

[15] For an overview of the co-operation of the Venice Commission with Ukraine see <http://www.venice.coe.int/site/main/Coop_UKR_E.asp>.

[16] See under I.

[17] Whereas the monitoring procedures in the Parliamentary Assembly and the Congress of Local and Regional Authorities are carried out in public, the monitoring procedure of the Committee of Ministers is held in a confidential manner.

The most influential and publicly known is the monitoring procedure of the Parliamentary Assembly. Starting in 1993, this procedure had undergone significant changes, which led to the adoption of resolution 1115[18] that set up a special Monitoring Committee[19] of the Assembly in 1997.

As a matter of principle, two Rapporteurs are appointed who are entrusted with the continuous monitoring of the reform process in a certain country. On the basis of the Council's standards, these Rapporteurs draw up a list of issues of potential areas of concern. The Rapporteurs visit the country concerned where they meet with representatives of the executive, legislative and judicial branches, as well as with opposition figures, civil society and the media.[20]

Subsequently, they prepare an assessment report and, following consultations with the respective member state, submit it to the Monitoring Committee and the Parliamentary Assembly, where the report is publicly debated. The reports also contain draft resolutions, which are voted on by the Assembly, and, if appropriate, recommendations to the intergovernmental Committee of Ministers.

The reports can also include recommendations as to whether sanctions should be imposed, in case commitments are not honoured. Possible sanctions are the non-ratification of the credentials of a national parliamentary delegation or the annulment of ratified credentials to the Council's Parliamentary Assembly. Should the member state continue to disobey its commitments, the Assembly may address a recommendation to the Committee of Ministers, requesting the suspension of the member state's representation in the Committee in accordance with Articles 8 and 9 of the Statute of the Council of Europe.

III. *The era of constitutional restructuring in Eastern Europe*

The Assembly's monitoring procedure accompanied the reform process of almost all new member states. The procedure for most of the states that acceded to the Council in the early 1990s was closed after finding that all their major commitments had been honoured.

However, for the majority of the new member states admitted to the organisation after 1995, the monitoring procedure is still ongoing and increasingly

---

[18] Parliamentary Assembly, Resolution 1115 (1997), Setting up of an Assembly committee on the honouring of obligations and commitments by Member States of the Council of Europe (Monitoring Committee).

[19] Previously, the Committee on Legal Affairs and Human Rights carried out the monitoring procedure as one of its multiple tasks.

[20] Jerzy Jaskiernia, The Parliamentary Assembly of the Council of Europe 303 (2003).

facing difficulties.[21] Several of these new members turned, at least partly, away from effectively pursuing the reform process. Therefore, the Council had to look for an efficient strategy to ensure that these states do not depart from their path of democracy.

1. *Involvement of the Venice Commission in the monitoring procedure*

Starting in 1995, it became obvious that the monitoring procedure of the Parliamentary Assembly itself could, in certain instances, not maintain the desired continuing influence on constitutional developments in the new member states.

An additional factor exacerbated this situation: constitution-making processes in Eastern Europe were to a great extent finalised in the late 1990s. The new challenge arising was the correct and effective implementation of the provisions contained in the recently adopted constitutions.[22] This, however, was not an easy task. Since most of the constitutions reflected a hardly worked out compromise between different political groups, the provisions were often unclear and subject to interpretation. Furthermore, efforts were made, most of the time by presidents of states, to amend "unfavourable" constitutional provisions in order for them to obtain more power and competencies under the constitution.

The monitoring procedure, embedded in the political organ "Parliamentary Assembly", was in need of an objective and legal expert body in order to make its concerns heard. Subsequently, the Parliamentary Assembly started to involve the Venice Commission in its assessment of whether a new member state had honoured its commitments. This involvement was eventually institutionalised in 1997.[23] Thus, in case the Assembly's Monitoring Committee detected worrisome constitutional developments or a significant delay in the honouring of specific commitments in a certain member state, it made a request to the Venice Commission to obtain a legal opinion on the subject matter. As a result, the Commission as a legal expert body evolved to an extended branch of the monitoring procedure.

The following sections illustrate achievements of this new interlinked institutional set-up, but also point to remaining challenges.

---

[21] Ten monitoring procedures are currently in progress: Albania, Armenia, Azerbaijan, Bosnia and Herzegovina, Georgia, Moldova, Monaco, the Russian Federation, Serbia and Ukraine, see Parliamentary Assembly, Doc. 11214, Progress of the Assembly's Monitoring Procedure, 30 March 2007, Summary, para. 2.

[22] See Venice Commission, CDL (1995) 10, The European Commission for Democracy through Law and the implementation of pluralist democracy, Memorandum by the President, Part A.

[23] See Annex to Parliamentary Assembly, Resolution 1115 (1997), article 9 Terms of Reference of the Monitoring Committee.

2. *The achievements*

The impact of this institutionalised involvement of the Venice Commission in the monitoring procedure will be illustrated by country-specific case studies, which cover two of the main areas of preoccupation on the Council's bodies – the abolition of the death penalty and the principle of separation of powers.

(1) *Abolition of the death penalty*

a) Ukraine

Ukraine committed itself to the abolishment of the death penalty within three years following its accession to the Council, as well as to the immediate establishment of a moratorium on the execution of death sentences.

From the start, the Parliamentary Assembly put emphasis on the need to abolish the death penalty in Ukraine. In the initial period, the Parliamentary Assembly focused on the establishment of an immediate moratorium on executions of the death penalty. Multiple actions were taken by the Assembly in this respect: Its Committee on Legal Affairs and Human Rights issued a special report[24] on the subject matter, and the Assembly subsequently held an extraordinary session adopting a resolution to consider the non-ratification of credentials of the Ukrainian parliamentary delegation at its next session.[25] A further resolution demanded an official declaration by the President and the Speaker of the Parliament of Ukraine, notifying the Council of Europe of the imposition of a *de jure* moratorium on executions.[26] Again the Assembly underscored the possibility of a non-ratification of the credentials of the Ukrainian delegation. As a preliminary outcome, the President of Ukraine confirmed a *de facto* moratorium on executions in late 1997.

In parallel to this monitoring process, a second instrument of the Council was initiated. Upon request by the Committee on Legal Affairs and Human Rights, the Venice Commission delivered an opinion on the issue of the abolition of the death penalty. In December 1997, the Commission came to the conclusion that the death penalty violates the new Ukrainian Constitution of 1996.[27] Subsequently, the Assembly referred in all of its documents to the expert view issued by the Venice Commission, pointing to the unconstitutionality of the death penalty.

---

[24] Parliamentary Assembly, Doc. 7745, Honouring of the commitment entered into by Ukraine upon accession to the Council of Europe to put into place a moratorium on executions of the death penalty.

[25] See on the issue of sanctions above, p. 160.

[26] Parliamentary Assembly, Resolution 1145 (1998), Executions in Ukraine, para. 12.

[27] Venice Commission, CDL-INF (1998) 1 rev, Opinion on the constitutional aspects of the death penalty in Ukraine.

In 1999, in absence of the establishment of a *de jure* moratorium, the Assembly announced that it would recommend that the Committee of Ministers suspend Ukraine's right of representation, in case no substantial progress in honouring this commitment would be made by the opening of its next session.[28]

In late 1999, upon request by members of the Ukrainian delegation to the Parliamentary Assembly, the Ukrainian Constitutional Court had to pronounce its decision on the constitutionality of a number of provisions of the criminal code providing for the death penalty. In its judgment, the Court explicitly referred to the opinion issued by the Venice Commission in December 1997 and declared the provisions in question unconstitutional. Consequently, the Ukrainian Parliament adopted legislative measures on the abolition of the death penalty in early 2000.[29]

b) Albania

Like Ukraine, Albania committed itself to the abolishment of the death penalty within three years following its accession, as well as to the immediate introduction of a moratorium on the execution of death sentences.[30]

Upon accession in June 1995, Albania introduced a moratorium on the execution of death sentences. However, this decision was not made publicly known since a broad spectrum of the population continued to be in favour of the death penalty during the transition phase.

The Parliamentary Assembly of the Council of Europe intensified its efforts, when in 1998 it became known that Albania had not honoured its commitment to abolish the death penalty by the agreed timeframe.[31] Consequently, the Bureau of the Assembly requested the Venice Commission to issue an opinion on the compatibility of the death penalty with the new Albanian Constitution adopted in 1998.[32] In March 1999, the Venice Commission declared the death penalty unconstitutional.[33]

---

[28] Parliamentary Assembly, Resolution 1179 (1999), Honouring of obligations and commitments by Ukraine, para. 15.

[29] Ukraine ratified Protocol No. 6 to the Convention for the Protection of Human Rights and Fundamental Freedoms concerning the abolition of the death penalty in 2000 (CETS No. 114) and Protocol No. 13 to the Convention for the Protection of Human Rights and Fundamental Freedoms, concerning the abolition of the death penalty in all circumstances (CETS No. 187) in 2003.

[30] Parliamentary Assembly, Opinion 189 (1995), Application by Albania for membership of the Council of Europe, para. 17 ii.

[31] Parliamentary Assembly, Doc. 8340 rev 2, Europe: A death penalty-free continent, Report of the Committee on Legal Affairs and Human Rights, Explanatory memorandum, para. 10.

[32] See <http://www.codices.coe.int> (Constitutions, Albania) for an English version.

[33] Venice Commission, CDL-INF (1999) 4, Opinion on the compatibility of the death penalty with the Constitution of Albania (see Annex 1).

Nine months after the publication of the opinion by the Venice Commission, the Constitutional Court of Albania pronounced itself on the issue and declared the death penalty unconstitutional[34] using, to a great extent, arguments brought forward by the Venice Commission.[35] As a result, Albania abolished the death penalty *de jure* in 2000.[36]

(2) *Separation of powers*

The principle of the separation of powers and the instalment of "checks and balances" in the constitution are the crucial issues in each constitutional system. With regard to the Eastern European countries, the problem became particularly apparent in the debate on the determination of competencies of the president, the government and the parliament; that is the question of whether to opt for a presidential or parliamentary system.

a) The case of Ukraine 1995–2004

Ukraine committed itself to drafting and adopting a constitution compatible with Council of Europe standards within one year following its accession in 1995.[37]

Three years later, the Parliamentary Assembly stated, based on a report prepared by its Monitoring Committee,[38] that "[i]n the transitional phase between a totalitarian and a democratic state, Ukraine has not achieved a clear separation between the judicial, legislative and executive powers. There is continuing control by the executive and a determination to seek and hold political power, sometimes illegally [. . .]."[39]

This statement held particularly true when, starting in 1999, then President Kuchma attempted to alter the constitution in his favour. He regarded the provisions related to the principle of the separation of powers enshrined in Ukraine's Constitution of 1996 as an obstacle to effective policy making. The presidential system of the new constitution, although mainly based on the semi-presidential system of France, reflected a compromise with regard to the competencies vested

[34] Constitutional Court of Albania, Judgment of 10.12.1999, nº 65; see <http://www.codices.coe.int> (Précis, ALB-1999–3–008) for an English version.

[35] See Paolo G. Carozza, *"My friend is a stranger": The death penalty and the global ius commune of human rights*, 81 Texas Law Review 1031, 1069 (2003).

[36] Albania ratified Protocol No. 6 in 2000 and Protocol No. 13 in 2007.

[37] Parliamentary Assembly, Opinion 190 (1995), Ukraine's application for membership of the Council of Europe, Ziff. 11 v.

[38] Parliamentary Assembly, Doc. 8272, Honouring of obligations and commitments by Ukraine.

[39] Parliamentary Assembly, Resolution 1179 (1999), Honouring of obligations and commitments by Ukraine, para. 3.

in the president, the government and the parliament. The uncertainty on whether the government was accountable to the president or the parliament was particularly troublesome. As a consequence, continuous conflicts between the president and the parliament and subsequent power struggles ensued.

Therefore, in early 2000, then President Kuchma decided to call a nation-wide referendum on a constitutional revision aimed at amending the 1996 Constitution. After his confirmed re-election in late 1999, he intended to strengthen his presidential powers to the detriment of the Parliament. Among the six issues put to the electorate were: a vote of no confidence against the Parliament, a proposal to amend the constitution in order to enable the president to dissolve the legislature, and a provision that the constitution could only be adopted through an all-Ukraine referendum.[40]

Kuchma pursued this undertaking despite the fact that the constitution authorises the president to introduce referenda on constitutional amendments only after a parliamentary approval with a two-thirds majority.[41]

Having followed the worrying developments in Ukraine through its monitoring procedure, the Parliamentary Assembly and its Secretary General made a request to the Venice Commission on the subject matter. One month prior to the referendum, the Commission rendered its opinion[42] on the envisaged questions, elaborating on 1) whether the Constitution could be amended through such a referendum; and 2) whether the proposed changes were constitutional and in compliance with international law.

On the first question, the expert body came to the conclusion that the referendum could not have the effect of directly amending the Ukrainian Constitution. The Commission referred to the appropriate chapter in the constitution and to the lack of a parliamentary endorsement of the envisaged referendum. With regard to the content of the referendum, the expert body concluded that the suggested changes to the constitution were partly unconstitutional and contrary to international norms.

The Constitutional Court of Ukraine, consulted by 100 Ukrainian deputies, endorsed the Commission's opinion, declaring that the referendum could not directly alter the constitution and that state bodies are bound by the constitutional provisions governing the procedures for amendments of the Constitution. Moreover, it declared two of the six questions of the referendum unconstitutional.

---

[40] See Parliamentary Assembly, Doc. 8666, Reform of the institutions in Ukraine, Explanatory memorandum, para. 25 ff. and Serhiy Holovaty, *Ukraine in transition: From the newly emerged democracy towards autocracy?*, 26 Review of Central and East European Law 267, 299–300 (2000).

[41] Article 156 para. 1 Constitution of Ukraine of 1996.

[42] Venice Commission, CDL-INF (2000) 11, Opinion of the constitutional referendum in Ukraine.

Shortly before the referendum, the Parliamentary Assembly adopted a recommendation to the Committee of Ministers in which it summarized the main concerns stressed by the Ukrainian Constitutional Court and the Venice Commission. In the recommendation's last paragraph the Assembly underlined that "[i]f the referendum results are implemented in a non-constitutional manner, or if the constitution were to be amended through non-constitutional means, it recommends that Ukraine's membership of the Council of Europe be suspended."[43]

Despite this international pressure, President Kuchma went ahead and submitted those four questions that were declared admissible by the Ukrainian Constitutional Court to the referendum. After the approval of these questions by the Ukrainian population, he submitted a proposal for the amendment of the constitution to the parliament. In turn, a group of deputies also submitted a proposal to the legislative branch.

Again, the Council's Monitoring Committee, having followed the ongoing developments, consulted the Venice Commission, which, in turn, rendered opinions on both of the proposals. In both proposals, the Commission highlighted its concerns as to the compatibility with international standards.

In the end, the presidential proposal, which was adopted in a first session by the parliament, could not gain the qualified majority required during the second voting.[44] Therefore, the attempt to centralise powers in the hands of President Kuchma failed.

b) The case of Moldova 1995–2000

In 1999, the Monitoring Committee of the Parliamentary Assembly decided to task the Venice Commission to closely monitor the constitutional developments in Moldova.

This came as the result of an initiative taken by the then President Lucinschi to transform the semi-presidential governing system of Moldova into a purely presidential system.[45] In this respect, Lucinschi had issued a presidential decree to hold a nation-wide referendum in May 1999. Despite the consultative character of this referendum and the clear constitutional provisions specifying that the president lacks the right to initiate a constitutional revision,[46] Lucinschi saw himself mandated by the population[47] to initiate such a constitutional reform.

---

43 Parliamentary Assembly, Recommendation 1451 (2000), Reform of the institutions in Ukraine, para. 11.

44 The proposal introduced by a group of deputies could not be submitted to the parliament, since the Constitutional Court declared some of the proposed changes unconstitutional.

45 Venice Commission, CDL-INF (2001) 3, Co-operation between the Venice Commission and the Republic of Moldova on constitutional reform, section 1, para. 1.

46 Article 141 Constitutional of Moldova.

47 56 percent of the 58 percent who casted their ballot approved Lucinschi's plan.

In order to forestall a presidential draft, 39 parliamentarians prepared a proposal aiming at strengthening the role and competencies of the government. Only a few weeks later, the Constitutional Committee established by the president submitted a draft constitutional amendment, which sought to strengthen the position of the president.

At the request of the Monitoring Committee, the Venice Commission analysed both proposals. It assessed the parliamentary draft as compliant with the constitution despite minor flaws in its provisions. With regard to the draft constitutional amendment proposed by the Constitutional Committee, however, the Commission expressed strong criticism. It came to the conclusion that the principle of the separation of powers was not fully respected in this draft because of a lack of balance of competencies between the president and the parliament. The Constitutional Committee amended its draft, partly in accordance with recommendations by the Venice Commission. However, it could not secure the parliament's approval.

The President of the Parliamentary Assembly appealed to the President of Moldova and the Speaker of the Parliament for the preparation of a joint draft of both political sides.[48] A Joint Commission was established, which was composed of three representatives of the Constitutional Committee of the president and three parliamentarians. Both sides requested a member of the Venice Commission to preside the Committee. By the end of May 2000, the Joint Committee had finalized its draft proposal,[49] which was considered a compromise between both positions.

In July 2000, the newly elected parliament adopted constitutional amendments that, to a large extent, incorporated those proposed by the Joint Committee, but were also significantly based on the first proposal made by the parliamentarians. President Lucinschi vetoed the draft proposal and sent it back to parliament, which, however, approved it at its second reading.[50] In the end, the adopted constitutional amendments strengthened the competencies of both the parliament and the government.

(3) *Assessment*

All four case studies illustrate that the political pressure being exercised by the Parliamentary Assembly was complemented, and therefore strengthened, by the objective and neutral legal expert opinion issued by the Venice Commission.

[48] Press declaration of the Council of Europe, 7 December 1999.

[49] Venice Commission, CDL-INF (2001) 3, Co-operation between the Venice Commission and the Republic of Moldova on constitutional reform, section 4.

[50] Venice Commission, CDL (2000) 55 rev, Law on the modification and the completion of the Constitution of the Republic of Moldova.

The monitoring procedure together with its Parliamentary Assembly followed the developments in the countries closely and acted as a "watchdog". At crucial moments, the Parliamentary Assembly involved the Venice Commission into the monitoring process as an objective legal expert body. Thus, the Commission evolved to an extended branch of the monitoring procedure.

With respect to the abolition of the death penalty in Ukraine and Albania, it should be noted that the opinions adopted by the Venice Commission influenced the judgments rendered by the two constitutional courts significantly. In the case of Ukraine, the Constitutional Court explicitly referred to the Commission's opinion and orientated its reasoning along the arguments brought forward by the Council's expert body. The case was brought to the Constitutional Court by members of the Ukrainian delegation to the Council's Parliamentary Assembly who belonged to opposition factions of the Ukrainian Parliament.

As to the principle of separation of powers, in both Ukraine and Moldova the presidents aimed to strengthen their role in the governing system to the detriment of the legislature. In both cases, the presidents intended to achieve the necessary constitutional amendments in an unconstitutional manner – through a referendum. Clearly, the interplay of the monitoring procedure and the Venice Commission ensured that the highest authorities in both countries were put under significant scrutiny in crucial periods. Furthermore, the Commission was able to put itself into a mediating role, bridging between the political fronts of the president and the parliament, in particular in the case of Moldova.

3. *The challenges ahead*

Despite the achievements outlined above, many challenges still lie ahead for the Council of Europe. This holds particularly true since many Eastern European countries still have significant shortcomings in the area of the organisation's fundamental standards. Specifically, the Council increasingly struggles with countries that have joined the organisation after 1995.

Two of these cases are illustrated in the following sections.

(1) *Russia and its commitment to abolish the death penalty*

One of the Council's main challenges is the abolition of the death penalty in the Russian Federation. In 2008, twelve years after its accession, the death penalty is still in the books of the Russian Federation and seems far from being abolished in the near future, in spite of Russia's firm commitment upon its accession.[51]

---

[51] Parliamentary Assembly, Opinion 193 (1996), Russia's application for membership of the Council of Europe, para. 10 ii.

As in the case of Ukraine, the Committee on Legal Affairs and Human Rights issued a special report on the progress made by Russia on the abolition of the death penalty. On the basis of this report, the Parliamentary Assembly stated that it will consider the non-ratification of the credentials of the Russian delegation, as well as a request to the Committee of Ministers for sanctions, in case of further executions of pronounced death sentences.[52]

When the Russian Parliament, the DUMA, asked President Putin to reintroduce the death penalty in 2002, the Council's Assembly expressed strong dismay.[53] Whilst recognising that the official moratorium on executions introduced by President Yeltsin in 1996 had been respected, the Assembly urged the Russian authorities to abolish the death penalty *de jure*. However, sanctions had not been mentioned by the Parliamentary Assembly.

The following monitoring report and its subsequent resolution of 2005 recalled that the original deadline to meet this commitment had expired in 1999. It also mentioned, though in a rather general way, that other countries which failed to respect this key commitment had been exposed to sanctions.[54] In its recommendation to the Committee of Ministers, the Assembly insisted on a speedy action by the Russian Federation on the commitment entered into.

On its part, the Council of Ministers agreed with the demand of the Assembly, but merely referred to regular consultations on this issue with the Russian Government. During the 2005 consultation, the Committee had insistently called on the Russian Federation to take the necessary steps to transform the existing moratorium on executions into a *de jure* abolition.[55] The Parliamentary Assembly, in its recommendation to the Committee of Ministers,[56] underlined that the death penalty has been abolished in all Council of Europe member states, with just one exception. Furthermore, the Assembly expressed its regret that more than ten years after accession, the Russian Federation retains the death penalty in its legislation. The Assembly also regretted that it had so far

[52] Parliamentary Assembly, Resolution 1111 (1997), Honouring of the commitment entered into by Russia upon accession to the Council of Europe to put into place a moratorium on executions, paras. 5–6.

[53] Parliamentary Assembly, Resolution 1277 (2002), Honouring of obligations and commitments by the Russian Federation, para. 8 ii.

[54] Parliamentary Assembly, Resolution 1455 (2005), Honouring of obligations and commitments by the Russian Federation, para. 13 i.

[55] Committee of Ministers, Reply to recommendation 10760 (2005), Honoring of obligations and commitments by the Russian Federation, para. 6.

[56] Parliamentary Assembly, Recommendation 1760 (2006), Position of the Parliamentary Assembly with regard to Council of Europe Member States and Observers which have not abolished the death penalty.

not received any clear indication from the Russian authorities, at the highest level, as to their intentions on this issue. It urged the Russian authorities to show the same determination and persuasiveness displayed by the other Council of Europe member states vis-à-vis public opinion, who had the political will and courage to abolish the death penalty despite the potential unpopularity of the measure. On the World Day against the Death Penalty, this call was repeated by the President of the Council's Parliamentary Assembly and the Secretary-General of the organisation.[57]

The continuing resistance to the *de jure* abolition of the death penalty has recently led to more serious concerns. In 1999, the Russian Constitutional Court decided that no death sentence could be rendered by the courts as long as the system of jury trials has not been established within the entire territory of the Russian Federation. However, the Criminal Procedural Code of 2001 extended jury trials to the whole of Russia except Chechnya, where it was scheduled to be introduced in January 2007. Shortly before the expiration of this deadline, in late November 2006, the State DUMA enacted law changing the date for introduction of jury trials in Chechnya to 1 January 2010. While this decision had the effect of extending the current *de facto* moratorium on sentencing people to death until 2010, it also signifies that courts in Russia can restart issuing death sentences once this new deadline has passed.

Thus, the monitoring procedure of the Parliamentary Assembly has not achieved one of its key objectives within the last 12 years – the abolition of the death penalty in the Russian Federation.

In contrast to the case of Ukraine, the Parliamentary Assembly explicitly referred to specific sanctions just once, and this only with a view to the establishment of an immediate moratorium. With respect to the *de jure* abolition of capital punishment, the Assembly has never made it clear that it will apply sanctions if this crucial commitment is not honoured. Moreover, it should be noted that the Assembly applied sanctions vis-à-vis the Russian Federation only once, namely because of grave human rights violations committed during the second war in the Republic of Chechnya.

Finally, the Venice Commission has never been asked by the Monitoring Committee or the Assembly for an opinion on the lack of implementation of this key commitment.

(2) *Azerbaijan 2002: Playing tricks with the Council*

At its accession to the organisation in 2001, Azerbaijan had to commit itself to reforms aimed at strengthening the independence of the legislature vis-à-vis the

---

[57] Council of Europe, Press release 575 and 576 (2006), 10 October 2006.

executive.[58] This commitment emerged as a result of an assessment pointing to a particularly weak position of the Parliament within the governing system.

With a view to honour this commitment, the Azeri presidential administration consulted the Venice Commission in September 2001 with respect to a draft constitutional law, which allegedly established additional guarantees to the exercise of a non-confidence vote of the legislature against the government.[59]

In its subsequent opinion, the Venice Commission stated that the introduction of a veritable right of the legislature to put a non-confidence vote to the executive required an amendment in the constitution itself, since this right would significantly alter the mechanisms of the governing system. The adoption of an additional constitutional law was not sufficient, the Commission argued. Given the function of a constitutional law as detailing provisions already contained in the constitution, this draft law could not introduce a non-confidence vote with legally binding consequences. In this vein, the Venice Commission clearly pointed out that this constitutional law could lead to a further destabilization of the institutional setup and conflicts between the branches of power.[60]

In June 2002, then President Heidar Alijev unexpectedly announced a decree to hold a referendum for the amendment of the constitution – scheduled for August the same year. With the referendum, the President intended to introduce 39 amendments to 24 constitutional articles with one single question to be put to the electorate. Among the planned amendments were changes of the presidential election system, the transfer of the president's powers to the prime minister in case of the president's early demission, the introduction of an individual complaints procedure before the constitutional court, and the establishment of an Ombudsperson.

Immediately after the announcement of Alijev's plan, one of the country Rapporteurs of the Monitoring Committee of the Council's Assembly raised the concern that such a significant number of changes be implemented with a single question and proposed that the 39 amendments be put to the voters in eight clusters. Furthermore, in his subsequent report, the Rapporteur pointed to the fact that the Azeri legislature was only informed about the holding and the content of this referendum at the time of the publication of the presidential

---

58 Parliamentary Assembly, Opinion 222 (2001), Azerbaijan's application for membership of the Council of Europe, para. 14 iii c.

59 Venice Commission, CDL-INF (2001) 26, Opinion on the draft constitutional law of the Republic of Azerbaijan on "Safeguards for the vote of confidence to the Cabinet of Ministers by the Milli Majlis", Annex.

60 Venice Commission, CDL-INF (2001) 26, Opinion on the draft constitutional law of the Republic of Azerbaijan on "Safeguards for the vote of confidence to the Cabinet of Ministers by the Milli Majlis", paras. 18–22.

decree.[61] He argued that for such far-reaching constitutional amendments the parliament should have been involved at a much earlier stage. Also, the Rapporteur expressed his concern at the period of only two months between the adoption of the decree and the date of the referendum. Given the high number of proposed alterations to the constitution, the population was, in his opinion, not able to fully capture the proposed changes.

His main criticism, however, focused on the fact that the Venice Commission – despite previous cooperation with Azerbaijan – had not been consulted. Moreover, the proposed amendments had not included the Commission's recommendations with a view to strengthening the legislature.

Although a few commitments made in 2001 had been honoured with the proposed constitutional changes,[62] a majority of the provisions led to a strengthened executive branch. The key criticism in this respect was that the amendment changed the transfer of the president's powers in case of his early demission: the changes would put the prime minister in charge, while the current constitution would have transferred the powers to the speaker of parliament after an early demission. As the president would have been authorized to appoint the prime minister against the will of the parliament, this move was likely to be used to transfer the executive power to a "pre-selected" successor. This assumption materialized with the decree of then President Heidar Alijev appointing his son Ilham Alijev *ad interim* to the post of the prime minister, and the successful candidature of Ilham in the presidential elections of October 2003.

Following the adoption and implementation of the constitutional amendments, the Parliamentary Assembly repeatedly stressed[63] the necessity to strengthen the parliament in order to establish its independence and control function vis-à-vis the executive and reiterated the commitment made by Azerbaijan in 2001.

In January 2004, the Assembly announced for the first time that it would consider the non-ratification of the credentials of the Azeri parliamentary delegation.[64] In a further report, the Monitoring Committee concluded that no reform steps had been taken in this respect. In its subsequent resolution of 2004, the Assembly stated that, with regard to the separation of powers, it was still waiting for the parliament to play its role in legislating and in overseeing

---

[61] Parliamentary Assembly, Doc. 9545 rev, Honouring of obligations and commitments by Azerbaijan, Explanatory memorandum, para. 46.

[62] E.g. the establishment of an Ombudsperson and an individual complaints procedure before the Constitutional Court.

[63] Parliamentary Assembly, Resolution 1305 (2002), Honouring of obligations and commitments by Azerbaijan, para. 7; Resolution 1358 (2004), Honouring of obligations and commitments, para. 7.

[64] Parliamentary Assembly, Resolution 1358 (2004), Honouring of obligations and commitments, para. 16.

the executive.[65] However, the Assembly did not continue to highlight possible sanctions in case of lacking reforms.

Thus, from late 2004 onwards, the Assembly's call for the establishment of a genuine separation of powers has slowly faded away. Much more emphasis was put on the question of whether parliamentary elections in 2005 and 2006 were conducted in compliance with democratic standards. This issue was considered by two reports of the Monitoring Committee and two subsequent resolutions by the Assembly.[66] Azerbaijan's failure to alter its governing system in order to strengthen the legislature was not even mentioned in one of the two resolutions. The most recent Assembly resolution of 2008 again focuses attention on electoral issues and touches only very timidly upon the fact that the legislature does not yet live up to its actual role.[67]

To sum up, seven years after Azerbaijan's accession its commitment to strengthen the legislature vis-à-vis the executive branch still remains to be honoured. Clearly, in 2002, the presidential administration purposely avoided to consult the Venice Commission with a view to the proposed constitutional changes. Because of the particularly short period between the announcement of the constitutional referendum and its actual conduct, the preparation of an opinion by the Venice Commission would not have been possible.

Finally, the Council's Assembly did not stick to its warning to annul the credentials of the Azeri delegation. Though it is understandable that elections constitute a main issue of concern, it should be noted that the electoral legislation and particularly its practice will continue to infringe the Council's main standards as long as no genuine balance has been established between the executive and legislative branches of power.

(3) *Assessment*

As can be seen from both case studies, the Council of Europe is still struggling with the Russian Federation on the abolition of the death penalty and with Azerbaijan with regard to its commitment to strengthen the legislature. Since the accession of the two countries, both commitments have been considered as crucial steps to be taken in their mutual reform process.

---

[65] Parliamentary Assembly, Resolution 1398 (2004), Implementation of Resolution 1358 (2004) on the functioning of democratic institutions in Azerbaijan, para. 6.

[66] Parliamentary Assembly, Resolution 1480 (2006), Challenge of credentials of the parliamentary delegation of Azerbaijan; Parliamentary Assembly, Resolution 1505 (2006), Implementation of Resolution 1480 (2006) on the challenge of credentials of the parliamentary delegation of Azerbaijan.

[67] Parliamentary Assembly, Resolution 1614 (2008), The functioning of democratic institutions in Azerbaijan, para. 5, second sentence: "Much remains to be done to ensure that the Parliament plays its role as a public forum for political debate".

The question thus arises why the Council has not been able to exert the desired impact on the constitutional developments in Russia and Azerbaijan. A response should take possible structural shortcomings of the Council's architecture into account.

In contrast to the four cases illustrating the achievements above, the Venice Commission has, in neither case, been able to play the mediating role it fulfilled in other circumstances.[68] In the case of the Russian Federation, the Commission has simply never been requested to provide its opinion on the long-overdue commitment. Even worse, in the case of Azerbaijan, the Venice Commission has been precluded from giving its expert opinion on the proposals made by the President due to the short notice of the referendum.

Thus, in cases when the respective state authorities are unwilling to cooperate with the Council's instruments in order to bring their constitutional systems in line with the fundamental standards of the organisation, or even work in the opposite direction, the monitoring procedure is too weak on its own to have the desired impact. The same applies if the political opposition is not sufficiently and solidly represented in national parliaments to develop alternative proposals to those of the presidential administration. In these cases, the legal expert opinion of the Venice Commission is needed as justification and advocacy tool for the Assembly's monitoring procedure, and indirectly also for the political opposition in the respective member state.

Furthermore, in both cases, the Parliamentary Assembly has not consistently used its means to consider and impose sanctions on the Russian Federation and Azerbaijan. In the case of Russia, sanctions have neither been considered nor imposed for the lack of the *de jure* abolition of the death penalty. Since the abolition of capital punishment is one of the main priorities of the Council, the organisation is weakened by the fact that Russia remains the only member unwilling to honour this commitment. Regarding Azerbaijan, sanctions have been mentioned initially but have never been imposed. This absence of the implementation of announced sanctions severely discredits the organisation as a whole.

On the basis of this analysis, the following steps are suggested to tackle these challenges.

Firstly, when member states are unwilling to pursue the democratisation path and honour their commitments, the Venice Commission ought to be more closely involved in the monitoring process and be asked to deliver a neutral legal opinion. Thus, the Assembly and its Monitoring Committee should carefully follow the developments in the respective member state and engage the Venice Commission

[68] See in particular the case studies of Ukraine and Moldova under III. 2. (2) a) and b).

more consistently at crucial moments. This should particularly apply to cases in which key commitments are overdue for a long period of time.

Secondly, the Commission should set up a "Quick Response Task Force" which could deliver a preliminary opinion at very short notice. This would prevent member states to adopt and implement constitutional amendments before the expert body is in a position to react. If member states realise that the Council is capable to respond to pertinent constitutional developments in a very short period of time, they will be forced to cooperate with the organisation at an early stage.

Finally, the Assembly needs to review and assess the use of its sanctions regime carefully. Currently, the standards which lead the Assembly to announce and/or impose sanctions are vague. Therefore, sanctions are applied in an inconsistent way. Moreover, it is unpredictable in which situations the Assembly will use sanctions at the parliamentary level, i.e. the non-ratification of the credentials of the respective national delegation to the Assembly, or in which situations it will go further and suggest the Committee of Ministers to suspend the member state at the inter-governmental level. In the light of these assessments, efforts should be undertaken to make use of the available sanctions in a more consistent and targeted manner.

IV. *Conclusion*

Until 1989, the constitutional law of the member states' was outside the purview of the Council of Europe. This changed drastically with the fall of the Berlin Wall Starting with the first accessions of post-communist countries in the early 90s, the organisation put itself into a new role and transformed itself into a trainer of these reform countries providing direct constitutional assistance.[69]

With its "commitments for membership" strategy, the Council enforced its fundamental standards and established criteria and benchmarks for progressive implementation by its new Eastern European members.

Furthermore, in order to live up to its new role in assisting new member states in their constitution building and enforcing processes, the Council established new structures and institutions, namely the monitoring procedure of the Parliamentary Assembly and the European Commission for Democracy through Law – the Venice Commission.

The organisation deserves to be praised for its achievements in assisting the new Eastern European members in their transition to democracy. As evidenced

---

[69] See also Günther Winkler, The Council of Europe: Monitoring Procedures and the Constitutional Autonomy of the Member States 522–524 (2006).

by the underlying analysis of the successful interaction of the Assembly's monitoring procedure with the Venice Commission, the Council was able to play an important role in politically difficult constellations. Crucial steps on the path to democracy have been illustrated by the case studies of Albania and Ukraine in the area of the abolition of the death penalty and those of Ukraine and Moldova in the sphere of separation of powers. Compared to non-member states of the Council, such as Belarus or countries in Central Asia, in which the process of abolition of capital punishment has just started and in which the presidential systems have been dangerously transformed into autocracies, the new member states of the Council of Europe have made significant progress.

The two mechanisms of the Council, the monitoring procedure of the Parliamentary Assembly and the Venice Commission, have worked hand-in hand very well: While the monitoring procedure exercises political pressure, the Commission delivers expert advice on which the monitoring procedure can build as an advocacy tool. Thus, in its role as a legal expert body, the Venice Commission progressively evolved to an extended branch of the monitoring procedure.

Nonetheless, important challenges remain. The continuing resistance by certain member states – illustrated, for example, by the case studies of the Russian Federation and Azerbaijan – in honouring key commitments does not only slow down the reform process in these countries. It also damages the credibility of the Council.

If the Council is to continue fulfilling its role as a trainer and crucial reform agent on the European stage, it ought to think about adapting its structure to the challenges posed by member states unwilling to pursue their reform path as promised at the moment of accession.

Therefore, three reform proposals to help the Council overcome these challenges are suggested:

Firstly, a complementary and efficient interaction of the Venice Commission with the Assembly's monitoring procedure is crucial. Precautions have to be taken to ensure that the Venice Commission is not circumvented by member states. In order to achieve this, the Commission needs to set up a rapid response mechanism, possibly in the form of a task force. The Assembly, on its side, is required to act as a watchdog and seize the expert body on pertinent constitutional developments and proposals, including those brought forward by the opposition. Only in such circumstances will the Commission be able to play its role as a mediating expert.

Secondly, when realising that key commitments are overdue for a significant period of time, the Parliamentary Assembly should request the Venice Commission to assess the reform steps already completed by the respective member state. On this basis, the member state should be encouraged to strengthen its co-operation with the Council. In particularly difficult cases, a recommendation should be adopted at the level of the Committee of Ministers requesting the respective state to collaborate with a view to fulfilling its commitments.

Finally, the Assembly needs to conduct a careful review and reform of the way it currently uses its sanctions regime. In this process, the Assembly should elaborate specific and transparent standards for imposing sanctions. This holds true as sanctions will only have the desired efficiency with member states if they are credibly imposed and enforced.

To conclude, it is desirable that the Council of Europe succeeds in effectively providing continued constitutional assistance to its new member states. To this end, however, the organisation must overcome the stated structural obstacles which presently hamper its ability to accompany new member states on their path to democracy.

The Duties of the Occupying Power: An Overview of the Recent Developments in the Law of Occupation

Charles H. B. Garraway

I. *Introduction*

The law of occupation has always been rather on the sidelines of the law of armed conflict. Of the four Geneva Conventions of 1949,[1] the Fourth, dealing, *inter alia*, with the law of occupation, is perhaps the least well known. Despite the fact that it grew out of the experiences of the Second World War in which large swathes of both Europe and Asia found themselves under occupation, revealing the inadequacy of the existing Hague law,[2] the Convention itself was little used in the second half of the 20th Century. Indeed, if anything, its efficacy was challenged in that in those cases where it might be most relevant, it was argued that it was not applicable. This was particularly true in the Occupied Territories where Israel has long argued that the situation in those territories does not fall within the ambit of Common Article 2 to the Conventions[3] because the Occupied Territories, prior to 1967, did not form part of "the territory of a High Contracting Party". The argument is based on the fact that Jordan's assertion of sovereignty over the West Bank was only recognized by two States,

---

[1] Geneva Convention for the Amelioration of the Condition of the Wounded and Sick in Armed Forces in the Field (Geneva Convention I), Geneva Convention for the Amelioration of the Condition of the Wounded, Sick and Shipwrecked Members of Armed Forces at Sea (Geneva Convention II), Geneva Convention Relative to the Treatment of Prisoners of War (Geneva Convention III), Geneva Convention Relative to the Protection of Civilian Persons in Time of War (Geneva Convention IV), all of 12 August 1949, reprinted *in* Documents on the Laws of War, 3rd ed. (Adam Roberts & Richard Guelff eds., 2000) 197, 222, 244 and 301 respectively.

[2] Regulations Respecting the Laws and Customs of War on Land, annexed to Hague Convention (IV) Respecting the Laws and Customs of War on Land, 18 October 1907 (Hague Regulations), reprinted *in* Roberts & Guelff, *supra* note 1, 73.

[3] Common Article 2 to the four Geneva Conventions of 1949 states that the Conventions "shall also apply to all cases of partial or total occupation of the territory of a High Contracting Party, even if the said occupation meets with no armed resistance."

the United Kingdom and Pakistan.[4] It should be stated that this position was generally condemned outside Israel and the Convention was deemed applicable by numerous resolutions of the United Nations Security Council and General Assembly[5] as well as by statements by the International Committee of the Red Cross. The application of the Convention was subsequently affirmed by the International Court of Justice in the "Barrier" case.[6]

Furthermore, in other cases where the law of occupation might have been thought to be applicable, it was supplanted by resolutions of the United Nations Security Council. Thus the NATO "occupation" of Kosovo after the conflict against Serbia and Montenegro in 1999 was governed by the terms of United Nations Security Council Resolution 1244 (1999),[7] establishing what amounted to a United Nations Administration through the United Nations Mission in Kosovo (UNMIK) supported by a NATO-led force, 'Kosovo Force' (KFOR). Nobody sought to apply the law of occupation other than as 'guidance' in the early days before UNMIK was able to exercise effective control.

It appeared therefore that at the turn of the century, the law of occupation was in some disarray. Its application was challenged both as a matter of law and, in long term occupations, as a matter of practicality. Furthermore, it was in danger of being superseded by the growing use of the United Nations to 'circumvent' its strict application.

However, all that was to change with the invasion of Iraq in 2003 by the Coalition led by the United States. Suddenly, the law of occupation again became relevant and the subject of both practical and academic interest. The reason for this was, to a large extent, political. The decision of the United States and their allies to 'go it alone' without the sought-after 'Second Resolution' from the United Nations Security Council[8] meant that the Council itself was split with Permanent Members lined up on both sides. There was therefore no question of a subsequent Security Council resolution 'legitimizing' the invasion and establishing a United Nations Administration to oversee the return to local government. Indeed, such a course of action would probably have been unacceptable to the United States Administration itself, which considered that it was acting in self

[4] See Geoffrey Watson, *The "Wall" Decisions in Legal and Political Context*, 99 AMERICAN JOURNAL OF INTERNATIONAL LAW 6, 12 (2005).

[5] See those cited in paras. 98–99 of the Advisory Opinion on the Legal Consequences of the Construction of a Wall in the Occupied Palestinian Territory, (The Barrier Case), International Court of Justice, July 9, 2004, 43 ILM 1009, 1037 (2004).

[6] See *supra* note 5.

[7] S/Res/1244 (1999) of June 10, 1999.

[8] Following up on United Nations Security Council Resolution S/Res/1441 (2002) of Nov. 8, 2002.

defence under Article 51 of the Charter[9] and was not prepared to leave what it saw as its own security in the hands of others. The apparent belief within the Pentagon that the invasion would be greeted with open arms by the Iraqis[10] and that an indigenous administration would soon be ready to take over the reins of government was quickly squashed as it became apparent that the machinery of government itself had collapsed. The Coalition Forces would have to take over responsibility for the running of the country themselves – at least in the short term. But on what basis? Initially, certainly in the United States, there was grave reluctance to accept the idea of 'occupation'.[11] However, there was little doubt but that the situation fell squarely within the definition contained in Common Article 2 and that therefore the Fourth Geneva Convention applied in full. This was recognised by the United Kingdom very early on[12] and also – though in slightly convoluted language – in United Nations Security Council Resolution 1483[13] which, in the Preamble, stated:

> [...] and recognizing the specific authorities, responsibilities, and obligations under applicable international law of [the United States and the United Kingdom] as occupying powers [...].

In paragraph 5 of the Resolution, the Council called upon:

> [...] all concerned to comply fully with their obligations under international law including in particular the Geneva Conventions of 1949 and the Hague Regulations of 1907.

A situation had now arisen which would test the law of occupation fully in that, unusually, it was accepted as applicable even by the occupying powers, it involved a situation not of temporary occupation of part of a territory but of the total occupation of a country requiring a rebuilding of the governmental structures,

---

[9] See Letter dated March 20, 2003 from the Permanent Representative of the United States of America to the United Nations addressed to the President of the Security Council, UN Doc. S/2003/351, which, whilst primarily relying on previous Security Council resolutions, also states that the actions of the Coalition forces were "necessary steps to defend the United States and the international community from the threat posed by Iraq".

[10] In an interview with NBC Meet the Press, Vice President Cheney, on March 16, 2003, stated: "I think things have gotten so bad inside Iraq from the standpoint of the Iraqi people, my belief is we will, in fact, be greeted as liberators." (*at* <http://www.mtholyoke.edu/acad/intrel/bush/cheneymeetthepress.htm>).

[11] Marc Grossman, Under-Secretary of State for Political Affairs in the State Department, speaking on Al-Arabiyya TV on April 25, 2003 said, "Obviously we consider ourselves to be liberators of Iraq, not the occupiers of Iraq". *At* <http://www.state.gov/p/us/rm/20058.htm>.

[12] See statement by British Prime Minister Tony Blair on April 14, 2003, Hansard, Column 616.

[13] S/Res/1483 (2003) of May 22, 2003.

and all of this was to be done under the supervision of the United Nations operating through Chapter VII resolutions from the Security Council.

Of course, history has not dealt kindly with the occupation of Iraq and there has been much criticism of the way that it was carried out. However, it has opened up a possible new chapter in the development of the law of occupation. It is now necessary to examine the law of occupation not just in isolation but also in conjunction with human rights law and United Nations law as developed by the Security Council. These three are at times uneasy bedfellows and it is perhaps encouraging that there is a growing willingness to look again at the law of occupation and test it against modern circumstances. Does it need change or can it be incorporated as it stands into the overall structure of international law in a manner that will assist those faced with similar conundrums? The International Committee of the Red Cross has itself initiated a project to examine these issues with a group of experts.[14]

II. *The notion of the law of occupation*

1. *The Hague Regulations of 1907 and the conservationist principle*

The original law of occupation had developed in somewhat different circumstances. Chief Justice John Marshall in *American Insurance Company v. Cantor* wrote as early as 1828:

> The usage of the world is, if a nation be not entirely subdued, to consider the holding of conquered territory as a mere military occupation, until its fate shall be determined at the treaty of peace.[15]

The words "not entirely subdued" are relevant here. Occupation was seen as a temporary control over part of a territory with the sovereign State continuing to exist and to operate in other parts of its territory. The provisions in the Hague Regulations of 1907 adopted this approach, and imposed two primary obligations on the occupier. First, the occupier could not gain actual sovereignty over the territory – that remained with the original sovereign. Second, the occupier was to leave intact as far as possible the existing legal and political structures within

[14] See International Humanitarian Law and the Challenges of Contemporary Armed Conflicts, document prepared by the International Committee of the Red Cross for the 30th International Conference of the Red Cross and Red Crescent, Geneva, November 26–30, 2007, *at* <http://www.icrc.org/Web/eng/siteeng0.nsf/htmlall/ihl-30-international-conference-101207/$File/IHL-challenges-30th-International-Conference-ENG.pdf>.

[15] American Insurance Company v. Cantor, 26 U.S. (1 Pet.) 511 at p. 542.

the territory. This is sometimes referred to as the "conservationist" approach.[16] Article 43 of the Hague Regulations states:

> The authority of the legitimate power having in fact passed into the hands of the occupant, the latter shall take all the measures in his power to restore and ensure, as far as possible, public order and safety,[17] while respecting, unless absolutely prevented, the laws in force in the country.

This principle is supplemented by Article 64 of the Fourth Geneva Convention:

> The penal laws of the occupied territory shall remain in force, with the exception that they may be repealed or suspended by the Occupying Power in cases where they constitute a threat to its security or an obstacle to the application of the present Convention. Subject to the latter consideration and to the necessity for ensuring the effective administration of justice, the tribunals of the occupied territory shall continue to function in respect of all offences covered by the said laws.
>
> The Occupying Power may, however, subject the population of the occupied territory to provisions which are essential to enable the Occupying Power to fulfil its obligations under the present Convention, to maintain the orderly government of the territory, and to ensure the security of the Occupying Power, of the members and property of the occupying forces or administration, and likewise of the establishments and lines of communications used by them.

Thus the United Kingdom Manual of the Law of Armed Conflict states:

> The law of armed conflict does not confer power on an occupant. Rather it regulates the occupant's use of power. The occupant's power arises from the actual control of the area.[18]

This reflects the definition of occupation to be found in Article 42 of the Hague Regulations:

> Territory is considered occupied when it is actually placed under the authority of the hostile army.
>
> The occupation extends only to the territory where such authority has been established and can be exercised.

It follows that the law of occupation imposes a series of constraints rather than a series of rights upon the Occupying Power.

The Hague Regulations themselves were concise and dealt specifically with "Military Authority over the Territory of the Hostile State" (Section III). The fourteen articles prevent forced informants (Article 44), oaths of allegiance to the

---

16 See Gregory Fox, *The Occupation of Iraq*, 36 Georgetown Journal of International Law 195, 236 (Winter 2005).

17 The authentic French text reads 'l'ordre et la vie publique'. This is incorrectly translated as 'public safety' and the meaning may perhaps be better reflected by use of the term 'civil life'.

18 The Manual of the Law of Armed Conflict, para. 11.9, 278 (UK Ministry of Defence ed., 2004).

Occupying Power (Article 45) and pillage (Article 47), whilst requiring respect for "family honor and rights, the lives of persons, and private property, as well as religious convictions and practice" (Article 46). The right of the Occupying Power to levy taxes is restricted to that required for the "needs of the army or of the administration of the territory in question" (Article 49) and the collection and disbursement of general tax revenues shall be "as far as is possible" in accordance with the rules of assessment and incidence already in force within the territory (Article 48) with receipts tendered (Article 51). Collective punishments are prohibited (Article 50) and requisitions limited (Article 52). Moveable State property may be seized and some private property linked to the war effort but, in the latter case, restoration and compensation must be made "when peace is made" (Article 53).

There are special provisions governing certain submarine cables (Article 54) and some cultural property (Article 56) but perhaps of most importance is Article 55, which provides that:

> The occupying State shall be regarded only as administrator and usufructuary of public buildings, real estate, forests, and agricultural estates belonging to the hostile State, and situated in the occupied country. It must safeguard the capital of these properties, and administer them in accordance with the rules of usufruct.

This is fully in accordance with the "conservationist" principle.

The Second World War raised different problems. First, there were the Axis occupations of Europe and the Japanese occupations in the Far East. Secondly, there were the Allied occupations of Germany and Japan at the end of the war. These were different, in that the earlier occupations were opposed and in many countries, Governments-in-Exile purported to represent the legitimate sovereign even when the territory of the State had been completely overrun. However, in the Allied occupations at the end of the war, this was not the case. The Allied Powers took over full governmental responsibility with no representatives of the original State remaining. Indeed, the Berlin Declaration of 5 June 1945 stated that there was "no central Government or authority in Germany capable of accepting responsibility for the maintenance of order, the administration of the country and compliance with the requirements of the victorious Powers."[19] There followed an extensive series of Control Laws designed to rebuild the country.

The problem that the Allies faced was that such complete subjugation of a State would normally in the past have led not to occupation but to annexation. However, the Allies had no wish to annex either Germany or Japan and indeed, it could already be argued that international law had reached a stage

[19] Berlin Declaration, 5 June 1945, printed in Robert Jennings, *Government in Commission*, 23 British Yearbook of International Law 112, 113–114 (1946).

where such annexation might be considered to be illegal. Certainly, it would be illegal today under the United Nations Charter.[20] On the other hand, clearly the restraints of the Hague Regulations would prove impracticable. The 1958 United Kingdom Manual on the Law of War on Land freely recognized this conundrum and stated:

> The position in Germany after the unconditional surrender has given rise to much controversy. It was probably not governed by the Hague Rules 42–56.[21]

The editors cited as authority Robert Jennings[22] and Lassa Oppenheim.[23] Jennings had stated that "to attempt to apply [the law of occupation] would be a manifest anachronism".[24]

2. *The Fourth Geneva Convention: retention of the conservationist approach*

In the light of this, it is perhaps somewhat surprising that in 1949, the Fourth Geneva Convention carried on the "conservationist" policy of its predecessor the Hague Regulations of 1907. Nevertheless, that was what was done. It should be recalled, however, that the Geneva Conventions were less concerned with the conduct of hostilities than with the protection of victims. Thus the conduct of occupation was inevitably viewed from the need to protect the persons and property of the inhabitants of the territory. This would inevitably lead to a conservationist approach. Furthermore, the intention was to build upon the provisions of the Hague Regulations, not to replace them.

The Fourth Geneva Convention lays down detailed provisions on the administration of the occupied territory, including the position of local officials, especially judges. It is recognized, however, that the Occupying Power is entitled to take measures to protect its own security and thus permits certain restrictions on civilians within the territory, including restrictions of movement, assigned residence and internment (Arts. 42, 43, 78). However, the latter two measures are seen as exceptional and may only be adopted subject to a regime similar to that applicable to prisoners of war under the Third Convention.[25] Other specific areas dealt with are schools (Art. 50), medical care (Art. 56) and protection of civilian medical facilities (Art. 57). In addition, there are articles dealing with

---

[20] Art. 2(4), United Nations Charter, reprinted *in* Basic Documents in International Law, 5th ed., 3 (Ian Brownlie ed., 2002).

[21] The Law of War on Land being Part III of the Manual of Military Law, para. 499, 140, note 2 (HMSO ed., 1958).

[22] *Supra* note 19.

[23] Lassa Oppenheim, International Law, 8th ed., Vol. II, 603, note 2 (1955).

[24] Jennings, *supra* note 19, 136.

[25] Section IV.

relief supplies, both in relation to the provision of such supplies (Art. 59), their protection (Art. 60) and arrangements for their distribution (Art. 61).

In keeping with the protective aim, there are also specific provisions dealing with labour (Art. 51 and 52) and protection of property (Art. 53). Linked to the provisions dealing with criminal justice and internment, there is in place a reasonably comprehensive system of protection for all those who find themselves within the designation of "protected person" under Article 4 of the Convention.

III. *The recent evolution of the law of occupation: The Case of Iraq*

1. *The current adequacy of the conservationist approach*

Whilst these provisions make sense in the context of the sort of occupation envisaged by Chief Justice Marshall,[26] the question must be asked as to their relevance in the modern context where sovereignty is increasingly giving way to human rights. In many cases of "intervention" today, the very aim of the intervention is to remove from power the existing administration – effectively a policy of 'regime change'. How can this be equated with the law of occupation in its traditional sense?

This article is not designed to examine the legality of intervention nor should that issue be directly relevant. The law of armed conflict, of which the law of occupation is a subset, is designed to bind both sides in a conflict equally, regardless of the rightness or otherwise of their cause. Thus it is irrelevant whether or not the occupation is as a result of aggression or action taken in self defence or in protection of human rights. The law should be the same. However, if the State authorities have ceased to exist as was the case in Germany – and later in Iraq – can the conservationist approach be workable? If not, how can the need for a rebuilding of the State organs be accommodated within the fundamental provisions designed to protect the rights of those within the occupied territory?

This conundrum came to the fore in Iraq. Whatever the rights or wrongs of the invasion itself under international law, there were few people who were sorry to see the back of Saddam Hussein. He had run one of the most repressive regimes in the world and there was little doubt that the people of Iraq – of all denominations and ethic origins – had suffered grievously at the hands of his regime. Nobody seriously wished to argue that, at the end of any occupation, power should be handed back to the Ba'ath Party. In that respect, the situation was similar to that faced by the triumphant Allies in Germany at the end of the Second World War. However, a strict interpretation of the Fourth Convention

---

[26] See *supra* note 15.

and the Hague Regulations would seem to imply exactly that and leave the hands of the Occupying Power tied.

2. *Blending UN law and the law of occupation*

The answer adopted was to rely on a combination of laws – a blending of UN law and occupation law. United Nations Security Council Resolution 1483 was adopted on 22 May 2003[27] and in its 27 operative paragraphs went into considerable detail on the reconstruction of Iraq. Indeed, in the Preamble to the Resolution, the Security Council "resolved that the United Nations should play a vital role in humanitarian relief, the reconstruction of Iraq, and the restoration and establishment of national and local institutions for representative governance." This was to be done through the appointment of a Special Representative who was given a specific remit "in coordination with the [Coalition Provisional Authority]". The Special Representative was required, *inter alia*, to carry out his duties:

> (c) working intensively with the [Coalition Provisional Authority], the people of Iraq, and others concerned to advance efforts to restore and establish national and local institutions for representative governance, including by working together to facilitate a process leading to an internationally recognized, representative government of Iraq; [...]
> (e) promoting economic reconstruction and the conditions for sustainable development, including through coordination with national and regional organizations, as appropriate, civil society, donors, and the international financial institutions; [...]
> (h) encouraging international efforts to rebuild the capacity of the Iraqi civilian police force;
> (i) encouraging international efforts to promote legal and judicial reform.[28]

What was envisaged thus was a partnership between the Coalition Provisional Authority (CPA) and the United Nations. This seemed to be acknowledged by the CPA, which cited Security Council Resolution 1483 as an authority for its actions as early as CPA Regulation No.1.[29] This was curious as Regulation No.1 is dated 16 May, several days before Security Council Resolution 1483 was actually adopted.[30]

The Secretary General appointed the experienced diplomat Sergio Viera de Mello as his Special Representative and it is interesting to speculate how that partnership might have evolved. However, it was not to be as on 19 August 2003,

27 See *supra* note 13.

28 Para. 8.

29 CPA Regulation 1, May 16, 2003, *at* <http://www.cpa-iraq.org/regulations/20030516_CPAREG_1_The_Coalition_Provisional_Authority_.pdf>.

30 Security Council Resolution 1483 was not adopted until May 22, 2003.

a suicide bomber attacked the UN Headquarters in Baghdad, killing de Mello and causing the withdrawal of most UN staff from Iraq. The United Nations effectively ceased to be a "player" on the ground.

3. *The CPA takes over the role of the UN Special Representative*

At this point the CPA sought to take over the role previously given to the Special Representative and proceeded to take steps to implement the provisions of Resolution 1483 through its own Regulations. The Security Council continued to monitor the situation and passed a series of further Resolutions, most notably perhaps Resolution 1511 on 16 October 2003.[31] However, the driving force was now the CPA and the legal basis for many of the subsequent Regulations adopted by the CPA is to be found not in the law of occupation but in the Security Council Resolutions. It can be argued that the authority in Resolution 1483 was granted not to the CPA itself but to the Special Representative, acting on behalf of the United Nations.[32] However, the Special Representative was tasked to act "in coordination with the Authority" and with the withdrawal of the United Nations, the CPA took it upon themselves to implement the provisions of the Resolution. In doing so, they clearly had to go beyond the constraints of the law of occupation but sought authority in the Resolution itself.

The argument remains as to whether the CPA were entitled so to do or whether the collapse of the UN presence effectively prevented the application of Resolution 1483. A strict legal approach might favour the latter but to permit suicide bombers to thwart the will of the international community in that way might be more dangerous in the long run than to permit the CPA to act unilaterally to implement the terms where the prime mover, the Special Representative, had been removed from the scene.

The CPA was faced with a number of key areas that required action. The first was that of governance. The occupation could not cease until there was an indigenous authority to whom power could be handed over but there was no authority under the law of occupation for such a construct, that law envisaging that power would revert to the original sovereign. It follows that for almost every action taken in this area by the CPA, ranging from the recognition of the Governing Council[33] through the dissolution and reconstruction of Govern-

---

[31] United Nations Security Council Resolution 1511, S/Res/1511 (2003) of Oct. 16, 2003.

[32] See Fox, *supra* note 16, 262.

[33] See CPA Regulation 6, Governing Council of Iraq, July 13, 2003, *at* <http://www.iraqcoalition.org/regulations/20030713_CPAREG_6_Governing_Council_of_Iraq_.pdf>.

ment Ministries[34] to the subsequent appointment of an Interim Government,[35] authority must be sought outside the law of occupation. These steps, by their very nature, involved changes to the *status quo ante* of a nature apparently prohibited by the law of occupation.

Similarly in the area of security, the CPA began by dissolving the existing Iraqi security forces and set about a root and branch restructuring.[36] A new police force was established and a new Iraqi Army – under Coalition command and control.[37] Again the intention was to ensure that when the occupation ended, the new government had the necessary means to exercise control itself. A withdrawal of Coalition forces without any indigenous forces in place would have led to a dangerous power vacuum. Yet, again, a strict reading of the law of occupation would not seem to permit this. The Fourth Convention prohibits the recruitment of individuals into the occupier's armed or auxiliary forces (Art. 51). Whilst it does not specifically prohibit the creation of indigenous security organizations, where these are under command of the Occupier and are to be used in a counter-resistance role, the legality under Geneva law of such forces must be questionable. However Security Council Resolution 1511 specifically referred to "the importance of establishing effective Iraqi police and security forces in maintaining law, order and security and combating terrorism."[38] Without such forces being created, it would have been impossible to fulfill the other requirements of the Resolution 1483.

4. *The law of occupation and the rebuilding of the economy*

Perhaps the most controversial area of CPA activity was the economy. The economy of Iraq was in dire straits prior to the invasion as a result of years of mismanagement, the war with Iran and UN sanctions following the abortive attack on Kuwait. That situation was made worse by the collapse of law and order in the early days of the occupation and the disintegration of much of the economic structure. The CPA was faced with a country, on paper rich in natural resources, but in reality heavily burdened with debt and without any economic foundations. Again, under a strict reading of the law of occupation,

[34] See, inter alia, CPA Order 2, Dissolution of Entities, May 23, 2003, *at* <http://www.iraqcoalition.org/regulations/20030823_CPAORD_2_Dissolution_of_Entities_with_Annex_A.pdf>.

[35] CPA Regulation 10, Members of Designated Iraqi Interim Government, June 9, 2004, *at* <http://www.iraqcoalition.org/regulations/20040609_CPAREG_10_Members_of_ Designated_ Iraqi_Interim_Government_with_Annex_A.pdf>.

[36] See CPA Order 2, *supra* note 34.

[37] See CPA Regulation 22, Creation of a New Iraqi Army, Aug. 18, 2003, *at* <http://www.iraqcoalition.org/regulations/20030818_CPAORD_22_Creation_of_a_New_Iraqi_ Army.pdf>.

[38] Para. 16. See also on this point Michael Schmitt & Charles Garraway, *Occupation Policy in Iraq and International Law*, 9 INTERNATIONAL PEACEKEEPING 27, 44 (2003).

the duty of the occupier was to maintain the *status quo ante* but that was quite clearly both impracticable and also counter to the interests of the inhabitants of the occupied territory. However, how far could the CPA go in reconstructing the economy? The problem lies as much as anything in the different economic philosophies at issue. Iraq was a centralized State-run economy. The CPA was dominated by Western experts in whose eyes such an economy was an anathema. There followed as much an ideological battle as anything else.

Many of the reforms introduced can be accepted as in accord both with the law of occupation and the interests of the population. These included perhaps the tax law provisions[39] and the reconstruction of the currency.[40] Other reforms merely brought Iraq into line with existing international practice.[41] However, some were more controversial. Although the planned privatization of much of Iraqi State owned assets was never fully implemented, concern was expressed at the Foreign Investment Law[42] which permitted foreigners to own up to 100% of any Iraqi enterprise with the exception of oil, banking and insurance. This opening up of investment goes far beyond anything to be found elsewhere in the Arab world and certainly no authority could be found for such a major change under the law of occupation. Whether this can be classed as a necessary step in "promoting economic reconstruction and the conditions for sustainable development" in accordance with Resolution 1483[43] must at least be open to question. It should be noted that the Foreign Investment Law specifically cites Resolution 1483 as authority.

IV. *The current status of the law of occupation: A third way?*

There will always be controversy over any study of the forest that is international law and it is therefore necessary to try to look beyond the individual trees in order to examine the greater picture. Where does the law of occupation stand today? It would seem that, prior to Iraq, two separate tracks were beginning to

---

[39] See, *inter alia*, CPA Order 38, Tax Strategy for 2003, Sept. 19, 2003, *at* <http://www.iraqcoalition.org/regulations/20030919_CPAORD_37_Tax_Strategy_for_2003.pdf>.

[40] See CPA Order 43, New Iraqi Dinah Banknotes, Oct. 14, 2003, *at* <http://www.iraqcoalition.org/regulations/20031014_CPAORD_43_New_Iraqi_Dinar_Banknotes.pdf>.

[41] See the amendment to the Iraqi Trademarks and Description Law of 1957, *in* CPA Order 80, Amendment to the Trademark and Descriptions Law No. 21 of 1957, April 26, 2004, *at* <http://www.iraqcoalition.org/regulations/20040426_CPAORD_80_Amendment_to_the_Trademarks_and_Descriptions_Law_No._21_of_1957.pdf>.

[42] See CPA Order 39, Foreign Investment, Sept. 19, 2003, *at* <http://www.iraqcoalition.org/regulations/20031220_CPAORD_39_Foreign_Investment_.pdf>.

[43] See para. 8(e).

appear. First, there were those occupations which did not meet with international support and to which the international community therefore argued that the law of occupation applied in its full rigour. Such cases were usually marked by the reluctance of the occupier to accept that position. The second strand were those occupations carried out with the assent of the international community or to which the international community was prepared to extend a degree of legitimacy. To these, attempts were made to remove the constraints of the law of occupation by the application of United Nations law in the form of Security Council Resolutions.

However, Iraq appears to indicate that a third track has appeared – occupations where the international community is not prepared to extend legitimacy but where it is accepted that a return to the *status quo ante* is neither feasible nor desirable. In such cases, it would appear that the occupiers remain bound by the constraints of the law of occupation except in so far as authorization has been given by the Security Council to loosen those constraints. Thus, in the preambles of all the Security Council Resolutions dealing with Iraq, the Council called "upon all concerned to comply fully with their obligations under international law including in particular the Geneva Conventions of 1949 and the Hague Regulations of 1907", whilst at the same time authorizing measures that effectively sidetracked some of those obligations. It should be noted that in Resolution 1483, the Security Council reserved to the Special Representative the lead role in applying such measures though his subsequent death led to the CPA taking that responsibility into its own hands.

This is not the place to go into a detailed analysis of the effect of Article 103 of the United Nations Charter and the relationship between the Security Council and the law of armed conflict. There are those who argue that the Security Council, regardless of Article 103, has no authority to override humanitarian provisions, certainly if they amount to fundamental norms.[44] However, there is also a pragmatic school that recognizes that account must be taken of political realities. In such cases as Iraq, a strict application of the law of occupation could lead to stalemate. It is hard to see how the transition to a new Iraqi Government could have been undertaken without exercising some of the extended powers given under the Security Council Resolutions. The restriction of any extension to such measures as were approved by the Security Council would seem to provide a sensible solution. The law of occupation remains as the baseline and no occupier has the right unilaterally to break free from its constraints. However, where those constraints are clearly not in the interests of the occupied territory

---

[44] See Terry Gill, *Legal and some Political Limitations on the Power of the UN Security Council to Exercise its Enforcement Powers under Chapter VII of the Charter*, 26 Netherlands Yearbook of International Law 33, 71 (1995).

itself and its people, those constraints may be relaxed but only by the Security Council acting under Chapter VII of the Charter.

V. *Conclusions*

There will be those who wish, in the light of the experience of Iraq, to review the whole of the law of occupation and indeed, as with other areas of the law of armed conflict, there may be specific provisions which do need reexamination. However, if anything, the experience of Iraq has validated the principles of the law though recognizing their limitations. Any attempt to reopen the substantive provisions could lead to a weakening of the protections, which they are designed to provide. The end could be worse than the beginning. The old divisions between the law of peace and the law of war are no longer as clear cut as they were in the 19th Century and already there is an increasing overlap between different legal systems. The complexities in the inter-relationship between human rights law and the law of armed conflict are already being recognized. Similarly, a *modus vivendi* needs to be drawn up between the law of armed conflict and United Nations law as reflected in the powers of the Security Council. The Iraq experience may have contributed to a greater understanding for the need for such an inter-relationship and indeed a greater appreciation of the way that the two legal systems can work together to the same end.

It may be argued that with the changing nature of conflict, the nature of occupation is changing too. If so the law must adapt to reflect the realities on the ground. If it does not do so, it risks being consigned to oblivion. The secret is how to adapt without removing the protections which the law applies. As with all developments, the first steps are usually tentative and almost always controversial. However, if the combination of occupation law and United Nations law can resolve some of the practical problems found in the pure application of either body of law on its own, then it is worth exploring further.

Peace-Building and the Role of International Tribunals

*Roberta Arnold**

I. *Introduction*

1. *Aims and objectives*

State-building is a concept which has recently been regaining importance, in particular following to the occupation of Afghanistan and Iraq and the defeat, respectively, of the Taleban and Saddam Hussein regimes. In order to function, a state needs to be constructed on three pillars: the legislative, executive and judiciary powers. In a post-conflict situation these can only exist and be operated if peace has first been re-established and kept. This was proven in particular in the Balkans[1] and Iraq[2] and more recently by the situation that followed the declaration of independence of Kosovo.[3]

The role of justice as an important tool for peace-building, peace-keeping and, therefore, for state-building has been recognised in particular during the last fifteen years, with the establishment of several international tribunals, in particular the two UN *ad hoc* tribunals – the International Criminal Tribunal for the Former Yugoslavia (ICTY) and the International Criminal Tribunal for Rwanda (ICTR) – and the permanent International Criminal Court (ICC).[4] For the first time international tribunals have been set up as an alternative

---

* The views expressed here are the author's solely. Special thanks go to Maj. Stefan Wehrenberg for his helpful comments.

[1] Michael E. Hartmann, *International Judges and Prosecutors in Kosovo: A New Model for Post-Conflict Peacekeeping* (2003), *at* <http://www.usip.org/pubs/specialreports/sr112.html>.

[2] *Saddam defence lawyer shot dead*, BBC News, June 21, 2006, *at* <http://news.bbc.co.uk/2/hi/middle_east/5101162.stm>.

[3] See UNMIK Online, *Recent events make it more challenging for UN to administer Kosovo – envoy*, Aug. 4, 2008, *at* <http://www.unmikonline.org/news.htm#1508>.

[4] This is not an exhaustive list. There are also, for instance, the Special Tribunal for Lebanon (for more information see <http://www.un.org/apps/news/infocus/lebanon/tribunal/>) or The Cambodia Tribunal (see for more info <http://www.cambodiatribunal.org/>)

"Chapter VII measure" under the UN Charter, with the aim of contributing to the reconstruction process of war-torn countries by means of adjudication of perpetrators of international crimes.[5] As highlighted by then UN Secretary General Kofi Annan, the underlying idea was that:

> the establishment of an international tribunal would bring about the achievement of the aim of putting an end to such crimes and taking effective measures to bring to justice the persons responsible for them, and would contribute to the restoration and maintenance of peace […] in this particular case, the Security Council would be establishing, as an enforcement measure under Chapter VII, a subsidiary organ within the terms of Article 29 of the Charter, but one of a judicial nature.[6]

By bringing to justice those responsible for outrageous crimes like those committed in the armed conflicts that affected the Former Yugoslavia and Rwanda, there was hope to help these countries in coming to terms with their past, thereby laying a new, "clean" ground as for the restoration of peace. The belief was that with the intervention of a neutral and independent international judiciary body, the victims would be encouraged to reconcile with the perpetrators, independently from their religious or ethnic background.

In reality, these efforts have proven more difficult than expected. Media have repeatedly reported about the disappointment of the former international prosecutor of the ICTY, Mrs. Carla Del Ponte, about the lack of cooperation and incapability – or unwillingness – of the responsible authorities to enforce arrest warrants.[7] As expressed in her speech of 15 December 2005:

> It is obvious to all informed observers that, in the first years after the indictments were issued, there was no political will, either from the local authorities in Republika Srpska or in Serbia, or from the international forces in Bosnia and Herzegovina, to arrest Karadzic or Mladic. It was perceived that arrest operations against either of them could undermine the stability of Bosnia and Herzegovina and the security of the international troops there.[8]

---

[5] UNSCR 827/1993 established the International Criminal Tribunal for the former Yugoslavia (ICTY), whereas UNSCR 955/1994 established the International Criminal Tribunal for Rwanda (ICTR).

[6] Report of the Secretary General pursuant to para. 2 of Security Council Resolution 808 (1993) (S/25704), para. 28 (May 3, 1993), *at* <http://www.un.org/icty/legaldoc-e/basic/statut/s25704index.htm>.

[7] *Serbia, smentito l'arresto di Mladic*, Corriere della Sera, Feb. 21 2006, *at* <http://www.corriere.it/Primo_Piano/Esteri/2006/02_Febbraio/21/mladic.shtml>; *Ratko Mladic is still at large*, BBC News, Feb. 22, 2006, *at* <http://news.bbc.co.uk/2/hi/europe/4739424.stm>.

[8] Carla Del Ponte addresses the Security Council (Dec. 15, 2005), *at* <www.un.org/icty/pressreal/2005/speech/delponte-sc-051215.htm>.

Only recently, after Mrs. Del Ponte's departure from the ICTY, Radovan Karadzic was eventually arrested and indicted for war crimes.[9] Moreoever, one can ask whether the fact that no verdict can now be released against former Serb President Slobodan Milosevic, who died on 11 March 2006 in his cell in Scheveningen (NL),[10] may leave some questions unanswered that, in the long term, may bring back turmoil and upheaval in the region.

One of the major sources of criticism directed at the UN *ad hoc* tribunals is the fact that the ICTY and the ICTR have been established by the UN Security Council, a political body, on the basis of a Chapter VII Resolution, which is automatically binding on UN member states. This may be one reason why some countries are not keen to cooperate. As a consequence, the courts' jurisdiction has been challenged on numerous occasions, e.g. in the notorious Milosevic trial, and accused of political manoeuvre. Therefore a lot of time has been invested in the creation of a truly international tribunal, based on an international agreement which was eventually reached at the conclusion of a lengthy, intensive but successful conference in Rome on 18 July 1998. The acceptance of the International Criminal Court (ICC) seems to have a much wider basis, thanks in particular to its reliance on the principle of complementarity,[11] which delegates the responsibility for ensuring the respect of international law back to the states, asking them to apply their domestic legislation.

The aim of this paper is to illustrate that independent from whether *international* tribunals will manage to 'catch the hearts of the population' of war-torn countries, they will certainly have a major impact on peace-building at the institutional level. Both national and international justice can be crucial in the re-establishment and reconstruction of a state. This paper, however, will focus only on international justice.

Two crucial elements of peace-building are the *implementation* and *enforcement* of international law. Implementation means the integration of international

---

[9] Dan Bilefsky, *Serbia provides details on the arrest of Karadzic*, INTERNATIONAL HERALD TRIBUNE EUROPE, July 22, 2008, *at* <http://www.iht.com/articles/2008/07/22/europe/serbia.php>; Anne Penketh, *As Europe celebrates arrest of Karadzic, hunt is on for Mladic*, THE INDEPENDENT, July 23, 2008, *at* <http://www.independent.co.uk/news/world/europe/as-europe-celebrates-arrest-of-karadzic-hunt-is-on-for-mladic-874844.html>.

[10] *Milosevic found dead in his cell*, BBC NEWS, March 11, 2006, *at* <http://news.bbc.co.uk/2/hi/europe/4796470.stm/>. See also the comments in the NEUE ZÜRCHER ZEITUNG, March 13, 2006, 1–3.

[11] See Roy S. Lee, *State's responses: issues and solutions*, *in* STATES' RESPONSES TO ISSUES ARISING FROM THE ICC STATUTE: CONSTITUTIONAL, SOVEREIGNTY, JUDICIAL COOPERATION AND CRIMINAL LAW (Roy S. Lee ed., 2005), 1, 13.

law into domestic legal systems,[12] whereas enforcement means the capability of enforcing or "giving teeth" to these rules by providing a legal remedy to the victims of breaches of these rules. International law has often been criticised for not being 'real' law since there is no authority capable of enforcing it. Although this position can be rebutted with the argument that norms shall be observed because they are valid and sensible, rather than out of fear of prosecution, the creation of these tribunals, particularly of the ICC, has dramatically changed this situation. The principle of complementarity, in particular, allows the ICC to resort to the cooperation of states in conducting investigations, enforcing arrest warrants and judicial sentences, thereby making it increasingly difficult for offenders to find safe havens.[13] Thanks to enforcement, coupled with implementation, the future promises the existence of an international legal system with stronger structures, providing better guarantees for the prevention of these crimes and, should a conflict erupt, the existence of a system already being in place, permitting much speedier reconstruction and peace-building.

In order to analyse the impact of international tribunals on peace building processes, this paper is structured as follows. After this brief introduction, part II looks at the differences characterising the creation and aims of the International Military Tribunal of Nuremberg (IMT) and the International Military Tribunal for the Far East (IMTFE) in the aftermath of World War II, which had a primarily "punitive" role.

Part III examines the role played by the more recent international tribunals, the ICTY, the ICTR and the ICC, in the implementation and enforcement of international law, thereby contributing to peace-building. Part IV considers the special case of the Special Iraqi Tribunal and the Special Court for Sierra Leone, whereas Part V offers conclusions.

2. *Philosophical views on the relationship between peace and justice*

There are different philosophical views with regard to the role of justice as a peace-building element. Hideaki Shinoda[14] analyses three different theories at the nexus between peace and justice: the "harmonious," "adversarial" and "conditional" theory.

---

[12] On the implementation of the ICC Statute and its effects, see in particular STATES' RESPONSES TO ISSUES ARISING FROM THE ICC STATUTE: CONSTITUTIONAL, SOVEREIGNTY, JUDICIAL COOPERATION AND CRIMINAL LAW (Roy S. Lee ed., 2005).

[13] See parts 9 and 10 of the ICC Statute.

[14] Hideaki Shinoda, *Peace-building by the Rule of Law: An Examination of Intervention in the Form of International Tribunals* (March 22, 2001), *at* <http://www.isanet.org/archive/shinoda.html#_ftnref11>.

The *first* consists in identifying a strong positive correlation between peace and justice. In his view, lawyers tend to have the "justice first, then peace follows" (*fiat iustitia sit pereat mundis*) attitude. Shinoda refers to Richard Goldstone who points to the political and judicial approach to the achievement of peace, highlighting the fact that the perspective of the victim is often left out of account.[15] He further criticizes the failure of IFOR (the Implementation Force in Bosnia) in arresting indicted war criminals, holding that "it is their job to go out and make the arrest."[16] He strongly rejects IFOR's notion of peace, advocating the "justice first" approach instead, and holds that "justice can be a useful tool for peacekeeping or peace building".[17] In sum, the "justice first, then peace follows" approach believes that peace can be consolidated through justice by exposing the truth without imposing collective guilt, by providing public and official acknowledgment of the victims, by accurately recording history, by curbing criminal conduct, by revealing systematic patterns of gross human rights violations and by *implementing efficient criminal justice*, which is one of the peace-building elements argued for in this paper.

The *second*, "adversarial" theory holds that the excessive pursuit of justice in an unstable society may undermine peace-building. According to Shinoda this is a widely held political opinion. He cites Stephen Krasner, a political scientist, who, in response to former US President Clinton's signing the Statute of Rome, identified the ICC as "the wrong instrument for dealing with large-scale war, devastation, destruction and crimes against humanity", emphasizing that "developing stable democratic societies and limiting the loss of human life require prudent political calculations, not judicial findings." In Krasner's view "Judgments about individual guilt can point in one direction, and judgments about political order and the promotion of peace and democracy can point in another." However, the judiciary may contribute to peace-building if trials "are conducted through national, not international, tribunals, and if they are designed to elicit the truth, as South Africa's was." The emerging argument, thus, seems to be that peace-building can only be attained by delegating primary competence to national criminal proceedings. As it will be argued in this paper, however,

[15] Richard J. Goldstone, *Assessing the Work of the United Nations War Crimes Tribunals, 33* Stanford Journal of International Law 7 (1997): "we have had illustrated the political approach which subscribes to the view that peace is more important and should be achieved if necessary at the cost of justice, and, on the other hand, we have had the approach from the perspective of the victim. In my opinion, it is the victim who is too often and too frequently left out of the equation and left out of account."

[16] Goldstone, *supra* note 15, 7–8.

[17] Richard J. Goldstone, *Justice as a Tool for Peace-making: Truth Commissions and International Criminal Tribunals*, 28 New York University Journal of International Law and Politics 501 (1996).

both national and international judicial institutions need to contribute to an efficient peace-building.

The *third* theory presented by Shinoda is that of an intermediate position. What he calls the "conditional" theory pursues further development of international tribunals, and at the same time warns against inappropriate implementation of legality due to ignorance of political considerations. The critical matter is how to take political factors into consideration. He cites as example David Scheffer, former US Ambassador-at-large for war crimes, who strongly supported the two *ad hoc* tribunals and the setting up of the ICC, but eventually opposed the Rome Statute. In a paper published in 1996, Scheffer had urged the Security Council to make efforts to strengthen a future international criminal court, which would be more cost-effective but weaker than the *ad hoc* tribunals.[18] Then he converted to the view that the Security Council shall hold exclusive power on the commencing of investigations, led mainly by the – unjustified – fear that U.S. senior officials, commanders, and soldiers could face international investigation and even prosecution without sufficient guarantees of fair, non politicised, trial standards. This theory, therefore, supports the importance of international tribunals in the peace-building process but warns against the negative effects that politics may have on their work, particularly if politicians have not been adequately informed about the tribunals' functioning system. This may have occurred, for instance, in relation to the ICTR, taking in consideration the strong opposition from the Rwandan government.[19] One should also recall that the Chief Prosecutor Carla Del Ponte was removed from the position as chief prosecutor of the ICTR following her intention to investigate crimes by the Tutsis and President Kagame.[20]

As described by Shinoda, these are the three prevailing positions reflecting the opposition between law-oriented and politics-oriented approaches to peace building. As already mentioned, however, a common position which can be found in all three theories is the recognition of the pivotal role of judicial institutions in the peace-building process.

3. *The notion of peace-building or post-conflict state building*

As implied by the composed structure of the term, "peace-*building*" can only be started once peace has been achieved. It corresponds to the stage that follows

[18] Reported by Shinoda, *supra* note 14.

[19] See Global Policy Forum, *UN Prosecutor Rallies UK Support to Investigate Rwandan Army* (Dec. 3, 2000), *at* <http://www.globalpolicy.org/security/issues/rwanda/2002/1204coop.htm>.

[20] John Hooper, *I was sacked as Rwanda genocide prosecutor for challenging president, says Del Ponte*, The Guardian, Sept. 13, 2003, *at* <http://www.guardian.co.uk/international/story/0,,1041177,00.html>.

peace-enforcement and it usually occurs in a peace-keeping stage. The difference between peace-keeping and peace-enforcement is that in the former case, the hosting state usually consents to the intervention of international troops under Chapter VI of the UN Charter, thereby permitting the fulfilment of their task in a relatively "peaceful" environment. Peace-enforcement, instead, is unilaterally decided by the Security Council on the basis of Chapter VII of the UN Charter. The consent of the receiving state is not required, the lack of which usually leads to confrontations and tensions, vesting the intervening UN troops with the clothes of a "third belligerent", allowed to resort to force to separate the warring sides. Peace-building cannot occur in a peace-enforcement environment, as there will not be the necessary local support. The belief of the local population in the necessity of the international intervention, be this a military force or an international tribunal, is a key element for success in the re-establishment of peace and democracy. Otherwise the outcome will be ongoing internal violence, as proven by the current events in Iraq.

Peace-building further requires the establishment of *judiciary, legislative and executive institutions*, with a democratic foundation. It is not the task of the UN intervening external forces to impose a foreign system, as this is in the responsibility of the local institutions and population. These, with the support of international experts, must re-establish a functioning system which, by taking into consideration local traditions, laws, and system, shall guarantee compliance with international legal standards. However, this task is not easy, as demonstrated for instance by the situation in Kosovo, which for years has retained an ambiguous status, by technically remaining a part of Serbia within the imperfectly integrated two unit federation of Serbia and Montenegro, but in fact being governed by a protectorate structure, the United Nations Interim Mission for Kosovo (UNMIK).[21] Moreover, both the ICTY and ICTR are led by principles and rules drawn from the common law system, without taking into consideration the civil law tradition of the former Yugoslavia and Rwanda.

For this reason, the *implementation* of international legal standards into domestic legal systems is a crucial element of peace-building. At the same time, unless there are functioning judiciary institutions which can, with the help enforcement agencies, *enforce* these rules, peace-building will be an unattainable task. Victims need to see that the perpetrators are being brought to justice, or else a system of "self-justice" emerges, running counter to peace-building. In this case, particular care needs to be taken of local customs and the reality of criminal prosecution *in loco*.

---

[21] On this problem see Leonard J. Cohen, *Kosovo: From Interim Status to Enhanced Sovereignty*, V Strategic Insights (January 2006), *at* <http://www.ccc.nps.navy.mil/si/2006/Jan/cohenJan06.asp>.

The theory presented in the next paragraphs holds that the judiciary can play a pivotal role in peace-building by promoting the implementation and enforcement of international law on a world-wide scale.

4. *The notions of implementation and enforcement*

Implementation comes from "implement", which means "the performance of an obligation" or "to put a plan or system into operation".[22] In public international law states either follow a *monist* or a *dualistic* tradition. The monist tradition implies that provisions of international law constitute an integral part of a nation's domestic legislation, whereas the dualist tradition requires the implementation of international norms into the domestic legal system.[23]

For instance, in a dualistic state, unless its domestic provisions address war crimes, a victim of breaches of international humanitarian law (IHL) will not be able to invoke them in front of a domestic court, even though these rules, such as the four Geneva Conventions of 1949 (GCs), may have acquired customary law status. This was, for instance, the case in South Africa, where the four GCs were ratified as early as 1952, but never implemented. Also attempts to invoke the 1977 Additional Protocols as customary international law during the armed struggle against apartheid failed. Now, however, the Republic of South Africa, thanks to adoption of the *Implementation of the Rome Statute of the International Criminal Court Act* by its Parliament in 2002, is fully capable of enforcing these provisions.[24]

In monist countries, on the other hand, implementation may nevertheless be important to refine those provisions of international law which may not comply with the principle of legality and which, therefore, require precise definitions in domestic legislation. Switzerland, for instance, had to introduce a specific provision on genocide in its criminal code (Art. 264) in order to implement the 1948 UN Convention on Genocide to comply with the principle of strict legality. A crucial factor in this respect is the implementation of humanitarian rules into military regulations and rules of engagement, which will be the tools to be consulted in specific cases by military servicemen.

Implementation has become pivotal for those states that have ratified the ICC Statute. In order to avoid the risk that the ICC seizes a case due to unwillingness or incapability to prosecute the case in their national courts, member states – both of a monist and dualistic tradition – have initiated complicated and

---

[22] The concise Oxford Dictionary (Robert E. Allen ed., 1991).

[23] Switzerland, e.g., is a monist country, whereas the UK has a dualist tradition.

[24] Hennie Strydom, *South Africa's implementation of the Rome Statute, in* States' Responses to Issues Arising from the ICC Statute: Constitutional, Sovereignty, Judicial Cooperation and Criminal Law (Roy S. Lee ed., 2005), 105, 105ss.

lengthy legislative processes to incorporate the ICC Statute's provisions into their domestic legislation.[25]

Implementation per se, however, may not be sufficient, unless coupled with *enforcement*. *Enforcement* means in general the activity of making certain that the laws of an area are obeyed. International criminal law norms for the punishment of war crimes are understood primarily as a means for the enforcement of humanitarian law. International criminal law can play a major role in this regard. In fact enforcement can be achieved in two ways: a) by resorting to *judiciary* institutions; or b) by resorting to police forces. International tribunals, in recent years, have played a crucial role in the enforcement of international law provisions by calling to justice persons accused of serious breaches of international law. By doing this, they have contributed to the eradication of negative elements of the society (as argued below), thereby facilitating the reconstruction phase of formerly war-torn countries. Enforcement of international law, however, is not simply done in courtrooms but also in the field, thanks to the cooperation of enforcement forces entrusted with the arrest of those indicted by the tribunals.

At the current stage there is no international police force allowed to intervene whenever international rules are breached. However, UN military forces are being increasingly endowed with such tasks, particularly in so-called peace-enforcement operations mandated by a UN Security Council Resolution under Chapter VII of the UN Charter. Unlike peace keeping troops, peace-enforcement troops have to re-establish peace with coercive military means. The UN peace-enforcement mandate may include the search for and arrest of those accused of international crimes.

However, without the establishment of judiciary and legislative institutions, it will be very difficult to promote peace-building, even with the existence of military and police forces. The role that can be played by international courts will be addressed next.

II. *The origins of international criminal justice: The "punitive" role of post WWII prosecutions at Nuremberg and Tokyo*

After the end of WWII, the Hague Conventions of 1907 proved to be an insufficient legal basis for the prosecution of crimes committed by the Nazis in Europe and by the Japanese in the Far East. Thus, most states enacted special national criminal legislation to address the matter. However, differences between the several national systems involved and the fact that these legislations only

---

[25] The impact of the ICC on the implementation of international humanitarian rules will be examined in details in Part III.

provided for the prosecution of the defeated parties, raised several concerns regarding procedural fairness. The Allies, faced with the moral duty to provide for justice, signed the 1943 *Moscow Declaration*.[26] This declaration established that the minor Nazi criminals would be judged by national courts administered by the Allies, in the countries of the commission of the crimes. The major war criminals, instead, whose offences had no particular geographic location, would be tried by a joint decision of the Governments of the Allies.

The 1943 *Moscow Declaration* was followed by the 1945 *London Agreement*,[27] which adopted the *Charter of the International Military Tribunal of Nuremberg* (IMT Charter). This was the first international treaty explicitly recognising the criminal character of IHL violations (crimes against peace, war crimes, and crimes against humanity.). Since the Geneva Conventions of 1949 had not been in force yet, the Charter was drawn from customary law and the principles contained in the Hague Conventions of 1907, particularly the Fourth. However, the latter did not *explicitly* provide for individual criminal responsibility. Thus, legitimacy to try individuals was drawn from the joint legal power of the Allied Powers, which allowed them to do jointly what any of them could have done individually. The competences of the single national criminal jurisdictions (the American, the Soviet, the French and the British) were converted into an international-quadripartite-one, embodied by the International Military Tribunal of Nuremberg (IMT). Another established principle was that individuals could be held criminally responsible for the violation of international obligations signed by their respective countries of origin.[28]

The International Military Tribunal for the Far East (IMTFE) had an analogous function. However, this was basically a tribunal of the victorious powers, too. Its Charter[29] was issued by order of General Douglas MacArthur, Supreme Commander for the Allied Forces in Japan in 1946.[30] It had jurisdiction over crimes committed by the Japanese and was composed of eleven members representing

---

[26] Source: DECADE OF AMERICAN FOREIGN POLICY: BASIC DOCUMENTS, 1941–49 (Prepared at the request of the Senate Committee on Foreign Relations by the Staff of the Committee and the Department of State, 1950), *at* <http://www.yale.edu/lawweb/avalon/wwii/moscow.htm>.

[27] Available *at* <http://www.yale.edu/lawweb/avalon/imt/proc/imtchart.htm>.

[28] *'Crimes against international law are committed by men, not by abstract entities [...] only by punishing individuals who commit such crimes can the provisions of international law be enforced'*. This argument was also followed by the ICTY AC in Prosecutor v. Tadic, Decision on the Defense Motion for Interlocutory Appeal on Jurisdiction, Case IT-94-1-AR72 (Oct. 2, 1995), paras. 80 et seq., *in* ANNOTATED LEADING CASES OF INTERNATIONAL CRIMINAL TRIBUNALS – VOL. 1: THE INTERNATIONAL CRIMINAL TRIBUNAL FOR THE FORMER YUGOSLAVIA 1993–1998 (André Klip & Goran Sluiter eds., 1999). See also *Tadic Jurisdiction Case*, AC, para. 128. For more, see ROBERTA ARNOLD, THE ICC AS A NEW INSTRUMENT FOR REPRESSING TERRORISM 90 (2004).

[29] Available *at* <http://www.yale.edu/lawweb/avalon/imtfech.htm>.

[30] For more details see Arnold, *supra* note 28, 90.

Australia, Canada, New Zealand, Great Britain, India, the US, the Philippines, China, the USSR, France, and the Netherlands.[31]

The contribution of minor and non-Western powers to its jurisprudence gives the IMTFE a special authority that the IMT, according to some, may have lacked. The so-called "Tokyo Trials" played a major role in developing the doctrine of command responsibility, particularly by enunciating the nowadays inapplicable principle of strict liability, which led to the death sentencing of General Yamashita.[32] These trials, however, had primarily a punitive role.

With regard to the Tribunal of Nuremberg, a major problem was the condemnation of the mass killing of German Jews under the provisions of the laws of war, which were only applicable to "protected persons", i.e. persons in the hands of an enemy power. Being of German nationality, German Jews could not avail themselves the protection granted by customary war crimes provisions to civilians. On the other hand the provisions on crimes against humanity required a link with an armed conflict and since the extermination of the Jews had begun prior to the outbreak of the conflict, not all the offences could be prosecuted under this heading.[33]

So it could be argued, that desire for justice or vengeance, rather than state building, was the primary aim of these trials. This, in a way, is understandable, since at the time it was not usually the task of the victorious party to help the defeated side to reconstruct its own country.

Today, this task is rather in the hands of international organisations like the UN, which, in recent years, has developed a new approach, considering the establishment of international tribunals as a peace-enforcement and peace-building tool.

---

[31] Manchuria, the People's Republic of Mongolia, Thailand, Cambodia, Burma, and Portuguese possessions in East Asia were not formally associated with the proceedings for political reasons.

[32] *In Re Yamashita*, 327 US 1, 14–16 (1945). On this see Roberta Arnold, *Command Responsibility: a case study of alleged violations of the laws of war at Khiam detention centre*, 7 JOURNAL OF CONFLICT AND SECURITY LAW 191, 203 (2002) and Roberta Arnold/Otto Triffterer, *Commentary on Art. 28 ICC Statute*, *in* COMMENTARY TO THE ROME STATUTE FOR AN INTERNATIONAL CRIMINAL COURT (Otto Triffterer ed., 2008).

[33] Judgement: The law relating to war crimes and crimes against humanity, *at* <http://www.yale.edu/lawweb/avalon/imt/proc/judlawre.htm>.

III. *The new "peace-enforcement" role of international tribunals*

1. *The ICTY and the ICTR*

a) *Impact on implementation of international law*

The ICTY and the ICTR can be considered the first "truly" international tribunals, since they were constituted on the basis of a Chapter VII UNSC Resolution and since their subject matter jurisdiction was drawn directly from international law.

The ICTY was established pursuant to UNSC Resolution 827/1993.[34] Its Statute[35] provides jurisdiction over grave breaches of international humanitarian law (Art. 2), violations of the laws and customs of war (Art. 3), genocide (Art. 4) and crimes against humanity (Art. 5), committed in the territory of the former Yugoslavia since 1991 (Art. 1). The ICTR, instead, was established pursuant to UN Security Council Resolution 955/1994.[36] According to its Statute[37] it has jurisdiction over genocide (Art. 2), crimes against humanity (Art. 3) and violations of Article 3 common to the four GCs and Additional Protocol II of 1977 (Art. 4), for acts committed in Rwanda and its neighbouring States between 1 January and 31 December 1994 (Art. 1).

The major difference between the two UN *ad hoc* tribunals and the Nuremberg and Tokyo Tribunals is that the former do not envisage trials in absentia and do not impose death penalties. It is a fundamental right of the accused to be present at the trial, in order to be able to defend him- or herself. Since the primary aim is peace-building, the death penalty would have been an inappropriate measure for reconciliation, considering in particular the fact that the death penalty, in several countries, also raises concerns with respect to human rights standards.[38] These standards played a fundamental role, too, in the drafting of the ad hoc tribunals' statutes. Other innovations were: a) the inclusion of genocide as a specific count; b) the detachment of crimes against humanity from the requirement of a nexus with an armed conflict and c) the criminalisation of breaches of International Humanitarian Law (IHL) provisions applicable to non-international armed conflicts.[39] The latter was a tremendous innovation introduced

---

[34] Available *at* <http://daccessdds.un.org/doc/UNDOC/GEN/N93/306/28/IMG/N9330628.pdf?OpenElement>.

[35] Available *at* <http://www.un.org/icty/legaldoc-e/index.htm>.

[36] Available *at* <http://daccessdds.un.org/doc/UNDOC/GEN/N95/140/97/PDF/N9514097.pdf?OpenElement>.

[37] Available *at* <http://www.un.org/ictr/statute.html>.

[38] On this see Amnesty International, *Rwanda: Ugandan President incites killings* (Jan. 26, 1998), *at* <http://web.amnesty.org/library/Index/ENGAFR470041998?open&of=ENG-384>.

[39] See Roberta Arnold, *The development of the notion of war crimes in non-international conflicts through the jurisprudence of the UN ad hoc tribunals*, Humanitäres Völkerrecht – Informationsschriften 134, 135 (2002).

by Judge Antonio Cassese, which opened the gates for a new interpretation of IHL. War crimes are subject to discretionary universal jurisdiction, meaning that every state is allowed to open criminal proceedings against suspected war criminals, even if the crime was committed on foreign territory, by a foreign national, or against a foreign national. The previous position was that to qualify as war crimes, breaches of IHL applicable to non-international conflicts may have jeopardised the principle of state sovereignty.[40] The establishment of the ICTR to adjudicate crimes committed within Rwanda, on the basis of a Chapter VII Resolution, was already viewed as a sort of "humanitarian intervention" in breach of this principle. However, the criticism was silenced by the fact that the Rwandese genocide was considered a threat to international peace and security, therefore justifying the intervention of the UN Security Council on the basis of Chapter VII of the UN Charter.

The emergence of this new doctrine in IHL was codified in the Rome Statute for an International Criminal Court, which explicitly provides for a list of war crimes applicable to acts committed in time of armed conflicts of non-international character (Art. 8). Due to the principle of complementarity most ICC member states have adopted implementing legislation explicitly providing for a list of war crimes applicable in this type of conflict. This means that in the last sixty years there has been a 180 degrees turnover, with the principle of state sovereignty no longer prevailing over considerations of international criminal justice. In this sense, the two *ad hoc* tribunals, by providing the basis of the ICC Statute and, indirectly, the domestic implementing legislations of a vast number of states, have played a major role in peace-building. Thanks to this change it will be possible to open proceedings against perpetrators of heinous crimes in civil conflicts, thereby creating the legal environment for the reconstruction of democracy in the affected regions. But what is the difference between the role played by the UN *ad hoc* tribunals and the ICC in peace-building?

At the international level, the ICTY and ICTR have had little impact on implementation. This is particularly due to the fact that they have *primary* jurisdiction, meaning that they can exercise priority by requesting a state to transfer case proceedings to them. This occurred, for instance, in the *Tadic Case*. Tadic had been arrested in Germany, but the ICTY requested a transfer of proceedings.[41] Similarly, there were two Rwandan cases which were transferred

---

[40] See *Ibid.*

[41] See Michael P. Scharf, Balkan Justice – The Story Behind the First International War Crimes Trial Since Nuremberg 96–101 (1997); Hans-Peter Kaul, *Germany: methods and techniques used to deal with constitutional sovereignty and criminal law issues, in* States' Responses to Issues Arising from the ICC Statute: Constitutional, Sovereignty, Judicial Cooperation and Criminal Law (Roy S. Lee ed., 2005), 65, 72.

from the Swiss military court to the ICTR.[42] Due to primary jurisdiction, national legislative powers feel little inclined to enact domestic implementing legislation. An exception, however, is provided e.g. by Art. 3 of the Greek law No. 2665, which provides for the direct application of the ICTY and ICTR Statutes. Similarly, Spain's Organisation Act 15/1994 specifies that not only is it compulsory to recognise the legality of the UN tribunals, but also to adopt domestic legislation compatible with it.[43]

Switzerland is a special case because jurisdiction on war crimes is vested in military courts. In the early Nineties, the Swiss Military Justice was entrusted with the investigation and adjudication of Mr. Niyonteze, a Rwandan national suspected of participation in the Rwandan genocide. The Swiss military judicial authorities, however, could not indict him for genocide, since Switzerland, notwithstanding its ratification of the 1948 Genocide Convention and its monistic tradition, did not have a specific provision on genocide in either its Military or Civil Criminal Code. Thus, to comply with the principle of strict legality, the Military judges had to abandon the charges on genocide.[44] As a consequence, in 2000 a specific provision on genocide (art. 264) was introduced to the Civil Criminal Code. In the future, everyone accused of participation in genocide shall be tried by civilian courts in Switzerland.

Among the drawbacks of the UN *ad hoc* tribunals are their locations in The Hague/Netherlands (ICTY) and Arusha/Tanzania (ICTR) – very distant from the place of occurrence of the crimes. Often the ICTY has been criticised for promoting justice in a country remote from the place of occurrence of the offences. Whereas the work of the UN *ad hoc* tribunals may have been in

---

[42] See the Federal Court's decision BGE 123 II 175. For another similar case, where proceedings were transferred from the Swiss military court to the ICTR, see BGE 1A.129/2001 of 3. September 2001 (www.bger.ch). For more details see Stefan Wehrenberg, *Die Kompetenzen und Zuständigkeiten der Militärjustiz zur Verfolgung von Kriegsverbrechen – Die Umsetzung des Römer Statuts als Chance zur Revision*, JUSLETTER (March 14, 2005), *available at* <http://www.blumlegal.ch/pdf/voelkerrecht/jl_%20140305_artikelsw.pdf>.

[43] "Paragraph 4 (of Resolution 827[1993]) [...] places upon all States the obligation to take any measures necessary under their domestic law to comply with the resolution and implement the Statute. It is not a matter of recognising the competence of the Tribunal [...] it is a question of adopting appropriate domestic measures, bearing in mind its special legal basis which is a resolution of an international organisation and not an international treaty. [...] The Act is based on a pre-existing body of conventional or customary law (IHL and the Genocide Convention) [...]. Since [...] *much of the Statute is self-executing*, the Act makes provision for its implementation only in respect of those matters which our Constitution stipulates must be the subject of Organisation Acts."

[44] Roberta Arnold, *Military Criminal Procedures and Judicial Guarantees*, JOURNAL OF INTERNATIONAL CRIMINAL JUSTICE 749, 760 (2005); Stefan Wehrenberg, *Art. 264 StGB, in* BASLER KOMMENTAR STRAFGESETZBUCH II, para. 40 (Marcel A. Niggli & Hans Wiprächtiger ed., 2003).

the headlines in its early working phase with echoes in the former Yugoslavia, the UN *ad hoc* tribunals have lost their importance in international media coverage, apart from a few cases such as the opening of the proceedings against former President Milosevic, or updated news about the arrest of those still wanted by the tribunals. The problem is probably even more accentuated in relation to the work of the ICTR. Whereas the Western world seems to still lay some interest in the events affecting the former Yugoslavia, thanks to the court's location in the heart of Europe and the deployment of Western peacekeepers in the region, the interest seems to have decreased with regard to the Rwandan court. Regarding the ICTR, the events affected a single, remote country, with minor impact on the Western world in terms of refugee flow. At the same time international staff is less attracted to apply to positions at the ICTR due to its location. It is therefore imaginable that reports about the work conducted in Arusha may have a minor echo not only in Europe, but also in Rwanda itself. But not only the Rwandan people, but probably also ordinary former Yugoslav citizens have been practically unable to follow the courts' work. Thus, the fact that until 1999, the ICTY did not translate its decisions and other relevant documents into Serbo-Croatian or other local languages can be seen as a major impediment, even though outreach activities are being organised regularly by the ICTY.[45] Therefore, their impact on the war's victims has been less effective than expected.[46]

b) *Impact on the enforcement of international law*

With regard to enforcement, the creation of the UN tribunals has ended 50 years of inactivity of international criminal justice. They also permitted to enforce the 1948 Genocide Convention for the first time. As said, the IMT and IMTFE Statutes did not encompass genocide as a crime per se, but as a form of crime against humanity which had to be committed in relation to an armed conflict. The possibility to *enforce* the law in front of an international tribunal has given IHL more teeth. As mentioned, the ICTY and ICTR were constituted on the basis of a Chapter VII UNSC Resolution, meaning that the recognition of their jurisprudence is binding on UN member states. For instance, Finland's Act on the Jurisdiction of the ICTY and on legal assistance to the International Tribunal of 5 January 1994[47] provides that:

---

45 Alison Smith, *A response to "A 'Special Court' for Sierra Leon's war crimes"* (Aug. 15, 2001), *available at* <http://www.globalpolicy.org/security/issues/sierra/court/2001/critique.htm>. More info on the outreach program of the ICTY is available *at* <http://www.un.org/icty/index-b.html>.

46 See the reference in Michelle Sieff, *A "Special Court" for Sierra Leone's war crimes* (2001), *available at* <http://www.globalpolicy.org/security/issues/sierra/court/2001/analysis.htm>.

47 Act on the Jurisdiction of the International Tribunal for the Prosecution of Persons Responsible for Crimes Committed in the Territory of the Former Yugoslavia and on Legal Assistance to

> For the purpose of implementing the obligations based on resolution No 827 of the UNSC, [...] this Act shall govern the recognition and *enforcement in Finland of decisions made by the Tribunal.*

In fact, enforcement is guaranteed by the compulsory cooperation provision provided by the ICTY and ICTR's[48] Rules of Procedure. Rule 11 of the Rules of Procedure and Evidence of both tribunals provides that:

> If, within 60 days after a request for deferral [...] the State fails to file a response which satisfies the Trial Chamber that the State has taken or is taking adequate steps to comply [...], the Trial Chamber may request the President to report the matter to the Security Council.

The UN Security Council's power to enforce sentences was already proven in the *Lockerbie Case*, when, hampered by Libya's reliance on the extradition law principle that allows states to refuse the extradition of their own nationals, it enacted resolutions compelling the Libyan authorities to extradite the suspects of the bombing of Pan Am Flight 103 over Lockerbie, moved by the pressures exercised by the US and the UK.[49]

Interestingly, though, Art. 7 of the Italian Law Decree No. 544 of 28 December 1991 provides for exceptions to the recognition of the ICTY's decisions if: a) the fact for which the judgement was rendered is not an offence under Italian law; b) for the same fact and the same person a final judgement has already been rendered in Italy.

This position is curious, since all the crimes contained in the ICTY Statute, being drawn from customary law, should be crimes also pursuant to Italy's domestic laws. Moreover, Art. 10(2) ICTY Statute provides that there are two situations in which a person who has been tried by a national court for acts constituting serious violations of IHL may be subsequently tried by the International Tribunal, namely if: (a) the act for which he or she was tried was characterized as an ordinary crime; or (b) the national court proceedings were not impartial or independent, were designed to shield the accused from international criminal responsibility, or the case was not diligently prosecuted.

Another enforcement-related problem is that in order to be able to hold trials against suspects of international crimes, it is necessary to have them physically

---

the International Tribunal (Jan. 5, 1994), *at* <http://www.icrc.org/ihl-nat.nsf/WebLAW?OpenView&Start=1&Count=150&Expand=52.5.1#52.5.1>.

48 See however the problems caused by the eight year delay in the adoption of the Italian implementing legislation for cooperation with the ICTR, reported by Roberto Bellelli, *Italian implementation of the Rome Statute and related constitutional issues, in* States' Responses to Issues Arising from the ICC Statute: Constitutional, Sovereignty, Judicial Cooperation and Criminal Law (Roy S. Lee ed., 2005), 215, 217.

49 For more details see Arnold, *supra* note 28, 12.

at the courts' site. The advantage of the two UN *ad hoc* tribunals, being UN institutions, is their possibility to resort to UN peace-keeping forces to track down the suspects. This alternative, true, may be obstructed by the legislation of the troops contributing nations (TCN) – e.g. Swiss peace-keeping troops are not allowed to engage in any type of peace-enforcement activity, including the tracking down of international criminals[50] – in particular by their rules of engagement. However there are other TCN which may be more inclined to support the UN in police-like activities. Particular mission mandates may specifically provide for law enforcement tasks to be conducted either by the military component of a peace support force, or jointly with a civilian police component or the national police force. For example, UN SC Resolution 1244 required the international security presence in Kosovo (KFOR) to ensure public safety and order until the international civil presence could take responsibility for this task.[51] For instance, among the various tasks of EUFOR, the European Union Force in Bosnia and Herzegovina (BiH), is to:

> provide support to the International Criminal Tribunal for the Former Yugoslavia (ICTY) and relevant authorities, including the detention of PIFWCs, and provide the security environment in which the police can act against the organised criminal network.[52]

The EU's intention to launch an EU military operation in BiH was welcomed by UNSC Resolution 1575, adopted unanimously on 22 November 2004. This authorised the Member States acting through or in cooperation with the EU to establish a multinational stabilisation force (EUFOR) as a legal successor to SFOR under unified command and control, which would fulfil its missions in relation to the implementation of Annex 1–A and 2 of the Dayton/Paris Agreement. EUFOR's mandate was extended by UNSCR 1639 (2005) on 21 November 2005.

Therefore, whereas the two UN *ad hoc* tribunals may have had little impact on the *implementation* of international law at domestic level, they had a rather

---

50 See art. 66a of the Swiss Federal Law on the Armed Forces and the Military Administration, RS 510.10, available at <http://www.admin.ch/ch/f/rs/510_10/a66a.html>. "(1) Le Conseil fédéral détermine dans chaque cas l'armement nécessaire à la protection des personnes et des troupes engagées par la Suisse ainsi qu'à l'accomplissement de leur mission. (2) La participation à des actions de combat destinées à imposer la paix est exclue."

51 See Kwai Hong Ip, *Peace Support Operations: establishing the rule of law through security and law enforcement operations*, and Gerhard Scherhaufer, *Military and legal aspects of PSO – the example of Austria's deployment with KFOR*, both *in* Practice and Policies of Modern PSO Within Contemporary International Law (Roberta Arnold & Geert-Jan Alexander Knoops ed., 2006).

52 <http://www.euforbih.org/mission/mission.htm>. PIFWC means "persons indicted for war crimes".

strong impact on the *enforcement* of international law. Thanks to their affiliation with the UN, they can rely on the support of UN mandated peace-enforcement missions to track down those responsible of international crimes and thus lay the foundations for reconstruction and peace-building.

Another advantage of the ICTY is that it operates in the capitals of the states of the former Yugoslavia through field offices, which provide a useful base to investigators to work and conduct interviews, as well as a capacity for liaising with local officials. Unlike the ICTY, however, which has authority under Chapter VII of the UN Charter, other types of international tribunals would need to conclude agreements with countries in which they wished to establish field offices.[53]

Finally, enforcement of international law by the UN tribunals is facilitated by the non-application of extradition rules. Like the ICC Statute, the ICTY and ICTR Statutes provide for the *surrender* of the suspect to the courts. This is a technically different procedure from extradition. Extradition takes place between two states, horizontally, whereas surrender occurs between a state and an international tribunal, vertically.[54] All these arrangements make sure that international law is *de facto* enforced and that offenders can find no safe haven, thereby contributing to peace-building.

The ICTY and ICTR also have had an impact on the enforcement of international law on the domestic level. For instance, in Switzerland they have influenced the jurisprudence of Military Courts. In *Public Prosecutor v Nyionteze*, the Military Tribunal was influenced by the ICTY/ICTR jurisprudence in establishing the nature of the conflict in Rwanda, the liability of civilian superiors for war crimes, the reliability of witnesses' declarations and the assessment of the nexus requirement of the offences with the armed conflict.[55]

In conclusion, due to their primary jurisdiction, the two UN ad hoc tribunals have provided little incentive to states to implement international law into their domestic legislation. On the other hand, however, they have influenced the jurisprudence on international criminal law and have laid the basis for the enactment of the ICC Statute, thereby having a major impact on the enforcement of international law.

---

[53] United States Institute of Peace, Special Report: Building the Iraqi Special Tribunal – Lessons from experiences in international criminal justice 5 (June 2004), *at* <http://www.usip.org/pubs/specialreports/sr122.pdf>.

[54] On the differences see Sylvia Helena Steiner & Tarciso Dal Maso Jardin, *Implementation of the Rome Statute in Brazil, in* STATES' RESPONSES TO ISSUES ARISING FROM THE ICC STATUTE: CONSTITUTIONAL, SOVEREIGNTY, JUDICIAL COOPERATION AND CRIMINAL LAW (Roy S. Lee ed., 2005), 179, 186ss.

[55] On this see Arnold, *supra* note 44, 749.

c) *The example of Rwanda: International jurisdiction versus traditional conflict resolution*

A good example for the need to have the acceptance of this 'legal intervention' by the local population is given by Rwanda. In Rwanda, there has been much reticence to accept the intervention of the ICTR. Thus, the *gacaca* system was introduced, to run parallel with the ICTR.[56]

Gacaca refers to a "traditional" Rwandan method of conflict resolution. This method of conflict resolution used to be applied to solve disputes concerning e.g. land rights, property damage, marital disputes, inheritance rights, et cetera. Meetings were convened between the litigating sides. *Gacaca* sessions were informal, non-permanent and *ad hoc*. They were presided over by community elders (*inyangamugayo*), with the primary aim to re-establish social order, after sanctioning the violation of shared values, through the re-integration of offender(s) into the community. During the colonial period, a western judicial system was introduced but *gacaca* remained an integral part of customary practice. With independence, *gacaca* became more institutionalized with local authorities sometimes assuming the role of *inyangamugayo* and *gacaca* sessions considering local administrative matters.[57]

Thus, the *gacaca* tribunals are legally established judicial bodies and the judges can impose sentences as high as life imprisonment. The Rwandan government re invented and transformed the existing mode of *gacaca*, in order to try the more than 100,000 genocide suspects overcrowding the country's prisons.[58] Organic Law No 40/2000 of 26 January 2001 established *gacaca* jurisdictions for the prosecution of genocide offences and crimes against humanity committed between 1 October 1990 and 31 December 1994. This law came into effect on 15 March 2001. It was done in particular to overcome the problem that most accused never had the chance to face trial proceedings. In fact, a decade after the genocide, neither the ICTR nor the twelve specialized genocide chambers established within Rwanda's Courts of First Instance (*Cours de première instance*) have managed to achieve maximal accountability for the crime of genocide and

---

[56] On 18 June 2002 the Rwandese government launched a new court system, called *gacaca*. It is named after and draws upon a customary system of community hearings used to resolve local disputes. The new *gacaca* tribunals, however, merge customary practice with a Western, formal court structure. They are legally established judicial bodies. *Gacaca* judges can impose sentences as high as life imprisonment. The Rwandese government re-invented and transformed the existing mode of conflict resolution, *gacaca*, in order to try the more than 100,000 genocide suspects who overfill the country's prisons. To learn more see Amnesty International, Rwanda: Gacaca, a question of justice (Feb. 17, 2002), *at* <http://web.amnesty.org/library/index/ENGAFR470072002>.

[57] *Ibid.*

[58] *Ibid.*

crimes against humanity. The ICTR has tried nine individuals in seven and a half years of operation, the Rwandan specialized genocide chambers slightly more than 7,000 in five and a half years.[59]

One of the primary aims of this re-invented court system, apart from emptying the overcrowded prisons, is to reconstruct the Rwandese society, torn by the armed conflict and the genocide, by locating the trial of those alleged to have participated in the genocide within the communities in which the offences were committed. The *gacaca* judges hearing the cases are selected in neighbourhoods and local residents initially aid the *gacaca* benches and general assemblies in listing the genocide victims and suspected perpetrators within their community. In a later phase, community members provide information about the genocide offences during the *gacaca* hearings. This system permits an expeditious call to justice of those responsible in the areas where the crimes were committed, facilitating the peace-building process.

As remarked by Amnesty International (AI), however, it is neither the ultimate panacea, as one should be aware that their overall supervision and coordination is under the control of the Department of *Gacaca* Jurisdictions, within the Supreme Court, and the Ministry of Justice. State authority – not local consensus – is the *modus operandi* of the new, in comparison to the older forms, of *gacaca* jurisdictions. International human rights standards dictate that these tribunals must be legally established and act in accordance with fair trial standards. These, however, dramatically affect the customary workings of *gacaca* sessions. The significant differences between the older, customary, and contemporary forms of *gacaca* raise the question as to whether these may affect justice, the uncovering of truth and national reconciliation. As pointed out by AI, if reconciliation lies in the personal interaction between victim and perpetrator, *gacaca*, as previously practiced, would promote it, whereas it is less clear whether the state-mandated *Gacaca* jurisdictions, focusing on retributive justice, will achieve the same result. Certainly, however, the introduction of this system was necessary given the ICTR's perception by the local population as being an international court in the hands of an international organisation, composed by international staff not necessarily aware of Rwandan culture and customs.

It becomes evident, therefore, that the combination of *implementation* and *enforcement* is a key tool for peace building, which, however, needs the conviction of the affected population. Only where justice is searched for with the aim of reconciliation, rather than mere punishment, peace-building will be successful.

[59] *Ibid.*

2. *The ICC*

a) *Impact on implementation of international law*

Unlike the ICTY and the ICTR, the International Criminal Court (ICC) was established on the basis of an international treaty which resulted from the United Nations Conference of Plenipotentiaries on the Establishment of an International Criminal Court held in Rome, Italy, from 15 June to 17 July 1998. More than 130 governments participated in the conference, making significant contributions to shaping the treaty, such as strengthening the provisions on gender crimes and the role of the independent Prosecutor. After five weeks of intense deliberations, 120 nations voted in favour of its adoption. Only 7 nations voted against it, including the USA, Israel and China; 21 abstained.[60] The Statute entered into force on 1 July 2002 and has currently reached 100 ratifications. The ICC has jurisdiction over war crimes, crimes against humanity and genocide. As soon as there will be agreement on a definition, it shall have jurisdiction on aggression, too.

The ICC's key feature is its basis on the principle of complementarity, meaning that it shall intervene only where a state proves to be unwilling or unable to conduct by itself proceedings against a person suspected of international crimes falling within its jurisdiction. Unlike the ICTY and ICTR, it is a permanent court with voluntary nature and jurisdiction over every offender holding the nationality of a member state or who has committed a crime on the territory of a member state. Non-member states have the opportunity to recognise the ICC's jurisdiction on an ad-hoc basis.[61]

The principle of complementarity is a major incentive for states to implement international legal standards into their domestic legislation, in order to avoid transfer of proceedings. It should be recalled, however, that the ICC Statute was the result of a political compromise and, therefore, it is not without flaws. For instance, it does not contain a ban on nuclear, biological or chemical weapons. The delayed repatriation of prisoners of war, a war crime under the III Geneva Convention, is not enlisted as a war crime under art. 8 ICC Statute.[62]

There is nothing in the Rome Statute, however, preventing member states to adopt stricter legal provisions. For instance, pursuant to the Rome Statute, only the forcible recruitment of children less than 15 years of age constitutes a war crime. Member states who are also parties to the *Optional Protocol to the*

---

60 For more info see *History of the ICC,* information by the Coalition for an International Criminal Court, available at <http://www.iccnow.org/?mod=icchistory>.

61 Lee, *supra* note 11, 12–13.

62 Available *at* <http://www.un.org/law/icc/statute/romefra.htm>.

UN Convention on the Protection of the Rights of Child,[63] however, have decided to implement this provision by fixing the minimum age limit of child recruitment at 18.

On the other hand, the ratification of the ICC Statute has permitted many states to fill gaps in their domestic legislations. For instance, Brazil had a particular deficit insofar as the legislation on war crimes was intended only to further military efficiency, with no concern to rules of IHL. The implementation of the Rome Statute was the right occasion to bridge this deficiency.[64] There were also problems in Germany, as reported by ICC's Judge Hans-Peter Kaul:

> Before June 30, 2002, the German commitment to international criminal law and justice were not fully reflected in substantive criminal law, with the notable exception of the crime of genocide [...] crimes against humanity and war crimes were only "somehow" punishable with the norms of the General Criminal Code. When the Rome Statute was adopted, Germany felt more and more the need to remedy the insufficiencies concerning the coverage of these crimes through a specific new draft law.[65]

But there are many more examples of states which, even though they are parties to the four Geneva Conventions of 1949, had missed the opportunity to implement them into domestic law, thereby making them inapplicable in front of domestic courts.

There are currently 37 out of the 100 ratifying member states which have adopted implementing legislation of the ICC Statute.[66] It shall be noted, however, that implementation is a complicated process requiring legislative reform, which often implies constitutional, sovereignty, judicial cooperation and criminal law issues.

Among the major debated issues are the questions of immunity of Heads of State, exceptions to extradition, on-site investigation, enforcement of arrest warrants, and enforcement of sentences.[67] Taking the example of Switzerland, the ratification of the ICC and the subsequent implementing process opened debates not only on the existence of a sufficient legal basis to prosecute international criminal offenders, but also on issues such as the legitimacy of adjudication of

---

[63] Optional Protocol to the Convention on the Rights of the Child on the involvement of children in armed conflict, entered into force Feb. 12, 2002, available *at* <http://www.unhchr.ch/html/menu2/6/protocolchild.htm>.

[64] Steiner & Dal Maso Jardin, *supra* note 54, 206.

[65] Kaul, *supra* note 41, 74.

[66] On national implementation see <http://www.icrc.org/ihl-nat.nsf/WebLAW2?OpenView&Start=1&Count=150&Expand=14.28#14.28>.

[67] On these problems see in general States' Responses to Issues Arising from the ICC Statute: Constitutional, Sovereignty, Judicial Cooperation and Criminal Law (Roy S. Lee ed., 2005).

civilians indicted by military rather than civilian tribunals and the moral duty to prosecute offenders who may have no close link to Switzerland other than presence on its territory. The outcome was the elaboration of a draft revision of the civil and military criminal codes.[68] A major change, probably motivated by the experiences made with the *Niyonteze Trial*[69] by the Swiss Military Justice authorities in trying to transfer the witnesses to Switzerland, has been the drafting of a special legislation on witness protection to be integrated in the Swiss military criminal procedure code.[70] Concerning the implementation of substantial criminal law, although prosecution of war crimes was already possible under existing general provisions of the military criminal code, the new draft proposal provides for specific war crimes definitions, in strict compliance with the principle of legality. Provisions on indirect command responsibility (for omission of intervention) have been refined and made explicit and, more importantly, specific provisions on crimes against humanity have been introduced in the civil penal code. On 15 December 2003, the Swiss parliament decided, however, to limit the jurisdiction of the Swiss Military Justice to war crimes which have a strong link („enger Bezug")[71] with Switzerland, in order to avoid an overload of cases, in the wake of the Belgian precedent. This decision was reversed by the Federal Council, due to the strong criticism of this requirement. Therefore the new law project will need to be revised again. The only requirement will be that the perpetrator should find him/herself on Swiss soil and that he/she cannot be extradited or surrendered to an international tribunal.[72]

b) *The impact on the enforcement of international law*

As the ICC will not have its own police force, one of the most important forms of cooperation is for states to comply with a request to arrest and surrender a person to the court.[73] For this purpose, each state party is obligated to provide full

[68] See above.

[69] See above.

[70] See Message concernant la modification de la procédure pénale militaire (Protection des témoins) and the Military Criminal Procedural Code (RS 322.1), both in Feuille Fédérale, Feb. 18, 2003, 693 respectively 743, *at* <http://www.admin.ch/ch/f/ff/2003/>.

[71] See Wehrenberg, *supra* note 42. For criticism on the 'close link' requirement, see the comments by Trial Watch, *at* <http://www.trial-ch.org/en/crc.html#2006>.

[72] For more information on this topic see the website of the Federal Department of Justice and Police, *at* <http://www.ejpd.admin.ch/ejpd/it/home/dokumentation/mi/2008/2008–04–23.html> (Media release of April 23, 2008).

[73] Robert Hage, *Implementing the Rome Statute: Canada's experience*, *in* States' responses to issues arising from the ICC Statute: constitutional, sovereignty, judicial cooperation and criminal law (Roy S. Lee ed., 2005), 52.

cooperation and assistance to the ICC to ensure that there will be no obstacles in executing its requests.[74]

There are three ways in which the ICC may adjudicate a case (see art. 13): a) a state party may refer to the prosecutor a situation in which crimes under the ICC Statute appear to have been committed; b) the Security Council may submit a case to the court on the basis of Chapter VII of the UN Charter; c) the prosecutor may initiate an investigation under art. 15 of the Statute.

Where the UN Security Council refers a case to the prosecutor under Chapter VII of the UN Charter, both member and non-member states will have to accept the compulsory jurisdiction of the ICC over such a situation, pursuant to art. 25 of the UN Charter.[75] This option ensures that the ICC will work as a "watchdog" over the enforcement of international law provisions. Coupled together with its provisions on "surrender" of indictees to the court, thereby permitting to avoid extradition law rules (Art. 102), it makes sure that international criminals will be barred from finding safe havens from prosecution.

The ICC is said to be only applicable to member states. There is, however, also the option to prosecute crimes committed by nationals of non-member states. For example, if someone commits a crime on the territory of a member state, he or she may be tried by the ICC, on the basis of territorial jurisdiction. Moreover, as mentioned above, the UN Security Council, whose resolutions are binding almost universally, may decide to refer a case to the ICC,[76] as it occurred in Chapter VII SC Resolution 1593 (2005), referring the situation of Darfur, Sudan, to the ICC Prosecutor. The latter UN Security Council Resolution specifically provided that the Security Council:

> Acting under Chapter VII of the United Nations Charter,
> 1. Decides to refer the situation in Darfur since 1 July 2002 to the Prosecutor of the International Criminal Court [...];
> 3. Invites the Court and the African Union to discuss practical arrangements that will facilitate the work of the Prosecutor and of the Court, including the possibil-

---

[74] Art. 86–87 of the Statute.

[75] On this see Lijun Yang, *Some Critical Remarks on the Rome Statute of the International Criminal Court, in* States' Responses to Issues Arising from the ICC Statute: Constitutional, Sovereignty, Judicial Cooperation and Criminal Law (Roy S. Lee ed., 2005), 281, 284.

[76] Also the government of the Central African Republic decided to refer the situation to the Prosecutor of the ICC, with regards to facts occurred during the conflict in 2002–2003. On this see the report of Amnesty International, Central African Republic: Referral to the International Criminal Court Should Be Accompanied by Judicial Reforms to Address Impunity, Jan. 12, 2005, as reported by Global Policy Forum at <http://www.globalpolicy.org/intljustice/icc/2005/0112car.htm>. The referral led, eventually, to the charges against Jean-Pierre Bemba, former Vice-President of the Central African Republic. For more info see OTP on Jean-Pierre Bemba surrender: this is a day for the victims (July 3, 2008), *at* <http://www.icc-cpi.int/press/pressreleases/396.html>.

> ity of conducting proceedings in the region, which would contribute to regional efforts in the fight against impunity;
> 4. Also encourages the Court, as appropriate and in accordance with the Rome Statute, to support international cooperation with domestic efforts to promotethe rule of law, protect human rights and combat impunity in Darfur;
> 5. Also emphasizes the need to promote healing and reconciliation andencourages in this respect the creation of institutions, involving all sectors of Sudanese society, such as truth and/or reconciliation commissions, in order to complement judicial processes and thereby reinforce the efforts to restore longlasting peace [...].

Thus, notwithstanding the binding character of its resolutions, there is the clear intent of the UN Security Council to find an agreement between the ICC and the domestic authorities, so as to facilitate the reconciliation and peace-building process. This may be viewed as a contrast to the establishment of the ICTY and the ICTR, which were also constituted as a peace-enforcement measure on the basis of a Chapter VII UNSC Resolution. Such intent is expressed under the second paragraph:

> Decides that the Government of Sudan and all other parties to the conflict in Darfur shall cooperate fully with and provide any necessary assistance to the Court and the Prosecutor pursuant to this resolution and, while recognizing that States not party to the Rome Statute have no obligation under the Statute, urges all States and concerned regional and other international organizations to cooperate fully;

At the same time, El Fatih Mohamed Ahmed Erwa, the Sudanese representative, expressed a rather negative view, considering the intervention of the ICC as a violation of state sovereignty and as a persistence of the Council in adopting 'unwise decisions' against his country, which only served to further complicate the situation on the ground:

> The positions over the ICC were well known. The Darfur question had been exploited in light of those positions [...]. Sudan was also not party to the ICC, making implementation of the resolution fraught with procedural impediments. As long as the Council believed that the scales of justice were based on exceptions and exploitation of crises in developing countries and bargaining among major Powers, it did not settle the question of accountability in Darfur, but exposed the fact that the ICC was intended for developing and weak countries and was a tool to exercise cultural superiority.[77]

The Council, by adopting the resolution, had once again ridden roughshod over the African position, he said. The initiative by Nigeria, as chair of the African Union, had not even been the subject of consideration. Also, the Council had adopted the resolution at a time when the Sudanese judiciary had gone a long

[77] See Press Release SC/8351, 5158th Meeting, *at* <http://www.un.org/News/Press/docs/2005/sc8351.doc.htm>.

way in holding trials, and was capable of ensuring accountability. Some here wanted to activate the ICC and exploit the situation in Darfur, according to the Sudanese government. Accountability was a long process that could not be achieved overnight. The Council was continuing to use a policy of double standards, and sending the message that exemptions were only for major Powers. The resolution would only serve to weaken prospects for settlement and further complicate the already complex situation. Thus, each time that a severe international crisis will lead the Security Council to refer a case to the ICC, in a pattern similar to the establishment of the two UN *ad hoc* tribunals, there may be the same drawbacks presented earlier on.[78]

Another matter of discussion has been the so-called "art. 98 agreements" with the US in order to grant immunity to US soldiers stationed abroad. It shall be noted, in this respect, that a US soldier found indictable for war crimes committed on the territory of an ICC member state, e.g. Afghanistan, could be called to the court, should Afghanistan place a request and prove to be incapable, because of lacking structures, to conduct an investigation itself. In this case it should actually be preferable for the US to have the guarantee of the ICC Statute having the power to intervene and overlook proceedings affecting its nationals, rather than having them tried under Afghan law. This situation, however, relates to armed conflict scenarios, which are different from post-conflict situations, when 'peace-keeping forces' are being deployed. The latter, in fact, are usually subject to so-called Status of Forces Agreements (SOFA), which guarantee the jurisdiction of the sending state. In peace-keeping frameworks, therefore, the art. 98 agreements do apparently not add anything new to what already constitutes common practice in this type of operations.

Another important provision of the ICC Statute is that state parties shall cooperate with the court in the enforcement of sentences. The ICC shall determine where a convicted person is to serve his/her sentence by selecting from a list of states that have agreed to accept such prisoners. In its function as a host state, the Netherlands has a duty to enforce prison sentences imposed by the ICC if no other willing state can be found.[79] The guarantee, by the ICC, that convicted persons will be subject to fair conditions of detention may also facilitate the reintegration process as part of the peace-building phase.

---

[78] See also Andreas R. Ziegler & Stefan Wehrenberg, *Welches internationale Gericht soll Verbrechen in Darfur beurteilen? Argumente für die Übertragung der Untersuchung an den Internationalen Strafgerichtshof*, Neue Zürcher Zeitung, Feb. 23, 2005, at 5.

[79] See Harry Verweij and Martijn Groenleer, *The Netherlands' legislative measures to implement the ICC Statute*, *in* States' Responses to Issues Arising from the ICC Statute: Constitutional, Sovereignty, Judicial Cooperation and Criminal Law (Roy S. Lee ed., 2005), 102.

3. *Lessons learned from the ICTY and ICTR – the Iraqi and Sierra Leone Special Courts*

a) *The Iraqi Special Tribunal: The legacy of a belligerent occupation*

On 10 December 2003, the Iraqi Governing Council adopted the Statute of the Iraqi Special Tribunal (IST). According to it, the IST shall be independent from any Iraqi government body and shall have jurisdiction over specified crimes committed by Iraqi nationals or residents between 17 July 1968 and 1 May 2003, i.e. the period of the Baath party rule. It is composed of nine appellate, at least five trial, and up to 20 investigative judges and up to 20 prosecutors, appointed by the Governing Council. The IST has jurisdiction over international crimes of genocide, crimes against humanity, and war crimes, which are defined in the Statute both explicitly and by reference to international conventions. It further covers three specified crimes under Iraqi law involving manipulation of the judiciary, squandering of public assets, and the pursuit of policies that may lead to the threat of war or the use of the armed forces of Iraq against an Arab country.

The Statute permits but does not require the Governing Council to appoint non-Iraqis as judges. It requires, on the other hand, that non-Iraqis be appointed to serve in "advisory capacities" or as "observers" to the Trial and Appeals Chambers, to the investigative judges, and to the prosecutors. This was one of the major issues discussed in the conceptualizing period of the tribunal. In some people's view, this could contribute significantly to its legitimacy and credibility in the eyes of the international community.[80]

Another issue was whether to make the death penalty available. Under current Iraqi law, as referenced in the IST Statute, death is an admissible penalty. On the one hand, a wide application of the death penalty may have a negative impact on the *reconciliation* process in Iraq, particularly if most of those prosecuted belong to a particular ethnic or religious group. In this respect, for instance, in Rwanda, where more than 6,000 genocide cases were prosecuted, the death sentence was carried out only once and it was subjected to a moratorium for six years. Others suggested that the rejection by the Iraqi Special Tribunal of the death penalty for Saddam Hussein and other leading figures would signal a major change in the Arab world, whereas life imprisonment would have the benefit of serving as a daily reminder that they have been punished for their crimes.

A particular problem is that this Special Tribunal has been almost exclusively financed by the US, that the judges were nominated by the administrative

[80] United States Institute of Peace, *Special Report – Building the Iraqi Special Tribunal: Lessons from Experiences in International Criminal Justice* (June 2004), *at* <http://www.usip.org/pubs/specialreports/sr122.html#lessons>.

authorities established by the US posterior to the occupation, and that the US soldiers who should be liable for the commission of human rights violations will not fall under its jurisdiction.[81] A further negative point, which may affect peace-building, is that prosecution by US judicial authorities of US military personnel is being delayed or, as proven by the Abu Ghraib facts, only the lower ranks are being called to trial.

At the same time, in Sierra Leone, where capital punishment is provided for by local law but not by the Special Court, Court officials emphasized that those convicted with imprisonment rather than death penalty will be forced every day of their lives to think about what they did, and believe this message has resonated with the population. So various discussions, primarily revolving around the edge between international judicial standards and local legal traditions, seriously took in consideration the impact that one or the other provision may have on peace-building in the affected areas and population.

b) *The Special Court for Sierra Leone: Towards a new generation of international tribunals?*

Following a ten-year civil war in Sierra Leone the Lomé Peace Agreement was achieved in 1999 under the aegis of the UN. The war had been fought between the Revolutionary United Front (RUF) backed by the then president of neighbouring Liberia, Charles Taylor, and the Armed Forces Revolutionary Council (AFRC) on one side, and the pro-government Civil Defense Force (CDF) on the other. The RUF used amputations and mass rape to terrorize the population and gain control of the country's lucrative diamond mines, but the CDF committed serious offences, too. Within the context of the dysfunctional condition of the national justice system since the end of the conflict, the Special Court for Sierra Leone was established in 2002 by agreement between the Sierra Leone government and the UN.[82] The court has a mandate to "prosecute persons who bear the greatest responsibility" for serious crimes committed during the Sierra Leone war since 1996.[83] In October 2000 the UN Secretary-General presented to the UN Security Council the working model of a hybrid court to be jointly administered by the UN and the Sierra Leone Government. In some

---

81 See Human Rights Watch, *Irak: Saddam vor Gericht, faires Verfahren fraglich* (Oct. 18 2005); Stefan Wehrenberg & Andreas R. Ziegler, *Der Prozess gegen Saddam Hussein: Faires Verfahren oder Siegerjustiz?*, JUSLETTER 4 (Nov. 28, 2005), available *at* <http://www.blumlegal.ch/pdf/voelkerrecht/Saddam_Jusletter28112005.pdf>.

82 Agreement between the United Nations and the Government of Sierra Leone on the Establishment of the Special Court for Sierra Leone, signed on 16 January 2002, *at* <http://www.sc-sl.org/scsl-agreement.html>.

83 Statute of the Special Court for Sierra Leone (SCSL Statute), art. 1(1), *at* <http://www.sc-sl.org/scsl-statute.html>.

experts' view, this type of tribunal will open the path to a new generation of international courts, able to deliver justice faster and cheaper than the two UN *ad hoc* tribunals. Since its opening on 3 June 2004, however, the Special Court for Sierra Leone has also received criticism, particularly in relation to its time and jurisdictional limitations, viewed by some as an obstacle to the delivery of justice. Certainly, though, the combination of local and international justice will permit it to acquire legitimacy and credibility in the eyes of the local population, therefore having a higher potential to contribute to the reconstruction phase of the country.[84]

The cooperation with international experts was required by the fact that Sierra Leone's criminal code did not incorporate violations of international humanitarian law, or crimes against humanity. Secondly, due to the ongoing civil war and its consequent economical collapse, the Government did not have the necessary financial resources to establish a tribunal of its own. But another very important reason, as highlighted by the Sierra Leone Ambassador to the United States, John Leigh, was to establish the credibility of the court. As he pointed out: "We don't want the court to be seen as victor's justice, and international involvement will prevent this perception."[85] Moreover, due to significant financial and personnel requirements, none of the Security Council members supported the establishment of another UN tribunal. Thus, a major difference between the latter and the Sierra Leonean court is that whereas the last two were created by the Security Council as a Chapter VII peace-enforcement measure, the first is created by an agreement between the UN and the Sierra Leone government and is staffed with both local and international judges and prosecutors.

Another advantage of the SCSL, in comparison to the ICTR and the ICTY, is its location in the country where the crimes were committed. This location will permit the victims to follow the proceedings more closely and will facilitate the implementation of international law into the Sierra Leonean domestic system, taking its traditions into account. In this regard, particular efforts to have an impact on the Sierra Leonean population were made with the establishment of a 'Public Affairs Unit', which engages and trains local media and produces audio and video summaries of the court's work. In addition, there is the Outreach Unit, which diffuses information about the court in the country through video screenings, discussion, and dissemination of written material. This work is substantiated with efforts by the Court to target particular sectors of society such as students

[84] In considering the framework, however, it should be born in mind, however, that UNAMSIL (the UN mission in Sierra Leone) represents, with its 17'000 blue helmets, the biggest ever peacekeeping mission sent into a country.

[85] See the reference in Sieff, *supra* note 46.

and conduct of trainings for civil society. It is also building local professional capacity through employment and training of Sierra Leonean staff.[86]

In relation to the outreach of judicial decisions, radio remains the main medium for the majority of Sierra Leoneans to learn about the court. There are weekly radio summaries of proceedings and there have been plans to develop an independent radio station that would focus on justice issues and provide detailed coverage of the court. On the other hand, attendance in the public gallery seems to be limited. Court staff has apparently recognized this problem and expressed the intention to intensify initiatives to expand attendance.[87]

At the same time, a drawback of the SCSL is its lack of Chapter VII powers and authority over third states to cooperate with it in surrendering suspects of international crimes. Some, in fact, have managed to flee to Liberia or other West African countries. Moreover, the Statute of the SCSL limits its jurisdiction to crimes committed in Sierra Leone, whereas the activities of the rebel group supported by Charles Taylor have extended to neighbouring Guinea. In fact, as reported by Human Rights Watch, inadequate and uncertain funding, and Nigeria's continued shielding of Charles Taylor – who was taken to custody only on 29 March 2006, three years after the release of the indictment – may have been two major obstacles to the court's ability to bring justice fairly and effectively.[88] However, these obstacles have more to do with the international political situation than with the intrinsic structure of the court.

Lack of funding is a problem that may affect every type of judicial institution, independently from whether this is domestic, international or mixed. The harbouring of offenders by third states is another matter that the creation of a permanent international criminal court, via the complementarity principle, is trying to counter by obstructing the existence of safe havens. But the structure of the Special Court, with its efforts to involve the local population and important sectors of the society, such as judges, lawyers, students, may be the winning formula to peace-building in the country. As observed by Human Rights Watch:

> During the trial phase, the Special Court is implementing a program of activity to make the court accessible to the Sierra Leonean population. It has one of the most successful outreach programs of any international or hybrid court to date, and may be considered a model for other such courts.[89]

[86] See Human Rights Watch Report, *Justice in motion, the trial phase of the Special Court for Sierra Leone* 4 (Oct. 2005), *at* <http://hrw.org/reports/2005/sierraleone1105/sierraleone1105.pdf>.

[87] *Ibid.*

[88] *Ibid.*

[89] *Ibid.*, 28.

Similarly to the Outreach Program of the ICTY,[90] the Special Court's Public Affairs Unit prepares video summaries twice a month and audio summaries once a week, using the knowledge of local staff to help identify developments that will likely be of the greatest importance or interest to Sierra Leoneans, therefore focusing on the summaries accordingly.[91] Additionally, the unit conducts training of local media on international law, which helps to ensure accurate reporting.[92] Court officials regularly meet with civil society in Freetown through the Special Court Interactive Forum, approximately once a month. Following suggestions that outreach to religious leaders was not adequate, the Outreach Unit expanded its efforts to include such religious leaders. This Unit also works with civil society members who monitor and report on court proceedings, permitting it to respond where necessary to developments in the trials. For example, on the basis of this feedback, the Outreach Unit sought to provide further explanation of the basis for closed proceedings at the court. Thanks to these efforts, Sierra Leone civil society generally praised the court's outreach efforts and responsiveness to civil society.[93]

A peculiarity of the Special Court, however, which is the subject of much debates between humanitarian and human rights lawyers, is the courts' jurisdiction not only over leaders, but also over children,[94] even though the Prosecutor David Crane mentioned that he does not intend to prosecute children but rather people who forced children to commit crimes during the country's war.[95] The problem of child soldiers is a widespread phenomenon in the country. Neither the ICC nor the ICTR or the ICTY have competence to try children. The ICC is only competent to try perpetrators aged over 18. Out of the principle of complementarity, the reasoning is that competence to try children under 18 or 15 shall be vested with national courts. This, however, may be an obstacle to the achievement of justice and peace-building. For instance, in Switzerland war crimes lie within the competence of military tribunals. These, however, pursuant to the Military Criminal Code, only have jurisdiction over offenders over 18 years of age. Those who are younger shall be tried in accordance with the special provisions on juvenile justice. However, the ordinary Criminal Code

---

90 For more information see the website <http://www.un.org/icty/index-b.html>.

91 Human Rights Watch interview with Special Court staff, Freetown, April 15, 2005.

92 Human Rights Watch interview with Special Court staff, Freetown, April 20, 2005.

93 See Human Rights Watch Report, *supra* note 86, 30.

94 See Art. 7 of the Statute of the SCSL, *at* <http://www.sc-sl.org/scsl-statute.html>.

95 Special Court for Sierra Leone, *Public Affairs Office, Press Release: Special Court Prosecutor Says He Will Not Prosecute Children* (Nov. 2, 2002), *available at* <http://www.sc-sl.org/Press/pressrelease-110202.pdf>. See in particular the Sam Hinga Norman Case No. SCSL-2004–014 (Formerly SCSL-2003–08), which, for the first time, saw an indictment for recruitment of child soldiers (para. 16), *at* <http://www.sc-sl.org/indictment-CDF.html>.

applicable to juveniles does not yet encompass war crimes. Assuming the presence of a teenager asylum seeker in Switzerland, suspected of the commission of war crimes, it would be impossible for the Swiss judicial authorities to try him/her for these offences. At best, the person could be tried under more general headings like murder. The impact of the sentence on the perpetrator and the victims, however, would not be the same as a conviction for war crimes.

But here the debate is whether child soldiers are victims themselves and whether, for this reason, they shall be exculpated from the commission of war crimes. In the authors' view this position, primarily supported by human rights lawyers, does not take into consideration the realities of war and the fact that in Africa and other countries, where children are enlisted to combat, the cultural and social situation may be different from the one existing in Western cultures. A 15 year old child may have a different maturity in Sierra Leone than in Switzerland or Italy. For the same reason there were several objections to the raising of the age limit from 15 to 18 for the prohibition of compulsory recruitment. Additional Protocol I to the four Geneva Conventions of 1949 allows for recruitment of children between 15 and 18 exactly for this reason. Similarly the ICC Statute, as a result of a compromise, decided to fix the age limit at 15 (Art. 8(2)(b)(xxvi)). What can be the impact of judicial proceedings in relation to conflicts fought primarily by soldiers under 18 years of age? Can this contribute to peace-building? In Sierra Leone the answer was to hold those responsible accountable regardless of their age. After receiving the draft Statute, the initial compromise position presented by the Government was that the Special Court should have jurisdiction over people aged over 17, i.e. the age at which a person takes on full adult criminal liability in Sierra Leone. UN officials, however, insisted that the Government shall include jurisdiction over juveniles. The conviction that this was the right position to adopt came from the belief that the people of Sierra Leone would not perceive the Court capable of dispensing justice should those aged between the ages of 15 and 18 be arbitrarily excluded from the jurisdiction of the Special Court. Thus, the compromise was reached to keep with Article 4 of Additional Protocol II to the Geneva Conventions, which states that belligerents do not include persons under age fifteen.[96] Moreover, it shall be recalled that the Special Court has jurisdiction only over offenders who bear "the greatest responsibility" for the atrocities committed in Sierra Leone, a threshold which must be reached prior to any indictments being issued. Thus, only a limited number of children, if at all, will fulfil this criterion. In fact, Art. 15(5) of the Statute calls the Prosecutor's attention to the desirability of assessing the responsibilities of child soldiers by the Truth and

96 Smith, *supra* note 45.

Reconciliation mechanism.[97] Moreover, there are special proceedings for those aged between 15 and 18 which take into account the age of the accused. There are in this regard a range of sentencing options which must be utilized should someone under the age of 18 be convicted, such as vocational training, but not imprisonment,[98] as spelt out in Art. 7 of the Statute.[99]

Another peculiarity of Sierra Leone is that parallel to the Special Court a Truth and Reconciliation Commission was installed. Sierra Leone's Parliament, after consultation with the UN High Commissioner for Human Rights, passed legislation in February 2000 calling for its creation. The UN Security Council suggested that because the court might dissuade perpetrators from disarming for fear of prosecution, the Truth and Reconciliation Commission might provide a better alternative for some combatants, particularly children.[100] It should further be mentioned that until now no child has been indicted by the Special Court.

There are also indications that Special Court decisions have been cited in domestic proceedings. Some members of the legal community also view the jurisprudence of the Special Court as being valuable for future prosecutions of crimes in the country and for the development of implementing legislation for the Rome Statute of the International Criminal Court.[101] All these aspects may prove the establishment of the international court as a winning tool for the peace building phase in the African country.

---

[97] Art. 15(5) of the Statute provides that: "In the prosecution of juvenile offenders, the Prosecutor shall ensure that the child-rehabilitation programme is not placed at risk and that, where appropriate, resort should be had to alternative truth and reconciliation mechanisms, to the extent of their availability."

[98] Smith, *supra* note 45.

[99] (1) The Special Court shall have no jurisdiction over any person who was under the age of 15 at the time of the alleged commission of the crime. Should any person who was at the time of the alleged commission of the crime between 15 and 18 years of age come before the Court, he or she shall be treated with dignity and a sense of worth, taking into account his or her young age and the desirability of promoting his or her rehabilitation, reintegration into and assumption of a constructive role in society, and in accordance with international human rights standards, in particular the rights of the child.
(2) In the disposition of a case against a juvenile offender, the Special Court shall order any of the following: care guidance and supervision orders, community service orders, counselling, foster care, correctional, educational and vocational training programmes, approved schools and, as appropriate, any programmes of disarmament, demobilization and reintegration or programmes of child protection agencies.

[100] See the reference in Sieff, *supra* note 46.

[101] See Human Rights Watch Report, *supra* note 86, 36.

IV. *Conclusions*

The establishment of the two UN *ad hoc* tribunals in the early Nineties has certainly paved the way for a new role of international tribunals, the aim of which is no longer to merely punish, as it was the case of the IMT of Nuremberg and the IMTFE in Tokyo, but to contribute more positively to the peace-building process by facilitating the implementation and enforcement of international law and by supporting the reconciliation of the victims with the offenders. With the ICTY and the ICTR, created as a Chapter VII peace-enforcement measure in alternative to the sending of military troops to sedate a conflict, the international community has definitely acknowledged the important role that the judiciary can play in the reconstruction of war-torn areas.

By assisting the affected countries in bringing to justice, indistinctively, *all* the perpetrators of international crimes, no matter what side they belonged too, international tribunals no longer appear as a tool to enforce "victors' justice". By assisting domestic courts in adjudicating the perpetrators, they give a chance to victims to come to terms with their past and to overcome their hunger for revenge, thereby avoiding an escalation of the hostilities. At the same time, offenders who will be treated according to fair trial and detention standards will be more inclined to reintegration and rehabilitation, thereby also contributing to peace-building between all the conflicting sides.

Different forms of international tribunals have been tried out to attain this goal: ad hoc tribunals, an international permanent criminal court or hybrid solutions like the Special Court for Sierra Leone. Which option is the best will very much depend on the circumstances. In some situations, as e.g. in South Africa, the best solution was apparently the establishment of a Truth and Reconciliation Commission. This, however, may have not been a sufficient tool in other areas like the Former Yugoslavia.

In any event, the common denominator to all these types of judicial or quasi-judicial authorities is that justice, particularly the one promulgated in accordance with international standards, is a key tool for peace-building. Their success, however, will depend on a good cooperation with the domestic authorities.

The thesis defended here is that the role of international tribunals is particularly important in relation to the enforcement of international law at both international and national level and the implementation of international legal standards into domestic legal systems. The two UN *ad hoc* tribunals, thanks to their establishment on the basis of a Chapter VII UNSC Resolution, could count on the full support of the UN, particularly in enforcing the law and trying to apprehend the suspects. Notwithstanding difficulties and failures, generally speaking it may be said that the ICTY's success is also due to the support of international peace-enforcement forces, which fulfilled the role of a police investigating force. Being binding on every UN member state, the Resolutions establishing the UN ad hoc tribunals further imposed on each state the obligation to fully cooperate with them, thereby facilitating enforcement.

However, because of their primary jurisdiction, the *ad hoc* tribunals have had little incentive for the implementation of international law into domestic legal systems. In this sense, the ICC has been far more effective. Because of the principle of complementarity, the ICC will very much depend on the cooperation of its member states. Cooperation will enable it to conduct on site investigations, arrests and enforce sentences. However, thanks to its possibility to intervene in situations where a state proves to be unable or unwilling to conduct investigations, it will give a strong incentive to states to implement the legal standards codified by the ICC Statute into their domestic systems. This ensures that in the long term, states will have a common legal standard, which will nevertheless take into account their own specific cultural and legal traditions. This will facilitate the prevention of conflicts and will allow the call to justice of those responsible of breaches of international law. Where the domestic system of member states has completely broken down due to a conflict, the ICC will be able to intervene and help these states to re-establish the judiciary system and rebuild the country. The advantage of the ICC, moreover, is its legitimacy and credibility, since it was created on the basis of an international treaty.

A very good example of an international tribunal contributing to peace-building is the Special Court for Sierra Leone, the aim of which is not simply to bring to justice the perpetrators, but also to train the local judicial authorities and the civil society in international law in order to promote peace among the population. For this reason special programmes were established to diffuse the outcomes of the judicial proceedings among the population, with discussion fora, radio programs, etc. Thus, the Special Court for Sierra Leone can bee seen as the forerunner of a new generation of international tribunals.

On the other hand the effects of the Iraqi Special Tribunal are quite discussable, since its establishment was not welcomed by all the parties involved in the conflict, particularly the Iraqi population, which perceives the US presence as an unlawful interference in their internal affairs.

In conclusion, it can be said that international tribunals can strongly contribute to peace-building, firstly by setting incentives for the implementation of international legal standards, thereby ensuring the existence of efficient legal systems at the domestic level, which prevents conflicts. Secondly, in situations where domestic judiciary systems have collapsed following a conflict, as it was the case in Iraq, international tribunals may be the right alternative to re-establish peace and order, although their efficiency will only be guaranteed if they will be granted local support. To do otherwise may imply the risk of escalating internal tensions. It is very important that in the regions or countries where peace should be re-established, the local population is convinced of the legitimacy and efficiency of these courts, which shall not be viewed as a tool of the victorious party to inflict their power, as it may be the case for the Iraqi Special Tribunal. Enforcement of international law may be the right approach in the initial phases of peace-building, when first of all some order must be re-established. In later stages, however, it is important to raise awareness among the local population about the importance to implement these standards into their domestic system, giving them the feeling that international humanitarian and human rights provisions provide for the protection of *universal* and not regional or western values.

Issues

Private Security and State-Building

William Reno

Old fashioned state-builders used private security forces, either as personal adjuncts or as hired mercenaries, in their efforts to control resources. As Mancur Olson pointed out in his formulation of "stationary bandits" as state-builders, those entrepreneurs who stayed in one place provided security to productive groups of people so that they could extract more resources from their "victims".[1] Before those "victims" asserted their own interests in this relationship, this was an essentially private application of coercion, much as racketeers coerce their targets. Charles Tilly's expression of "state-building as organized crime" shows how this private security – the exercise of coercion through the use or the threat to use violence as an element of an excusive transaction – can lead to state-building.[2] In its pure form, private security is not a public good since each person who receives protection pays for it in separate transactions. Those who do not pay can be excluded from its benefits and may even become its targets. In contrast, while state officials may show predatory tendencies, the entire community still benefits from the order that government police or soldiers provide. Of course purveyors of private security might decide that they are better off behaving like a state, as Robert Bates, Olson, and Tilly saw in the incentives for racketeers to become governments.[3] But in the final analysis in this formulation, state-building and private security are integrally linked.

Contemporary experience also shows that states can evolve into private security organizations, as in the early 2000s when Liberia's President Charles Taylor used his office to intimidate the citizens of Liberia while he managed the proceeds of a personal business empire that overshadowed internal state revenues by close

---

[1] Mancur Olson, *Dictatorship, Democracy and Development*, 87 (3) American Political Science Review 567–76 (1993).

[2] Charles Tilly, *War Making and State Making as Organized Crime, in* Bringing the State Back In 169–91 (Peter Evans, Dietrich Rueschemeyer & Theda Skocpol eds., 1985).

[3] Robert Bates, Prosperity & Violence: The Political Economy of Development (2001); Mancur Olson, Power and Prosperity: Outgrowing Communist and Capitalist Dictatorships (2000).

to a factor of ten.[4] Taylor or his successor might have followed Olson's path to become a stationary bandit who recognized that the welfare of his victims was also his interest. But in contemporary international society the transition of such a private security agency to a real state in the sense of providing citizens with public goods, much less with the sorts of services and the forms of administration that are conventionally associated with states in the 21st century is problematic. Long before this evolution could commence in the Liberian case, an American-led diplomatic and military coalition forced Taylor from office into Nigerian exile in 2003, and in 2006 from exile to answer charges of crimes against humanity before the Special Court of Sierra Leone.[5] Tilly's criminals and Olson's bandits did not face international tribunals or armed peacekeeping interventions, or international opinion that views modern repetitions of old fashioned state-building as exploitation and systematic violations of basic human rights.

Today, private security forces cannot initiate state-building on their own. But what about pre-existing state uses of private security? Historically, established rulers made deals with private syndicates to exercise coercion on their behalf. Karen Barkey found that the 17th century Ottoman authorities hired bandit gangs to help control truculent subjects.[6] Some contemporary state rulers hire private security companies, or what people in the business call private security companies (hereafter, PSCs)[7] that provide expertise usually associated with the militaries of states to defend their regimes. These PSCs have been responsible for reducing overall levels of violence and in creating conditions for orderly state administration in some important cases. Aspirants to state power also have hired PSCs. The French mercenary Bob Denard overthrew four regimes in the Republic of the Comoros between the 1970s and 1990s for his clients. Mark Thatcher, the son of the former British Prime Minister, was implicated in a plot in 2004 to overthrow the government of Equatorial Guinea and install an exiled politician in its place.[8]

---

[4] Liberian domestic revenue estimates (c. $60 million) from International Monetary Fund, *Liberia: Selected Issues and Statistical Appendix*, 7, 41–42 (Feb. 25, 2003); estimates of commerce under Taylor's personal control (c. $500 million) from United Nations Security Council, *Report of the Panel of Experts appointed pursuant to Security Council resolution 1395 (2002), paragraph 4, in relation to Liberia* (April 11, 2002).

[5] *The Prosecutor v. Charles Ghankay Taylor* (Special Court for Sierra Leone, March 17, 2003), copy of the original in the author's possession.

[6] Karen Barkey, Bandits and Bureaucrats: The Ottoman Route to State Centralization (1994).

[7] See International Peace Operations Association, *at* <http://www.ipoa.org>, Private Security Company Association of Iraq, *at* <http://pscai.org>, and British Association of Private Security Companies, *at* <http://www.bapsc.org.uk>.

[8] Adam Roberts, The Wonga Coup: Guns, Thugs and a Ruthless Determination to Create Mayhem in an Oil-Rich Corner of Africa (2006).

Post-Second World War uses of private security in state and international politics, however, expose limits to the practice. Machiavelli's warning still applies half a millennium later: "The mercenary captains are either capable men or they are not; if they are, you cannot trust them, because they always aspire to their own greatness, either by oppressing you, who are their master, or others contrary to your intentions; but if the captain is not skilful, you are ruined in the usual way."[9] Denard bore out the warning, as from 1978 to 1989 he ran the Comoros through a front-man while he converted to Islam and called himself Said Mustapha Madjoub. Denard's 1995 coup was met with a French paratroop intervention and a condemnation of his old patron, the French foreign minister Jacques Foccard who distanced himself from Denard as the mercenary went from being an agent of French power to become a threat to France's international image and to order in the regions where he operated.[10] Likewise, it is unlikely that a successful coup in Equatorial Guinea in 2004 would have survived international outrage, just as Nigerian threats reversed a coup in neighboring São Tomé in 2003 that involved members of apartheid ear South African security forces.

Freelance mercenaries face the reality that contemporary nationalist passions leave rulers to fear popular perceptions that they are kept in power only through the efforts of foreigners. They also face an international effort to ban the hiring of private individuals or firms to fight in inter-state wars or in wars of national liberation. These included the Organization of African Unity's 1977 Convention for the Elimination of Mercenarism in Africa, Article 47 of the 1977 Protocol I of the Geneva Conventions, and the 1989 International Convention against the Recruitment, Use, Financing and Training of Mercenaries. But these conventions did not foresee that even states that were signatories to these agreements would hire PSCs to fight in their civil wars and that powerful states would use them in their foreign military interventions, including in those defined by the UN and other international organizations as peacekeeping operations.

In contemporary international society private security forces and their leaders cannot become states in their own right, in contrast to their old historical roles. Existing state uses of private security also face severe limits. But states and private security have not parted ways. Contemporary examples of state uses of private security abound (besides the ill-fated Thatcher and Denard adventures), usually under the rubric of the PSC that are beholden to interests of powerful states. Moreover, almost all PSCs declare their respect for the sovereignty of existing states. These features turn the exercise of private coercion in the international realm into a tool that reinforces the existing system of states. Private security neither threatens states (as opposed to regimes) nor signals a significant shift

---

[9] Nicolo Machiavelli, The Prince (1977), Chapter XII.

[10] Jacques Foccart, Foccart Parle: entretiens avec Philippe Gaillard, vol. 2 (1997).

in the exercise of coercion in the international realm. In fact, its contemporary uses reinforce the current hierarchy of state power in the international system. The real systemic effect of private security comes through this means, and it is reflected in the ways that the reinforcement of this hierarchy influences how sovereignty is applied.

I. *The Argument*

This analysis of the relationship of private security to state-building recalls the findings of Janice Thomson. She saw that state officials used private agents of coercion in the international system to extend their states' power well into the 19th century. For example, the US government backed filibusters, or entrepreneurs who organized private military actions in foreign countries, in the 1800s to influence developments in weaker states, especially in Central America and the Caribbean.[11] It was only in 1923 that British colonial authorities ended their contract of the British South Africa Company to run Rhodesia (Zimbabwe). American officials used private contractors to train Saudi armed forces soon after the Second World War. Thus private security has long had a role in reinforcing the international state system, especially in its periphery. It has helped to shore up client regimes and bolster their local control over and capacity to manage state-like functions on the diplomatic and economic margins of international society, especially when organized at the behest of officials in more powerful states.

Recent literature on private security stresses this close connection between this phenomenon and officials in powerful states, especially in the US and Great Britain. It focuses on the impact of private security on the capabilities of state military capabilities, and the interconnecting networks of private security contractors and key politicians. It pays less attention to *variations* in its impact on the capabilities of *different kinds of states*.[12] In contrast, the analysis here finds that private security in the control of officials in the US and Britain significantly strengthens the military capabilities and political influence of these powerful countries. Moreover, these outsiders' promotion of the use of private security in the poorest and most politically unstable countries of the world extends the influence of bureaucracies and the ideas about governance that hold sway in these powerful states. In most countries where private security forces intervene, private security helps to reinforce the institutions and practices of state politics in places where states might otherwise collapse. Thus PSCs have become key elements of international, especially US and British, interventions in chaotic and

---

[11] Janice Thomson, Mercenaries, Pirates, and Sovereigns (1994).

[12] For example, Deborah Avant, The Market for Force: The Consequences of Privatizing Security (2005); Ken Silverstein, Private Warriors (2000).

impoverished countries. PSCs flourish in circumstances where public opinion in powerful countries pressures officials to be seen to do something about wars and humanitarian emergencies while the same public would punish officials who sent national militaries to the remote and desolate margins of the world. These wary and prudent officials also appreciate the dangers of provoking local nationalist passions through the provocative direct use of foreign armies to restore order. These same officials also avoid heated debates in legislatures that would accompany the commitment of their own militaries and use PSCs to shield them from potential liabilities of poor planning and mission failure. A PSC presence in military logistics, training, intelligence analysis and other tasks conventionally associated with state militaries also helps officials in powerful countries consolidate commercial, political, and personal ties with local authorities.

This role of PSCs in the foreign policies of powerful countries shapes the PSC industry at organizational and cultural levels. This process further subordinates private security to the services of the contemporary system of states and creates formidable barriers of entry to PSC firms and potential employees from outside the militaries of the wealthiest industrial states. Even within this category of states, Anglo-American military ideas, culture and national interests assert an overriding influence on almost all other private security enterprises that engage internationally with foreign governments. This is an outgrowth of the fact that the United States and the United Kingdom possess the world's only militaries with truly global reach. These states dominate the PSC market to such an extent that they can impose not only their regulatory framework, but also their preferred military cultures among PSC managers and employees, many of whom are known to their employers through past military service or policy networks. The most competitive PSCs are those headed by retired members of the US and British militaries. Companies like Military Professional Resources (MPRI) and Blackwater in the US and Aegis in Britain gain commercial advantages from their employees' and their contractors' deep understandings of the cultures of the US and British militaries and from their managers' political and military network connections to state decision-makers. These firms are able to reassure clients that they understand and will adhere to the delicate political parameters of their missions that state officials define. Moreover, extensive US and British engagement in Iraq and Afghanistan simply offer vastly more opportunities for contracts, compared to any other set of clients and in the world. Astute PSC commercial analysts recognize the impact of this political context on their industry, laud the competitive advantage that this situation gives them, and strategize to consolidate their advantages through more assiduous attention to their clients' political interests.[13]

[13] Dominick Donald, After the Bubble: British Private Security Companies after Iraq (2006).

Thus the destabilizing freelance PSC activities in small, weak states of the sort that Bob Denard and Mark Thatcher undertook emerge as isolated incidents. These incidents incur the wrath of officials in powerful countries and serve as negative examples to firms that seek long-term markets for their services. Other isolated examples in which PSCs took the initiative to intervene included Executive Outcomes, a South African firm with British financial backers that operated in Angola from 1992 to 1996 and in Sierra Leone from 1995 to 1996. Sandline International attempted to operate in Papua New Guinea in 1997 and was associated with a clandestine effort to aid the return of an ousted elected government to Sierra Leone from 1997 to 1998. But even in these cases, PSCs were careful to declare that they would sign contracts only with recognized governments (which in the case of Sierra Leone and Sandline included the exiled, democratically elected government that it helped to return to power with tacit British backing).[14] The Papua New Guinea venture involved a contract with an incumbent Prime Minister, but provoked resistance from the country's regular army and ire from officials in neighboring Australia. Since then, many of the employees and managers of these firms (apart from some who became involved in the Equatorial Guinea fiasco in 2004 and Sao Tome in 2003) have integrated into the larger framework of the Anglo-American PSC industry or have left the business.

II. *Private Security and Strong States' Redefinition of the Sovereignty of Weak States*

PSCs assumed a more significant role in US military strategy under the Clinton Administration. Les Aspin, Clinton's Secretary of Defense, announced that in the absence of a peer rival, the US would reduce troop strength, but not its capacity to engage in overseas interventions. One mission of the US military would be to organize multilateral interventions in weak or failing states, with PSCs playing key roles as providers of logistics for peacekeeping forces, local security, and training for indigenous police and soldiers. This policy was in line with Clinton's Presidential Decision Directive 25, issued soon after the decision to withdraw American troops from Somalia, to minimize the political and financial costs of intervention without abdicating a US role in managing conflicts in poor and chaotic countries.[15] When Donald Rumsfeld became Defense Secretary under the

[14] Select Committee on Foreign Affairs, House of Commons, Summary of Conclusions and Recommendations, *Sierra Leone, Second Report*, February 1999, HC-116, *at* <http://www.publications.parliament.uk/pa/cm199899/cmselect/cmfaff/116/11613.htm>.

[15] PDD 25 summary, *at* <http://www.gmu.edu/departments/t-po/peace/pdd25.html>.

new Bush Administration in January 2001, he shared much of this assessment, though he did not believe that the US could count on other states to commit forces for the types of interventions that he contemplated. He also focused more on containing China, a potential future peer power, and favored strengthening the direct operational capabilities of US armed forces.

Official perspectives changed on 11 September 2001. Those attacks showed that non-state actors could threaten a major state. President George W. Bush declared: "The events of September 11, 2001 taught us that weak states, like Afghanistan, can pose as great a danger to our national interest as strong states."[16] British Foreign Secretary Jack Straw shared this assessment: "no one can doubt that a primary threat to our security is now posed by groups acting outside formal states, or from places where no state functions at all. It is no longer possible to ignore misgoverned parts of a world without borders, where chaos is a potential neighbour anywhere from Africa to Afghanistan."[17] Even prior to the 11 September attacks, the 1998 bombings of US embassies in Kenya and Tanzania exposed the threat of weak and collapsing states to the powerful. The 1998 attacks were planned in Somalia, which has lacked a central government since 1991, and parts of Kenya's Indian Ocean coast where government control is weak. The 2000 attack on the US warship *USS Cole* originated in Yemen, a country that had friendly relations with the US but which also had a government that exercised only weak oversight over the activities of most of its citizens.

Responding to this threat meant building a capacity to fight adversaries in territories that states do not necessarily control, or recognizing the need in Rumsfeld terms, to "conduct war in countries we are not at war with (safe havens)" and to fight enemies that are not members of regular military forces, including organized crime and extremist groups that are enablers of terrorism.[18] President Bush put the policy in gentler terms, declaring: "America encourages and expects governments everywhere to help remove the terrorist parasites that threaten their own countries and the peace of the world. If governments need training or resources to meet this commitment, America will help."[19] Though this policy challenges some key norms of sovereignty such as the right of recognized rulers of states to freedom from external intervention, it shores up other core norms. In particular, the policy demands "the actual transformation of an unstable or aggressive state into one which is both stable and willing to adhere to the norms

[16] George W. Bush, National Security Strategy of the United States 3 (2002).

[17] Jack Straw, *Order Out of Chaos: the Challenge of Failed States*, *in* Re-ordering the World: the Long-term Implications of September 11 98 (Mark Leonard ed., 2002).

[18] Department of Defense, Quadrennial Defense Review Report, vi (Feb. 6, 2006).

[19] Mike Allen, *Inaction Is Not an Option: Bush Offers Military Aid in Continuing Terror War*, Washington Post, March 12, 2002, at A1.

of the international community," wrote Steven Metz and Raymond Millen.[20] US and other Western interventions into the affairs of these weak states can come as invitations to local rulers to strengthen their authority as partners with these outsiders who are so keen to boost state capacities to actually rule over people within their territories.

This doctrine links the safety of citizens in powerful countries to the capacity or political will of rulers in poor countries to exercise control over their own citizens and to conduct adequate surveillance over who and what enters and leaves their countries to reduce threats to powerful countries. In short, states are expected to be able to provide guarantees concerning the behaviour of citizens and to abide by agreements with other states. Sovereignty-as-guarantee fits classic notions of the emergence of states in the international system and the positive functional role of this definition of sovereignty in assisting that transformation. This doctrine also claims a right of external enforcement, expressed as regime change through military means ("pre-emptive warfare"), which it defines as a defensive response where hostile rulers actively protect threatening non-state armed groups. The doctrine's overall effect is to insist that all regimes conform to minimal standards of internal governance that powerful states define.[21]

The right of rulers to rule as they see fit without obstruction from outsiders, and the association of sovereignty with a right of non-intervention, which post-911 strategic doctrines of powerful states are beginning to foreclose, is a recent innovation in international relations that dates to the end of the colonial era. Previously, European states claimed a right to rule territories and people who did not have what Europeans considered "civilized governments", or as in the case of several North African countries in the 1880s, were incapable of repaying private international loans. The right of stronger states to claim the territories of weaker neighbours through conquest only came under serious attack in the League of Nations Covenant after the First World War and more definitively after the horrors of Nazi conquest during the Second.[22] Recent strategic doctrine developments in powerful states now pose serious challenges to what Robert Jackson calls "negative sovereignty", or the freedom from external intervention,

[20] Steven Metz & Raymond Millen, *Intervention, Stabilization, and Transformation Operations: The Role of Landpower in the New Strategic Environment,* 35 Parameters 42 (Spring 2005).

[21] This is not a purely Anglo-American doctrine. Pre-emptive warfare is a prominent feature of the French *LOI No. 2003–73 du 27 janvier 2003 relative à la programmation militaire pour les années 2003 à 2008 (1).*

[22] Kalevi Holsti, Taming the Sovereigns: Institutional Change in International Politics 275–99 (2004).

and what Robert Kasner calls "organized hypocrisy", or the intentional non-acknowledgement of internal incapacities of weak states.[23]

This doctrine of intervention to bolster the capabilities of states and force conformity to a standard of governance is difficult to apply. One institute estimates that over two billion people, almost a third of the world's population, live in "countries that are in danger of collapse."[24] The coverage of US International Military Education and Training (IMET) program extends to 46 of 47 sub-Saharan African states, excluding only Zimbabwe.[25] Nine African states participate in the Pentagon's Trans-Sahara Counterterrorism Initiative and six in the East Africa Counterterrorism Initiative. These operations focus on drug interdiction, strengthening border controls and domestic surveillance of extremist groups. Since stationing large numbers of US soldiers in these countries would be provocative to local people and politically and financially burdensome to US politicians, these operations make heavy use of PSC contractors.

This doctrine defines state-building in ways that combine military and non-military tasks. NATO doctrine based upon experiences in Bosnia and Kosovo after 1995 provides an explicit role for the inclusion of non-governmental organizations, local authorities and private contractors as force multipliers into combined war-fighting and post-war reconstruction.[26] It is into this niche that many PSCs try to fit, such as in Provincial Reconstruction Teams in Afghanistan that combine military personnel, NGOs and contractors in counterinsurgency strategies that involve local service provision, intelligence collection and military operations. It is this niche that the PSC security analyst noted above identifies the most rapid growth in demand for PSC services on the battlefield. In particular, he identifies the difficulties that many NGOs find in fitting into these new roles: "The sector's insistence on retaining the perception of political neutrality and humanitarian impartiality means that it is extremely reluctant to be in any way associated with government activity [...]. Might this then be an opportunity for the private sector, which would be far readier to work to governments' directions?"[27]

State-building operations already provide opportunities for PSCs outside of formal military programs. They include counter narcotics programs under Department of Defense auspices, Department of Treasury financial surveillance

---

[23] Robert Jackson, Quasi-states: Sovereignty, International Relations and the Third World (1990); Robert Krasner, Sovereignty: Organized Hypocrisy (1999).

[24] *The Failed States Index*, Foreign Policy 50–54 (May/June 2006).

[25] United States Department of State, Military Assistance, *at* <http://www.state.gov/documents/organization/60649.pdf#search=%22IMAT%20Africa%20military%20training%22>.

[26] North Atlantic Treaty Organization, NATO Civil-Military Co-Operation (CIMIC) Doctrine (2003).

[27] Donald, *supra* note 13, 3–4.

programs, and Drug Enforcement Agency anti-drug operations. The Department of State operates the IMET program. These programs are designed to increase the capabilities and degrees of civilian control over militaries. They also aim to create institutional and personal links between US and foreign militaries. All incorporate PSCs in their operations too. US-based Military Professional Resources Inc (MPRI) operates the Department of Defense's Africa Center for Strategic Studies and the African Contingency Operations and Assistance Program to, according to company literature, "increase African capacity to fight terrorism and to prevent, mitigate, and resolve crises, conflicts, and regional instability."[28]

These operations offer PSCs more opportunities to work for US and British government clients. For example, DynCorp received a $35 million US State Department contract to train 4,000 Liberian soldiers under the rubric of the UN mission in that country. The firm offers $118,000 per year to recruits, but requires that they hold US passports and drivers licenses. This firm also trains police in Iraq (salary: $120,000), Afghanistan ($100,000) and East Timor ($98,000).[29] MPRI advertises that it has been contracted to "implement an Action Plan for the national defense structure, with the goals of reprofessionalizing the armed forces, developing competence among civil leaders in defense, disengaging the military from civil government functions, and improving the standing of the armed forces among the people" in Bosnia, Iraq and Afghanistan, essentially as an agent of US policy makers and strategic planners.[30]

This also means that these firms must abide by regulatory frameworks of those strong states upon which their commercial fortunes depend, or as the analyst above terms it, "work to governments' direction" and gain the confidence of their civilian and military clients. PSC contracts with the US government, for example, must conform to the International Traffic in Arms Regulations (ITAR) under State Department administration. ITAR registered companies must apply for licenses before signing contracts with foreign clients.[31] British officials model their regulations on the US licensing regime, and also cite the need to balance growing tasks without increasing the size of British armed forces.[32] In contrast, French and South African regulations, and positions of organizations like the United Nations and African Union focus on the suppression of mercenary activ-

[28] MPRI, *at* <http://www.mpri.com/site/int_africa.html>.

[29] DynCorp web site, *at* <http://www.policemission.com>.

[30] <http://www.mpri.com>.

[31] The US Arms Export Control Act (1968) under which ITAR operates is found *at* <http://www.fas.org/asmp/resources/govern/aeca00.pdf>.

[32] House of Commons, Foreign Affairs Committee, Foreign Affairs – Ninth Report, Session 2001–2002 (July 23, 2002), *at* <http://www.parliament.the-stationery-office.co.uk/pa/cm200102/cmselect/cmfaff/922/92202.htm>.

ity.[33] While firms from these countries exist and do bid on contracts in places like Iraq and Afghanistan and elsewhere, they have to contend with hostile elements of their own governments' administrations, and they generally lack the depth of connections to contracting government officials that the Anglo-American firms enjoy. This difference in regulatory approach, along with US and British dominance in major interventions in Iraq and Afghanistan give Anglo-American PSCs the advantage of favorable official relations with the dominant UN Security Council members that are engaged in the creation of peacekeeping and post-conflict reconstruction missions.

III. *Warfare and the Anglo-Americanization of Private Security*

The US decision to invade Afghanistan in 2001 and Iraq in 2003 created an even larger role for PSCs in the course of applying new security doctrines. In Afghanistan, PSC employees helped release special operations forces and other specialized military units for targeted missions and sped up military deployment to Iraq in preparation for the 2003 invasion. Whether in preventative deployments as in Africa or retaliatory operations in Afghanistan, PSC employees needed to be able to operate complex technologies to keep the new weapons operating and provide other services that low-paid regular soldiers were abandoning for more lucrative salaries in the civilian world.[34] This market expansion, however, raises the threshold of skills needed and draws from a more limited labor pool.

The White House's decision to invade and occupy Iraq in 2003 with as few regular troops as possible reinforced doctrinal shifts and further boosted the demand for PSCs, or as an industry analyst put it: "The war in Afghanistan opened the door to more widespread employment of independent security contractors, and then Iraq kicked that door off it's hinges, stomped on it, burned it, and scattered the ashes."[35] A year after the invasion Rumsfeld reported that about 20,000 PSC employees worked for 60 companies active in Iraq.[36] By March

---

[33] Links to regulatory instruments are found *at* <http://www.PSCs.hemscott.net/legal.html>.

[34] Peter Singer, Corporate Warriors: The Rise of the Privatized Military Industry (2003); Deborah Avant, *The Privatization of Security and the Change in the Control of Force*, 5 International Studies Perspectives 153–57 (2004).

[35] Robert Young Pelton, Licensed to Kill: Hired Guns in the War on Terror 97 (2006).

[36] Letter, Donald Rumsfeld to Representative Ike Skelton (D-MO), Attachment: Discussion Paper Private Security Companies Operating in Iraq (May 4, 2004). For a list of security companies doing business in Iraq, see <http://travel.state.gov/travel/cis_pa_tw/cis/cis_1763.html>.

2006, the PSC presence had grown to 181 firms, employing over 48,000 people.[37] This increased the proportion of PSCs to regular military personnel by over ten times the level of the first Gulf War. The tasks of occupation of Iraq required that more of them work in jobs such as protection of VIPs and infrastructure put them in the line of fire. This bolstered the revenues of these firms. Prior to British deployment in Iraq in 2003, British PSCs reportedly grossed about £200 million a year. A year after the start of the war, they accounted for about 40 percent of all firms operating in Iraq and grossed an estimated £1 billion.[38] US firms accounted for most of the remaining activity (with two from Australia and one each from Korea, Hong Kong, India and a South Africa – British hybrid), with the four largest taking contracts worth about $950 million in the first year of the war.[39]

This involvement has been lethal, with 444 deaths from March 2003 to the middle of July 2008. Of these, 40.5 percent were Americans, and 10.5 percent involved British citizens. The remaining half of deaths involved PSC employees from 37 other countries. It is significant in light of differing military cultures and regulatory regimes that the substantial formal military deployments of Italian, German, Danish and French soldiers either in conflicts in Iraq or in Afghanistan is accompanied by the deaths of only six citizens from these countries from among this PSC toll.[40] The overall death rate for the estimated 60,000 PSC employees deployed to mid-2006 showed the seriousness of their engagement, as it stood at .52 percent, compared to .15 percent for the estimated 1.5 million US soldier deployments to Iraq during the same period. These figures underline the Anglo-American dominance in the PSC market, with Nepalese (20 casualties to July 2008) and South African PSC members (23 casualties to July, 2008) playing important ancillary roles, with the addition of 34 Turkish casualties (that appear to be accounted for largely by attacks on truck drivers.)

The changes in US security and military doctrines, their wide application, and the death toll among PSC employees highlights the ambiguity of equating PSC employees with the ill-defined mercenary label and the difficulty of separating military from non-military tasks. The dispersed nature of insurgency warfare in Iraq and Afghanistan, and the extension of counterinsurgency even to friendly states and regions that do not now see active combat blur distinctions between offensive military tasks and support operations. In April 2004, for example, an employee of the Hart Group (UK) was killed and four wounded while fighting

---

[37] United States Government Accountability Office, Rebuilding Iraq: Actions Still Needed to Improve the Use of Private Security Providers 2 (June 13, 2006).

[38] *Mercenaries: the Baghdad Boom*, Economist, March 25, 2004, 31.

[39] David Isenberg, A Fistful of Contractors: The Case for a Pragmatic Assessment of Private Military Companies in Iraq (2004).

[40] PSC and other contractor casualties can be found *at* <http://icasualties.org/oif/Civ.aspx>.

insurgents that they encountered during a logistics operation. Employees of Control Risk Group (UK) and Triple Canopy (US) fought a battle for several hours. Several days earlier Blackwater (US) repulsed an attack of the Badr Brigades, using a company helicopter to supply ammunition and evacuate a wounded US Marine.[41] The first US combat casualty in Afghanistan was a CIA contractor, Johnny "Mike" Spann, hired as an interpreter for prisoner interrogation and who was killed on 25 November 2001. Combat engagement extends to PSCs serving private clients. For example, in March 2004 CNN Journalist Tucker Carlson reported that his DynCorp (US) security detail gave him an AK-47 as they commandeered an Iraqi gas station.[42]

IV. *The Anglo-American Military Culture of Private Security*

The Iraq and Afghan markets for PSCs reinforce the closer alignment of interests between PSCs and the US and British governments. This extends advantages to firms with Anglo-American military cultures and builds on earlier preferences of firms and clients for Anglo-American military expertise. An informant explained that firms that operated in Iraq from 2003 sought former British soldiers since "they have been fighting since they joined their armies" and many had counterinsurgency experience from British operations in Northern Ireland.[43] Initially American employees were seen as less able to undertake the "cultural acclimatization" necessary to operate efficiently in new settings and as less fit or adaptable to physical hardship. Moreover, many American soldiers to 2003 had less counterinsurgency experience than their British counterparts, though this would change as the US military deployment in Iraq encountered growing local resistance and American military strategists began to reconsider their earlier strategies.

The US Department of Defense recognition of the recruitment of American soldiers to PSC work is reflected in the 2005 approval of a $150,000 bonus for Special Operations Forces members who reenlist for six additional years, which was "devised to stem an exodus of senior sergeants, petty officers and warrant officers to higher-paying civilian jobs."[44] This reflects the competition to retain

[41] Dana Priest & Mary Pat Flaherty, *Under Fire, Security Firms Form an Alliance*, Washington Post, April 8, 2004, at A1.

[42] Tucker Carlson, *Hired Guns*, Esquire (March 2004).

[43] Observations in this section are drawn from the author's research and encounters with PSCs in Sierra Leone (1995–96, 2001, 2005), Kosovo (2002) and regions of Sudan under the control of the Sudan People's Liberation Army (2003).

[44] Thom Shanker, *Pentagon Sets Bonuses to Retain Members of Special Operations*, New York Times, Feb. 8, 2005, at A4.

soldiers against private sector salaries that can range as high as $200,000 a year for high risk forward security and VIP guard duties. This flood of skilled labor and the rising standards of PSC firms have enabled PSCs to weed out employees who draw negative attention to their clients for human rights abuses and unwarranted uses of force. Though drawing upon the manpower of the armed forces of the US and Britain and bidding up salaries, this flood of skilled workers helps to discipline the PSC market and to serve US and British government interests in using employees to bolster weak state capacities without provoking resistance among local populations or generating negative publicity in policy makers' home countries.

Several "problem children" incidents illustrate how the US and British official interests shape the private security industry. In late 2005, employees of a British firm posted video on a personal website that appeared to show them firing shots at Iraqi motorists, set to the soundtrack of Elvis Presley's song "Mystery Train." This video quickly spread to other internet sites and generated considerable commentary.[45] This incident followed the revelation that a British PSC employed a former South African death squad leader to guard the Iraqi Labor Minister. This story became public when the employee was killed in an insurgent bomb attack on his hotel, which maimed another South African who had testified before his country's truth commission that he had murdered nine anti-apartheid activists and bombed between 40 and 60 homes. These revelations promoted the South African government to launch investigations of its citizens who worked for PSCs in violation of the 1998 Regulation of Foreign Military Assistance Act, which bans South African citizens from participating in armed conflicts for private gain. This legislation was applied against the two owners of a firm contracted to provide police training and oil field protection in Iraq, after they were arrested in Zimbabwe for alleged connections to the Thatcher-backed coup plot in Equatorial Guinea.[46] Such anti-PSC sentiment generally is not found among US and British officials, and they are able to leave their South African counterparts to help separate the public relations problems out of the industry from among the estimated 2,000 to 4,000 South Africans who worked for PSCs in Iraq as of 2006.[47]

This evolving industry standard meant that those who wanted to remain in the business have to divorce themselves of past associations that would hint of controversy or that posed direct threats to regimes in weak states, regardless of

---

[45] Video *available at* <http://movies.crooksandliars.com/Aegis-PSD.mov>.

[46] Graeme Hoskin, *They Kill Foreigners Because they Can*, Daily News [Cape Town], Feb. 17, 2005, 1.

[47] Peter Leon & Kevin Williams, *When Intentions and Consequences Clash*, Business Day [Johannesburg], Aug. 31, 2006.

whether they actually had a hand in such activities or not. The association in the media of Tim Spicer, the CEO of Aegis, with Simon Mann, and Nick du Toit, among the founders of Sandline International, responsible for interventions in Sierra Leone and Papua New Guinea in the 1990s, brought unwanted attention, even though this firm was very strict in working only within the constraints of internationally recognized regimes. Perhaps not so happily for Spicer (even though he was not connected to these events), Mann and du Toit were among the 60 jailed in Zimbabwe in March 2004 in connection with the plot to overthrow Equatorial Guinea's government, a rare instance of contemporary private security forces threatening a recognized regime. Meanwhile, Sandline announced that it was closing on 16 April 2004, while Spicer rose in prominence in Aegis before its 14 May announcement of a successful bid on a $293 million Pentagon contract to provide security services in Iraq. Even so, Sandline's claims that it aided British policy in its dealings in West Africa in the 1990s found considerable support in facts, and illustrated the extent to which that firm's officers recognized the importance of adhering to the discipline of working within the bounds of state policies as a prerequisite for long-term commercial success.

The capacity to attract clients is not readily available to skilled military veterans of other countries who might otherwise venture into the international PSC market. The collapse of the Soviet Union initially generated concerns that shrinking militaries in that region would flood the market with cheap private fighters along with their old armies' weapons. While these weapons became a significant factor in numerous wars, the expected flood of fighters did not appear. Contractor deaths in Iraq, for example, include only four Russians, three Poles and only one Ukrainian among the 444 reported job-related deaths to July, 2008.[48] One PSC manager noted that Russian Spetsnaz [специального назначения or "special purpose troops"] veterans tend to exhibit a "congenital inability to follow instructions" and often try to circumvent bureaucratic procedures whenever possible. This author has observed Russian Special Forces and OMON (Отряд милиции особого назначения) veterans in African conflict zones that conform to suspicions among others in the field of conflict that these workers are associated with high alcohol consumption and uneven job performance.[49] It is likely that language and cultural differences play a significant role in this exclusion too.

---

[48] <http://www.icasualties.org>.

[49] This includes smoking while fueling aircraft and drinking before piloting aircraft in SPLA-held Sudan. It should be noted, however, that in 2001 the author encountered sober Russian employees entering Paddy's Bar in Freetown, Sierra Leone. They started fighting only after heavy drinking later in the evening, but were not the most drunken in the room.

Tight personal ties between regulators, clients and PSCs in the US and Britain further narrows the PSC market. The preference among state officials for PSCs that understand their own political priorities and security establishment cultures offers advantage to insiders. For example, Blackwater, a major sub-contractor for DynCorp in Iraq, announced in February 2005 that Cofer Black had been appointed its new Vice Chairman. Black, a former Coordinator for Counter-Terrorism at the US Department of State, had previously run the CIA's Counter-terrorism Center.[50] MPRI occupies the advantageous position of influencing the writing of the the US Army manual, *Contractors on the Battlefield*.[51] Diligence LLC was founded by William Webster, formerly head of both the FBI and the CIA. Joe Allbaugh, one of its co-chairmen, was Bush's campaign manager in 2000.[52] MPRI's president, Carl Vuono, was US Army Chief of Staff (1987–93) and played a role in reorganizing the US Army after the Vietnam War. British firms boast similar connections. Col. Tim Spicer organized Aegis Defense Services and won a $293 million Pentagon contract to coordinate PSCs in Iraq. As noted above, Spicer earlier played a role in Sandline International, which was involved in a Foreign Office effort in the late 1990s to provide military aid to the civilian government of Sierra Leone in contravention of UN sanctions against arms shipments.[53]

These connections work to the detriment of firms outside the Anglo-American official sphere. This means entrepreneurs and would-be PSC employees decide whether they need to seek partnerships with firms from one of these two states or simply join favored firms as contractors or as individual employees. Access to the most lucrative contracts requires conformity to the official US and British standards of military behavior. By extension, PSCs have to pay very careful heed to US and British policy interests.

V. *The Conservative Bias of Private Security*

The close integration of private security and strong state interests, especially since the 911 attacks, show the extent to which states, and especially strong states, continue to dominate the reshaping of international relations. US and British applications of post-911 strategic doctrines to strengthen the capabilities of weak states has opened up new business opportunities for PSCs. They are hired to

---

50 Press Release, *at* <http://www.blackwaterusa.com/btw2005/articles/pr1.html>.

51 Found *at* <http://www.usafa.af.mil/jscope/JSCOPE00/Campbell00.html>.

52 Isenberg, *supra* note 39, 39.

53 Letter from Cogressional Representative Marty Meehan (D-MA) to Donald Rumsfeld, *at* <http://www.house.gov/apps/list/press/ma05_meehan/NR040811PentagonIraqContractLetter.html>.

engage directly in "state-building" operations specifically designed to bring the exercise of coercion under the more exclusive control of recognized governments in weak states. This serves the interests of most incumbent regimes in weak states that are happy to receive additional outside support – that melds together the influence of official and private foreigners in their view – to exercise power in their own realms. It also serves the interests of strong states as it reinforces the capacity of rulers to guarantee outsiders that they can be held responsible for the behavior of people within their own realms, including those who outsiders define as terrorists. This capacity to provide guarantees – to fulfill treaty obligations and to be held accountable, and thus subject to deterrence by more powerful states – is the essence of the classic exercise of sovereignty as it became defined in the process of state-building in early modern Europe.[54]

These developments would seem to reinforce trends toward a greater equality of rights and expectations, if not capabilities, among sovereign actors that began with the era of decolonization. In fact, they do the reverse, as they expose the importance of a steep hierarchy of capabilities among sovereign states. The world's strongest military powers, the US and Britain, prove able to harness PSCs to impose their standards of governance on regimes that previously either lacked the political will or capabilities to control their own states' citizens and territory. Many have good reason not to do this on their own; either because they are averse to stirring up domestic opposition among local strongmen or they fear aggravating factional splits within their own regimes. But as doctrines of preemptive warfare become influential among powerful states (in the sense even that officials in powerful states claim for themselves the right to force officials in weak states to administer more effectively) and regimes in weak states perceive the external dangers to them that the activities of non-state armed groups on their own territory can bring, most choose to allow outsiders to help reconstruct their state according to standards that US and British outsiders determine. The alternative is far worse; to be seen as obstructive or even become a target for "regime change" as a consequence of strangers' use of one's territory to attack a third party. The targets of preemptive warfare of this sort are groups that undermine state authority and the direct beneficiaries are regimes that rule weak states.

The culture of PSCs is important in this process of state-building. In a macro-social equivalent to the widespread adoption of the QWERTY keyboard configuration, the spread of one standard of operation – say, a British or American bureaucratic design for customs services, militaries or police – blocks the adoption of competing standards. Cultural domination in the PSC sector prevents other clients from gaining easy access to competing services, and even blocks the development of such an alternative. This helps to reinforce the power of the

[54] Charles Tilly, Coercion, Capital, and European States, AD 990–1992 167 (1992).

world's strongest states, both in terms of direct influence over the organization of the weak and through personal networks. PSCs play increasingly important roles in mediating both of these avenues for influence and power in what looks more and more like a pre-20th century application of sovereignty in the service of maintaining an international system of states, but now against the threat of global insurgents who challenge the state paradigm.

Women's Human Rights in the State-Rebuilding Process

*Hilary Charlesworth**

The protection of human rights has an uncertain place in the theory of state-building. The Brahimi report referred briefly to the potential role of 'human rights experts' in complex peace operations,[1] but it did not provide any detail of what this might mean. The practice of state-building has also illustrated the tenuous position of human rights norms, with priority typically given to achieving immediate political stability over the protection of human rights.[2]

The human rights of women are often regarded as a sub-set of the human rights applicable in state-building, but they have become increasingly prominent over the last decade. The United Nations regularly emphasises the significance of talk of human rights in ameliorating the position of women in 'post-conflict' societies. For example, UNIFEM's strategies for women in the reconstruction of Afghanistan and Iraq are couched in terms of rights[3] and the mandate of the UN Peacebuilding Commission recognises the importance of women's involvement in post-conflict settlements.[4] The protection of women's rights was also endorsed by United States President, George W. Bush, as one major benefit of the invasions of and subsequent state-building exercises in Afghanistan and Iraq.[5]

In this chapter, I examine the way that the vocabulary of women's human rights has been translated into two state-building exercises of the past decade – East

* Thanks to Sue Harris-Rimmer for assistance with updating the references. Parts of this chapter are drawn from Hilary Charlesworth, *'Worlding Women' in International Law, in* Gender and Global Politics in the Asia-Pacific (Bina D'Costa & Katrina Lee-Koo eds., 2009).

1 UN Doc. A/55/305, S/2000/809 (2000).

2 See generally The UN, Human Rights and Post-Conflict Situations (Nigel D. White & Dirk Klaasen eds., 2005).

3 See <http://www.unifem.org/afghanistan>; <http://www.womenwarpeace.org/iraq/iraq.htm>.

4 SC Res 1645 (December 20, 2005).

5 See Karen Engle, *Liberal Internationalism, Feminism, and the Suppression of Critique: Contemporary Approaches to Global Order in the United States*, 46 Harvard International Law Journal 427 (2005).

Timor and Iraq. The former is an example of UN state-building efforts and the latter undertaken effectively outside an international institutional framework. Conclusions are then drawn from these two case studies pointing to a series of common problems faced by women in states that are being rebuilt. I argue that, despite rhetorical commitment by the international community, women's rights are typically sidelined in the process of state-building and that 'rebuilt' states can both create and reinforce women's inequality.

I. *East Timor*

The international rebuilding of East Timor began in 1999 after the East Timorese voted for independence following 24 years of Indonesian occupation. The vote against integration with Indonesia prompted severe violence and destruction of the infrastructure of East Timorese society. After creating a peacekeeping force, International Force East Timor (INTERFET), the UN Security Council established the United Nations Transitional Administration in East Timor (UNTAET) to oversee the transition to statehood.[6] East Timor finally became a new state in May 2002.[7]

At first sight, UNTAET might be seen as an example of women's rights-sensitive nation-building. In establishing UNTAET, the Security Council emphasised the 'importance of including in UNTAET personnel with appropriate training in international humanitarian, human rights and refugee law, including child and gender related provisions'.[8] This was the first such reference in the mandate of a comparable body and was regarded as implementing the UN's commitment to 'mainstreaming' gender perspectives in peace operations.[9]

Women in East Timor live within a traditional, patriarchal culture, where customary practices accord them a separate, and lesser, role in society. They had however been deeply involved in the independence struggle against Indonesia and had suffered all types of violence, much of it because of the low status of

---

6 SC Res 1272 (1999) on the Situation in East Timor. An interim United Nations presence had been provided for earlier in 1999 in the May agreements between Indonesia, Portugal and the United Nations about the conduct of the elections. See Agreement between the Republic of Indonesia and the Portuguese Republic on the Question of East Timor, May 5, 1999, Art. 6, *at* <http//www.un.org/peace/etimor99/agreement(agreeFrame_Eng01.html>.

7 The United Nations still has a presence in East Timor. On Feb. 25, 2008, the Security Council, by resolution 1802 (2008) extended the mandate of the United Nations Integrated Mission in Timor-Leste (UNMIT) for one year.

8 SC Res 1272 (1999) on the Situation in East Timor, para. 15.

9 See the *Windhoek Declaration and the Namibia Plan of Action on 'Mainstreaming a Gender Perspective in Multidimensional Peace Support Operations'* (May 31, 2000).

women and the sexual stereotypes with which they were burdened. Rape, forced sterilisation and sexual slavery were common in the occupation period.[10] After the 1999 referendum, the Indonesian military and local militias abducted women and many individual and mass rapes occurred.[11] Women related to pro-independence activists appear to have been targeted for sexual violence.[12] The UNTAET era was also marked by considerable domestic violence. Violence against women by male family members was estimated to constitute 40% of all offences committed in East Timor during the year 2000.[13] One possible explanation for the increase of family violence was the unemployment rate of 80% in urban areas. Violence within the family became a way for men to reassert their domestic power.

East Timorese women's groups regularly invoked the language of human rights during the state-building process to make claims about the employment of women, the representation of women in public life, the high rate of female illiteracy and the issue of violence against women. Another concern raised by the women of East Timor was that of accountability for the crimes committed against them during the Indonesian occupation and its aftermath.

Few East Timorese women played formal roles in the state-building process. An administrative unit devoted exclusively to gender issues was included in the original structure proposed for UNTAET in November 1999 but it was not implemented because of competing budget priorities.[14] It took the intervention of two senior women UN officials, Angela King (Assistant Secretary-General and Special Adviser on Gender Issues and the Advancement of Women) and Mary Robinson (United Nations High Commissioner for Human Rights), to ensure the creation of a Gender Affairs Unit (GAU) in April 2000. The GAU was eventually responsible for some significant initiatives in East Timor, but the delay in establishing it seriously affected its operations. Funding that had initially been allocated for the payment of gender affairs officers was redistributed, and no program or operational budget was created even when the GAU was reinstated. Thus, preliminary tasks that should underlie the functions of the GAU, such as

---

[10] The *Report of the Commission for Reception, Truth and Reconciliation in East Timor* (2006) provides significant evidence of sexual violence during the occupation (see in particular Chapter 7.7), *at* <http://www.ictj.org/en/news/features/846.html>. See also *UNIFEM Timor Leste Country Report, at* <http://www.unifem-eseasia.org/projects/Cedaw/countryprogramme_timor.html>.

[11] Report of the Independent Commission of Inquiry on East Timor to the Secretary-General, UN Doc. A/54/726 (2000); Seth Mydans, *Sexual Violence as a Tool of War: Pattern Emerging in East Timor*, New York Times, March 1, 2001.

[12] Susan Harris-Rimmer, *East Timorese Women and Transitional Justice, in* Global Issues: Women and Justice 335, 339 (Sharon Pickering & Caroline Lambert eds., 2004).

[13] Maggie O'Kane, *Return of the Revolutionaries*, Guardian Weekly, Jan. 15, 2001.

[14] Sherrill Whittington, *Gender and Peacekeeping: The United Nations Transitional Administration in East Timor*, 28 Signs: Journal of Women in Culture and Society 1283 (2003).

an assessment of the impact of the post-referendum violence, or identification of different needs of men and women, were delayed.

UNTAET established a Special Panel for Serious Crimes to try acts of international criminality occurring after the 1999 referendum. The Panel's decisions with respect to crimes against women have been criticised however[15] and women's groups have called, so far unsuccessfully, for an international criminal tribunal to provide greater accountability for crimes.

Overall, UNTAET's achievements relating to women were the product of uncoordinated pressures, rather than the result of long-term planning. There was implicit recognition in various public statements made by the Transitional Administrator, Sergio Viera de Mello, that East Timorese men and women had quite different experiences under the Indonesian regime, and also that gender was a significant factor affecting their opportunities in the transitional and independence eras, but this was not reflected in resource or management terms. The employment of women in UNTAET in particular suggests failures in planning and execution. East Timorese women's groups sought an assurance that one third of the East Timorese people employed by the UN would be women. A directive issued by the Transitional Administrator, after intense lobbying by the major women's organisation, REDE, stated that 'a minimum of all national and district hiring shall comprise 30% women within every classification/level of employment.'[16]

But in the end this commitment was not achieved: 33% of the international civilian officials working for UNTAET were women but women comprised only 11% of the UNTAET East Timorese staff. Women were represented in even lower numbers in the civilian police and peacekeeping force in East Timor, composing 4% and 2.4% respectively.[17]

Significant in East Timor was the reaction of local groups to assertions of women's human rights. Traditional law and indigenous practices that disadvantage women can be reinforced by religious conservatism and also by patriotic expressions of cultural pride by male leaders.[18] This phenomenon was evident in East Timor, and was mixed with an ambivalent attitude to the UN's presence, combining gratitude and resentment. Thus in his 2001 New Year's speech

---

[15] Harris-Rimmer, *supra* note 12.

[16] UNTAET internal memo (Sept. 7, 2000).

[17] Hilary Charlesworth & Mary Wood, *Women and Human Rights in the Rebuilding of East Timor*, 71 Nordic Journal of International Law 325 (2002).

[18] See e.g. Heather Wallace, *Gender and the Reform Process in Vanuatu and Solomon Islands*, 51 Development Bulletin 23 (March 2000); Suzette Mitchell, *Women in Leadership in Vietnam*, 51 Development Bulletin 30 (March 2000); Anne Hellum, *Human Rights and Gender Relations in Postcolonial Africa: Options and Limits for the Subjects of Legal Pluralism*, 25 Law and Social Inquiry 635 (2000).

to the nation the resistance leader and now Prime Minister, Xanana Gusmão criticised what he called the "obsessive acculturation to standards that hundreds of international experts try to convey to the East Timorese, who are hungry for values."[19]

Gusmão went on to acknowledge that some of the 'standards' that UNTAET aspired to entrench in law and in administrative practice in East Timor were universal in the sense that they were recognised as such in international law. However, he implied that the standards relating to the rights of women, particularly the right of women to determine their own lives, did not find natural affinity or reflection in East Timorese culture. These standards were regarded by Gusmão as difficult to absorb locally. Gusmão also suggested that the values and the process by which international standards, especially with respect to women's human rights, were being introduced into East Timorese society were beset by strong elements of colonial attitudes amongst the international workers, and unthinking receptiveness by some East Timorese.

A response to this approach was given by Milena Pires, Deputy Speaker of the National Council in August 2000. Pires spoke of problems caused by a combination of traditional culture with religiously-based social conservatism. She observed that:

> cultural discourse is invoked frequently to quash attempts to introduce discussions on women's rights into the East Timorese political equation. The incompatibility between East Timorese culture and what is popularly cited as a western feminist imposition is used to dismiss even the notion that Timorese women's rights may need to be nurtured and defended so as to become a reality. Undermining the importance of women's human rights because it only considers half of the East Timorese population is another argument put forward to prevent its elaboration.[20]

These types of arguments were invoked against various proposals to boost the political representation of women in East Timor, not only by the East Timorese but also by UN officials. For example, a public debate about quotas for women was ignited by a proposal to entrench in law a requirement for political parties to field women in at least 30% of their nominated representative positions for election to the Constituent Assembly which was responsible for drafting the Constitution. Some influential UNTAET officers were opposed to the proposal, arguing that quotas infringed the concept of free and fair elections.[21] The proposal

---

[19] *Available at* <http://www.pcug.org.au/~wildwood/JanNewYear.htm>.

[20] Milena Pires, *Strategic Development Plan for East Timor* (paper presented at CNRT Conference, Dili, August 2000).

[21] See Jonathan Morrow & Rachel White, *The United Nations in Transitional East Timor: International Standards and the Reality of Governance*, 22 AUSTRALIAN YEARBOOK OF INTERNATIONAL LAW 1 (2002).

was ultimately defeated in the National Council in March 2001, although in the end 27% of the seats in the Constituent Assembly were held by women.[22]

After broad community consultation, a Gender and Constitutional Working Group prepared a Charter for Women's Rights.[23] The Charter sought the prohibition of all forms of discrimination and the adoption of positive measures to promote equality. It demanded the protection of women's right to live free from any form of violence, both public and private and regulation of the dowry system to prevent violence against women. The Charter also sought a guarantee of women's participation in traditional decision-making processes. The Constitution however contains only a few traces of the Charter's provisions, for example its reference to non-discrimination on the basis of gender in access to political positions.[24]

State-building in East Timor under international auspices did not give adequate attention to the involvement of East Timorese women and has produced very limited gains for them. Women are poorly represented in public life and in governmental positions, domestic violence remains at extremely high levels and women have little hope of economic freedom.[25] The waves of unrest and violence in East Timor since 2006 have led women's groups once again to appeal to the international community for support in ensuring women's involvement in decision-making, equality of access to employment, reform of the police and public service and ending impunity for human rights violations against women.[26]

II. *Iraq*

State-building in Iraq is a response to the political and physical chaos caused by the 2003 invasion by the United States and its partners in the 'Coalition of the Willing'. David Frum, a former speech writer in the Bush White House,

[22] The Law on the Election of the National Parliament, passed in December 2006, included a mandatory quota that one in every four candidates be a woman. The 2007 Presidential and Parliamentary elections saw a slight increase in women elected under this new quota system (27.69%). One woman, Lucia Lobato, ran for President and was placed fifth in the vote out of eight candidates. Female candidates from most parties signed on to a 'Women's Political Platform'. See further *at* <http://www.unifem.org/attachments/stories/200707_TimorLeste_WomensPoliticalPlatform.pdf>.

[23] The Charter appears in 2 (5) La'O Hamutuk Bulletin (August 2001): <http://www.laohamutuk.org/Bulletin/2001/Aug/bulletinv2n5.html>.

[24] Section 63. See also sections 6j, 16 and 17.

[25] UNDP, *Timor-Leste Human Development Report* 15–17 (2006).

[26] See letter from Rede Feto (Women's Network) Timor Leste to Ian Martin, Special Envoy of the UN Secretary-General for Timor Leste (July 7, 2006).

reported that he was asked in 2002 to sum up in a sentence or two the best case for invading Iraq.[27] One proposal he devised as a rationale for military action was for President Bush to promote the appeal of democracy and women's rights to Muslim world. This plan was abandoned because the White House was concerned that the call for women's rights would destabilise some of Washington's most important allies in the Middle East.

Women have however featured increasingly in the official White House material on state-building in Iraq and officials have often stated that "women's rights are at the core of building a civil, law-abiding society, a pre-requisite for true democracies."[28] This commitment has been haphazardly observed. The Iraqi government in exile, created by the United States before the invasion, had three women out of 65 members. Only three of 25 members of the Iraqi Governing Council established by the United States'-led Coalition Provisional Authority after the invasion were women and there was a single woman in the Cabinet. No women served on the 24 member constitutional drafting committee that produced the interim Constitution. The Iraq Interim Government, appointed from 1 July 2004, had six women out of thirty members.

The pressures against the participation of women in state-building are to some extent a product of the ambivalence of the United States. For example, the Coalition Provisional Authority was reluctant to support Iraqi women's groups' call for a 50% quota for women's seats in the National Assembly responsible for drafting an interim Constitution in 2004[29] because it was regarded as inconsistent with United States anti-affirmative action policies. A far greater problem for women however has been local hostility to their involvement in public life, particularly from religious groups.[30] Coalition officials tended to postpone overt support for women until the time that proper security was established, making it much harder to involve women after conservative religious and community leaders become entrenched in power.[31]

In the end, the interim Constitution prescribed a *goal*, rather than a quota, that 25% of the seats should be held by women; the election regulations however mandated that a third of people on electoral lists should be women. This was an important step, though it was considerably less than the percentage sought by

[27] David Frum, The Right Man: The Surprise Presidency of George W. Bush (2003).

[28] E.g. Paula Dobriansky, *Women and the Transition to Democracy: Iraq, Afghanistan, and Beyond*, Heritage Foundation Lecture to the Conservative Women's Network (April 11, 2003).

[29] See e.g., Letter from Basma Fakri, President, Women's Alliance for a Democratic Iraq (May 12, 2004), *at* <http://www.womenwagingpeace.net/content/articles/ElectionCommissionLetter.pdf>.

[30] Swanee Hunt & Cristina Posa, *Iraq's Excluded Women*, Foreign Policy (July/Aug. 2004).

[31] Ibid.; Isobel Coleman, *Women, Islam, and the New Iraq*, Foreign Affairs 24, 35 (Jan./Feb. 2006).

Iraqi women's groups. Most women candidates refused to campaign in public in the lead up to the January 2005 elections; one woman candidate was assassinated and one kidnapped. Of course concerns about violence were held by men also, but the violence against women was regarded as having religious support. In the end, women won 25.45% of the seats in the legislature.[32] The 55-member committee established to draft the Constitution, however, included only eight women; five were members of the main Shiite party, and two came from the Kurdish Alliance. There was a single independent woman member.

The 2005 Iraqi Constitution includes specific reference to women's rights to vote and to stand for election[33] and prohibits gender discrimination.[34] It includes an aspiration, rather than a requirement, that voting laws enable 25% of the Council of Representatives to be women for a transitional period.[35] The Constitution's commitment to equality before the law[36] is potentially undermined by the declaration that Islam is "a fundamental source of legislation"[37] and that "[n]o law that contradicts the established provisions of Islam may be established".[38] Depending on the interpretation of *Sharia* law that is adopted, the Constitution could invalidate civil laws similar to those adopted by Iraq in 1959 which accorded women equal rights in relation to marriage, divorce and inheritance.[39] Another troubling provision of the Constitution gives individuals a choice of personal status law.[40] It is not clear what would happen for example if there was a conflict between spouses over the law to apply in a divorce. The Constitution provides for an independent judiciary,[41] but it also mandates the appointment of clerics and religious judges to the Federal Supreme Court.[42] The nature of the appointments of these religious judges will be very significant in the interpretation of the Constitution.

---

32 See <http://www.ipu.org/parline-e/reports/2151.htm>.

33 Article 20.

34 Article 14.

35 Article 47.

36 Article 14.

37 Article 2. The religious parties argued strongly that Islam be recognized as *the* source of legislation, while the Kurds and secular groups supported a reference to Islam as *a* source. The indefinite article was finally used after pressure from the United States. See Coleman, *supra* note 31, 30.

38 Article 2.

39 An attempt was made by the Iraq Governing Council in 2003 to overturn the 1959 personal status law and replace it with *Sharia* law. A resolution adopted by the Council to this effect was eventually vetoed by Paul Bremer, head of the Coalition Provisional Authority, after intensive lobbying by Iraqi women's groups.

40 Article 39.

41 Article 19.

42 Article 89.

The invasion of Iraq has replaced a secular regime with a government of strong religious affiliation. Rebel groups also are characterised by a commitment to fundamentalist religion. The major protagonists in the chaotic process of state-building are at best ambivalent and at worst hostile to the involvement of women. Moreover, the continuing violence in Iraq has destroyed daily domestic security, leaving little space for women's lives.[43]

III. *Conclusions*

State-building is often regarded as process that has the capacity to deliver a new dispensation for women. Simona Sharoni has observed that "while in some instances, political conflict may complicate women's lives and set back their struggles for gender equality, in a different context and under different circumstances, a heightened political conflict may become a springboard for gender equality".[44] She notes, for example, that in Ireland "far from being mutually exclusive or irreconcilable, feminism and nationalism are presented as two complementary movements wh[ich] seek to radically transform existing social and political relationships and structures as a stepping stone for the future envisioned nation".[45]

Over the last decade, the international state-building industry has embraced the language of women's human rights, supporting women's capacity "to take their rightful and equal place at the decision-making table in questions of peace and security".[46] But the cases of state-building of East Timor and Iraq illustrate the complexity of the translation of the worthy public statements about the equality of women in modern state-building. Cynthia Enloe has suggested a series of questions for feminist inquiries in international relations that are useful in the context of women and state-building: Where are the women in state-building and what women are there? How did these women get there and what do they

---

43 See further Women for Women International, *Stronger Women, Stronger Nations: 2008 Iraq Report, at* <http://www.reliefweb.int/rw/RWFiles2008.nsf/FilesByRWDocUnidFilename/RMOI-7CF2MK-full_report.pdf/$File/full_report.pdf>.

44 Simona Sharoni, *Paper presented to a World Bank conference on Gender, Armed Conflict and Political Violence*, 1 (June 10–11, 1999).

45 Ibid., 7.

46 Press Release from the United Nations Secretariat on the Secretary-General's address to the special meeting of the Security Council meeting on women and peace and security, UN Doc. SG/SM/7598 (Oct. 24, 2000).

think about their position?[47] Unlike some state-building ventures,[48] women in East Timor and Iraq had little representation in the peacemaking and state-building process after conflict and they have been unable to alter the asymmetry of power relations. In both East Timor and Iraq, attention to women's human rights has largely been the product of the work of women's groups, with the support of particular individuals within UNTAET and the Coalition Provisional Authority respectively. With limited spheres of influence in respect of official policy, these groups used international and local networks to pressure state-building institutions to take women's concerns seriously. They have contended with official attitudes of scepticism, hostility or resentment towards what have been seen as marginal or subversive distractions. Most women's groups in East Timor and Iraq express great frustration with their inability to affect the post-conflict settlement. The examples of East Timor and Iraq suggest three major issues for women in the state-rebuilding process.

IV. *Women's rights v local cultures*

A significant issue in both countries has been the fact that talk of women's rights was associated with imposed, international standards, inevitably in tension with some local cultures. In East Timor, gender roles assigning men to a public world of politics and employment and women to a private world of home and family pervade social and economic relations. They are supported by religious doctrine, low levels of education and traditional practices. The situation in Iraq is more complex. Despite the oppressive nature of Saddam Hussein's regime, Iraqi women generally benefited from its secular approach to personal status laws.[49] The UN Arab Development Report noted in 2002 that Iraqi women rated highest among Arab women on UN measures of 'gender empowerment' because of their significant political participation.[50] The 2003 invasion of Iraq, among other things, has allowed an assertive masculine traditionalism to re-claim authenticity and authority.

Noah Feldman, an American constitutional lawyer who worked with the Coalition Provisional Authority, has concluded from his experience in Iraq that

---

[47] Cynthia Enloe, Maneuvers: The International Politics of Militarizing Women's Lives 294 (2000).

[48] See e.g. Sumie Nakaya, *Women and Gender Equality in Peacebuilding: Somalia and Mozambique*, *in* Building Sustainable Peace 143 (Tom Keating & W. Andy Knight eds., 2004).

[49] See Gihane Tabet, Women in Personal Status Laws: Iraq, Jordan, Lebanon, Palestine, Syria 11–12 (July 2005).

[50] UNDP, *Arab Human Development Report* (2002). In 2002, women held almost 20% of parliamentary seats in Iraq compared to the 3.5% average for Arab states.

international standards should not be imposed or even influence new democracies.[51] New constitutions, he has argued, should "get off the ground through a process of adoption by localized self-interest, not out of episodic external pressure that will soon be lifted."[52]

Feldman's prescription of deference to "localized self-interest" in the context of women's rights however allows particular local male elites to define the substance of state-building. Women's rights are unlikely to appeal to self-interest of such elites. Feldman's argument also assumes that there is one set of 'local' views that should be respected and ignores the role and aspirations of 'internal reformers' within state-building societies.[53]

The respect claims to culture generally attract from the international community are based on a monolithic view of 'culture', assuming that it has no internal diversity. We often see such an assumption made in the context of religious culture, as though religion cannot have "a critical tradition or commitment to rights".[54] It is thus important to be aware of the politics of the culture being invoked as part of state-building. For example, whose culture is being invoked? What is the status of the interpreter of culture? In whose name is the argument being advanced? And, who are the primary beneficiaries of the claim?[55] The cultures of the international communities involved in state-building also require close scrutiny. Very few women hold senior positions in agencies concerned with state-building, an absence that sends a strong message in post-conflict societies. Evidence from the last decade of state-building also shows an institutional insouciance or forgetfulness about the position of women, with mistakes being repeated in subsequent missions.[56]

V. *Limited definitions of human rights*

A second concern for women in state-building is the way that relevant international human rights standards are defined. Representation of women has

---

[51] Noah Feldman, After Jihad: American and the Struggle for Islamic Democracy 29–33 (2003).

[52] Ibid., 29–30.

[53] Madhavi Sunder, *Enlightened Constitutionalism*, 37 Connecticut Law Review 890, 892 (2005).

[54] Ibid., 895.

[55] Arati Rao, *The Politics of Gender and Culture in International Human Rights Discourse, in* Women's Rights Human Rights 167 (Julie Peters & Andrea Wolper eds., 1995).

[56] See e.g. Hilary Charlesworth & Christine Chinkin, *Regulatory Frameworks in International Law, in* Regulating Law 246 (C. Parker, C. Scott, N. Lacey & J. Braithwaite eds., 2004); Tammy Smith, *Post-War Bosnia and Herzegovina: The Erosion of Women's Rights under International Governance*, 3 (2) Critical Half 38 (2005).

been the major concern addressed, albeit superficially and inadequately, by the international community, with intense debate about the legitimacy and impact of quotas for women. Other problems women face in particular contexts tend to be obscured. For example Sumie Nakaya points to the lack of attention paid to the gendered impact of the ethnic partition models used in state-building in Bosnia-Herzegovina and Kosovo.[57] Moreover the right to equality in international law invoked in state-building has essentially remained tethered to a limited, procedural, account of non-discrimination. Structural discrimination against women in times of peace has been exacerbated in times of conflict; for example women's lack of access to adequate housing is made worse when infrastructure is destroyed during fighting.[58] A more useful analysis of inequality thus may be in terms of oppression and domination, rather than in terms of discrimination in the distribution of social goods. Iris Marion Young notes that "[w]hile discriminatory policies sometimes cause or reinforce oppression, oppression involves many actions, practices, and structures that have little to do with preferring or excluding members of groups in the awarding of benefits."[59] This suggests an understanding of equality and inequality that would attend to structures of oppression and domination. Linking the idea of equality with non-domination also allows consideration of the history and context of inequality and relative distributions of power.

A related problem is the tendency in state-building to emphasise civil and political rights over economic, social and cultural rights.[60] This is of course an issue for men as well as women, but discrimination against women in areas such as access to land or inheritance of housing and property will make lack of attention to economic and social rights even more serious for them. It is striking that, when post-conflict truth commissions have found evidence of violations of such rights, they have generally not proposed that reparation be paid to redress the breaches.[61]

The international institutional understanding that the empowerment of women depends simply on the inclusion of women in various spheres of public life means that there is inadequate attention paid to the gendered nature of the rules of the game that women are required to play. We need to rethink traditional structures of public and private life, such as ideas of economic activity

---

[57] Nakaya, *supra* note 48, 146.

[58] See Report of the United Nations High Commissioner for Human Rights, UN Doc. E/2008/76 (2008), para. 41.

[59] Iris Marion Young, Justice and the Politics of Difference 195 (1990).

[60] See Christine Chinkin & Hilary Charlesworth, *Building Women into Peace: The International Legal Framework*, 27 Third World Quarterly 937 (2006).

[61] See Report of the United Nations High Commissioner for Human Rights, *supra* note 58, para. 51.

and value, to accommodate women's lives. We also must consider the effects of the unequal balance of domestic labour which limits the capacity of women to operate in the public, political sphere.

State-building relies on the human rights concept of self-determination. In international law, self-determination accords a people the right to autonomy, freedom from alien oppression and the right to choose an economic, political and social system "free from outside intervention, subversion, coercion or constraint of any kind whatsoever".[62] Once external self-determination has been achieved and internal self-determination is guaranteed, it is assumed that all members of the group will equally benefit, in other words that the terms 'self' and 'peoples' are homogenous. Individual and group aspirations and goals, both before and after the achievement of self-determination, are subsumed within those of the self-determining unit.

This assumption of group identity and commonality is of course open to challenge. The notion of a self-determining unit collapses many forms of diversity, but most particularly that of sex. The consequences of this limited definition are evident in the fact that apparently successful claims to self-determination typically fail to deliver the same level of personal freedom and autonomy for women as for men, despite in many cases an historical association between nationalist and feminist movements and a high degree of participation in the decolonization process. Indeed, in many cases achievement of national self-determination has led to deterioration in the position of women.

VI. *Narrow conceptions of gender*

A third problem for the protection of women's human rights in state-building is its relationship to the flawed 'gender mainstreaming' enterprise endorsed by international institutions.[63] There have been important analyses of the failure to implement gender mainstreaming projects in state-building.[64] But perhaps more significant is the international consensus that the concept of 'gender' is simply about women. For example, Security Council Resolution 1325, the high water mark of UN concern with gender and peace, used the term 'gender perspective' in peace negotiations to refer to giving attention to the special needs of women

[62] The wording is taken from a General Assembly Resolution on Afghanistan after the Soviet invasion in 1979. GA Res. ES-6 2 (Jan. 14, 1980).

[63] See Hilary Charlesworth, *Not Waving but Drowning: Gender Mainstreaming and Human Rights*, 18 Harvard Human Rights Journal 1 (2005).

[64] E.g. Lori Handrahan, *Rhetoric and Reality: Post-Conflict Recovery and Development – the UN and Gender Reform*, *in* The UN, Human Rights and Post-Conflict Situations 404, 414–418 (Nigel D. White & Dirk Klaasen eds., 2005).

and girls during repatriation, supporting local women's peace initiatives, and protecting the human rights of women and girls in any new legal order.[65] This account of gender does not include the significance in state-building of male gender identities and patterns of behaviour which are assumed to be standard, normal and immutable. Unless state-building addresses the gendered structures of power and domination in a society, it will inevitably fail women.

[65] Oct. 31, 2000. This approach is also evident in UN implementation of the resolution: see Report of the Secretary-General on Women, Peace and Security, UN Doc S/2006/770 (2006).

The Significance of Cultural Heritage for State Stability and its Protection by Public International Law

Kerstin Odendahl & Mayte Peters

The destruction of the Buddha statues of Bamijan by soldiers of the Taliban Regime in March 2001 and, two years later, the looting of the National Museum in Baghdad during the Second Gulf War were met with widespread disbelief and shock. In both cases, the pieces of art that had been destroyed or stolen were important historic objects forming part of the cultural heritage of Afghanistan and Iraq respectively. Yet the question remains – *why* exactly was the loss of this heritage such a disaster?

Cultural heritage does not only consist of "old stones". It is a much wider concept, entailing both tangible and intangible elements, and gaining its relevance for society through political implications stemming from its function for collective memory and identity. Considering that state stability depends on the social acceptability of stable state institutions, cultural heritage has a significant role with regard to state stability.

I. *The significance of cultural heritage for state stability*

From a political science viewpoint, states can be defined "as multidimensional arenas in which different groups compete for resources by using all kinds of means – technological, organisational, ideological – to occupy strategic nodes in the distribution of power."[1] In a stable state, political and legal institutions will be able to effectively implement a set of rights and obligations governing the distribution of resources in an efficient, predictable manner that is able to

---

[1] Eric R. Wolf, *Comments on state, identity, and violence, in* The State, Identity and Violence: Political Disintegration in the Post-Cold War World 61, 61 (R. Brian Ferguson ed., 2003).

stabilise expectations. Cultural heritage is in turn essential for the social acceptability of state institutions.

The significance of cultural heritage for state stability stems from its fundamental role for the communication of a specific collective memory, which forms the basis of collective identity. Cultural heritage may have implications for state stability in two major respects. First, the state itself needs to be based on a certain cultural heritage in order to gain legitimacy with state-actors. Secondly, the state needs to provide for stability by averting de-stabilising opposition from culturally heterogeneous non-state actors, who may exploit cultural heritage for political purposes by tying cultural heritage to certain identity markers.

1. *Cultural heritage, collective memory and collective identity*

In every society, culture serves as the central provider of meaning and identity. It shapes and preserves a society's collective memory, based on which a social order is established and maintained. Collective memory comprises communicative and cultural memory.[2] While the communicative memory of a society essentially consists of the life-memory of its living members and disappears with their death, cultural memory is based on ceremonial communication and gains its validity in the long-term. It is specific for each community and entails a particular inventory of tangible and intangible cultural heritage, in the care of which it stabilises and communicates its self-perception.

Cultural heritage can act as a carrier of collective memory in many ways. Both tangible and intangible cultural heritage are relevant in this respect. The past is transmitted into the present through old buildings, libraries and historical landmarks as well as through myths, fables, language, music, systems of value and political or legal traditions.[3] The list of cultural heritage is practically endless as every society has different means of transmitting knowledge across time.

In this context the term *heritage* describes the relationship between remembering and identity.[4] Identity is never punctual but rather the result of unique processes that have culminated, through gradual development, in the status quo. According to Manuel Castells, identity is "the process of construction of meaning on the basis of cultural attribute, or related sets of cultural attributes,

---

[2] Jan Assmann, Das kulturelle Gedächtnis: Schrift, Erinnerung und politische Identität in frühen Hochkulturen 342 pp. (2002).

[3] Jan Assmann, *Kollektives Gedächtnis und kulturelle Identität, in* Kultur und Gedächtnis 9, 15 (Jan Assmann & Tonio Tölscher eds., 1988).

[4] Peter Wagner, *From Monuments to Human Rights: Redefining "Heritage" in the Work of the Council of Europe, in* Council of Europe, Forward Planning: The Function of Cultural Heritage in a Changing Europe, 9–28, 16, *at* <http://www.coe.int/t/e/cultural_co-operation/heritage/resources/ECC-PAT(2001)161.pdf>. See also Pierre Nora, Zwischen Geschichte und Gedächtnis (1990).

that is/are given priority over other sources of meaning."[5] The prioritisation of meaning cannot be decided randomly; rather, it needs to be logically explained and justified. This is where cultural heritage comes into play.

Cultural heritage can be seen as an essential basis for a functioning collective identity.[6] Though no clear-cut definition of the term "cultural heritage" exists, there are strong arguments for a wide understanding of the concept. Essentially, cultural heritage forms "symbolic markers that imply a normative definition of inclusion and exclusion. The included needs an additional quality: it has to be loved. To guarantee such affective stability, a third element is needed: the symbolic representation of the normatively and emotionally shared."[7] In this sense, cultural heritage functions as a medium for communication, as a means for the transmission of values, ideas, and collectively shared knowledge, about or based in the past, on which a group bases its consciousness of belonging and character. Thus, according to ethnologist Clifford Geertz, who underlines the significance of symbols with regard to religion, "holy symbols have the function to connect the ethos of a people – style, character and condition of its life, its ethics, aesthetical direction and mood – with its worldly understanding – the image it holds of things in their pure state, its ideas on order in the widest sense. Religious imagination and practices lend intellectual credibility to the ethos of a people."[8]

As cultural memory always carries certain messages, a society's cultural memory will rarely be based on the past as it actually occurred. Instead, it is the *meaning* certain events hold for a society that determines their entering the collective conscience or not.[9] By emphasising a cultural heritage that is essentially liberal, for instance – by incorporating democratic ideas into the education system or granting a certain set of democratic rights – a society automatically distances itself from non-democratic systems of value and forms of governance. The same is true for other forms of government.

This is a consequence of the open character of cultural heritage; the spectrum of interpretation and communication of this heritage is endless. Certain elements

[5] MANUEL CASTELLS, THE POWER OF IDENTITY 6 (1997).

[6] ALBERT F. REITERER, SOZIALE IDENTITÄT: ETHNIZITÄT UND SOZIALER WANDEL: ZUR ENTWICKLUNG EINER ANTHROPOLOGISCHEN STRUKTUR 158 (1998).

[7] Klaus Eder, *Integration through Culture? The Paradox of the Search for a European Identity, in* EUROPEAN CITIZENSHIP BETWEEN NATIONAL LEGACIES AND POSTNATIONAL PROJECTS, 222, 223 (Klaus Eder & Bernhard Giesen eds., 2001).

[8] As cited in Hans G. Kippenberg, *Was sucht die Religionswissenschaft unter den Kulturwissenschaften?, in* KULTURWISSENSCHAFT: FELDER EINER PROZESSORIENTIERTEN WISSENSCHAFTLICHEN PRAXIS 240, 257 (Heide Appelsmeyer & Elfriede Billmann-Mahecha eds., 2001) [translated here by Mayte Peters].

[9] JAN ASSMANN, DAS KOLLEKTIVE GEDÄCHTNIS 129 (1985).

of cultural heritage, both tangible and intangible, will be selected according to present (political) needs to transport a specific set of norms and values constitutive of collective identity. Already existing cultural heritage will be interpreted accordingly.

2. *The significance of cultural heritage for institutional and social stability*

Each state claims for itself a national flag, a national hymn, (a) national language(s), and/or a national history.[10] One could say that political coherence is based on an "artificial community"[11] which is achieved through the constant communication of a common cultural heritage.[12] The state and its institutions provide the system that communicates this cultural heritage, thus creating state- or citizenship-based commonality.[13] Through the symbolic reference to a specific past, the state may portray its existence as a logical consequence of historical developments, thus legitimising its status quo. The symbols used are provided by both tangible and intangible cultural heritage.

While a specific cultural heritage is used to legitimise state institutions, it is also crucial that these institutions are able to effectively organise cultural plurality at the sub-state level. Thus, the relationship between state stability and cultural heritage works two ways: first, institutions must be based on a specific cultural heritage. Second, the integration of culturally heterogeneous groups into this institutionally organised society depends on the ability of state institutions to provide a political and legal order around which cultural plurality can be organised.

---

[10] As is stated in an Official Indian Government Commentary: "The National Flag, the National Anthem and the National Emblem are three symbols through which an independent country proclaims its identity and sovereignty, and as such they command instantaneous respect and loyalty. In themselves they reflect the entire background, thought and culture of a nation." *Official Indian government commentary*, cited in Raymond W. Firth, Symbols: Public and Private 341 (1973).

[11] See Anthony D. Smith, The Ethnic Revival (1981); Ibid., National Identity (1991); and Benedict Anderson, Imagined Communities: Reflections on the Origins and Spread of Nationalism (1991); Eder, *supra* note 7, 230.

[12] Eder, *supra* note 7, 229–230.

[13] See K.W. Deutsch, Nationalism and Social Communication (1953). Cultural heritage is not only of importance for states but also for regional identities like the European identity. This view is not shared by everyone, see, for example, Paul-Lukas Good & Kai Spiekermann, *Liberalismus und Rechtsstaat: Thesen zur EMRK und europäischer Identität, in* 30 Jahre EMRK-Beitritt der Schweiz: Erfahrungen und Perspektiven 19, 24–25 (Patrick Sutter & Ulrich Zelger eds., 2005).

a) *The implications of cultural heritage for institutional stability*

In a stable state, both political and judicial systems must be historically justified in order to be effectively "understood" by at least the ruling, yet ideally also the ruled population. In any case, institutions will be the direct result of historical cultural developments.[14] A historically justified state identity has certain implications for state actors who wish to exercise authority within it.

Identity bears certain restrictions for state institutions. Cultural heritage will determine the state's adherence to human rights standards and the existence or absence of stable democratic institutions by shaping people's norms, value systems and political expectations. A state's nature, idiosyncrasy, societal norms, its national security doctrine and policies are directly affected by its cultural environment.[15] On the institutional level, cultural heritage will directly influence legislation and political decision-making processes.

A key point to be made with regard to cultural heritage is legitimacy, though it must be noted that social legitimacy is not necessarily a prerequisite of state stability.[16] It may be technically sufficient for legitimacy to be restricted to state actors.[17] However, many states' political and legal systems practically depend on social legitimacy to function, as many democratic states can be said to have a culture of protest, with institutionalised rights to oppose the government under certain circumstances. The fact that political ruptures often go hand in hand with the destruction of physical monuments, the re-writing of history books or the re-naming of public streets and places emphasizes this relationship.[18]

In any case, stable states must base their political and legal institutional order on a cultural set of norms and values that are historically grown, representative, specific and constitutive of the state. State institutions must be seen as effective in the sense that they can withstand present and future political or social developments, thus providing a frame of reference that "works" with regard to

---

[14] See Peter Häberle, Europäische Rechtskultur: Versuch einer Annäherung in zwölf Schritten 17–18 (1994); Georg Burckhardt, Kulturstaat und Menschheitskultur 21 (1958): "Thus, also the state, including its laws and the habit of its people, is in the widest sense, essentially subordinated under the term culture in terms of law and organised economy." [translated here by Mayte Peters].

[15] Constantine P. Danopoulos & Dhirendra Vajpeji, *Introduction: Notes and Concepts, in* Civil-Military Relations, Nation-Building, and National Identity: Comparative Perspectives 1, 4 (Constantine P. Danopoulos & Dhirendra Vajpeji eds., 2004).

[16] Sebastian von Einsiedel, *Policy responses to state failure, in* Making States Work: State Failure and the Crisis of Governance 13, 19 (Simon Chesterman, Michael Ignatieff & Ramesh Thakur eds., 2005).

[17] Martin Kriele, Einführung in die Staatslehre: Die Geschichtlichen Legitimitätsgrundlagen des Demokratischen Verfassungsstaates 19 (1994).

[18] An example of this is the toppling of Saddam Hussein's Statue in Baghdad on April 9, 2003, which caught world-wide attention.

the allocation of resources and political conflict resolution. This means that the cultural heritage of a state's society, its specific historical "experience", society's political and cultural status quo, and its corresponding hopes and aspirations are combined to shape a valid and legitimate value system on which a judicial order can be based.[19] Without such reliability, legal and political decisions lose their legitimacy and binding force. State stability may thus be threatened, either through opposition from its population or from outside intervention under certain circumstances provided for by international law.

b) *The implications of cultural heritage for social stability*

Today, the traditional model of the culturally homogeneous nation state,[20] along with its various political and legal implications, is increasingly contested[21] as mobility of people and capital cause physical and cultural boundaries to become more and more porous.[22] While state institutions are based on a historically specific cultural heritage, they also need to provide an effective forum of articulation for a culturally heterogeneous state population in the present.

Cultural pluralism within a state's boundaries may have concrete implications for state stability, as cultural heritage may be exploited for political purposes. Different groups may present cultural heritage in a way that either legitimises a status quo or induces change.[23] In the former case, the cultural heritage should ideally depict the present as a logical consequence of the past, thus conveying a sense of belonging and continuity. Regarding the latter, change may be induced by drawing on a past that should be overcome, or on a previous condition which should be re-established.

---

[19] Peter Häberle, Verfassungslehre als Kulturwissenschaft 590 (1998).

[20] Craig Calhoun, *Nationalism, political community and the representation of society: or, why feeling at home is not a substitute for public space*, 2 European Journal of Social Theory 217–31 (1999).

[21] Kevin Robins, *A Cultural Policy for European Cosmopolitanism, in* Transcultural Europe: Cultural Policy in a Changing Europe, 254–283, 273 (Ulrike Hanna Meinhof & Anna Triandafyllidou eds. 2006); Habermas for instance notes that the state with a nationally homogeneous population has always remained fiction. Jürgen Habermas, *Geschichtsbewusstsein und posttraditionale Identität, in* Eine Art Schadensabwicklung 166 (Ibid., 1987).

[22] Seyla Benhabib, The Claims of Culture: Equality and Diversity in the Global Era 184 (2002).

[23] This played a decisive role in the destruction of cultural heritage in the French or the Chinese Cultural Revolutions for instance. Even Saddam Hussein is said to have tried to legitimise his power by emphasising Iraq's ancient past. See Gertjan Dijkink, National Identity and Geopolitical Visions: Maps of Pride and Pain 121 (1996). The same rhetoric pattern was already used in Athens 300 B.C., see Patrick Sutter, Die politische Ordnung Athens: Im Lichte von Aristoteles und im Vergleich zum heutigen Forschungsstand 77 (2005).

Drawing on certain cultural markers is a powerful social mobilising factor that has fuelled conflict numerous times.[24] Yet the existence of ethnically different nationalities within a state does not automatically lead to conflict. Instead, conflict arises when identities are threatened in their core, or when identity can be linked to economical or political claims. For instance, language legislation can play a role regarding ethnic containment by automatically disadvantaging certain linguistic groups, or influence the management of linguistic diversity in general, by assigning languages different roles in such areas as education, administration, or access to state funds.

Legislation involving cultural heritage will attain its significance regarding the ethnic composition of the population, the nature of democratisation processes, the country's international ambitions etc. Essentially, it may serve to influence a state's national identity.[25] State institutions provide the grounds for cultural freedom (or non-freedom), peaceful pluralism, the need for cultural assimilation etc., through the communication of a certain cultural heritage. State stability will depend on the willingness of those affected to accept these rules and regulations.

Essentially, stable states' political institutions should provide and implement a set of rules that organise cultural pluralism in such a way as to avert conflict. Non-protection of cultural heritage may be seen as a threat to a particular identity; whether state stability is thus threatened will ultimately depend on whether predictable and historically legitimised state institutions provide for effective means of political articulation. Under these circumstances, social acceptability of a state's legal and political systems may be high even if the cultural heritage on which the state is based differs substantially from cultural groups' within its

---

[24] See for instance Karl-Heinz Kohl, *Ethnizität und Tradition aus ethnologischer Sicht, in* IDENTITÄTEN: ERINNERUNG, GESCHICHTE, IDENTITÄT 3, 269, 277 (Aleida Assmann & Heidrun Friese eds., 1998); Adrian Hyde-Price, *Reflections on Security and Identity in Europe, in* SECURITY AND IDENTITY IN EUROPE: EXPLORING A NEW AGENDA 22, 25 (Lisbeth Aggestam & Adrian Hyde-Price eds., 2000); David Maybury-Lewis, *Tribalism, ethnicity and the state, in* THE STATE, IDENTITY AND VIOLENCE: POLITICAL DISINTEGRATION IN THE POST-COLD WAR WORLD 96, 97 (R. Brian Ferguson ed., 2003). Yet it must also be asked "how conflict produces culture, not just [...] how cultural differences promote conflict", see Kay B. Warren, *Introduction: Revealing Conflicts across Cultures and Disciplines, in* THE VIOLENCE WITHIN: CULTURAL and POLITICAL POSITION IN DIVIDED NATIONS 1, 3 (Kay B. Warren ed., 1993).

[25] Priit Järve, *Language Battles in the Baltic States: 1989–2002, in* NATION-BUILDING, ETHNICITY AND LANGUAGE POLITICS IN TRANSITION COUNTRIES, 73, 75–76 (Farimah Daftary & François Grin eds., 2003). As is stated in the Latvian language act of 1992: "One of the main prerequisites for the existence of the Latvian nation and for the preservation and development of its culture is the Latvian language. During the last decades there has been a marked decrease in the use of the Latvian language in state affairs and social life; therefore it is necessary to establish special measures for the protection of the Latvian language". <http://www.iom.ch/www/migrationweb/legislation/countries/la/Latvia_language_eng.html>, cited in Järve, 93.

midst. Ideally, expectations of the state's population are themselves stabilised through effective governance that is not only historically justified, but also strengthens its acceptability through its ability to provide stability for a culturally heterogeneous state population.

II. *Instruments of public international law for the protection of cultural heritage*

Given the significance of cultural heritage for state stability and the general importance of stable states for the functioning of public international law, the question arises whether international legal instruments effectively provide for the protection of cultural heritage. An analysis of the current legal situation shows that the level of protection depends on the type of cultural heritage. Tangible cultural heritage is far better protected than intangible cultural heritage.

1. *The legal definition of the term "cultural heritage"*

Legally, the term "cultural heritage" ("patrimoine culturel", "patrimonio cultural", "Kulturerbe") is difficult to define. A clear-cut definition does not exist, even though the expression is rather old. It originates in the French Revolution. It was Puthod de Maisonrouge, a Member of Parliament, who demanded the protection of the French "patrimoine national" during the tumults of 1791.

Since the mid forties of the 20th century the expression is to be found in several international conventions. Many of them employ the term cultural heritage (or inheritance) without defining its content. Several examples can be mentioned: article II (2c) of the UNESCO-Constitution of 1945[26] states that UNESCO will maintain, increase and diffuse knowledge by assuring the "conservation and protection of the world's inheritance of books, works of art and monuments of history and science". The preamble and Article 2 of the Paris Convention of 1970[27] establish the moral obligation of every state to respect "its own cultural heritage and that of all nations". The two Additional Protocols to the Geneva Convention of 1977[28] (Articles 53 and 16 respectively) aim at the protection

[26] Constitution of the United Nations Educational, Scientific and Cultural Organization, 16 November 1945, 4 U.N.T.S. 275.

[27] Convention on the Means of Prohibiting and Preventing the Illicit Import, Export and Transfer of Ownership of Cultural Property, 14 November 1970, 10 ILM 289 (1971).

[28] Protocol Additional to the Geneva Conventions of 12 August 1949, and Relating to the Protection of Victims of International Armed Conflicts (Protocol I), 12 August 1977, 1125 U.N.T.S. 3; Protocol Additional to the Geneva Conventions of 12 August 1949, and Relating to the Protection of Victims of Non-International Armed Conflicts (Protocol II), 12 August 1977, 1125 U.N.T.S. 609.

of "historic monuments, works of art or places of worship which constitute the cultural or spiritual heritage of peoples".

For the purposes of various conventions the expression cultural heritage is considered to comprise exclusively tangible heritage. This conception is particularly evident in the World Heritage Convention of 1972.[29] Its Article 1 states that for the purposes of the convention only monuments, groups of buildings and sites shall be considered as cultural heritage. A similar approach can be found in the UNESCO Convention on the Underwater Cultural Heritage of 2001.[30] In its Article 1 underwater cultural heritage is defined as "all traces of human existence having a cultural, historical or archaeological character which have been partially or totally under water, periodically or continuously, for at least 100 years such as sites, structures, buildings, artefacts and human remains, together with their archaeological and natural context; vessels, aircraft, other vehicles or any part thereof, their cargo or other contents, together with their archaeological and natural context; and objects of prehistoric character". Such a terminology is liable to be misunderstood since the correct term for tangible cultural heritage is "cultural property" ("bien culturel", "bien cultural", "Kulturgut").

Fortunately, the terminology of other conventions is more accurate. It shows that cultural property is only a part of the cultural heritage. A good example is the preamble of The Hague Convention of 1954.[31] It states that "damage to cultural property belonging to any people whatsoever means damage to the cultural heritage of all mankind". Another example is Article 5 of the European Cultural Convention of 1954.[32] It reads: "Each Contracting Party shall regard the objects of European cultural value placed under its control as integral parts of the common cultural heritage of Europe".

The only international document offering an abstract description of the term cultural heritage is the Mexico City Declaration on Cultural Policies.[33] Its article 23 provides a rather clear and complete definition: "The cultural heritage of a people includes the works of its artists, architects, musicians, writers and scientists and also the work of anonymous artists, expressions of the people's spirituality, and the body of values which give meaning to life. It includes both tangible and intangible works through which the creativity of that people finds

[29] Convention for the Protection of the World Cultural and Natural Heritage, 16 November 1972, 11 ILM 1358 (1972).

[30] Convention on the Protection of the Underwater Cultural Heritage, 6 November 2001, 41 ILM 40 (2002).

[31] Convention on the Protection of Cultural Property in the Event of Armed Conflict, 14 May 1954, 249 U.N.T.S. 240.

[32] European Cultural Convention, 19 December 1954, ETS No. 18.

[33] Adopted at the World Conference on Cultural Policies Mexico City, 26 July–6 August 1982.

expression: languages, rites, beliefs, historic places and monuments, literature, works of art, archives and libraries".

Thus, cultural heritage is a wide legal concept. It comprises both tangible and intangible elements of culture. The expression "heritage" indicates that the term refers only to cultural elements of the past having a significance for the present.[34] Contemporary cultural trends or possible future cultural developments do not belong to the cultural heritage of a people.

2. *The existing legal instruments of protection*

a) *The protection of tangible cultural heritage*

Tangible cultural heritage or "cultural property" consists of two groups of objects: movable and immovable ones. Both are endangered by destruction, decay, change or negligence. Moreover, movable objects are threatened by the removal from their countries of origin, i.e. by their illegal export. Public international law offers several legal instruments to protect the tangible cultural heritage from both kinds of threat.

aa) In times of war

The oldest legal instruments are to be found in the law of war.[35] For many centuries, cultural property of the enemy was considered as a legitimate loot of war. The victor was entitled to remove the cultural objects of the defeated nation and to transport them to his own territory. Objects of cultural value were considered as war trophies, as a symbol of victory. At the same time, the removal as well as the destruction of cultural property was a means to humiliate or even to destroy the enemy by depriving it from essential elements of its own history and culture. This legal situation changed after the Napoleonic wars (1792–1815) with the conclusion of the peace treaties at the Vienna Congress. For the first time in history, the act of removing cultural property was fundamentally condemned. Each Party was obliged to return the works of art to their place of origin.[36] In the meantime, the prohibition of removing cultural property in times of war has become part of customary international law.[37]

---

[34] For further details see Kerstin Odendahl, Kulturgüterschutz. Entwicklung, struktur und dogmatik eines ebenenübergreifenden Normensystems 389 pp. (2005).

[35] Odendahl, *supra* note 34, 107 pp.; Rainer J. Schweizer, Kay Hailbronner & Karl-Heinz Burmeister, Der Anspruch von St. Gallen auf Rückerstattung seiner Kulturgüter aus Zürich 76 pp. and 156 pp. (2002).

[36] Dorothy Mackay Quynn, *Art Confiscation of the Napoleonic Wars, in* Law, Ethics and the Visual Arts 6 (John Henry Merryman & Albert E. Elsen eds., 1998).

[37] For further details see Stanislaw E. Nahlik, *La protection internationale des biens culturels en cas de conflit armé*, 120 (I) Recueil des Cours de l'Académie de Droit International de la Haye 86 (1967).

In the 19th and 20th century the law of war was gradually codified. The most important treaties were the 15 conventions of The Hague of 1899 and 1907.[38] Three of them contained some rules on the protection of cultural property in armed conflicts: The Hague Conventions I and IV on the Laws and Customs of War on Land (1899/1907) and the Hague Convention IX on the Bombardment by Naval Forces in Time of War (1907). They all prohibited the removal of cultural objects. Destruction of immovable cultural property was prohibited as well, except in case of military necessity.

But the rules of The Hague were not able to prevent the terrible destructions of movable and immovable goods during the First and the Second World War. It became evident that a special convention containing detailed and specific provisions was needed. The Hague Convention of 1954[39] is therefore a milestone in the history of the protection of cultural property in armed conflicts. It differentiates between "safeguarding" and "respect". The term "safeguarding" refers to the cultural property situated within the own territory. The states Parties are obliged to protect it against the foreseeable repercussion of an armed conflict by taking such measures as they consider appropriate (Article 3), especially by making it bear a distinctive emblem so as to facilitate its recognition (Articles 6 and 16). "Respect" has to be given to the cultural property situated within the own territory as well as within the territory of other states Parties. Each state Party has to refrain from any use of the property and its immediate surroundings or of the appliances in use for its protection for purposes which are likely to expose it to destruction or damage in the event of armed conflict, and to refrain from any act of hostility, directed against such property (Article 4). Protocol I to the Hague Convention of 1954[40] establishes special provisions for movable cultural property. Its removal is prohibited; in case of an illicit export it has to be returned to its country of origin. Protocol II to the Hague Convention, signed in 1999,[41] aims at specifying some of the rules of the Hague Convention, especially the still existing exemption provision of "military necessity".

Altogether, the law of war offers the most detailed and elaborated rules on the protection of cultural property. Some improvements might still be made;[42] but in general the system established is sufficiently effective.

---

[38] The texts of all 15 Conventions of the Hague of 1899 and 1907 are available *at* <http://www.lib.byu.edu/~rdh/wwi/hague.html>

[39] Convention on the Protection of Cultural Property in the Event of Armed Conflict, 14 May 1954, 249 U.N.T.S. 240.

[40] Protocol to the Convention on the Protection of Cultural Property in the Event of Armed conflict, 14 May 1954, 249 U.N.T.S. 358.

[41] Second Protocol to the Hague Convention of 1954 for the Protection of Cultural Property in the Event of Armed Conflict, 26 March 1999, 38 ILM 769 (1999).

[42] Odendahl, *supra* note 34, 128.

bb) In times of peace

The law of peace, in contrast, has not yet reached the same level of protection. The first conventions on the safeguarding of cultural property in times of peace were not signed until the mid-20th-century. The most famous treaty is the World Heritage Convention of 1972.[43] The states Parties have the opportunity to submit an inventory of the most valuable cultural and natural property situated in their territories to the World Heritage Committee. If the Committee considers the property being of outstanding universal value it adds it to the "World Heritage List" (Article 11 (2)). The state Party, on whose territory the object is situated, has the duty to ensure its identification, protection, conservation, presentation and transmission to future generations (Articles 4 and 5). The other states Parties are obliged to offer their help upon request (Articles 6 and 7). In case of a serious and specific threat the Committee may enter an object on the "List of World Heritage in Danger" (Article 11 (4)). As a consequence, international assistance is strengthened.

Even though the World Heritage Convention has been accepted almost worldwide and is seen as a great success, there are still serious shortcomings: The obligations imposed on the states are rather weak, and there is no possibility to oblige the states to protect the world heritage situated in their territories. The Committee may only put pressure on the state concerned by threatening to delete the object from the World Heritage List. In practice, the Convention would not be able to prevent the destruction of monuments of outstanding universal value.

For Europe, the legal situation is somewhat different. The Council of Europe has passed several conventions obliging the states Parties to protect cultural property situated in their territories. The most important examples are the Convention of Granada of 1985[44] and the Convention of Valetta of 1992.[45] Both aim at the protection of specific types of cultural property: the architectural heritage on the one hand, and the archaeological heritage on the other hand. The conventions of the Council of Europe set forth much stronger obligations than the World Heritage Convention does. States Parties have to institute a legal system for the physical protection of the cultural objects according to their ability. But the treaties apply only to the members of the Council of Europe. In other parts of the world, particularly in Africa, Asia and Latin America, conventions contain-

---

[43] Convention for the Protection of the World Cultural and Natural Heritage, 16 November 1972, 11 ILM 1358 (1972).

[44] Convention for the Protection of the Architectural Heritage of Europe, 3 October 1985, ETS No. 121.

[45] European Convention on the Protection of the Archaeological Heritage (Revised), 16 January 1992, ETS No. 143.

ing far-reaching legal obligations for the safeguarding of cultural property have not yet been elaborated.

The analysis shows very clearly that the physical protection of cultural property in times of peace is still primarily in the hand of the state. The question whether cultural property is safeguarded or not remains part of state sovereignty and is, in general, not subject to internationally binding rules.

This result, however, does not apply to one aspect of the protection of movable cultural property: the protection of its ties to the country of origin. Two important worldwide treaties, the UNESCO Convention of 1970[46] and the UNIDROIT Convention of 1995,[47] oblige states to prohibit and prevent the illicit import, export and transfer of ownership of cultural property as well as to return cultural property to the countries of origin. Unfortunately, only a handful of countries have joined both conventions, so that there is a discrepancy between legal theory and practice.

cc) In a case of state succession

A succession takes place when one state is replaced by another in the responsibility for a territory. In most cases, the succession of states is the consequence of a dismemberment of states. In such a case many questions arise, among them the distribution of movable cultural property of the predecessor state between the different successor states. The international community has tried to solve this difficult problem with the help of a treaty, the Vienna Convention of 1983.[48] The general rule stipulates that the movable property of the predecessor state, connected with the activity of the predecessor state in respect of the territory to which the succession of states relates, shall pass to the successor state. Thus, the convention aims at safeguarding the ties between movable property, especially cultural objects, and the territory concerned. The Vienna Convention of 1983 has not entered into force since the necessary number of ratifications has not yet been reached. In practice, states have tried to solve each case of state succession with a special treaty. Again, a discrepancy between legal theory and practice is revealed.

Altogether, several legal instruments for the protection of cultural property, i.e. the protection of tangible cultural heritage, do exist. They provide particularly strong provisions in times of war. In times of peace and in other situations, in contrast, the protection offered by international conventions is rather weak.

---

[46] Convention on the Means of Prohibiting and Preventing the Illicit Import, Export and Transfer of Ownership of Cultural Property, 14 November 1970, 10 ILM 289 (1970).

[47] UNIDROIT Convention on Stolen or Illegally Exported Cultural Objects, 24 June 1995, 34 ILM 1330 (1995).

[48] Vienna Convention on Succession of States in Respect of State Property, Archives and Debts, 8 April 1983, 22 ILM 306 (1983).

b) *The protection of intangible cultural heritage*

The protection of intangible cultural heritage is even less developed. It was not until the beginning of the 21st century that the first treaties were signed. All of them have been drafted under the auspices of UNESCO.

The first to mention is the Convention on the Safeguarding of the Intangible Cultural Heritage of 2003,[49] which entered into force on 20 April 2006. It contains the obligation of states Parties to take the necessary measures in order to ensure the safeguarding of intangible cultural heritage and to strengthen solidarity and cooperation at regional and international levels in this area. The convention encourages the exchange of information, experience and joint initiatives to this end. It establishes two lists, the "Representative List of the International Cultural Heritage of Humanity" and the "List of International Cultural Heritage in Need of Urgent Safeguarding". The convention emphasizes that the safeguarding of intangible cultural heritage is a complex process involving many actors, commencing with the communities and groups that are its very lifeblood. The new convention is the first worldwide treaty providing for the protection of intangible cultural heritage.[50]

The second treaty is the Convention on the Protection and Promotion of the Diversity of Cultural Expressions of 2005.[51] It reinforces the ideas enshrined in the UNESCO Universal Declaration on Cultural Diversity of 2001,[52] stipulating that cultural diversity is a "common heritage of humanity" and that its protection must be considered "an ethical imperative, inseparable from respect for human dignity". The ultimate goal of the convention, which entered into force on 18 March 2007, is to provide all countries with the means to protect and promote the diversity of cultural expressions within and outside their territories. The convention has a strong focus on economic and development issues.[53] The treaty aims at recognizing the equal importance of cultural and economic aspects of development. The dual cultural and economic nature of goods and

---

[49] Convention For the Safeguarding of the Intangible Cultural Heritage, 17 October 2003, UNESCO, Records of the General Conference, 32nd Session, Vol. 1, 53–62.

[50] For more details see Kerstin Odendahl, *Die Bewahrung des immateriellen Kulturerbes als neues Thema des Völkerrechts*, 15 Schweizerische Zeitschrift für internationales und europäisches Recht 445 (2005).

[51] Convention on the Protection and Promotion of the Diversity of Cultural Expressions, 20 October 2005, UNESCO, Records of the General Conference, 33rd Session, Vol. 1, 83–95.

[52] UNESCO Universal Declaration on Cultural Diversity, 2 November 2001, UNESCO, Records of the General Conference, 31st Session, Vol. 1, 61–64.

[53] See Christoph Beat Graber, *The New UNESCO Convention on Cultural Diversity: A Counterbalance to the WTO?*, 9 Journal of International Economic Law 553–574 (2006).

services has a significant impact on the rights and duties of states as set out in the convention.[54]

It remains to be seen whether these new instruments will enhance the safeguarding and the promotion of intangible cultural heritage. In any case, the new tendency in public international law to protect not only tangible but also intangible elements of cultural heritage is a step in the right direction and a necessary addition to the existing legal instruments.

3. *The impact of the legal instruments on the stability of states*

The question remains whether the existing legal instruments for the protection of cultural heritage have an impact on state stability. In other words: Do the treaties strengthen or weaken the significance of cultural heritage for the stability of states?

The answer is ambiguous. It is clear that, even if there is still much to be done, the treaties have led to an improved protection of tangible cultural heritage. Moreover, it is to be expected that the new generation of conventions aiming at the protection of intangible cultural heritage will have similar consequences. But all the treaties mentioned above do not intend to protect cultural heritage solely because of its importance for state stability. As the wording of the preambles of the different treaties shows, the reasons for promoting cultural heritage are manifold. There are only a few treaties, especially those signed over the last years, which take into account the significance of culture for state stability. A good example is the recently adopted Convention on the Protection and Promotion of the Diversity of Cultural Expressions of 2005. Its preamble contains, inter alia, the following passage: "Emphasizing the importance of culture for social cohesion in general [...]". Thus, the international legal instruments for the protection of cultural heritage do not directly contribute to state stability but they enhance it in an indirect way: By promoting cultural heritage in general, they are able to strengthen collective memory and collective identity. Both constitute essential elements of state stability.

However, the intensity of this indirect effect is not always the same. It depends on the scope of protection of each convention. Treaties aiming at the safeguarding of cultural heritage of worldwide value contribute little to state stability. The most famous example is the World Heritage Convention of 1972. It protects only objects of "outstanding universal value". Cultural goods of national or regional significance are not protected, even if they might be particularly important for the national identity and, therefore, for the stability of states. Only if the object

---

[54] For more details see Sabine von Schorlemer, *Kulturpolitik im Völkerrecht verankert: Das neue UNESCO-Übereinkommen zum Schutz der kulturellen Vielfalt*, 53 Vereinte Nationen 217 (2005).

of an important national and regional value is of an outstanding universal value as well, the World Heritage Convention might help to strengthen the stability of the prevailing state. Still, it should not be overlooked that many objects on the World Heritage List did not have an outstanding national value until they were put on the list and broad public awareness in that state was drawn towards that object.

Treaties protecting cultural heritage regardless of its territorial significance are far more important. The conventions passed by the Council of Europe, for example, which oblige the states Parties to protect their architectural and archaeological heritage, lead to the safeguarding of objects that each state considers important for its own cultural identity. Thus, the cultural heritage at the national level is strengthened.

Finally, the territorial scope of the conventions should be highlighted. The treaties of major importance for state stability, i.e. those protecting cultural heritage of national or regional value, are often regional treaties. Most of them form part of the conventions of the Council of Europe and are therefore not applicable to states in other continents. This means that the existing legal instruments do not have any binding effect in many parts of the world, especially not in Africa, Asia or Latin America.

III. *Conclusion*

In every society, culture serves as the central provider of meaning and identity. The term cultural heritage in this context describes the relationship between culture, remembering and identity. Cultural heritage consists of tangible and intangible elements of culture belonging to the past but being of importance for the present. It plays an eminent role in the process of identification with a society and with a territory, and attains its importance for states due to its significance for collective memory and identity. By offering symbols of a common identity and history, cultural heritage contributes actively to the stability of states. However, the significance of cultural heritage in this respect is often underestimated.

Undoubtedly, the influence of cultural heritage factors on state stability or dismemberment will vary according to a unique interplay of innumerable factors. The implications of cultural heritage for state stability differ from state to state, according to numerous factors like historical stability,[55] degree of cultural

[55] This is the case in former colonies or communist states, for instance. See James Mayall, *The legacy of colonialism, in* MAKING STATES WORK: STATE FAILURE AND THE CRISIS OF GOVERNANCE 36–58, 57 (Simon Chesterman, Michael Ignatieff & Ramesh Thakur eds., 2005); Hyde-Price, *supra* note 24, 22, 25.

pluralism, or democratic culture. The political and legal systems of a state need to fulfil the functions of historical legitimacy and coherence. State stability is only possible if a significant proportion of the population living under the auspices of the state, or at least the political elite, sees its interests sufficiently represented. When no historically justified, reliable institutional methods of conflict resolution exist, cultural heritage may be politically exploited and state stability threatened, depending of course on the degree of the dispute and the possibilities of the population to protest.[56] In any case, the past plays a significant role in shaping the political environment in the present.

Given the significance of cultural heritage, public international law has developed many legal instruments for its protection. The first special treaties were concluded in the mid-20th-century. While all treaties of the 20th century aimed only at the protection of tangible cultural heritage, the new generation of treaties signed at the beginning of the 21st century also protect intangible cultural heritage. Yet the influence of these conventions on state stability should not be overestimated. Two reasons are to be mentioned: First, the international protection of cultural heritage is far from being comprehensive. Second, the existing conventions do not intend to protect cultural heritage specifically because of its importance for state stability. They only enhance it indirectly: By promoting cultural heritage in general, they strengthen essential elements of state stability.

Currently, the protection of cultural heritage for reasons of state stability remains primarily an issue of domestic law – even if the stability of states is of crucial importance for the functioning of public international law in general. As the sad examples of Iraq and Afghanistan show, domestic law may not always be sufficient.

[56] This ability may be limited by the use of force by state authorities, for instance.

Processes

What the Neighbours Think: State-building, Esteem and Political Culture

Kai Spiekermann

When people attempt to found a state, each potential citizen faces a fundamental decision which determines the success of the whole undertaking: Each individual either chooses to contribute to the process of state-building in a spirit of public responsibility – or chooses not to contribute and to promote immediate self-interest rather than the public good. If most individuals contribute, the necessary public goods to found a state can be provided. If most individuals do not contribute, state-building fails.

It would be too simplistic to describe this choice situation as a conflict between altruists and egoists. In the process of state-building, the stakes are high. Making the wrong choice can be lethal, and sometimes cooperating in such a process is not only altruistic, but also naive. One of these fundamental decisions to be taken concerns the means of self-defence. No one saw that more clearly than Thomas Hobbes. In 'Leviathan', Hobbes argues at length that individuals must rationally choose to give up their 'right to everything', i.e. their unlimited right to defend themselves with any means, to give way to the foundation of the state.[1] Hobbes surely describes the problem in too dramatic terms, leaving only a choice between murderous anarchy and maximal state power. His core problem, however, remains a challenge even today. Sacrificing (most of) one's own means of self-defence is essential to set up the state, but it is also extremely dangerous unless all other citizens do so as well. Even if people are willing to found the state and contribute, they face a dilemma of cooperation. Therefore, categorizing choices as 'egoistic' or 'altruistic' does not capture the full depth of the problem.

The dilemma described is a special case of a general type of problems. Since Mancur Olson's ground-breaking book 'The logic of collective action', these problems are called *collective action problems*.[2] The problem of creating state

---

1 Thomas Hobbes, Leviathan ([1651] 1996).

2 Mancur Olson, The Logic of Collective Action: Public Goods and the Theory Of Groups (1965).

authority is probably the most important instance of a collective action problem in the process of state-building. But it is by far not the only one.[3]

This essay focuses on the problem of establishing security and state authority as the most fundamental collective action problem of state-building. It contains five sections. The first section gives a brief account of the theory of collective action and prisoners' dilemmas. The second deals with the analysis of weapons decommissioning as a collective action problem in state-building. Then the article moves on to discuss reasons for cooperation. Section 3 explains the assumptions of the framework. In the fourth section, the concept of esteem as an incentive to obey social norms is introduced. Finally, social norms and esteem are connected with the notion of 'political culture'.

I. *The Theory of Collective Action Problems and Prisoners' Dilemmas*

Collective action problems can occur when more than one individual has to contribute towards the production of a public good. The good is 'public' in the sense that it is impossible to exclude non-contributors from its use.[4] The problems emerge when

- the production of the good is beneficial for all individuals,
- while it is even more beneficial for each single individual to withhold the own contribution for each level of contribution provided by all other individuals.[5]

That is, each individual wants the public good to be produced. If the good is produced, then the individual benefit from the good is higher than the individual costs of contribution towards the production of the good for each participant. The problem is that individuals also have the option to withhold their contribution (they 'defect') while they can still benefit from the public good produced by the contributions of other individuals (and if no one else contributes, it is still better not to be the only contributor). If this option of 'free-riding' is more attractive than contributing, we have a collective action problem. As a result, no rational individual contributes and no public good is produced. Individual

[3] This article gives more examples below.

[4] The second characteristic of an ideal public good is that it is non-rivalrous. However, this condition is seldom perfectly satisfied.

[5] It is also possible that contributing is beneficial for certain (often small) group sizes, but not for the optimal group size. This leads to an undersupply of the public good. Further complications arise if individuals have heterogeneous thresholds. We omit these refinements for the sake of simplicity.

rationality prevents individuals from producing the public good, even though all individuals would be better off if the public good was produced.

A formal analysis uses marginals to make this point. Let *MB* be the marginal benefit derived by one individual if she decides to contribute, given the decisions of all other individuals. In other words: *MB* is the additional utility derived from the good if the individual contributes, compared to the utility the individual derives by free-riding. Let *MC* be the marginal costs of contribution, i.e. the additional cost for the individual to increase the contribution by one unit. The collective action problem occurs if for all levels of individual contribution *MC* > *MB*, i.e. the additional costs to contribute one more unit are always higher than the additional benefits from contributing one more unit, compared to free-riding.

Figure 1 demonstrates this point graphically. The slope of *MC* is positive, because it is assumed that individuals have increasing opportunity costs for each additional unit of contribution. Contributing small amounts induces only comparatively small sacrifices elsewhere, contributing massively implies that individuals forego other activities that are very valuable to them. The slope of *MB* is zero in figure 1, representing the assumption that each additional unit of contribution increases the benefit for the individual by the same amount. Other assumptions for the shape of *MC* and *MB* can also be plausible, but these refinements are not necessary to demonstrate the general point. In figure 1, the marginal costs of contribution *MC* are always higher than the marginal benefit of contribution *MB*. Therefore, the individual minimizes the losses and chooses to contribute nothing. Since all individuals reason in the same vein, no one contributes and the public good will not be provided.

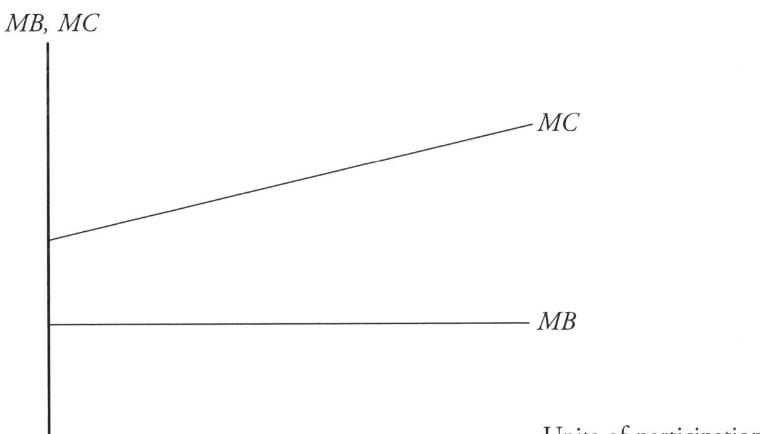

Figure 1 The problem of collective action in a marginal analysis.

Table 1 The standard prisoners' dilemma.

	Player 2	
Player 1	Cooperate	Defect
Cooperate	3, 3	0, 4
Defect	4, 0	1, 1

There is a link between the problem of collective action and prisoners' dilemmas. In fact, a two-person one-shot prisoners' dilemma can be described as a collective action problem with two individuals. A prisoners' dilemma occurs when two individuals have a binary choice between cooperation and defection. This results in four possible constellations, as shown in table 1. The cells in the table show the payoffs for individual 1 and individual 2.[6] Higher numbers represent outcomes that offer higher payoffs over outcomes with lower numbers. We assume that both players are strict payoff maximizers, such that they always prefer higher to lower payoffs. For instance, player 1 prefers an outcome where she defects while player 2 cooperates (payoff 4 for player 1) over a situation where both cooperate (payoff 3 for player 1).

In the prisoners' dilemma, rational players do not cooperate. Why not? Assume that you are player 1: If you think that your opponent cooperates, your best choice is to defect in order to achieve the highest payoff. To the contrary, if you think that your opponent defects, it is better to defect as well, to secure the third highest payoff instead of the worst outcome. This is vice versa also true for player 2. Therefore, it is the dominant strategy for both players to defect, no matter what the other player does. This results in the third best outcome for both players, which is mutual defection.

For both players, this result is unsatisfying. If they could agree to cooperate, they could both reach their second best outcome. But as long as there is no enforcement mechanism to secure cooperation, rational players do not cooperate. They prefer to defect, no matter what the other player does. Many authors have argued that it is rational to cooperate in a prisoners' dilemma despite the given incentive structures. Game theorists reject these arguments.[7] The prisoners' dilemma is *defined* in such a way that individuals choose defection over

[6] The values in the cells are payoffs. However, payoffs can be interpreted as ordinal preferences, i.e. a payoff of 3 only means that it is strictly preferred by the individual over a payoff of 2, but nothing is implied about the strength of the difference, as the measurement is not cardinal. The payoffs can but need not be of a pecuniary nature. They can be interpreted as a general preference relation under the assumption that individuals maximize their payoffs.

[7] Ken Binmore, *Reciprocity and the Social Contract*, 3(1) Politics, Philosophy & Economics 5 (2004).

cooperation. If individuals choose to cooperate nevertheless, they do not play a prisoners' dilemma. The question is not: 'Why do individuals cooperate in a prisoners' dilemma?'; it is rather 'What kind of game are cooperating individuals playing?'.

I want to clarify this idea by distinguishing between the *given* and the *effective* payoff matrix.[8] Assume that a scientist designs a lab experiment in which subjects face a prisoners' dilemma. At least the scientist believes that his experimental setup puts people into such a dilemma. Thus, the *given* payoff matrix is the one set up by the researcher. However, if the scientist finds that many people cooperate in his experiment, one can conclude that the *given* payoff matrix is not the *effective* payoff matrix. The individuals' behaviour shows a preference towards cooperation. Thus, their *effective* payoff matrix is not a prisoners' dilemma, but a different game tilted towards cooperation. In general terms: The *effective* payoff matrix is the one which really guides the behaviour of people, while the *given* payoff matrix is the one assumed to be true based on the observed payoff structures.

Ideally, given and effective payoff matrix are identical. This is most likely the case if people behave in the way the researcher predicts with the given payoff matrix. Often, however, people do not behave as predicted. For instance, even though we expect defection in theory, a substantial percentage of people cooperate in prisoners' dilemmas.[9] Or rather: Even though we think that people face prisoners' dilemmas (given payoff matrix), they must in fact perceive the situation differently, and their behaviour shows that they operate on the basis of different payoffs, i.e. their effective payoff matrix differs from the given payoff matrix. Later in this paper, one effect which drives a wedge between given and effective payoff matrix will be discussed.

If two individuals face an effective one-shot prisoners' dilemma, rational individuals choose defection. What happens when more than two individuals are involved? A multi-person prisoners' dilemma emerges. Multi-person prisoners' dilemmas are even more difficult to resolve. While game theorists are at least able to show that mutual cooperation can be a Nash equilibrium in *infinite* two-persons prisoners' dilemmas (in contrast to the one-shot prisoners' dilemma, the players can build up cooperation over time in infinite two-person prisoners' dilemmas),[10] there are good theoretical reasons to be pessimistic about multi-

[8] A similar distinction was proposed by Harold J. Kelley & John W. Thibaut, Interpersonal Relations: A Theory of Interdependence (1978). It was recently used by Peter Kollock, *Transforming Social Dilemmas: Group Identity and Co-operation, in* Modelling Rationality, Morality, and Evolution (Peter A. Danielson ed. 1998).

[9] David Sally, *Conversation and Cooperation in Social Dilemmas: A Meta-Analysis of Experiments from 1958 to 1992*, 7 Rationality and Society 58 (1995).

[10] Robert M. Axelrod, The Evolution of Cooperation (1984).

person prisoners' dilemmas. If there are many players, and if each of these players finds non-cooperation to be the dominant strategy, then cooperation is unlikely to emerge because it is impossible to reciprocate against defectors in a targeted way. This holds true even though all individuals realize that mutual cooperation would produce a higher payoff for all. Multi-person prisoners' dilemmas are collective action problems. Even though all individuals want to produce the public good from a collective perspective, they are individually better off to free-ride on the efforts made by others.

II. *Weapons Decommissioning as a Collective Action Problem*

Imagine a contemporary scenario. Let A be a state in the early phase of state-building. Maybe A has been a 'failed state', making an attempt to re-establish working institutions. Maybe A has gone through a civil war. In any case, the people of A face the challenge to reinstate state authority and to provide security and welfare for its citizens.

In A, the private ownership of firearms and other weapons poses a threat to peace and security. Therefore, the people in A (or the newly established authorities) pursue a programme to decommission weapons. Each owner of weapons faces a difficult choice: He (or she!) can either surrender the weapons in the hope that most citizens do the same and a more peaceful future results. Or he can choose to keep his 'Kalashnikov' hidden in his garden shed, either because he thinks that others will either keep their weapons themselves, or because he wants to gain an advantage over others who are foolish enough to surrender their firearms.

This situation is a collective action problem and a multi-person prisoners' dilemma. All citizens are better off if all citizens surrender their private weapons arsenal. However, each single citizen is even better off if she keeps her weapons hidden, regardless of what the other citizens do with their rifles: If they do turn them in, it is still better to keep one's own weapon and be one of the few who still has firepower. If the others do not turn in their weapons, it is imperative not to be the only one without a gun. Thus, the dominant strategy is to hold on to one's weapon. Table 2 displays this incentive structure for one individual. The numbers in the table represent payoffs for individual X; payoffs for all other individuals are omitted, but all other individuals have identical payoff structures. The table shows two extreme scenarios only. Individual X expects two possible worlds: either one in which no other individual decommissions, or one in which all others decommission. The situation is a prisoners' dilemma because for both scenarios X prefers non-cooperation over cooperation. But it is assumed here that the results from these two specific scenarios hold generally: Whatever proportion

Table 2 Decommissioning of weapons as a prisoners' dilemma.

	All other individuals	
	Decommission	Keep weapons
X decommissions	3	0
X keeps weapon	4	1

of other individuals turn in their weapons, it is always individually rational not to turn in one's own weapon.[11]

In our case, country A would be a much safer place if everyone turned in the weapons. However, this knowledge alone is not enough to induce cooperation. If individuals perceive the choice situation as described in the payoff matrix in table 2, cooperation will not emerge.

Can a system of sanctions help to overcome the challenge posed by a multi-person prisoners' dilemma? Sanctions could be used to change the payoffs, making defection costly. The problem with sanctions is that their production is also a multi-person prisoners' dilemma because the provision of sanctions is costly. While all individuals prefer a state with sanctions rather than one without (since sanctions would guarantee the higher payoffs in the upper-left corner of table 2), each single individual finds that she is even better off if others invest time and money to provide sanctions, while she just rakes in the rewards without helping to put the sanctions in place. This shows that the attempt to implement sanctions to coordinate social behaviour in a multi-person prisoners' dilemma leads to an infinite regress of prisoners' dilemmas. Therefore, sanctions cannot explain the emergence of cooperation.

These results look rather bleak – and they are strange, given that existing states have faced many collective action problems in the form of prisoners' dilemmas which have been solved. In fact, the enforcement of most social norms is a potential prisoners' dilemma. We rely on the fact that our fellow citizens comply with the valid formal laws and with many informal social norms that we take as a matter of course, even if they cannot be effectively enforced. As we have seen now, they are anything but a matter of course, and for a state in the making the challenges posed by collective action problems threaten its very existence. However, there are mechanisms to explain why cooperation can emerge despite the challenges posed by collective action problems.

[11] This implies that the table could be extended to report X's reaction for each proportion of other cooperating individuals.

Table 3 Decommissioning of weapons as a cooperation game.

	All other individuals	
	Decommission	Keep weapons
X decommissions	4	1
X keeps weapon	3	0

Why do individuals cooperate despite collective action problems? The answer must be that individuals do not perceive these situations as collective action problems. Rather they see reasons to cooperate where social scientists only see reasons to defect, i.e. the *perceived* payoff structure is suited to induce cooperation, while the *given* payoff structure indicates a collective action problem. The interesting question is now: How does this gap between assumed and perceived payoff matrix come about? In different words: Which incentives have researcher falsely ignored in their given payoff matrix? In the following paragraphs, it will be argued that there are psychological processes which make the existence of cooperation games much more likely than the existence of prisoners' dilemmas in the provision of public goods.

Let us return to the example of weapons decommissioning from above. If the perceived payoff matrix is the one displayed in table 2, then there will be no decommissioning whatsoever. While this may sometimes be an appropriate analysis, it is surely too pessimistic to assume that such processes have to fail out of necessity. It is more likely that fortunate circumstances can change the perceived payoff matrix towards a cooperation game as displayed in table 3. Table 3 shows payoffs such that individuals always have an incentive to cooperate, i.e. to surrender their weapons, regardless of the decisions taken by other individuals. Thus, mutual cooperation is the result. In the following section one possible and – in the author's opinion – plausible explanation on how collective action problems like the decommissioning problem can be turned into cooperation games will be introduced.

III. *Local Knowledge and Cooperation*

To set up the argument, the decommissioning example must be enriched with three additional assumptions. The first assumption is that all agents share the view that there is a norm requiring people to turn in their weapons. Moreover, the agents believe that the enforcement of this norm is desirable from a collective perspective. This is not surprising, given the problem of collective action. The agents know that they are better off if all of them cooperate and therefore they are in principle in favour of a norm inducing mutually cooperative behaviour.

The problem is that agents have no rational reason to comply with the norm as long as the payoff structure looks like table 2.[12]

The second assumption specifies the difficulties arising when the state tries to enforce norms. I have argued above that sanctioning is a collective action problem itself, because the production of sanctions is costly. However, suppose the state can solve this collective action problem. Assume (for example) that our state receives international help to set up a police force and that the new policemen are motivated and well-paid enough to do their job. Even though the state is now in principle able to enforce the norm demanding the decommissioning of private weapons, a problem remains: weapons are easy to hide. It is practically impossible to send policemen from door to door and ask everyone to surrender their weapons at gunpoint. Even if it was feasible it would be very ineffective, as the weapons would soon disappear, forcing the police to perform door-to-door house-searches – an utterly unrealistic scenario. If the police knew exactly who owns a weapon, sanctioning would be possible. But since they do not, the state is not in the position to enforce decommissioning.

The third assumption opens a way out of the dilemma. Even though it is rather unrealistic to assume that the state has knowledge about gun owners, it is rather likely that there exists *local knowledge* about who has a rifle hidden in the garden shed. In other words: It is assumed that people do know whether their neighbours hide guns. Let us further assume that this local knowledge remains local because there is an unwritten norm that neighbours do not report each other to the police for illegal gun ownership.

In such a situation, the odds seem to be set against a successful decommissioning of weapons. While there is good news that a norm against gun ownership is in principle embraced, there seems to be little hope that the state can enforce this norm, given the difficulties to find illegal weapons. Nevertheless, this article argues that such scenarios are not only common, but also often resolvable. All functional states are indeed solving collective action problems successfully every day. Open societies simply do not have the means to enforce the compliance with all norms directly – unless we introduce an Orwellian system of observation, we cannot constantly force all people to adhere to all valid norms. Opportunities for free-riding are plenty. Take a much more harmless example such as public littering. For each citizen there are enough opportunities to litter without being seen. In many situations, littering is much easier than carrying one's litter to the next bin. Nevertheless, most people do not litter in public places.[13] Why? There are at least two possible explanations. Either individuals are motivated by a feeling

---

[12] For an analysis of social norms see CRISTINA BICCHIERI, THE GRAMMAR OF SOCIETY (2006).

[13] Raymond R. Reno, Robert B. Cialdini & Carl A. Kallgren, *The Transsituational Influence of Social Norms*, 64(1) JOURNAL OF PERSONALITY AND SOCIAL PSYCHOLOGY 104 (1993).

of duty which goes beyond utilitarian calculations. Or individuals perceive a certain social pressure inducing them to comply with a norm even though they realize that they cannot be forced to comply. In both cases, the payoff matrix would change such that individuals prefer cooperation over defection.

This paper deals with the second motivation to comply with norms: the social pressure felt by individuals to comply with norms. Recently, the concept of 'social norms' has been discussed by legal theorists,[14] but also by sociologists[15] and by philosophers and economists.[16] Social norms are norms which are part of the political culture and usually obeyed without direct state enforcement. This paper argues that the existence of social norms demanding cooperative behaviour is one – and often the most plausible – explanation why collective action problems can be solved against all odds. In this sense it is shown that a successful process of nation-building depends not only on good institutions and economic development, but also on the right 'political culture'.

IV. *What the Neighbours think: Esteem as an Incentive*

In our example, the decommissioning of weapons cannot be enforced by the state, because the state neither has the knowledge nor the means to enforce. However, there is local knowledge who owns illegal weapons, and even though neighbours do not report each other, neighbours can exercise pressure on each other when norms are violated. This pressure is exercised in the form of esteem. Geoffrey Brennan and Philip Pettit[17] have developed an economic and philosophical framework to analyse how the desire for esteem affects human actions. The concept of esteem is particularly useful to explain the emergence and stabilization of social norms in the wake of collective action problems.

Brennan and Pettit start with the assumption that people desire to be held in esteem by other people and that this desire is sufficiently strong to change people's behaviour. Since people want to be held in high esteem, they adapt their actions such that other people approve of their behaviour. Esteem is usually not expressed in words or action. Rather, it is the perceived attitude others hold towards us. If, for instance, I try to show good table manners when I dine with colleagues in an expensive restaurant, I do this because I do not want to make

[14] Richard H. McAdams, *The Origin, Development, and Regulation of Norms*, 96(2) Michigan Law Review (1997); Robert C. Ellickson, *Law and Economics Discovers Social Norms*, 27(2) Journal of Legal Studies (1998).

[15] E.g. James S. Coleman, Foundations of Social Theory (1990).

[16] In particular Geoffrey Brennan & Philip Pettit, The Economy of Esteem: An Essay on Civil and Political Society (2004).

[17] Brennan & Pettit, *supra* note 13.

a fool of myself. Even though it is rather unlikely that my colleagues would openly criticize me for putting my elbows on the table, I make assumptions about their attitudes towards me if I do. Thus, my behaviour is guided by the attitudes I believe others are going to have towards me if I act in a certain way. Would I strictly stick to the same rules if I was alone at home? Most people do not. Table manners are not legally binding, and they are almost impossible to enforce. Nevertheless, they are often adhered to, in particular if other people are present. The reason is that we desire to be held in esteem by other people, and that there are certain social norms of good behaviour whose violation is punished with diminished or negative esteem.

Esteem is in many ways a special good. It can neither be stored nor saved. It cannot even be exchanged or traded, at least not directly. We can only hold someone in high esteem if we think that the person truly deserves it. We hold someone in esteem for virtuous acts, not for acts that are intentionally done for the mere sake to be held in esteem. In an almost Kantian fashion, 'good will'[18] is rewarded with esteem, while merely instrumental behaviour is not. The result is similar if we look from the perspective of the 'esteemed' person. To be held in esteem is only valuable if you think that you are held in esteem because you have acted with virtue. Esteem is worthless if it is used for instrumental reasons. If people intentionally heap praise on me because they want me to change my behaviour, I might be cajoled, but I am not held in true esteem.

People hold other people in esteem according to certain norms of good behaviour. Suppose, as Brennan and Pettit do, that these norms are universally accepted by all relevant agents. There are a multitude of social norms. Some of them regulate minor issues like table manners, others deal with elementary questions of social interaction. Regarding state-building, we are talking about core norms which form the 'cement of society'.[19] These norms are part of a country's or a society's political culture. One fundamental norm influencing the functioning of any legal system is the norm that law-abidance is a virtue. In a society valuing this norm, transgressors are at least punished with disesteem from other citizens, even if other sanctions cannot be provided. By contrast, in a society where transgressing the laws is a peccadillo, the effects of esteem do not support the enforcement of laws. Such a society is more likely to fail in its most basic functions. In other words: A political culture where law-abidance is seen as a virtue has much better chances to install and maintain a well-working legal system.

Let us return to the example of weapons decommissioning. This is a formidable example for the failure of state enforcement. However, if we take the effects of

---

[18] Immanuel Kant, Grundlegung zur Metaphysik der Sitten ([1785], 1984).

[19] Jon Elster, The Cement of Society: A Study of Social Order (1989).

esteem into account, we can see how decommissioning can succeed nevertheless. We have made the assumption that there is local knowledge about illegal gun ownership. We have also assumed that neighbours tend not to report each other to the police. However, even if neighbours do not report each other, they can have different attitudes towards neighbours with illegal weapons. If this society honours a social norm which condemns the ownership of illegal weapons, there is a chance that the collective action problem can be solved.

If citizens hold each other in esteem for turning in weapons, while they hold each other in disesteem for hiding weapons, then there exists an additional incentive to abide by the laws and to take part in the decommissioning. A simple formal decision model clarifies this argument. Let there be one citizen who currently owns an illegal weapon. This citizen has to trade off several considerations. On the one hand owning the weapon produces a certain level of utility W ($W > 0$), because owning the weapon increases his security. At the same time, there is a probability to be discovered by the police p ($0 < p < 1$) and be fined with a fine F ($F > 0$). As I have argued above, the expected value of the fine pF is neglectable compared to the utility derived from the weapon.

Therefore,

$$W > pF. \tag{1}$$

His neighbours know that he owns an illegal weapon. While he can be certain that they would not tell the police about it, he knows that they disapprove of his behaviour or hold him in disesteem. If he were to turn in his weapon, however, they would hold him in high esteem. Let the difference between the disesteem for illegal ownership and esteem for turning in the weapon from all neighbours be ΔE. Adding the effect of esteem to inequality (1) gives

$$W \,{}^{>}\!/\!{}_{<}\, pF + \Delta E, \tag{2}$$

where the direction of the inequality depends on the strength of the esteem effect, the probability and severity of a fine, and the utility derived from owning a weapon. The point is: If the difference between positive esteem for turning in one's weapon and negative esteem for keeping it is sufficiently high, the incentive to decommission can be strong enough, despite the collective action problem. Whether the esteem incentive is indeed strong enough depends on several factors:

- The utility derived from weapon ownership W must be low. This is usually the case if citizens are reasonably save even without weapons. In violent anarchy no one will surrender her weapon.

- The risk p to be caught by the police owning an illegal weapon and the incurring fine F can tip the decision towards decommissioning but in itself these factors are usually not strong enough to induce norm compliance.
- The strength of the esteem effect ΔE depends on the number of neighbours knowing about the weapons, on their level of interest, on the psychological disposition of the agent to care about being held in esteem, and, crucially, on the prevalent norms in this society.

While all factors deserve to be treated in detail, this paper focuses on the last point, in particular on the effect of social norms and the link to the notion of political culture.

V. *Esteem and Political Culture*

With formal sanctioning being out of question, social pressure remains the most plausible incentive to induce cooperation, i.e. to motivate people to turn in their weapons as required. However, this mechanism can only work if there is a consensus among all or at least a strong majority of citizens regarding the norms that determine the standards for esteem-worthiness. If there is no universally accepted norm that weapons have to be surrendered, then owners of weapons are not held in disesteem by the neighbours, and there is no incentive to take part in the decommissioning programme. By contrast, if there are such norms and if the transgression of such norms is widely seen as disgraceful, then the desire for esteem is an excellent incentive to resolve the collective action problem. Esteem is particularly suited to solve collective action problems because it can be 'produced' without costs, as Brennan and Pettit point out. Holding someone in high or low esteem happens without effort, as these attitudes come naturally. The costless nature of esteem avoids the infinite regress following from the attempt to solve the problem with sanctions as discussed above.

The set of social norms which determines the esteem processes can be interpreted as a society's political culture. Thus, define political culture as a set of social norms which is accepted by a large majority of agents. 'Accepted' means that the agents think that it is normatively desirable that people obey these norms. The transmission mechanism which makes political culture relevant for aggregate behaviour is the individual desire for esteem. As described above, individuals adapt their behaviour to increase the esteem they receive. The esteem they receive, in turn, is determined by how well they comply with the relevant social norms. Since the relevant social norms constitute the political culture of that society, political culture influences the behaviour of individuals.

This setup creates a link between the research on esteem and the extensive literature dealing with political culture and its effects. Political culture research (PCR) takes the attitudes, beliefs and values held by citizens as an explanatory variable to predict different aggregative outcomes. Robert Putnam, for example, argues that the quality of administration and consequently economic success of regions in Italy is determined by their political cultures.[20] This explains the stunning differences between Italy's north and south, according to Putnam. The bulk of PCR literature, however, deals with the relation between political culture and the transition to democracy. PCR claims that there is an association between the values, attitudes and beliefs held by the citizens, and the success to create a well-functioning democracy. More specifically, Inglehart asserts that an orientation towards 'civic values' is positively associated with years of continuous democracy.[21]

How can the research on political culture be useful for the discussion of state-building as a collective action problem? The answer is twofold. Firstly, the general structure of explanation is similar. Both PCR and the esteem approach take political culture, understood as the set of accepted social norms, as an explanatory variable to predict the outcome of aggregative processes. Secondly, the themes 'stability of democracy' and 'state-building' are related regarding the research questions they are facing. As shown above, state-building can be analyzed as a collective action problem. In the same vein one can argue that the success of a democratic system depends on the solution of certain collective action problems – democracy is a public good that would cease to work if no one would be willing to contribute beyond narrow self-interest. For these reasons it is useful to link PCR and the esteem analysis of state-building.

Johnson argues that PCR faces serious conceptual problems, because proponents of PCR have never bothered to develop a theory explaining the underlying causal mechanisms on which their claims are based:

> Proponents of PCR offer no plausible account – causal, functional, or otherwise – of how political culture 'works', of how it motivates individual action or generates persistence or change in aggregate political or economic behavior.[22]

---

[20] Robert D. Putnam, Robert Leonardi & Raffaella Nanetti, Making Democracy Work: Civic Traditions in Modern Italy (1993).

[21] Robert Inglehart, *The Renaissance of Political Culture*, 82(4) American Political Science Review 1203 (1988). Some new research puts Inglehart's claims into question. See Edward N. Muller & Mitchell A. Seligson, *Civic Culture and Democracy: The Question of Causal Relationships*, 88(3) American Political Science Review 635 (1994).

[22] James Johnson, *Conceptual Problems as Obstacles to Progress in Political Science – Four Decades of Political Culture Research*, 15(1) Journal of Theoretical Politics 87, 103 (2003).

The author of this paper concurs with Johnson's critique. If we really want to understand how political culture shapes political outcomes, we have to look at the transmission mechanisms between these two realms. Fortunately, the concept of esteem offers us such a transmission mechanism. While most research on political culture remains vague when it comes to the explanation of the phenomena they predict, this paper offers an analytic account of how political culture influences political outcomes. It does not only offer a 'macrotheory' of aggregate outcomes, but also a 'microtheory' of individual choices and actions in Schelling's sense.[23]

The effect of political culture on aggregate political behaviour becomes most apparent when we look at collective action problems. If the prevalent political culture contains norms that demand cooperation despite material incentives to free-ride, agents are rewarded with positive esteem if they cooperate. Therefore, a rational agent chooses cooperation if the esteem incentive outweighs the material incentive to free-ride. A political culture which embraces cooperation as a value is better prepared to solve collective action problems, because free-riders are punished with disesteem and cooperators are rewarded with positive esteem.

The concrete example of weapons decommissioning demonstrates this point. In our case, each single person decides whether she surrenders her weapon or not. The analysis so far has shown that state sanctions alone are unsuited to reinforce decommissioning, because the risk to be caught is tiny. However, if this society rewards cooperation in the decommissioning programme with positive esteem, then the calculation can change, as in inequality (3):

$$W < pF + \Delta E \qquad (3)$$

Here the difference in esteem for cooperation and defection ΔE is strong enough to induce cooperation. While the given payoff matrix looks like a multi-person prisoners' dilemma (table 2), the perceived payoff matrix is a cooperation game (table 3). The desire to be held in positive esteem drives a wedge between these two matrices. Assume that a cooperating person receives positive esteem on the level 1, while a defector receives negative esteem –1. Taking esteem into account shows how the prisoners' dilemma is turned into a cooperation game, as displayed in table 4.

---

[23] Thomas C. Schelling, Micromotives and Macrobehavior (1978).

Table 4 Transformation of a prisoners' dilemma to a cooperation game.

	All other individuals	
	Decommission	Keep weapons
X decommissions	3 + 1 = 4	0 + 1 = 1
X keeps weapon	4 – 1 = 3	1 – 1 = 0

Under these assumptions, the positive esteem received for turning in one's weapon always outweighs the incentive to free-ride and keep the weapon. Some will object that the effect of esteem in such processes is overstated. The reply to this objection is twofold. Firstly, it is not argued in this paper that the desire for esteem is always the crucial factor to induce cooperation in collective action problems. It is merely claimed that it is one factor among others. Nonetheless this paper argues, secondly, that the desire for esteem (or similar phenomena of social pressure) is often the best explanation why people comply with norms which are otherwise unenforceable. The scenario of weapons decommissioning demonstrates the dilemma. State-building requires cooperation in situations where state enforcement is simply not a viable option. Unless we want to argue that state-building fails out of necessity, we have to answer the question why individuals sometimes cooperate nevertheless. The individuals' desire to be esteemed for norm compliance is one possible answer.

The upshot is that the success of weapons decommissioning in particular, and state-building in general, is contingent on the prevalent political culture. In a political culture where owning weapons (even illegally) is seen as desirable, no one will be motivated to turn in their rifle, because there is no positive esteem to be earned for doing so. However, if there is a widespread agreement that undermining the prospects for peace by hiding illegal weapons is shameful, the chances to succeed with disarmament are much higher, because cooperating people are held in esteem, defectors in disesteem.

VI. *Conclusion*

Successful state-building depends – among many other factors – on a prevalent political culture which is supportive of certain civic virtues. Institutions and state authority are important factors for successful state-building. Nonetheless, no state can be based on state power and enforcement only. Citizens have to be willing and able to cooperate and comply with norms even when no immediate enforcement is feasible. In the case of weapons decommissioning, the state simply lacks the knowledge and means to enforce it. Instead, citizens must be motivated to disarm through different mechanisms. The desire for esteem is such a mechanism. However, the effect of this desire hinges on the norms held in society. These norms comprise the political culture.

One could think of many other examples to demonstrate how political culture affects the cooperativeness of individuals through the desire for esteem. A particularly drastic instance is the support for terrorists within a population. Consider the ETA in Spain or the so-called 'insurgency' in Iraq. These groups often depend on the logistic and ideological support from ordinary citizens. In a society where the support of terrorists is positively evaluated by many people, terrorists are likely to be successful. By contrast, if an overwhelming majority of citizens rejects terrorism, then there will be strong incentives not to support the terrorists. In these cases, political culture is an important factor for the success of fighting terrorism.

The methodological advancement in the analysis of political culture in terms of esteem lies in the development of a microtheory of action. Brennan's and Pettit's 'Economy of Esteem' serves as the basis to explain how political culture as an aggregative concept changes the behaviour of individual agents. Gaining a better understanding how the decisions of individuals lead to outcomes on the macro-level is one of the most interesting methodological tasks for the social sciences. Since individuals are the entities who reason and make decisions, we need to understand individual motivations to advance our analysis of social processes.

The objective is not to reduce the social sciences to a science of individual action. Rather, the challenge lies in understanding how the individual and the social level are linked. In the case of state-building, Thomas Hobbes was already very much aware of this tension. Maybe the most remarkable trait of Hobbes's political theory is the contrast between the meticulous analysis of individual behaviour on the one hand, and the entirely anti-individualistic result on the other hand. We do not need to embrace Hobbes's totalitarianism to appreciate this paradigmatic tension. But we should learn from Hobbes that the social sciences must analyse individual behaviour to understand aggregative outcomes.

Comparative Law and the 'Proceduralization' of Constitution-Building Processes

*Andrea Lollini & Francesco Palermo**

I. *Introduction*

In the contemporary world, state and/or nation-building is increasingly substituted by constitution-building. Whereas previous centuries have been the time of the states and of the nations, this is the era of the constitution. When based on the rule of law, state and nation exist only through the constitution, and only the constitution is the reference point for the (re-)establishment of a nation. In modern liberal democracies, it is the constitution, not the state nor the nation, that establishes and guarantees the unity of a people, as pointed out by Dolf Sternberger in his concept of *Verfassungspatriotismus*.[1] A people is what its constitution is. Therefore, the study of state and nation-building in contemporary democracies (or democracies-in-the-making) is in the first line the study of constitution-building.

The analysis of constitution-building-processes, however, is all but a simple task. For ages, and particularly when state and nation were more important than constitutions, lawyers have basically avoided the problem.[2] Especially in the continental legal tradition, the theory of the *pouvoir constituant* excluded every further attempt to seriously investigate the genesis of constitutions, since it treated the establishment of a constitution as a formal act, created by an unlimited power, which took logical and legal priority over the constitution itself.[3] Therefore, the

* This essay has been discussed and written together by Andrea Lollini (with the main responsibility for paragraphs III and IV.2) and Francesco Palermo (for paragraphs I, II, IV.1 and V).

[1] D. Sternberger, Verfassungspatriotismus (1990).

[2] Compare O. Pfersmann, *in* Droit constitutionnel 93 (L. Favoreau et al. eds. 2001), who maintains that the constituent power cannot be considered a legal phenomenon. "The elaboration of a constitution does not depend on law, it creates the law".

[3] See in particolar J. E. Sieyes, Exposition raissonnée des droits de l'homme et du citoyen, quoted by G. Burdeau, Traité des Sciences Politiques (vol. IV) 172 (1971). For a comprehensive analysis see Cl. Klein, Théorie et practique du pouvoir constituant (1993). For the distinction between

process of constitutional formation, its (unconceivable) limits, its procedures, its contents, were considered to fall outside of the realm of legal analysis.

Such a comfortable but simplistic approach is put under stress in contemporary constitution-making (i.e. the drafting of a constitution) and constitution-building (i.e. the more general process of establishing and implementing a constitution) and it needs to be revised profoundly. Over the last decades, a clear tendency is emerging towards a fragmentation in the process of constitution-making (and, more broadly, constitution-building). Both in peaceful contexts and in several post-conflict arenas, the (pre-legal) constitution-making *moment* is being substituted by constitution-making *processes* and finally by the establishment of (legally defined) constitution-making *procedures*. As a consequence, the constitution is no longer a mere and single act of political will, but a more complex series of constitutional facts and acts, including political, judicial and international conditionality, and in the end it becomes a legally-driven process and procedure.[4] Contemporary constitutions are thus the outcome of a process of stratification of formal and material legal acts, increasingly supported by comparative elements due to the interplay of actors both internal and external to the domestic arena. Such a process, thus, can no longer be neglected in the legal analysis.

Taking this background as its starting point, this essay develops two main research hypotheses. First, it argues that contemporary constitutionalism is marking the end of the traditional constitution-making approach, where the constitution was seen as a single legal act created by an unlimited political power. The exclusiveness of the political constitution-making is being substituted by a larger variety of constitutional factors, is involving a plurality of actors with different legitimacies, and is diluting the constitution-making moment over a longer period of time. This clearly emerges from the analysis of recent constitution-building processes that have been exaggerating the (return to the) traditional, political-only method of constitution formation (the provocative cases of the EU on the one hand and of Afghanistan and Iraq on the other will be considered later in this chapter). These processes tend to fail when marked by an excess of simplification, which is no longer compatible with today's reality.

Secondly, the paper maintains that comparative law is the procedural matrix of modern constitution-building. In other words, there is no modern constitution-building nor constitution-making without a massive use of comparative (and international) law. This does not (and should not) mean legal transplants from one country to another, but simply that, in an interconnected world, constitu-

---

original constituent power and derived constituent power (basically coinciding with the power to amend the constitution) see firstly R. Bonnard, *Les actes constitutionnels de 1940*, Revue du droit public 48 ss (1942).

[4] See La "manutenzione" costituzionale (F. Palermo ed., 2007).

tionalism can no longer be but interconnected. The role of comparative (and international) law in constitution-building processes and in the elaboration of constitution-building procedures is thus the litmus test for the end of the age of the *pouvoir constituant* as well as a necessary step in contemporary constitutionalism. Comparative law, of course, is not "law", but a method – at present the most appropriate interpretative method[5] – to understand legal phenomena: it does not, as such, produce law, but it helps understand the new dynamics underpinned by constitution-building processes.

This paper argues that such dynamics are increasingly becoming procedural – thus legal – instead of being merely political, and this trend is demonstrated (and supported) by comparative law, which at the same time provides the common ground for the circulation of the procedural method.

II. *"Comparativization" of constitution-building and the procedural method*

1. *Meaning and scope*

Recent constitution-building processes tend to be exposed to strong international and comparative influence. While the former is not at all a novelty, as shown by an increasing amount of cases in which post-conflict constitutions have been approved under international pressure and have sometimes even been dictated by the international community,[6] attention needs to be paid to the phenomenon that could be labeled as "comparativization" of the constitution-making process.

---

[5] As correctly pointed out by P. Häberle, *Grundrechtsgeltung und Grundrechtsinterpretation im Verfassungsstaat*, JuristenZeitung 913 ss (1989), comparative law should be considered as the fifth methodology for legal interpretation, in addition to the classical four identified by Savigny in the 19th century (literal, systematic, historical and teleological interpretation).

[6] The variety of cases ranges form post-war Germany, Japan and Italy, to – more recently – Namibia, East Timor, Bosnia and Herzegovina and other Balkan countries (not to mention Kosovo), Cambodia, Cyprus, etc. For a comprehensive overview see H. Tourard, L'internationalisation des constitutions nationales (2000), and (shorter) N. Maziau, *Le costituzioni internazionalizzate. Aspetti teorici e tentativi di classificazione*, Diritto pubblico comparato ed europeo (DPCE) 1397 ss (2002-IV). For a tentative classification of the types of interaction between domestic constitutions and international "standards" see D. Maus, *L'influence du droit international contemporain sur l'exercice du pouvoir constituant, in* Le nouveau constitutionnalisme. Mélanges en l'honneur de Gérard Conac 87 ss (J.-C. Colliard & Y. Jégouzo eds., 2001). The Author distinguishes between three possible situations: strong interaction (when domestic law is bound to be in line with international provisions), medium interaction (where mere compatibility of domestic law with international requirements is demanded) and weak or soft interaction (where a process of gradual harmonization is required).

Unlike international law, which is an autonomous branch of law, implemented by international organizations, by the states, and by the international community as a whole, comparative law is not normative, but rather a methodology. "Comparativization" of the constitution-making process means therefore that constitutions of the last wave[7] are adopted under a factual influence of experiences, legal solutions and practices elaborated elsewhere. Comparativization of the constitution-making processes is thus a less visible phenomenon than internationalization, but not less important. On the contrary, it requires contemporary analysts of constitutional developments to be trained in comparative methodology, thus avoiding either a too simplistic understanding of today's constitutionalism, or – even worse – gross mistakes in superficially applying the comparative method, e.g. by suggesting rudimental forms of legal transplants that are deemed to fail, causing bigger problems than those that they are aimed at resolving.[8]

2. *The procedural method in constitution-building*

Comparativization in constitution-building means both that increasing attention is paid to foreign experiences, drawing comparative consequences from the functioning of institutions and from procedures adopted elsewhere, and that foreign institutions, case-law and global tendencies achieve such an authority that makes them a pre-normative factor in the process of adopting a constitution. Apart from the circulation of specific institutional solutions, what seems to be the main consequence of the phenomenon of comparativization of constitution-building is the dissemination of a method. More or less voluntarily, almost all processes of constitutional formation of the last "generation" of constitutions (i.e. those drafted over the last 30 years) have been following a common matrix in adopting constitutions that can be called "the procedural method".

Such a method indicates an overall tendency of the constitutions of the last generation (beginning with the cases of Portugal 1976 and Spain 1978)[9] to be

---

[7] A convincing classification of constitutional waves (and constitution-making processes) is provided by J. Elster, *Constitutionalism in Eastern Europe. An Introduction*, 58 University of Chicago Law Review 447 ss (1991), who distinguishes between seven clusters or waves of constitutions ranging from the post-revolutionary constitutionalism of the 18th century to contemporary post-cold war transitions.

[8] See on this phenomenon G. Ajani, *By Chance and Prestige: Legal Transplants in Russia and Eastern Europe*, 43 American Journal of Comparative Law 93 ss (1995), and G. Ajani, *The Transplant of Vague Notions, in* Liber Amicorum Z. Peteri 17 ss (H. Szilágyi István, Paksy Máté eds., 2005).

[9] In both cases, in fact, constitutional transition towards democracy was carried out through a negotiated political platform involving the former regimes and the new democratic political forces. Portugal and Spain, in other words, can be considered the first examples of multi-phase and procedural transition to a new constitutional order. See e.g. G. de Vergottini, Le origini

drafted in a new way, abandoning the (exclusiveness of the) classical, political method of the past. In particular, all recent constitutions have been drafted taking more and more distance of three inherent features of past constitutionalism. First, the elaboration and even the adoption of a constitution is no longer a temporarily unified moment. Constitutional assemblies or their functional equivalents tend to adopt a constitution through a coordinated series of constitutionally relevant moments and acts, making it difficult to clearly determine when the "constitutional big bang" takes place. Second, the exclusive political legitimacy of constitution-givers is being integrated by a number of other actors, representing different stakeholders, interests, categories, forms of legitimacy (e.g. Courts, international organizations, NGOs, experts, pressure groups, and in the end constitutionalism itself).[10] Such an inclusive approach is transforming constitution-making from a political agreement into a more complex – and often slower – process of incorporation of different constitutive elements into a constitution, performing a broader integrative function as compared to the past, where societal integration was delegated exclusively to the political representation, and marks the end of the political myth of exclusiveness of political decision-making. Third, and consequently, the very essence of a procedural approach to constitution-making (and, more broadly, to constitution-building) makes it illusory to believe that a constitution is the product of a free, unlimited constituent power. Not only political, but also international and comparative conditionality is playing an immense role in the process of adopting a constitution.

Thus, instead of the rooted idea of constitution-making as a temporarily unified, political and unrestricted activity, a new practice is being established, based on different – in some cases totally different mechanisms and approaches, requiring new systematic and comparative tools to be analyzed and fully understood. Such new mechanisms are in the first place a temporally diluted process for the adoption of a constitution, also requiring procedural rules for governing the different stages of constitution-making and therefore constraining constitution-giving into rules on the production of rules.

Second, new constitutions tend to be the result of a process of constitutional stratification, of slow sedimentation of constitutionally relevant acts, facts and judicial decisions, and even the very texts of new constitutions can be the

della seconda repubblica portoghese. 1974–1976 (1977) and Una costituzione democratica per la Spagna (G. de Vergottini ed., 1978). See briefly R. Jiménez Asensio, Apuntes para una historа del constitucionalismo español 173 ss (1992) as well as R. Morodo, La transición política (1984) and Transición política y consolidación democrática. España (1975–1986) (R. Cotarelo ed., 1992).

[10] On these developments see the papers published under the title *Back to Government? The Pluralistic Deficit in the Decision-making Process and Before the Courts*, 12 (2) Indiana Journal of Global Legal Studies 409 ss (2005).

product of a plurality of constituent acts, such as in the case of South Africa and other experiences of poly-phase adoption of constitutions, normally through transitional texts.[11]

Third, even though the rhetoric of constitutional discourse survives, underlying the absolute freedom of constitution-givers in determining the contents of a constitution, all recent constitutional-formation processes and increasingly even the very texts of new constitutions tend to make reference to their embedment into international and comparative standards. By doing so, the constitutions of the present generation show, as a matter of fact, that they are grounded on a double legitimacy: internal and external. The international community and (sometimes vague) comparative standards are being considered as a source of legitimacy in a way that becomes increasingly similar to the internal political process. Recent constitutions are thus also grounded on the acceptance by the international community, by showing that international standards and comparative best practices have been followed. In other words, the basic law elaborated through such a poly-phase and pluralistic constitution-making process has to persuade not only the country's citizens, but also other states and the international community as a whole. Thus, constitution-building, the complex process for the adoption of a constitution and for its penetration into the society, is becoming bi-directional, being addressed to the inside (the national political community and society) as well as to the outside (international and comparative acceptance of the adopted text). If and where peculiar solutions are adopted, there is a sort of a moral obligation to justify them in comparative terms.[12] Moreover, such moral obligation quickly becomes political as international and comparative acceptance is the requirement, for states in transition, to be admitted in the international community and particularly in some international organizations.[13]

An empirical verification of such a profound shift from the classical to the present constitution-making model would require an in-depth analysis of the

---

[11] Other examples can be found in the cases of Malawi, Namibia, Hungary, etc. See below.

[12] As appeared to happen e.g. when the 'Israeli Basic Law: the Government' was amended in 1992 in order to introduce the popular election of the Prime Minister (a provision that was changed after only one electoral round), as testified in the *travaux préparatoires*. See on this regard H. Stellman, *Electing a Prime Minister and a Parliament: The Israeli Election 1996*, Parliamentary Affairs 648 ss (1997).

[13] On this phenomenon, regarding the admission to what the author labels "the three geo-juridical areas of Europe" (OSCE, Council of Europe, European Union), see R. Toniatti, *Los derechos del pluralismo cultural en la nueva Europa*, 58 (II) Revista vasca de administración pública 17 ss. (2000). For the more specific case of the admission to the Council of Europe see J.-F. Flauss, *Les conditions d'admission des pays d'Europe centrale et orientale au sein du Conseil de l'Europe*, 5 European Journal of International Law 1 ss (1994). As regards the accession to the EU see among others C. Pinelli, *Conditionality and Enlargement in Light of EU Constitutional Developments*, 19 European Law Journal 354 ss (2004).

"comparative supermarket" of models on the one hand, as well as a broad mapping of the case-law produced by the constitutional courts. As to the first aspect, it is self-evident that the comparativization of constitution-building offers a broad spectrum of "comparative shopping" in the huge supermarket of models offered by the foreign best practices, ranging from the classical, post-colonial idea of legal transplants (i.e. importation of successful legal institutes and instruments normally due to a previous colonial domination or to the prestige of foreign solutions) to a more complex and modern idea of foreign law as metabolized through the activity of international bodies or institutions,[14] or through the use of comparative law as a parameter in judicial decisions or in authoritative scholarly pieces. As to the role of courts (particularly constitutional courts) in the constitution-building processes, the increasingly proactive judicial approach that is marking the recent constitution-building processes might also be seen both as a reason and as a product of the comparativization of legal systems.[15] In fact, constitutional courts have recently proved to be particularly attentive to the comparative method[16] and the increasing role of the courts as determinant hermeneutical actors in constitution-making and constitution-building processes[17] has consequently increased the attention paid to comparative achievements. In some cases, such as South Africa, constitutional courts also play a fundamental role – expressly recognized by the rules on the adoption of a constitution – in the very drafting of a constitution, thus explicitly recognizing constitutional adjudication and certification as one of the factors for the legitimacy of the constitution to be adopted. Sometimes, constitutional courts are explicitly vested with the power to initiate the constitution-amending procedure, such as in Ecuador and Panama. In other, more numerous cases, constitutional courts do not play any formal role in the drafting of the constitution, and therefore the judicial use of comparative law is to establish ex-post legitimacy of the constitution vis-à-vis the international community. Constitutional adjudication is therefore one of the key-determinants that prove the growing influence of comparative law as a critical factor of constitution-building and as a process of drafting a constitution and above all of legitimizing it, both internally and externally.

---

[14] An interesting and particularly effective example is represented by the role played in Europe by the Council of Europe's Commission for Democracy through Law (so-called Venice Commission). See <http://www.venice.coe.int/site/dynamics/N_Subject_ef.asp?T=13&L=E>.

[15] See P. Häberle, *Funktion und Bedeutung der Verfassungsgerichte in vergleichender Perspektive*, Europäische Grundrechte-Zeitschrift 685 ss (2005).

[16] For a broad overview and several country examples see Corti nazionali e comparazione giuridica (G. F. Ferrari & A. Gambaro eds., 2006).

[17] Constitutional courts have been defined as "permanent constitution-makers" by L. Pegoraro, Lineamenti di giustizia costituzionale comparata 128 (1998).

Such a deep analysis, however, would exceed the limits of this essay. Our goal is not to provide an overambitious new theory of constituent power, but more modestly to propose only a possible hint as to the interconnection between the changing function of constitution-building and the hermeneutical role of comparative law. To this end, the following pages will focus on some telling examples of the dissemination of the procedural model in constitution-making and constitution-building (due both to comparative authority and to international imposition) (III.1. and III.2.). To verify the hypothesis according to which the procedural and thus comparative method in constitution-building has become inherent in today's constitutionalism, some "negative" examples of a return to a merely political constitution-making will also be discussed (IV.). Finally, some tentative, comparative conclusions will be drawn from the aforementioned cases, arguing that the comparative method is becoming the backbone of contemporary constitution-building (V.). A method that, being increasingly and capillary diffused, becomes a comparative model.

III. *The procedural model: selected case studies*

The evolution from merely political constitution-making, typical of the *bourgeoise* revolution, to a more complex constitution-making process is well known in legal analysis.[18] In other words, it is commonly accepted that in complex and pluralistic societies constitution-making and constitution-building are the product of complex and pluralistic processes that necessarily include different actors. The

---

[18] See The Paradox of Constitutionalism: Constituent Power and Constitutional Form (M. Loughlin & N. Walzer eds., 2007); J. Elster, Constitutionalism in Eastern Europe, cit., L. Mezzetti, Teoria e prassi delle transizioni costituzionali 275 ss (2003); Constitutionalism in Africa. Creating opportunities, Facing Challenges (J. Oloka Onyango ed., 2001); R. Sacco, *Il costituzionalismo africano*, Diritto pubblico comparato ed europeo 3 ss. (2000); G. de Vergottini, Le transizioni costituzionali 131 ss (1998); F. Venter, *The Emergence of Constitutionalism in Southern Africa in the late XX century, in* International Conference on African Constitutions 11 ss (V. Piergigli & I. Taddia eds., 1998); R. Sacco, M. Guadagni, R. Aluffi Beck-Pecoz & L. Castellani, Il diritto africano (1996); P. F. Gonidec, *Le constitutionnalisme africain*, Revue Juridique et politique indépendance et coopération 23 ss (1996); Id., Les systèmes politiques africains (1996). For an empirical research of the genetic phase of the African State during decolonisation see D. M. Lavroff, Les systèmes constitutionnels en Afrique noire. Les Etats Francophones (1976) and A. Cabanis & M. L. Martin, Les Constitutions d'Afrique francophone. Évolutions récentes (1999). See also V. T. Le Vine, *The Fall and Rise of Constitutionalism in Africa*, 35 (2) The Journal of Modern African Studies 181 ss (1997) and A. Bourgi, *L'évolution du constitutionnalisme en Afrique: du formalisme à l'effectivité*, 52 Revue françiase de droit constitutionnel 721 ss (2002).

purpose of this paper is to demonstrate first, that more recent constitutional transitions also made a further step in this regard, moving from constitution-making *processes* to constitution-making (and constitution-building) *procedures* and, second, that this further evolution has been deeply influenced by the comparative method. The slow but constant evolution of "mere" processes into legally defined procedures means that these processes are gradually assisted by more (and more sophisticated) legal guarantees.

To show this evolution, we discuss three sets of comparatively relevant examples of recent procedural constitution-building: On the one hand, the establishment of pluralistic arenas as well as multi-phase constitution-making processes (1.) and recent internationally imposed constitutions (2.) prove evidence that there is a growing consensus towards pluralism, comparativization and proceduralization of constitution-building. On the other hand, the failure of the opposite approach, i.e. apparently political-only constitution-making processes demonstrates that this can no longer be the time for a simplistic, monistic constitution-making taking place outside of predetermined legal guarantees (IV.).

1. *Pluralistic arenas and multi-phase constitution-building: Constitutional forums, multiparty negotiations, Round Table Talks. The cases of South Africa, Namibia and Poland*

One of the most visible steps in the shift from the classical, political-only constitution-making (constitutional assemblies and alike) to a more complex and pluralistic constitutional process and, in the end, constitutional procedure, is the establishment of new types of decision-making *forums*, such as the so-called *Round Table Talks* or *Multi-Party Negotiations.*[19]

This new type of (no longer merely political but not yet fully procedural) constitution-making spread out in the eve of the post-1989 constitutional transition. Important European examples are the cases of Bulgaria, Hungary, Poland, Czechoslovakia and East Germany.[20] In Africa, the experience of multi-party negotiations during the constitutional transitions in Namibia and South African should be mentioned. All these forums became the (new) political space where, generally without democratic legitimation, fundamental decisions were made on radical amendments to the old constitutions or general agreements were reached on new constitutional texts. Moreover, in several cases the forums made it possible to reach a compromise on the subsequent constitution-making process,

[19] See P. Paczolay, Constitutional Transition and Legal Continuity, 8 CONNECTICUT JOURNAL OF INTERNATIONAL LAW 559, 560 ss (1993).

[20] See J. Elster, *supra* note 18, 455; R. Ludwikowski, *Mixed Constitutions Product of an East-Central European Constitutional Melting Pot*, 16 BOSTON UNIVERSITY INTERNATIONAL LAW JOURNAL 1 ss (1998).

allowing a sort of negotiated constitution-making procedure, thus submitting the further constituent steps to legal rules.[21]

The most relevant and better known example in this regard is certainly South Africa, whose constitution-making (and subsequently constitution-building) represents one of the most complex processes that ever took place, and might therefore serve as a comparative model. Even though the final democratic constitution of 1996 was formally adopted by the Parliament meeting as constitutional assembly, many fundamental decisions have been negotiated long before the establishment of the constitutional assembly. A number of multi-party forums, such as the Conference for Democratic South Africa (Codesa I and II), as well as the multi-party negotiating process (MPNP), took place even before the first democratic election in 1994. These forums, composed by delegates of the *de facto* constituent actors (political parties, liberation movements and organisations) reached an agreement on a number of constitution-making steps, such as the 1993 Interim Constitution, the establishment of a Constitutional Court, and the 34 fundamental constitutional principles that were guiding (and binding for) the subsequently elected constitutional assembly. The Constitutional Court has been vested with the power to verify and formally certify that the final Constitution was in line with the 34 fundamental constitutional principles.[22] It is worth noting that such a control was carefully carried out by the Constitutional Court. The judges, in fact, refused to certify the first constitutional text and forced the constitutional assembly to re-write some sections of the final Constitution based on the 34 principles.[23] The South-African experience is a clear example of the mentioned fragmentation of the constitution-making process (multi-step elaboration of the Constitution by limiting the previously exclusive power of a political body) as well as of its gradual transformation into a constitution-making procedure.

Even before the South African experience, an analogous constitution-making procedure has been experimented with in the same geopolitical area during the constitutional transition in Namibia. The South African apartheid regime, having the administrative control over the territory of today's Namibia, negotiated the

[21] A. Arato, Forms of Constitution Making and Theory of Democracy, 17 CARDOZO LAW REVIEW 191, 230 (1995).

[22] S. Gloppen, South Africa: the Battle Over the Constitution (1997); H. Ebrahim, The Soul of a Nation. Constitution Making in South Africa (1998); R. Spitz & M. Chaskalson, The Politics of Transition. A Hidden History of South Africa's Negotiated Settlement (2000); P. Strand, Decisions on Democracy. The Politics of Constitution – Making in South Africa 1990–1996 (2000); H. Klug, Constitution Democracy. Law, Globalism and South Africa's Political Reconstruction (2000).

[23] M. Chaskalson & D. Davis, Constitutionalism, the Rule of Law and the First Certification Judgment, 13 (3) SOUTH AFRICAN JOURNAL ON HUMAN RIGHTS 430 ss (1997).

political transition and partly also the content of the new Constitution with the former Namibian liberation movements (*South West Africa People's Organisation* – Swapo) and with international actors: the UN, Canada, the US, Germany, France and the United Kingdom.[24] These countries (the so-called "Western Contact Group") started a multilateral negotiation with the South African government and the liberation movements in 1982, under the supervision of the UN. The result of such a multilateral negotiation led to the approval of a number of fundamental constitutional principles which had to be imperatively introduced in the Constitution. The procedural character of the Namibian constitution-making process was already laid down in UN Resolution no. 435/1978, through which the Security Council established a procedural path in order to reach and maintain peace between the parties and to conduct further constitutional negotiations. The 1982 principles crystallised some fundamental constitutional decisions, such as the elaboration of a Bill of Rights, the establishment of a constitutional Court, the safeguarding of property rights, preservation of judicial independence, and the guarantee of a multiparty political system.

The cases of South Africa and Namibia clearly demonstrate that procedural constitution-making (and constitution-building) can accommodate diverse and to some extent conflicting internal and external constraints and thus perfectly fits in the "comparativization" of solutions and procedures that marks the present era.

Another interesting example in this regard comes from the Polish constitutional transition, which lasted eight years. In a very unstable political context, the 1989 Round Table Talks (RTT) made it possible to reach agreements on the rules to be applied to the first semi-free elections and to negotiate some major amendments to the 1952 socialist Constitution. After that, a set of profound constitutional amendments was passed by the new *Sejm* in April and December 1989 in order to address the economical and political challenges posed by the transition from a communist to a liberal regime. Most of the *interim* constitutional amendments foreshadowed the new constitutional framework that was adopted only in 1997.[25] In particular, the "December amendments" changed the country's name from Polish People's Republic into Republic of Poland, abolished

---

[24] M. G. Erasmus, *The Impact of the Namibian Constitution on the nature of the State, its Politics and Society: the Record after ten years, in* The Constitution at Work. 10 Years of Namibian Nationhood 6 (M. Hinz, S. K. Amoo & D. Van Wyk ed., 2000); M. Wiechers, *Namibia: the 1982 Constitutional Principles and their Legal Significance, in* Ibid., 1 ss; J. Dugard, The South Africa/Namibia Dispute (1973); D. Van Wyk, *The Making of Namibian Constitution: Lessons for Africa*, 24 CILSA 341 ss (1991); G. J. Naldi, Constitutional Rights in Namibia (1995).

[25] M. Brzezinski, The Struggle for Constitutionalism in Poland (1998); D. H. Cole, *Poland's 1997 Constitution in Its Historical Context*, 1 St. Louise-Warsaw Transatlantic

the provisions on the leading role of the "Party", eliminated the clauses on the socialist economy, cancelled the constitutional mandate of political and military alliance with the Soviet Union and introduced forms of private ownership by providing the constitutional basis for a new market economy. Alongside the 1990 economic reforms, these amendments allowed Poland to start a deep post-socialist transformation.[26] Due to a political stalemate, in 1992 another substantial constitutional revision had to be approved. The so-called 1992 "Small Constitution" provided a deep change in the state power structure, aiming to achieve a more balanced relationship between the states powers. In 1992, President Walesa tried to introduce a "Charter of Rights and Freedoms" integrating the Small Constitution. However, the sudden dissolution of the *Sejm* by Walesa himself and the call for new elections made it impossible to adopt the Charter as the new Polish Bill of Rights.

As Mark Brzezinski pointed out, the organs constituted in previous regime such as the Ombudsman and the Constitutional Tribunal played a fundamental role during the constitutional transition. In particular the Constitutional Tribunal has been "instilling normative characteristics into Polish constitutionalism and developing constitutional doctrine in accordance with its understanding of the supra-positive principles of a state ruled by law".[27] In several judgements from 1990 onwards, the Constitutional Tribunal established progressively "independency of the judicial review as a fundamental character of Polish constitutionalism", enforced transitional clauses on separation of powers "preventing [for example] the *Sejm* from delegating to the President the power to remove regular court judges for political reasons",[28] reinforcing the *Rechtsstaat* clause of the Constitution (as amended in December 1989). The eight years constitution writing process came to an end in April 1997, when the National Assembly approved the draft Constitution. The Constitution was successively ratified by a popular referendum.

The trend of the proceduralised constitution-building process is partly visible in some other post-socialist constitutional transitions. Here the phenomenon of the RTTs needs to be taken into closer consideration.

Generally the RTTs were organs enabled to start the constitutional negotiation between the "former enemies". They made it possible to take two types of

---

Law Journal, 1 ss (1998); M. Wyrzykowski, *Le riforme costituzionali in Polonia*, 3 Quaderni Costituzionali 386 ss (1992).

26 R. Ludwikowski, Constitutional Culture of the New East-Central European Democracies, 29 Georgia Journal of International and Comparative Law 1, 2 ss (2000).

27 Brzezinski, *supra* note 25, 158.

28 *Ibidem*, 163. J. Elster, *Constitution Making in Eastern Europe: Rebuilding the Boat in the Open Sea, in* Il futuro della Costituzione 209 ss (G. Zagrebelsky, P. P. Portinaro & J. Luther eds., 1996).

constitutional decisions: (a) the establishment of new electoral laws, which in many circumstances deeply influenced the creation of the following constitutional assembly; (b) the revision of a large number of articles of the socialist constitutions. In many cases these revisions survived the following constitution-making processes, being incorporated into the new "democratic" texts.

It must be pointed out that the RTTs took place before the formal establishment of the constitutional assembly, thus widening the timing and the type of the decision-making procedure of the new constitutions. Essentially the RTT model has been widely experimented with in Poland, Bulgaria, Hungary, Czechoslovakia and East Germany.[29] It is important to note that fragmented constitution-making *procedures* have been a useful tool in order to come to terms with complicated political impasses. In particular, when agreements among different constituent actors have to be reached, the multiple-step procedure has generally been successful in establishing a convergence between originally antithetic positions: giving up radical positions and being ready for compromise (the foundations of constitution-making processes) often requires postponing critical decisions.

Two main comparative lessons can be learned from the mentioned examples. Firstly, the RTTs cannot be fully understood as isolated experiences. Both in Africa and in Central-Eastern Europe, there has undoubtedly been a circulation of comparative models. "Domino" effects, "imitation", as well as a largely similar configuration of the political transitions requiring to be dealt with throughout negotiated constitutional agreements, underscore common constitutional law trends. Secondly, several analogies can also be observed with regard to the content of the agreements provided by the RTTs: in all cases the outcome was an entrenched constitution, a guaranteed bill of rights and a broad judicial review, and this was also due to the fact that in all mentioned cases a deep comparative analysis was carried out with respect to both the procedural and the substantial aspect of constitution-making.

2. *New imposed constitutionalism and the model of transitional justice*

Another important factor common to several contemporary constitutional transitions is the phenomenon of *new imposed constitutionalism*. In the past decades, scholars elaborated the notion of *imposed constitutionalism*.[30] This was essentially referred to the German and Japanese constitution-making (and constitution-building) processes after WWII because of the massive involvement of allied forces in the decision-making on the new constitutional order. In the following years, the notion of imposed constitutionalism has been largely used in order

---

[29] See J. Elster, *supra* note 18, 455 ss.

[30] See N. Feldman, *Imposed Constitutionalism*, 37 Connecticut Law Review 857 ss (2005).

to describe the post-colonial constitution-making in Africa, where a direct or indirect involvement of the former colonial states in drafting post-colonial constitutional texts took place.[31]

Today the phenomenon of imposed constitutionalism is slightly changing. As in the past, some constitutional transitions take place after violent conflicts. But in more recent times, several transitions are being "guided" and "mediated" by the international organisations, through the involvement of foreign *puissances* or NGOs. Looking at the involvement of international organisations, the consequences of the intervention in post-conflict reconfiguration of the constitutional systems are different than in the past. The cases of Bosnia,[32] Kosovo,[33] East Timor,[34] Cambodia and Sierra Leone[35] are evocative examples of this trend. Interim or permanent constitutions of these countries have been drafted in post-conflict arenas under the formal control of UN-supported international peace-keeping and peace-building interventions. Military and political actors such as NATO, the United Nations, international NGOs as well as single foreign states exercised pressure, imposed time frames, and delivered technical and financial support in order to produce new constitutions.

The direct influence of international constitutional models, patterns and standards has been remarkable in shaping the way to deal with the so called *transitional justice*,[36] in organizing the constitution-making (and constitution-building) process itself, as well as in introducing international standards and models of organisation of state powers, thus intensively using the comparative method. In particular, as to the international role in establishing a transitional justice process, in all the mentioned countries the transitional agreements, the interim constitutional drafts, and the final constitutions embodied different forms of transitional retributive justice models. In particular, so-called "mixed tribunals" (composed by international judges appointed by the UN and selected national

[31] Ibid.

[32] J. Woelk, *Federalism and Consociationalism as Tools for State Reconstruction? The Case of Bosnia and Herzegovina*, in FEDERALISM, SUBNATIONAL CONSTITUTIONS, AND MINORITY RIGHTS 177 ss (A. Tarr. R. Williams & J. Marko eds., 2004). See also J. Marko, *Five Years of Constitutional Jurisprudence in Bosnia and Herzegovina: A First Balance* (No. 7/2004), *at* <www.eurac.edu/edap>.

[33] GORDISCHER KNOTEN KOSOVO/A: DURCHSCHLAGEN ODER ENTWIRREN? (J. Marko ed., 1999).

[34] R. GARRISON, THE ROLE OF CONSTITUTION-BUILDING PROCESSES IN DEMOCRATISATION. CASE STUDY: EAST TIMOR, INTERNATIONAL INSTITUTE FOR DEMOCRACY AND ELECTORAL ASSISTANCE (2005).

[35] A. ADEBAID, BUILDING PEACE IN WEST AFRICA: LIBERIA, SIERRA LEONE AND GUINEA BISSAU (2002); A. BUNDU, DEMOCRACY BY FORCE? A STUDY OF INTERNATIONAL MILITARY INTERVENTION IN THE CIVIL WAR IN SIERRA LEONE FROM 1991–2000 (2001).

[36] See for the concept L. Bickford, *Transitional Justice, in* THE ENCYCLOPEDIA OF GENOCIDE AND CRIMES AGAINST HUMANITY (vol. 3) 1045 ss (D. Shelton ed., 2004).

judges)[37] have been established in the mentioned countries, although each tribunal or special court adopted different structures and procedures. Common elements, however, are the mixed composition and the retributive approach, enforcing the international principle of the "duty to prosecute" international crimes.[38] Whereas in many transitional experiences alternative models of conflict resolution (such as the Truth Commissions models) have been experimented with, in post-conflict areas that experienced a UN intervention retributive systems have been chosen:[39] Even if in East Timor and Sierra Leone Truth Commissions have been established together with the UN-sponsored special courts, the retributive system has been dominant.

By dealing with the crimes committed by previous regimes and by enforcing judicial machineries of truth recovery, sensitive political and social elements such as the notion of collective memory of the past can be influenced deeply. The "truth" and the "memory" of the past become, inevitably, the substantial platform on which the new democratic constitutional systems can be created. In this perspective, transitional justice is also perceived as a "tool" for the de-legitimisation of former criminal governments, oligarchies and political forces

---

[37] A. Lollini, *La giustizia di transizione: il principio del duty to prosecute come una nuova variabile di eterodeterminazione dei processi costituenti?, in* Guerre e minoranze 323 ss (G. Gozzi & F. Martelli eds., 2004).

[38] New Approaches in International Criminal Justice: Kosovo, East Timor, Sierra Leone & Cambodia (K. Ambos & O. Mohamed eds., 2003); D. Boyle, *Quelle justice pour les Khmers rouges?*, 40 Revue trimestrielle des droits de l'homme 773 (1999); S. Linton, *Cambodia, East Timor and Sierra Leone: Experiments in International Justice*, 12 Criminal Law Forum 185 (2001); D. Boyle, *Establishing the Responsibility of the Khmer Rouge Leadership for International Crimes, in* Yearbook of International Humanitarian Law, Vol. V, 167 ss (A. McDonald ed., 2002); A. J. Buckley, *The Conflict in Cambodia and Post-Conflict Justice, in* Post-Conflict Justice 635 (C. Bassiouni ed., 2002); M. J. Matheson, *United Nations Governance of Post-Conflict Societies: East Timor and Kosovo, in* Id., 523; H. Strohmeyer, *Collapse and Reconstruction of a Judicial System: the United Nations Missions in Kosovo and East Timor*, 95 American Journal of International Law 46 (2001); Id., *Building a New Judiciary for East Timor. Challenges of a Fledgling Nation*, 11 Criminal Law Forum 259 (2000). See also Transitional Justice. How Emerging Democracies Reckon with Former Regimes (N. J. Kritz ed., 1995); J. Zalaquett, *Balancing Ethical Imperatives and Political Constraints: The Dilemma of a New Democracies Confrontating Past Human Rights Violations*, Hastings Law Journal 1425 (1992); R. Siegel, *Transitional Justice: A Decade of Debate and Experience*, in: 20 Human Rights Quarterly 433 (1998); L. Huyse, *Justice after Transition: On the Choices Successor Elites Make in Dealing with the Past, in* International Criminal Law and procedure 51 (J. Dugart & J. Van Wyngaert eds., 1999); M. Smiley, *Democratic Justice in Transition*, 99 Michigan Law Review 1332 (2000).

[39] See for example *Agreement Between the United Nations and Royal Government of Cambodia Concerning the Prosecutions under Cambodian Law of Crimes Committed During the Period of Democratic Kampuches*, June 2003; Matheson, *supra* note 38, 523; A. J. M. Mc Donald, *Sierra Leone's Uneasy Peace: The Amnesties Granted in the Lomé Peace Agreement and the United Nation's Dilemma*, 13 Humanitäres Völkerrecht 11 (2000).

responsible for the conflicts. In other words, transitional justice is perceived as a key element of the post-conflict constitutional transitions. Its enforcement implies (a) the control over the solidification of some "material" elements of the post-conflict democracies; (b) the reconfiguration of the unity of political bodies fragmented by the previous conflicts; and (c) the de-legitimisation of former political forces and the contextual legitimisation of new ones. It thus seems fair to say that through the "imposition" of transitional justice retributive systems, a new "soft" form of "imposed" constitutionalism is implemented.

"Alien" influence on constitution-making processes has taken place, in the last decade, throughout more "classical" expedients. Over the last decade, external influence on constitution-making processes has often been exercised with the assistance of internationally controlled transitional authorities, such as in Kosovo,[40] in East Timor and in Cambodia. International forces sponsored more or less representative political bodies empowered to draft the new constitutions (generally under tight time constrains), largely inspired constitutional structures and substantial rights as well as administrative transitional body ruled by (or with considerable assistance of) international organisations.

The case of Timor is an evocative example of this international influence over the constitution-making process. When Indonesia left East Timor after the victory of independentist forces in the 1999 referendum, Indonesian militias were responsible for horrible crimes following the atrocities committed during the years of Indonesian control over Timor. With Security Council Resolution no. 1272, the UN decided to establish the United Nation Transitional Administration in East Timor (UNTAET). Despite of the concrete need for international intervention due to the dramatic situation of the country after the departure of Indonesian forces, the UN mission assumed the formal and practical control of a peace-keeping intervention, thus marginalizing autochthons organisations, despite of the presence of East Timorese organised political forces (such as the *Concelho*

[40] When Kosovo authorities unilaterally declared independence in February 2008, the process for the adoption of the new Constitution was particularly speedy and at first glance it was conducted without international involvement: a constitutional commission was formed, the text was drafted in less than two months, was subsequently approved by the Assembly and promulgated by the President and it entered into force on June 15, 2008. However, the case of Kosovo is an outstanding example of the modern trend of constitution-making processes based on international and comparative guidance. In fact, the constitution was largely based (particularly on issues such as the protection of minority rights) on the international plan known as "Ahtisaari plan" (after the name of the Special Envoy of the UN Secretary-General on Kosovo's future status) as well as on the Constitutional Framework adopted by the UN mission (UNMIK) in 2001, and so was the composition of the constitutional commission. Moreover, the Constitution was certified in April 2008 by the International Civilian Representative. Finally, the procedure for the adoption of the Constitution after the unilateral declaration of independence was just the final stage of a much longer process that *de facto* begun when Kosovo was put under UN administration in 1999.

Nacional da Resistancia Timorense) that were ready to cooperate in the constitution-building process. The reason was that in peace-keeping operations the UN had to be careful not to side with any of the "factions" until the establishment of political structures that were acceptable to "both" sides. The problem was that the "side" responsible for the conflict was not in the country anymore. As a consequence, until the establishment of the Constitutional Assembly in August 2001, all National Consultative Councils were under control of the UNTAET (and its Chairman Sergio Vieira Mello) and vested with very limited powers of intervention and with no veto power over UNTAET decisions.[41] In this context the timetable for the constitution-making process in East Timor had to be decided under UN control and within a very tight deadline. The constitution had to be drafted by the Constitutional Assembly within 90 days from its election. More "progressive" and articulated constitution-making processes, based on idea of interim constitutions with middle term power-shared government proposed by the NGO Forum, were rejected.

The Constitutional Assembly elections produced a clear victory of the *Fretilin* Party. The Assembly immediately started the drafting procedure and public consultation process. The original timetable was ultimately extended by the Constitutional Assembly to seven months. Only 15 months elapsed from the debate on the timetable to the adoption of the Constitution by the Constitutional Assembly in March 2002. The Constitution was finally approved on March 22, 2002.

IV. *Back to simplification and constitutional failures: the EU, Afghanistan and Iraq*

In contemporary constitutionalism one can observe the spreading of a procedural method in constitution-making and constitution-building. As the mentioned examples show, the shift towards such a procedural way for the adoption of new constitutions is largely conditioned by comparative imitation and international imposition. It might thus be argued that procedural rules comply better with the requirement of pluralism, which is the core of contemporary constitutionalism. In simple words, a procedural constitution-building seems to better accommodate the fundamental constitutional requirement of pluralism in the process of drafting a new constitution.

This seems to be confirmed *a contrariis* by three recent examples where to some extent a more traditional process of constitution-building has been tried, with rather unsatisfactory results. Provocatively, the experiences of the EU, of

---

[41] See Garrison, *supra* note 34, 11; L. Appicciafuoco, *Timor Est: processo costituente e transizione verso la democrazia*, Diritto pubblico comparato ed Europeo, Vol. II, 516 (2002).

Afghanistan and of Iraq will be analysed together albeit the immense difference among them, because in all these cases the attempt was made to elaborate a constitution by means of a "less procedural" process. Of course, to a great extent all three constitution-making processes can and must be seen as a long-run process; especially the case of the EU that represents *the* landmark example of a constitution-building through stratification of constitutional moments and fragmentation of the constitution-making process. However, the unsuccessful last step, the failure of the attempt to reach a "constitutional big bang" by means of the Treaty establishing a constitution for Europe (and to some extent even the stalemate provoked by the Irish "no" to its "light" successor, the Lisbon Treaty), seems to be evidence that this last step was not in line with the pluralistic, comparative and procedural process that marked the constitutional evolution of the EU until then, thus failing due to an excessive simplification that modern constitutionalism can no longer accept.

The provocative joint analysis of the constitutional processes in the EU, in Afghanistan and in Iraq seems to confirm our hypothesis for two main reasons. First, all these recent cases can not be labelled as only political constitution-making processes. On the contrary, they all present a large set of elements that are common to the modern constitutional processes: plural legitimacy (at least compared to previous regimes), multi-phase constitution-making, a certain degree of proceduralization in drafting and in adopting the text. All this testifies that these elements are unavoidable in contemporary processes of constitution-making. Second, even if constitution-making was somehow successful in all cases, the constitution-building failed. Among the reasons for that, the excessive stress of the political, sovereignty-oriented constitutional process might also have played a role, showing that the nostalgia for simplistic processes of constitution adoption might be counter-productive.

1. *The European Union: A Permanent Constitution-Building?*

The issue of the constitutionalization of the EU is the source of a never-ending debate among lawyers. Supporters of a more formalistic view, according to which the EU is still an international organization regulated by "normal" international treaties, tend to deny the possible existence of a European constitution, due to the lack of the formal and substantial elements of a constitution: people and sovereignty. Supporters of a substantive view, on the contrary, maintain that the EU already has a constitution in functional terms. The two approaches are mirrored in two well known judicial decisions: the so called *Maastricht*-decision of the German federal constitutional court[42] and the *Les Verts* case of the Euro-

[42] BVerfGE 89, 155 (1993). The court expressly pointed out that without a State there cannot be a constitution, and without a people there cannot be a State.

pean Court of Justice (ECJ).[43] In any event, it is undisputed that the EU has a constitutional law even without a formal constitution, and that the relationship between domestic and European law needs to be read in constitutional terms.

For the purposes of this essay, suffice here to say that the EU constitution-building process is perhaps the most significant and self-evident demonstration of the points to be made. First, constitution-building is clearly separated from any sort of state and nation-building. Second, it is being realized through a series of (legally and logically) connected acts and facts of constitutional relevance[44] over a long period of time. The interconnection of all these many constitutional moments make it impossible to tell when the constitutionalization has started and whether it has ended, and this gives rise to endless debates between those who support the idea that a constitution has already been established and those who support the opposite view. Third, this process is creating a stratification of constitutionally relevant acts (particularly through the case-law of the courts) which functionally substitute formal moments of constitutional "big-bang". Fourth, and more important for our purposes, the evolution of EU constitutional law is intimately linked to the comparative method. It can be argued that EU constitutional law is nothing but comparative constitutional law, as implicitly or explicitly affirmed first by the ECJ (elaborating the very comparative concept of the common constitutional traditions),[45] and subsequently also in the Treaties:

---

[43] ECJ, 23–4–1986, case 294/83, *Parti ecologiste "Les Verts"*, ECR, 1339, where the court defined the European Community as "a community based on the rule of law, inasmuch as neither its member States nor its institutions can avoid a review of the question whether the measures adopted by them are in conformity with the *basic constitutional charter, the Treaty*" (at 23, emphasis added).

[44] Besides the founding treaties, in the last two decades there has been a spill-over of constitutional documents, adopted at an ever closer time distance: from the Single European Act (1986) to the treaties of Maastricht (1992), Amsterdam (1997) and Nice (2000), the Charter of fundamental rights of the EU (2000) the Treaty establishing a Constitution for Europe (2004) and the Lisbon Treaty (2007). These constitutional developments have been followed by significant constitutional amendments in almost all Member States.

[45] Beginning with the landmark fundamental rights decisions in *Stauder v. City of Ulm* (ECJ, 12–11–1969, case C-29/69, ECR, 419) and *Internationale Handelsgesellschaft* (ECJ, 17–12–1970, case C-11/70, ECR, 1125), For a clear exposition of the reasoning see ECJ, 21–9–1989, joined cases 46/87 and 227/88, *Hoechst AG v. Commission*, ECR 2859. As to other fields of law where the ECJ has drawn comparative inspiration on the common constitutional traditions see among others the following leading cases: ECJ, 14–12–1965, *Morina v. Parliament*, case 11/65, ECR 1357, ECJ, 17–5–1973, *Pericolo v. Council*, case 58, 75/72, ECR, 511, ECJ 13–2–1979, *Granaria*, case 101/78, ECR 623, ECJ, 28.4.1979, *Lütticke v. Commission*, case 4/69, ECR 339, ECJ, 15–6–1976, *Mills*, case 110/75, ECJ 977, ECJ, 7–6–1972, *Sabbatini*, case 20/71, ECR 345, ECJ, 7–6–1972, *Bauduin*, case 32/71, ECR 363, ECJ, 30–1–1974, *Louwage*, case 148/73, ECR 81, ECJ, 12–7–1957, *Algéra*, case 7/56, ECR 83, ECJ, 4–7–1963, *Alvis*, case 32/62, ECR 107, ECJ, 3–3–1971, *Riva*, case 2/70, ECR 97, ECJ, 24–10–1973, *Balkan-Import-Export*, case 5/73, ECR 1091.

in particular, article 6.2 of the Treaty establishing the European Union (TEU) recognizes the international and comparative method of the constitution-building in the EU, by stating that the Union, founded on principles that are common to the Member States (art. 6.1. TEU), shall draw its protection of fundamental rights from the European Convention on Human Rights and other international instruments as well as "from the constitutional traditions common to the Member States, as general principles of Community law".

A recent attempt to unify the constitutional documents by (trying to) establish a clearer constitutional "big-bang" through the adoption of the constitutional treaty (Treaty establishing a Constitution for Europe) has failed after its rejection by the voters in France and the Netherlands in 2005, regardless of the fact that it has been drafted by a pluralistic body, the Convention for the future of Europe (which was at least much more pluralistic than the Inter-Governmental Conference, the ordinary Treaty-amending organ). Following the debacle of the constitutional treaty, a new and less ambitious attempt was made in order to merge the existing treaties, to adopt the Charter of Fundamental Rights and to give legal personality to the EU, by means of the Lisbon Treaty, adopted in December 2007 and carefully avoiding the term "constitution". Nevertheless, and regardless of its ratification by the vast majority of the Member States, the ratification Treaty has not been approved in the referendum held in Ireland in June 2008.[46]

This seems to confirm that constitution-building in the European Union is an intimately pluralistic phenomenon[47] that cannot stand an excess of simplification (particularly coming to the fore in referendums on the ratification) and top-down, political imposition. The comparative nature of the process requires a degree of complexity (in terms of procedures, time-frames, involved actors) that cannot be reduced to a traditional, simplistic process of approval. At least for the time being, constitution-building in the EU will have to remain a pluralistic, procedural, step-by step, multi-layered process. The case of the EU is, of course, an extreme example of the new, comparative method in constitution-building, but precisely for this reason it is particularly telling with regards to contemporary trends and evolutions. If our hypothesis is correct, the attempt to make a political, final step in the constitution-making process, represented by the adoption of the constitutional treaty, has failed not because of the lack of the political momentum but rather due to the opposite reason: too much

---

[46] Amendments to the Treaties require ratification by all Member States. On the ratification procedures see The European Constitution and National Constitutions: Ratifications and Beyond (A. Albi & J. Ziller eds., 2007).

[47] See on that also M. Dani & F. Palermo, *Towards An Ever More Complex Union: An Epilogue, in* An Ever More Complex Union 313 (R. Toniatti, F. Palermo & M. Dani eds., 2004).

of a political step, symbolized by a (quasi)-traditional constitution-making, is not compatible with the most prominent example of modern constitution-building tendencies, consisting in the plurality of actors, a diluted time frame, and complex procedural constraints. In other words, the most recent stages in the European constitution-making process, while largely prepared following the pluralistic openness of contemporary constitutionalism (particularly due to the establishment of two "conventions" that drafted the Charter of Fundamental Rights and the Constitutional Treaty respectively), failed precisely in the moment when pluralism ended: the requirement for an oversimplified, political-only final step in the ratification process impairs the pluralistic and process-oriented foundations of the constitution-making at the European level.

2. *Afghanistan and Iraq: too little attention to the comparative achievements?*

The recent constitution-making processes in Afghanistan and Iraq might serve as additional examples of this trend. As already mentioned, in both cases several key-elements of the contemporary, procedural constitution-making have been followed: the drafting of both constitutions took place in different steps and interim texts were adopted, the legitimacy of the constituent assemblies was much broader than it was during the previous regimes, and the processes that led to the approval of the constitutions were at least to some extent regulated by procedural rules, generally implying democratic elections.

However, in the end of the process the classical, political method emerged, the constitutions were adopted without sufficient involvement of the (political, ethnic, religious) minorities and constitution-building was left to the merely majoritarian, political/electoral process. This might be one of the reasons why the implementation of the recent constitutions is so difficult. Moreover, both constitution-making processes have been carried out in a quasi "mechanical" way, and this raises questions about the awareness of the political bodies about the constitutional *enjeux*.

The post-Taliban constitutional transition in Afghanistan has been divided in some constitutional steps implemented in a short time frame. The extremely problematic political and social situation of the country would have called for a much more articulated procedure, but the constitution-making process has been widely inspired by the "classical" method of constitution writing. The constitution has been perceived as a legal text adopted by a political body (more or less representative) and not as a document drafted through negotiated procedures among different social and political actors. The first Afghan constitutional step has been represented by the "Bonn agreements" signed in December 2001 during the UN-sponsored talks in Germany in which the Northern Alliance commanders also took part, as well as Afghan military factions and Afghan delegates. The agreements established an *Interim Authority* to rule the country in the aftermath of the military intervention. The Pasthun anti-Taliban leader Hamid Karzai became Chairman of the Interim Authority.[48] The two additional pre-constitutional steps were first made in June 2002, when the *Emergency Loya Jirga* established the *Transitional Authority of Afghanistan*, and second in 2004, when a "fully representative government" was formed after free elections. The agreements also stipulated that the new constitution would be adopted by the *Loya Jirga* (the Grand Council) within 18 months after the establishment of the Interim Authority.

It is important to note that the Bonn agreements provided for a non-elected Constitutional Commission enabled to draft a new constitutional text to be submitted to the *Constitutional Loya Jirga* (CLJ) which was planned to be convened in October 2003. In April 2003, President Karzai appointed the nine members of the Constitutional Drafting Commission as well as 35 members of the Constitutional Review Commission empowered to control the adoption of the new text by the *Constitutional Loya Jirga*.[49] The UN provided all technical and financial support for the whole constitution-making process. In July 2003, President Karzai issued a decree on the convening of the CLJ. That decree stipulated that CLJ would be composed by 500 delegates, 344 of which elected by the district representatives. Fifty delegates had to be appointed by the President of the Loya Jirga. In November 2003, the Constitutional Commission released the final draft of the proposed constitution. In a very short time frame, the last segment of the constitution-making process was started. In December 2003, the *Loya Jirga* was convened in Kabul in order to discuss and ratify the proposed draft. As a "constitutional *fiat lux*" the new text was suddenly presented to the public in early November 2003 by the Constitutional Commission. The *Loya Jirga* ratified the new Constitution on January 4, 2004. The constitution represents a compromise between Islamic hardliners and moderate reformists; the text does not include an explicit reference to the *Sharia* on the assertion that no Afghan law could be contrary to the beliefs and provisions of Islam.

Many commentators noted that the post-Taliban constitutional project is far from being satisfactory, due to a variety of reasons. The extremely problematic social, political and economical background made it difficult to write the new Constitution, and poses enormous difficulties to the effectiveness of the text. However, even if the new constitution-making process has been a remarkable step forward in terms of democratic involvement compared to the five past Afghan

---

[48] See H. Tavis, *Freedom or Theocracy? Constitutionalism in Afghanistan and Iraq*, 3 Northwestern University Journal of International Human Rights 4 (2005).

[49] C. Schneider, *The International Community and Afghanistan's Constitution*, 7 Peace, Conflict and Development: an Interdisciplinary Journal (2005), *at* <http://www.peacestudiesjournal.org.uk>.

constitutions, many political decisions weakened the idea of finding a constitutional common ground. In this perspective, the adopted constitution-making process, profoundly influenced by international actors and encapsulated within very tight deadlines,[50] was too short and somehow "mechanic", and thus unfit to comply with the complexity of the social, political and religious issues to be addressed. This seems to be confirmed by the fact that, despite UN efforts to set up public consultation processes, most of the rural Afghans never heard of the constitutional process and the new text is totally unknown to them.

The Iraqi constitution-making process has been even more controversial.[51] Like in Afghanistan, the extremely complicated and dramatic political background has been coped with by means of an internationally-run constitutional engineering[52] process that only superficially influenced the Iraqi political body.

In April 2003, in the aftermath of the war, a Coalition Provisional Authority (CPA) was established as a temporary administration for Iraq under the formal control of United States, the United Kingdom and Ireland. The UN Security Council Resolution no. 1483/2003 formalised this *de facto* situation empowering the CPA as administrative authority in the country. Ambassador Paul Bremer war named CPA's Chairman on May 6, 2003. On July 13, 2003, with the consent of the CPA occupying powers, an Iraqi Governing Council (IGC) was established. The Council represented the first step towards the transfer of powers from the international authority to an Iraqi representative institution. After a period of co-administration of the two authorities, in November 2003 an agreement was reached between the CPA and IGC in order to recognise a new transitional administration to take control over Iraq. Furthermore, a few weeks before the agreement, a new UN Security Council Resolution was adopted.[53] The UN Resolution welcomed "the decision of the Governing Council of Iraq to form a preparatory Constitutional Committee to prepare for a Constitutional Conference that will draft a Constitution to embody the aspirations of the Iraqi people and *[urges] it to complete this process quickly*" [emphasis added]. The Iraqi Governing Council, still a non-elected body, promulgated the so-called Transitional Administrative Law (TAL) on March 8, 2004. This text, broadly perceived as an Interim Constitution, was in fact approved by the GCI some weeks before, in February 2004. It lays down several constitutional principles establishing

---

[50] See Feldman, *supra* note 30, 858.

[51] See M. Lattimer, *Minority Participation and New Constitutional Law*, 12 International Journal on Minority and Group Rights 227, 234 ss (2005).

[52] On the notion of "constitutional engineering" see G. Sartori, Comparative Constitutional Engineering. An Inquiry into Structures, Incentives and Outcomes (1994); Public International Law & Policy Group and The Century Foundation, *Establishing a Stable Democracy Structure in Iraq: Some Basic Considerations*, 39 New England Law Review, 53 (2004).

[53] UN Security Council Resolution 1511/2003.

that Iraq will be a republican federal democracy (art. 4), that Islam will be the religion of the state (art. 7), and that fundamental rights will be protected (Chapter II, art. 10–23). Article 30 provided for a tight deadline concerning the election of a representative National Assembly (between December 2004 and January 2005), the drafting of a new Constitution, as well as the controversial provision of article 61 concerning the general referendum for its adoption. The most debated provision was that of article 61(d), according to which "the general referendum will be successful and the draft of the Constitution ratified if a majority of the voters approve and if two-thirds of the voters in the three or more governorates do not reject".[54]

Following the general election of January 30, 2005, the newly elected Transitional National Assembly has been empowered, under article 60 of the Transitional Administrative Law, to draft a new constitutional text. The new Transitional Government, chaired by Ibrahim Jaafari, started its office in April 2005. Only five months later, a constitutional draft was submitted to a general referendum and it was eventually approved. Under the new Constitution, in December 2005, general elections were called and a new Parliament was elected.

The recent constitution-making processes in Afghanistan and Iraq were governed by tight deadlines. Like in other post-conflict experiences, the draft constitutions have been written by a relatively small group of people with limited transparency, participation and consensus-building strategies. Consequently, several perplexities arose on the issues of national unity, stability and consensus: an even more serious problem in countries fragmented in ethnic and religious cleavages and perturbed by extremist forces.

Even considering the dramatic political background, the Iraqi and Afghani constitution-making processes may be seen more as a necessity than as an opportunity. Both processes have been started and guided by external time constraints, an overall goal that in the end was prevailing over internal requirements. It is too early to assess the outcomes of both experiences. However, the chosen types of constitution-making seem to be characterised by a sort of "mechanical" approach, typical for classical ideas based on the notion of constituent power exercised by a more or less representative political body in a delimited time.

---

[54] United States Institute of Peace, Iraq's Constitutional Process: Shaping a Vision for the Country's Future, Special Report no. 132 (Feb. 2005).

V. *Concluding Remarks*

Two main hypotheses are at the heart of this paper. First, recent constitution-making and even more the subsequent constitution-building processes have been and still are undergoing profound changes. Despite their apparently profound differences, the modern constitution-building processes share a common trend towards pluralism, which in legal terms means proceduralization of the adoption of the constitution. Therefore, the very nature of the process of adopting a constitution is becoming a legal phenomenon which can no longer be neglected by the legal analysis. Second, the comparative method plays a twofold role in this trend. On the one hand, it influences procedures and solutions adopted in the course of the most recent constitutional wave; on the other hand, it provides interpretative tools to systematically understand the process of mutual interdependence of constitution-building.

As to the first achievement of the analysis, the development of ever more sophisticated procedures to deal with the creation of a constitution is the consequence of several factors, in particular of the complexity of modern society, of the interconnection of legal solutions and, not least, of the insufficiency of the political process to cope with all these aspects. Therefore, particularly in highly conflictive societies, procedures represent the most reliable guarantee in order to safeguard the involvement of different, sometimes even incompatible actors in the process of the adoption of shared basic rules, by guaranteeing and implementing from the very beginning the basic principle according to which constitution-building cannot be a matter for political majorities and has to include (past, present or future) minorities. Also for international actors, more and more involved (to an obviously different extent) in drafting new constitutions, procedures represent the best guarantee that the new principles are gradually accepted and incorporated by all the social strands. Instead of imposing radical and homogeneous solutions without considering their impact on very different social contexts, the procedural method, together with fragmentation of the constitution-making and its dilution over a relatively long period of time, makes it likely that constitutions can really be "built" (thus accepted by the society) instead of simply "made" (thus often limited to political elites). Again, this is not at all a novelty, but rather an evolution of the rule of law, which to some extent is the rule of procedures. It is the plurality of actors that makes it necessary to adopt legal rules on the adoption of legal rules.

As to the role of the comparative method, it helps identify the ongoing shift from a mere constitution-making (political) process to a more complex constitution-building (pluralistic) procedure. Comparative law is not normative, but rather an interpretative method. It makes visible what the mere analysis of single cases leaves undiscovered. In addition, comparative law is the methodological foundation that can connect solutions and best practices, and it is therefore *the* interpretative method of today's interconnected world. For the purposes of this paper, it must be emphasized that the best practice comparatively developed regarding constitution-building processes is the process itself, or, rather, the procedure. Precisely because the transplant of substantive solutions has proven to be unsuccessful, it is now the procedure that constitutes the common ground for the circulation of models and best practices.

List of Authors

Roberta Arnold, former legal adviser in the Section on the Laws of Armed Conflict of the Swiss Armed Forces at the Federal Defence Department, is candidate military investigating magistrate, holding the rank of legal officer, within the Swiss Military Justice. She has written her Ph.D. thesis on *The ICC as a new instrument for repressing terrorism*. She is editor of several books on international humanitarian law and peacekeeping law.

David Chandler is Professor of International Relations at the Centre for the Study of Democracy (CSD) at Westminster University. He is the author of a number of books including *Empire in Denial: The Politics of State-building* (2006) and is the founding editor of the *Journal of Intervention and Statebuilding*.

Fairlie Chappuis is a Research Assistant at the Geneva Centre for the Democratic Control of Armed Forces (DCAF). Her work focuses on security sector governance and reform especially in West Africa. She holds graduate degrees in Security Studies (Geneva Graduate Institute of International and Development Studies) as well as Political Studies and Philosophy (University of Auckland, New Zealand).

Hilary Charlesworth is an Australian Research Council Federation Fellow and Director of the Centre for International Governance and Justice at the Australian National University (ANU). She also holds an appointment as Professor of International Law and Human Rights in the College of Law, ANU. She was Co-Editor of the *Australian Yearbook of International Law* 1996–2006 and is a member of the Board of Editors of the *American Journal of International Law*.

Simon Chesterman is Global Professor and Director of the New York University School of Law Singapore Programme, and an Associate Professor of Law at the National University of Singapore Faculty of Law. From 2004 to 2006 he was Executive Director of NYU's Institute for International Law and Justice, of which he remains a senior fellow.

Charles H. B. Garraway, former Stockton Professor at the Naval War College, Newport, is a Visiting Professor at King's College, London. A former military legal officer, he is an Associate Fellow at Chatham House, a Visiting Fellow at the Human Rights Centre, University of Essex and a Member of the International Humanitarian Fact Finding Commission.

Marlies Glasius is a Research Fellow at the Centre for the Study of Global Governance (London School of Economics) and a Lecturer at LSE's Government Department. She is also Lecturer in International Relations at the University of Amsterdam. In 2003–2004 she was coordinator of the Study Group on Europe's Security, and from 2000–2003 she was the first managing editor of the *Global Civil Society Yearbook*, of which she continues to be an editor.

Heiner Hänggi is Assistant Director and Head of Research at the Geneva Centre for the Democratic Control of Armed Forces (DCAF). He is also an Associate Professor of Political Science at the University of St. Gallen (Switzerland) and an Associate Fellow at the Geneva Centre for Security Policy (GCSP). His recent research and publications focus on the concepts of security sector reform and security governance in post-conflict peacebuilding.

Monika Heupel is a Research Associate at the Center for Transnational Relations, Foreign and Security Policy (Free University Berlin). From 2005 to 2008 she was a Post-Doc Fellow at the United Nations University, Tokyo, the Carnegie Endowment for International Peace, Washington D.C., and the German Institute for International and Security Affairs, Berlin. She holds a Ph.D. from the University of Bremen, Germany, and a MA from the University of Warwick, UK.

Denisa Kostovicova is a Lecturer in Global Politics at the Government Department and a Research Associate at the Centre for the Study of Global Governance, London School of Economics and Political Science. She held Junior Research Fellowships at Wolfson College, Cambridge, and Linacre College, Oxford. Her research interests include nationalism and democratisation in a global age, post-conflict reconstruction and security, and European integration of the Western Balkans.

Andrea Lollini is Lecturer in Comparative Constitutional Law at the Political Sciences Faculty of University of Bologna (Italy). She is also Research Fellow at the Institut des Hautes Etudes sur la Justice of Paris.

Ann C. Mason holds a Ph.D. in Political Science from Yale University and is currently Executive Director of Fulbright Colombia. She was Professor at the Political Science Department at the Universidad de los Andes in Bogotá from 1997–2005, and Department Chair during the last four years. Her research interests focus on the state and security in Colombia and the Andean Region.

Kerstin Odendahl is Professor of Public International Law and European Law at the University of St. Gallen (Switzerland). She has written her Habilitation thesis on the protection of cultural property. She was Visiting Professor at the University of Paris I, Panthéon-Sorbonne (France), at the Georgetown University Law Center in Washington D.C. (USA) and at the University of Oviedo (Spain).

Francesco Palermo is Associate Professor at the University of Verona School of Law, Director of the Institute for Studies on Federalism and Regionalism at the European Academy in Bolzano/Bozen and Adjunct Professor at the Vermont Law School. He is currently Senior Legal Adviser to the OSCE High Commissioner on National Minorities.

Mayte Peters is working on her Ph.D. thesis in International Relations at the University of St. Gallen (Switzerland), focusing on the significance of culture in the process of European integration.

Julia Raue has written her Ph.D. thesis on the Council of Europe's impact on constitutional developments in Eastern Europe. Since 2003, she works at the United Nations Office of the High Commissioner for Human Rights where she currently supports the United Nations Special Rapporteur on the independence of judges and lawyers. She is also Lecturer in international human rights law at the University of St. Gallen (Switzerland).

William Reno is Associate Professor at Northwestern University. He is a specialist in African politics and the politics of "collapsing states." His research focuses on the organization and behaviour of non-state armed groups and their relations with global actors. He holds a Ph.D. in Political Science from the University of Wisconsin.

Kai Spiekermann is Assistant Professor at The University of Warwick, Department of Philosophy. He studied international relations and philosophy in St. Gallen (Switzerland) and Konstanz (Germany), and took his Ph.D. at the London School of Economics and Political Science. His research is concerned with issues at the intersection of philosophy, politics, and economics, in particular social norms, cooperation, complex social systems, and theories of rationality.

Patrick Sutter, Ph.D. in Law (University of St. Gallen, Switzerland), Partner of Kessler Wassmer Giacomini & Partner, attorneys-at-law, in Schwyz, and Lecturer in Public Law at the University of Zurich (Switzerland), is founding co-editor of the Journal *Sicherheit & Recht / Sécurité & Droit* and Legal Expert in the Staff of the Head of the Swiss Army.

Index

Legal Aspects of International Organization

1. S. Rosenne, *Procedure in the International Court.* A Commentary on the 1978 Rules of the International Court of Justice. 1983 ISBN 90-247-3045-7
2. T.O. Elias, *The International Court of Justice and Some Contemporary Problems.* Essays on International Law. 1983 ISBN 90-247-2791-X
3. I. Hussain, *Dissenting and Separate Opinions at the World Court.* 1984 ISBN 90-247-2920-3
4. J.B. Elkind, *Non-Appearance before the International Court of Justice.* Functional and Comparative Analysis. 1984 ISBN 90-247-2921-1
5. E. Osieke, *Constitutional Law and Practice in the International Labour Organisation.* 1985 ISBN 90-247-2985-8
6. O. Long, *Law and Its Limitations in the GATT Multilateral Trade System.* 1985 ISBN 90-247-3189-5; Pb: 0-86010-959-3
7. E. McWhinney, *The International Court of Justice and the Western Tradition of International Law.* The Paul Martin Lectures in International Relations and Law. 1987 ISBN 90-247-3524-6
8. R. Sonnenfeld, *Resolutions of the United Nations Security Council.* 1988 ISBN-90-247-3567-X
9. T.D. Gill, *Litigation Strategy at the International Court.* A Case Study of the Nicaragua versus United States Dispute. 1989 ISBN 0-7923-0332-6
10. S. Rosenne, *The World Court.* What It is and how It works. 4th revised ed. Prepared with the assistance of T.D. Gill. 1989 *For the 5th revised ed., see below Volume 16*
11. V. Gowlland-Debbas, *Collective Responses to Illegal Acts in International Law.* United Nations Action in the Question of Southern Rhodesia. 1990 ISBN 0-7923-0811-5
12. Y. Beigbeder, *The Role and Status of International Humanitarian Volunteers and Organizations.* The Right and Duty to Humanitarian Assistance. 1991 ISBN 0-7923-1190-6
13. A.B. Avanessian, *The Iran-United States Claims Tribunal in Action.* 1993 (also published in *International Arbitration Law Library*) ISBN 1-85333-902-4
14. R. Szafarz, *The Compulsory Jurisdiction of the International Court of Justice.* 1993 ISBN 0-7923-1989-3
15. Y.Z. Blum, *Eroding the United Nations Charter.* 1993 ISBN 0-7923-2069-7
16. S. Rosenne, *The World Court.* What It is and how It works. 5th revised ed. 1994 ISBN 0-7923-2861-2
17. P.H.F. Bekker, *The Legal Position of Intergovernmental Organizations.* A Functional Necessity Analysis of Their Legal Status and Immunities. 1994 ISBN 0-7923-2904-X
18. S.A. Voitovich, *International Economic Organizations in the International Legal Process.* 1994 ISBN 0-7923-2766-7
19. S.A. Alexandrov, *Reservations in Unilateral Declarations Accepting the Compulsory Jurisdiction of the International Court of Justice.* 1995 ISBN 0-7923-3145-1
20. M. Hirsch, *The Responsibility of International Organizations Toward Third Parties.* Some Basic Principles. 1995 ISBN 0-7923-3286-5
21. A.S. Muller, *International Organizations and their Host States.* Aspects of their Legal Relationship. 1995 ISBN 90-411-0080-6
22. T. Kanninen, *Leadership and Reform.* The Secretary-General and the UN Financial Crisis of the late 1980s. 1995 ISBN 90-411-0102-0
23. C. Tomuschat (ed.), *The United Nations at Age Fifty.* A Legal Perspective. 1995 ISBN 90-411-0145-4
24. R. Frid, *The Relations Between the EC and International Organizations.* Legal Theory and Practice. 1995 ISBN 90-411-0155-1
25. M.M. Martin Martinez, *National Sovereignty and International Organizations.* 1996 ISBN 90-411-0200-0
26. M. Pomerance, *The United States and the World Court as a 'Supreme Court of the Nations': Dreams, Illusions and Disillusion.* 1996 ISBN 90-411-0204-3
27. E. Denters, *Law and Policy of IMF Conditionality.* 1996 ISBN 90-411-0211-6
28. P. van Dijck and G. Faber (eds.), *Challenges to the New World Trade Organization.* 1996 ISBN 90-411-0236-1

29. C. Peck and R.S. Lee (eds.), *Increasing the Effectiveness of the International Court of Justice.* Proceedings of the ICJ/UNITAR Colloquium to Celebrate the 50th Anniversary of the Court. 1997 ISBN 90-411-0306-6
30. B. Conforti, *The Law and Practice of the United Nations.* 1996 ISBN 90-411-0233-7
31. N.L. Wallace-Bruce, *The Settlement of International Disputes.* The Contribution of Australia and New Zealand. 1998 ISBN 90-411-0567-0
32. B. Fassbender, *UN Security Council Reform and the Right of Veto.* A Constitutional Perspective. 1998 ISBN 90-411-0592-1
33. R.A. Wessel, *The European Union's Foreign and Security Policy.* A Legal Institutional Perspective. 1999 ISBN 90-411-1265-0
34. A.D. Efraim, *Sovereign (In)equality in International Organizations.* 2000 ISBN 90-411-1310-X
35. P. van Dijck and G. Faber (eds.), *The External Economic Dimension of the European Union.* 2000 ISBN 90-411-1383-5
36. B. Conforti, *The Law and Practice of the United Nations.* Second Revised Edition. 2000 ISBN 90-411-1414-9
37. N.M. Blokker and H.G. Schermers (eds.), *Proliferation of International Organizations.* Legal Issues. 2001 ISBN 90-411-1535-8
38. K.G. Bühler, *State Succession and Membership in International Organizations.* Legal Theories *versus* Political Pragmatism. 2001 ISBN 90-411-1553-6
39. E. Riesenhuber, *The International Monetary Fund under Constraint.* Legitimacy of its Crisis Management. 2001 ISBN 90-411-1577-3
40. Mohammed Sameh M. Amr, *Role of the International Court of Justice as the Principal Judicial Organ of the United Nations.* 2003 ISBN 90-411-2026-2
41. T. Gill (ed.), *Rosenne's The World Court.* What It Is and How It Works. 6th revised edition. 2003 ISBN 90-04-13633-9
42. B. Conforti, *The Law and Practice of the United Nations.* Third Revised Edition. 2005 ISBN 90-04-14308-4
43. H. Olasolo, *The Triggering Procedure of the International Criminal Court.* 2005 ISBN 90-04-14615-6
44. N. Blokker and N. Schrijver (eds.), *The Security Council and the Use of Force.* 2005 ISBN 90-04-14642-3
45. R. Zacklin, *The Amendment of the Constitutive Instruments of the United Nations and Specialized Agencies.* 2005 ISBN 90-04-14800-0
46. M.E. Footer, *An Institutional and Normative Analysis of the World Trade Organization.* 2006 ISBN 90-04-14961-9
47. K. Manusama, *The United Nations Security Council in the Post-Cold War Era.* Applying the Principle of Legality. 2006 ISBN 90-04-15194-X
48. C. Stahn and G. Sluiter (eds.), *The Emerging Practice of the International Criminal Court.* 2008 ISBN 978-90-04-16655-4
49. J. Raue and P. Sutter (eds.), *Facets and Practices of State-Building.* 2009 ISBN 978-90-04-17403-0

MARTINUS NIJHOFF PUBLISHERS – LEIDEN / BOSTON